Understanding Humanitarian Diplomacy

This book introduces readers to the development, principles, and philosophy of humanitarian diplomacy, before demonstrating how it works in practice, using a range of case studies from humanitarian work in the field.

Humanitarian diplomacy seeks to create avenues to persuade decision makers and opinion leaders to act, at all times, in the interests of vulnerable people and with full respect for fundamental humanitarian principles. This book considers the historical evolution of humanitarian diplomacy, its theoretical underpinnings, its relationship with classic diplomacy, international law, and the greater ecosystem in which it exists, and the characteristics and attitudes essential for humanitarian diplomats. The book also draws on a range of first-hand experiences to showcase humanitarian diplomacy's success in solving humanitarian issues. In doing so, it draws attention to the challenges faced by humanitarian workers and serves as an invaluable roadmap for aspiring humanitarians.

Bringing an excellent balance of theory and practice, this book will be a perfect guide for students and practitioners looking to understand the historical, philosophical, legal, and practical foundations of humanitarian diplomacy.

Hafize Zehra Kavak is a senior specialist at Turkish Red Crescent Academy. She completed her PhD in Sociology with the dissertation "Humanitarian Diplomacy Activities of Turkish NGOs in the Middle East and Islamic Countries." She conducts valuable research but has also published, edited, and translated numerous works in the humanitarian aid field. She has also worked for humanitarian aid projects in various countries such as Ethiopia, Lebanon, Macedonia, Palestine, and Türkiye.

Routledge Humanitarian Studies
Series editors: Alex de Waal, Dorothea Hilhorst,
Annette Jansen and Mihir Bhatt
Editorial Board: Dennis Dijkzeul, Wendy Fenton,
Kirsten Johnson, Julia Streets and Peter Walker

The Routledge Humanitarian Studies series in collaboration with the International
Humanitarian Studies Association (IHSA) takes a comprehensive approach to
the growing field of expertise that is humanitarian studies. This field is concerned
with humanitarian crises caused by natural disaster, conflict or political instability
and deals with the study of how humanitarian crises evolve, how they affect
people and their institutions and societies, and the responses they trigger.

We invite book proposals that address, amongst other topics, questions of
aid delivery, institutional aspects of service provision, the dynamics of rebel
wars, state building after war, the international architecture of peacekeeping,
the ways in which ordinary people continue to make a living throughout crises,
and the effect of crises on gender relations.

This interdisciplinary series draws on and is relevant to a range of disciplines,
including development studies, international relations, international law,
anthropology, peace and conflict studies, public health and migration studies.

Authoritarian Practices and Humanitarian Negotiations
Edited by Andrew J Cunningham

Depoliticising Humanitarian Action
Paradigms, Dilemmas, Resistance
Edited by Isabelle Desportes, Alice Corbet and Ayesha Siddiqi

Humanitarian Futures
Challenges and Opportunities
Randolph C. Kent

Forced Migration and Humanitarian Action
Operational Challenges and Solutions for Supporting People on the Move
Edited by Lorenzo Guadagno and Lisette R. Robles

Understanding Humanitarian Diplomacy
Principles and Practice
Edited by Hafize Zehra Kavak

For more information about this series, please visit: www.routledge.com/Routledge-
Humanitarian-Studies/book-series/RHS

Understanding Humanitarian Diplomacy

Principles and Practice

Edited by Hafize Zehra Kavak

Routledge
Taylor & Francis Group

LONDON AND NEW YORK

Designed cover image: Getty Images

First published 2025
by Routledge
4 Park Square, Milton Park, Abingdon, Oxon OX14 4RN

and by Routledge
605 Third Avenue, New York, NY 10158

Routledge is an imprint of the Taylor & Francis Group, an informa business

British Library Cataloguing-in-Publication Data
A catalogue record for this book is available from the British Library

ISBN: 978-1-032-82147-4 (hbk)
ISBN: 978-1-032-82146-7 (pbk)
ISBN: 978-1-003-50318-7 (ebk)

DOI: 10.4324/9781003503187

Typeset in Times New Roman
by SPi Technologies India Pvt Ltd (Straive)

Contents

Figures

Tables

Contributors

Halil Kürşad Aslan is an Assoc. Prof. Dr. in Political Science and International Relations. He has a PhD dissertation with the title of *International Labor Migration from Rural Central Asia: The Potential for Development in Kyrgyzstan and Uzbekistan.* His areas of interest include global political economy, foreign policy analysis, humanitarian diplomacy, research methods, and Eurasian politics.

Cihat Battaloğlu is a humanitarian aid expert and has a PhD in international relations. Previously worked as a research assistant in Qatar University, as a researcher in the SESRIC, and as Head of External Relations and Partnerships in the Turkish Red Crescent. He is currently employed as the Senior International Research & Development Coordinator for Qatar Museums.

Orhan Battır is a lecturer in Political Science and International Relations. Completed his PhD in international relations with a dissertation *Humanitarian Diplomacy as an Instrument of Turkish Foreign Policy.* Produced numerous works in various issues such as Turkish foreign policy, the Middle East, regional policy, soft power, humanitarian diplomacy and human rights.

Murat Çemrek is a professor of Political Science and International Relations. He is the founding director of Akhmet Yassawi International Kazakh-Turkish University's Eurasian Research Institute. Served as assistant coordinator on the Institute of Strategic Thinking; directed Erol Güngör Turkic Diaspora Research and Analysis Center and also the Center for Global and Regional Studies.

Michael David Clark is Senior Partner and Advisor at Global Aid Pro. He is a humanitarian diplomacy specialist and has worked in more than seventy conflict and disaster zones in humanitarian relief operations. Clark is currently working as an advisor and lecturer in the humanitarian aid sector. He also has a PhD in Law.

John Zacharias Crist, the translator and English proofreader of the book, is a graduate of Indiana University. He taught one year in the USA before relocating to Türkiye in 2009. His works include the digitization of James Redhouse's Ottoman Turkish dictionary for LexiQamus, the translation of Nouman Ali Khan's *Divine Speech*, and Hayreddin Pasha's *Ġazavāt* from the text's original Ottoman Turkish manuscript.

Clare Dalton is the former Head of ICRC in the United Arab Emirates. She previously led Humanitarian Diplomacy for the ICRC, and has also held several field posts. She has a MSc in Conflict and Development and an undergraduate degree in Anthropology.

Alpaslan Durmuş is the founder of the Center for Educational Consultancy and Research (EDAM). He served as the Chairman of the Board of Education of the Ministry of National Education in Türkiye (2016-2019). In March 2020, he assumed the role of founding president of Turkish Red Crescent Academy.

Fadi Farasin is an international development specialist, researcher and author. In addition to holding in a managerial position in an international organization, Farasin is an accomplished international development specialist with more than ten years of experience in humanitarian aid, crisis prevention and recovery, advocacy, conflict resolution, and socioeconomic growth in developing countries.

Aygün Karakaş has served as the Honorary Consul of the Republic of the Gambia in Istanbul since 2020. He also served as president of the Türkiye-Gambia Business Council until 2018. Karakaş is currently engaged in various humanitarian projects implemented mainly on the commercial level throughout Africa.

Kerem Kınık is a MD. He is the Former President of the Turkish Red Crescent (TRC). Directed numerous humanitarian aid projects in conflict and disaster zones. Served as the president of TRC from 2016 to 2023, as a representative on IFRC's Governing Board from 2015 to 2017 and as IFRC Vice President in charge of operations in Europe and Central Asia from 2017 to 2022.

Mehmet Akif Kireçci is a professor of Political Science and International Relations. Some of his research interests include geopolitics, Orientalism, comparative politics and Turkish foreign policy. Kireçci is a member of the Turkish Fulbright Commission's board of directors and Deputy Chairman of the Turkish National Commission for UNESCO.

Kaan Namlı is a PhD candidate of International Relations. He boasts a rich résumé of involvement in humanitarian aid distribution and reconstruction projects. Namlı served as Head of Partnerships and Movement Relations at the Turkish Red Crescent and currently is the Humanitarian Representative to Türkiye at MSF.

Kaan Saner is the director of the International Relations Department of Turkish Red Crescent. He took part in various humanitarian relief operations. Served as a Functional Specialist for NATO's International Security Assistance Force in Kabul. He worked in Nigeria and South Sudan as a Movement Cooperation Delegate for the ICRC in 2016.

Hugo Slim served as the head of ICRC's Policy and Humanitarian Diplomacy (2015 to 2020), as Chief Scholar of the Centre for Humanitarian Dialogue in Geneva (2003 to 2007), and also as a member on the executive boards of Oxfam and CAFOD. He is currently a Senior Research Fellow at Oxford.

Tore Svenning is a member of the Norwegian Red Cross. He served in many countries throughout the world for humanitarian projects. He was also involved in diplomatic activities in both New York- and Geneva-based UN institutions and local organizations. He was the Former Secretary of the Standing Commission of the Red Cross and Red Crescent.

İzzet Şahin is a member of international humanitarian aid organization IHH's board of trustees. Şahin has managed humanitarian aid projects in more than thirty countries and has played a central role in securing freedom for thousands of prisoners of war and hostages in Syria.

Segâh Tekin is an Assoc. Prof. Dr. in Political Sciences and International Relations. Tekin served as a visiting researcher in São Paulo University's International Relations Institute and attended numerous projects in Türkiye, Germany, and Brazil. She has worked in international relations with Latin America, the USA, and the Iberian Peninsula, specializing in religious and humanitarian issues.

Selen Turp is a Political Sciences and International Relations expert. She worked with Assalam Community Foundation in field operations in Zanzibar and completed an internship in the Turkish Red Crescent Society. She continues her involvement in issues related to humanitarian diplomacy, foreign policy, immigration policy, Middle Eastern politics, and non-governmental organizations.

Hakan Ünay is a PhD candidate in Sociology. Ünay is currently working to complete his PhD in Sociology with a focus on migration and refugee studies. He currently serves as a researcher in the Migration Research Foundation of Türkiye, concentrating on issues related to borders, migration and border control, globalization, and diplomacy.

Foreword

Hafize Zehra Kavak

As humanity began its collective march into the twenty-first century, humanitarian diplomacy entered into the vernacular of international relations and, more specifically, gained increasing currency among international humanitarian relief organizations. Despite its novelty, however, all human communities have engaged in rudimentary forms of humanitarian diplomacy since time immemorial. Indeed, just as man is in need of forging bonds of solidarity with others to flourish, he empathizes with the plights of others and will often make sacrifices, even giving his own life for those he loves.

The theory on which this concept is based and the practices that it has begotten have developed in a world that has borne witness to shifts in traditional poles of influence, some of which having collapsed completely. This has in turn led to a revolution in how political power is perceived—we find ourselves living in a world that wrought by unimaginably tragic human crises that have engulfed Bosnia, Rwanda, Syria, Arakan, and Palestine as well as long-term, convoluted humanitarian catastrophes throughout the globe. The impact that globalization has had on transportation, communication, culture, and countless other aspects of daily life has likewise fueled these crises to cut across national and regional borders in ways never before seen, thus forcing the entire human race to experience the repercussions of their collective actions first hand. Indeed, as providence would have it, we now find ourselves in a world whose problems—greatly exacerbated by globalization—now require global responses that incorporate economic, cultural, artistic, and various other elements, lest they be unable to offer viable solutions to such cataclysmic humanitarian issues.

It is in this new international modus operandi—one in which civilian organizations play an equally vital a role as do official actors in ensuring that the necessary philanthropic response is given—that humanitarian diplomacy has gained ascendency. Used in assorted contexts by diverse individuals, this term has been imbued with different connotations both in practice and in the literature written on it. To equate humanitarian diplomacy strictly to humanitarian relief, to deem only those activities undertaken by civil actors to constitute humanitarian diplomacy, and to accept humanitarian diplomacy as an auxiliary facet to the multidimensional nature of general diplomacy are but a few examples of these different perceptions.

Whereas we claim neither to have conclusively settled the current confusion in how humanitarian diplomacy is articulated nor to have devised a final, end-all definition for it in this book, we have striven our utmost to introduce a holistic approach reflective of the diverse articulations dominating the field. This holistic approach is a tapestry woven from the contributions of countless scholars and enriched by the experiences of prominent actors who have distinguished themselves with their work in the international humanitarian field.

***

In this book, we have attempted to shed light on how the conceptual, theoretical, and institutional dimensions of humanitarian diplomacy have developed over time. To this end, we have explored the theoretical approaches and the first-hand experiences shared by main humanitarian actors. It will, however, be helpful to present a preface delineating which questions have been addressed by the scholars contributing to this book in their respective chapters. This will help readers understand not only the structure of this book but the journey that it underwent as it came into fruition.

Mehmet Akif Kireçci's chapter on the epistemological, historical, and theological underpinnings of concepts frequently discussed in the field, among which include *human, humanitarianism, philanthropy,* and *humanitarian aid,* astutely accomplishes this arduous task. In this introductory chapter, Kireçci engages in a historical and theological discussion on the epistemological foundations of the words *human* and *insān* in their own respective linguistic and etymological contexts of Latin and Arabic. This discussion is important considering that the concepts fundamental to humanitarianism that drive one to rush to the aid of his fellow man solely out of a shared humanity are predicated on these very words. Following this discussion, Kireçci proceeds to describe the epistemological and theological foundations on which humanitarianism is based, underscoring teachings and generational wisdom from different cultural milieus and specifically from Christianity and Islam theology. Kireçci further buttresses this work with examples of practices instituted and implemented in different cultures during the development and consolidation process that took place in the middle of the nineteenth century and the resulting institutionalization efforts undertaken to mitigate the impact of crises brought on by war and natural disaster. This chapter concludes with a discussion on how diplomacy has expanded to encompass multilateral conferences and organizations, parliamentary diplomacy, international activities undertaken by transnational and national entities, unofficial relations between non-government entities and on how the scope, standards, and goals of diplomacy have changed. This chapter concludes with a discussion on (*i*) how humanitarian diplomacy grew to encompass much more than simply bilateral relations, (*ii*) how its scope, strata, and goals have changed, and (*iii*) how humanitarian diplomacy has solidified into an integral part of international relations.

Beginning his chapter with what Kireçci described as the birth of a new field, Orhan Battır argues that humanitarian tragedies, given how the human component is often overlooked in the international system, give rise to de facto situations requiring the collaborative efforts of both traditional official actors and civilian groups. Drawing a correlation between the development of humanitarian diplomacy and such de facto situations, Battır delves into the historical realities that gave birth to humanitarian diplomacy and analyzes the relationship between humanitarian and classic diplomacy. This chapter examines how the international diplomatic system was significantly overhauled to better reflect the new post-WWII status quo and how globalization compelled diplomacy to change both in theory and practice. From there, Battır compares the historical development of these two forms of diplomacy, the actors involved in their respective developmental process, the goals the seek to accomplish, and the methods and means they employ to achieve these goals. To further improve readers' understanding of how classic and humanitarian diplomacy are related and interact with one another, Battır addresses not only each form of diplomacy's strengths and weaknesses but also where they oppose and overlap with one another. His exposé on how humanitarian diplomacy is understood in the literature and on the ground will serve as an illuminating guide while engaging in the subsequent discussions seeking to devise a shared conceptualization of humanitarian diplomacy. Here, we must underline that although humanitarian diplomacy tends to be equated with humanitarian aid, it is much more than that—it is a human-centric approach that produces solutions to humanitarian issues on the international level.

Though not included in the English version of this book, the IFRC's *Humanitarian Diplomacy Policy* and accompanying *Explanatory Memorandum* form the bedrock of this book. Since all of the authors contributing to this work espouse the IFRC's definition of humanitarian diplomacy, interested readers are directed to these two aforementioned documents for further reading, as a firm grasp of them will facilitate a deeper understanding of the concepts and discussions presented throughout the chapters.

In his chapter, Kaan Saner explores the legal and ethical foundations on which activities undertaken by humanitarian diplomacy actors are based, paying particular attention to the opportunities they afford and potential areas for growth and expansion. By virtue of its focus on international humanitarian and human rights law, this chapter aspires to serve as a valuable resource for all involved in humanitarian diplomacy. In addition to enumerating the rights vulnerable individuals have during times of conflict and crisis, Saner discusses how these rights can be preserved. Taken all together, this chapter furnishes a concrete basis on which those engaged in humanitarian diplomacy can formulate robust arguments to persuade decision makers to embrace their causes.

In their collaborative chapter, Hakan Ünay and Murat Çemrek explore the international environment that, spurred on by globalization, would give birth to humanitarian diplomacy. This chapter discusses how globalization not only enhanced humanitarian diplomacy's currency on the international arena despite being such a new field but also served to accelerate the identification of crisis environments in need of humanitarian diplomacy endeavors. Before bringing their chapter to a close, Ünay and Çemrek engage in a case study of the humanitarian diplomacy enterprises undertaken by Türkiye, evaluating how her efforts have affected the very course of globalization itself.

In the following chapter, Segâh Tekin shares her findings and reflections on seemingly unending crises and the subsequent long-term repercussions that arise as a result. Tekin's work is of immense importance because the dominant international political climate has produced many of these crises. As prevailing humanitarian diplomacy practices have made abundantly clear, localities in need of such efforts are those in which the normal flow of life and provision of public services are not simply disrupted temporarily during the occasional emergency situation but those in which health services, education, infrastructure, and the food supply chain suffer a systemic collapse brought about by successive, long-term armed conflict, natural disasters, and humanitarian crises. This chapter discusses ways to mitigate the effect of problems that have become deeply entrenched in places plagued by protracted, multilayered crises and how humanitarian diplomacy helps preserve human life under such dire conditions.

Up until this point chapters have expounded upon the historical, political, and legal foundation on which humanitarian diplomacy stands. Subsequent chapters will concentrate on actors involved in humanitarian diplomacy and the issues they are expected to face.

In their chapter, Halil Kürşad Aslan and Selen Turp discuss the actors making up what they have come to dub the humanitarian relief ecosystem: (*i*) humanitarian diplomats, (*ii*) decision-makers, and (*iii*) aggrieved populations. Notably, Aslan and Turp include official actors as humanitarian diplomacy actors, holding that all actors, whether civilian or otherwise, who act in the best interests of vulnerable individuals and in adherence to fundamental humanitarian principles may be considered humanitarian diplomats. Finally, the authors discuss strategies to execute reform that enhance the effectiveness of humanitarian efforts.

The next two chapters—the first written by Hugo Slim and the second by Cihat Battaloğlu and Fadi Farasin—initiate discussion on the proficiency levels, expertise, aptitude, character traits, attitudes, and approaches of humanitarian diplomats. Whilst Slim focuses on the specific traits humanitarian diplomats need in order to ensure the effective execution of humanitarian diplomacy, Battaloğlu and Farasin highlight the necessity of promoting a culturally sensitive approach among the numerous stakeholders so that they will be able to collaborate effectively in diplomatic affairs. Clare Dalton, after touching upon the various characteristics and skills essential for a humanitarian diplomat, embarks on a discussion of how this new form of diplomacy has impacted the field of diplomacy as a whole, highlighting both the opportunities it affords to humanitarian diplomats and the potential risks it poses.

Michael David Clark subsequently evaluates the findings he reached in his doctoral dissertation in his chapter. In doing so, Clark characterizes humanitarian diplomacy as a powerful tool to increase the effectiveness of humanitarian action. He further emphasizes the importance of diplomacy in humanitarian relief efforts, underlining that "to be a humanitarian is to be a diplomat." Kaan Namlı then accentuates the need to protect humanitarian relief workers and ensure that aid reaches its intended destination. Humanitarian diplomacy, he argues, not only guarantees the safety of relief workers operating in crisis zones under otherwise perilous conditions and that of aid items but also protects the interests of vulnerable individuals. Namlı focuses first on how humanitarian diplomacy helps eliminate the myriad risks and threats posed to relief workers and aid items. He then emphasizes the need to include the different facets of humanitarian discipline in the literature, arguing this to be equally as important as using humanitarian diplomacy to help protect relief workers and aid items. Finally, drawing on his experiences as former Chairperson of the Türkiye – Gambia Business Council and Honorary Consulate of The Gambia in Istanbul, Aygün Karakaş discusses how the private sector can contribute to ongoing and prospective humanitarian efforts.

To recap, chapters have thus far discussed the various means that official and civilian actors engaged in humanitarian diplomacy can employ to safeguard the interests of vulnerable groups.

***

We have now arrived at the part of our book that deals with the theoretical discourse surrounding humanitarian diplomacy. Here, we turn our focus toward specific cases in which humanitarian diplomacy practices are directly impacted by subjective realities and situations confronted in the field. In this section, we concentrate on the experiences and wisdom that different organizations and institutions have gained while engaged in humanitarian diplomacy on the international level. We have attempted to draw attention to how these organizations have contributed to the theoretical development of humanitarian diplomacy and the interaction between theory and practice.

In his chapter, Tore Svenning examines the experiences of the International Committee of the Red Cross (ICRC), exploring in what ways this committee has been involved in humanitarian diplomacy not only in situations requiring them to sit at the same table as armed forces during ongoing conflicts but also in different capital cities and international platforms. Given that it serves as a referential text for humanitarian diplomacy, we have included an interview that we conducted with Christopher Lamb, one of the architects of the Humanitarian Diplomacy Policy Document. Bolstered by Lamb's work in humanitarian diplomacy in Palestine, Bangladesh, Geneva, and New York City, this interview not only offers a glimpse into the humanitarian diplomacy efforts engaged in by the IFRC but also sheds light on the discussions headed by the IFRC to formulate a definition for humanitarian diplomacy. The interview also highlights parallels between classic and humanitarian diplomacy, the characteristics of humanitarian diplomats, and the opportunities created by humanitarian diplomacy.

Founded during the midst of the Bosnia War, IHH Humanitarian Relief Foundation has been involved in human rights and humanitarian aid campaigns in Türkiye and the wider world. İzzet Şahin explains IHH's humanitarian efforts in Syria and Libya in his chapter, where he provides concrete examples of the types of negotiations in which humanitarian diplomats participate, the different outcomes of these negotiations, and the various parties and interests involved.

We further explored the more than 150 years' worth of humanitarian diplomacy in which the Red Crescent has been involved both domestically and abroad. Originally known as the *Ottoman Society for Helping Wounded and Sick Soldiers*, the Turkish Red Crescent has participated in arbitration, negotiations, collaboration, and advocacy over its long existence. In their chapter, Kerem Kınık and Hafize Zehra Kavak present the Red Crescent's vision of humanitarian diplomacy, showcasing real-world examples of humanitarian diplomacy at work. These include reuniting families and locating missing persons, establishing communication channels between prisoners of war and their next of kin, providing legal and social services to displaced individuals, distributing humanitarian aid to civilian victims, protecting and evacuating civilians caught in conflict and war zones, transferring sick and wounded individuals out of conflict and war zones for medical treatment, and executing prisoner exchanges.

***

Every part of this book was conceived and brought together with the utmost diligence and care. We have surveyed infographics that we believe will aid readers to gain a more thorough grasp of humanitarian diplomacy's conceptual framework, that summarize the different facets of the subject, and that underline key points. These include "The Milestones in Humanitarian Diplomacy," "A Comparison of Humanitarian and Classic Diplomacy," and "The Traits of Humanitarian Diplomats." Chapters describing examples of practice included both historical and contemporary photographs accompanied by captions to aid readers comprehend the wider context.

In addition to safeguarding the interests of vulnerable individuals, humanitarian diplomacy offers effective solutions to the emerging problems that humanity, as a whole, is expected to face and overcome in the near future. It is our sincerest hope that this work might serve as a roadmap for the widespread comprehension, promulgation, and adoption of basic humanitarian principles for all people and that humanitarian diplomacy.

We have endeavored to present a portrait detailing the scholastic and ideological foundations of humanitarian diplomacy both to members of the wider humanitarian community seeking to enhance the professional competence levels of all involved and to selfless volunteers working side by side with other civilian and official actors. How well we have succeeded in this venture of ours, we leave to our readers' discretion.

Hafize Zehra Kavak
June 2024—Istanbul

Preface and Acknowledgements

Understanding Humanitarian Diplomacy: Principles and Practice is the English edition of *Kuramdan Uygulamaya İnsani Diplomasi*, originally published in Istanbul in 2023 by the Turkish Red Crescent Academy. This English version has been revised and updated to offer a more comprehensive narrative on humanitarian diplomacy so that it might be used as a primary source by those interested and actively engaged in the field.

A diverse group of scholars and field professionals have lent their hand in further enriching this work since the initial publication of the Turkish version. As the English version is largely derived from the original Turkish text, I wish to acknowledge those who contributed to the initial work. Accordingly, I would like to express my gratitude to director of publications Alpaslan Durmuş, coordinator of publications Fatma Sena Yasan, publication secretaries Zahide Ekmekci and Meryem Esra Varol, diplomacy editor Eren Paykal, Turkish language editor Gökçe Eser, and graphic editor Nevzat Onaran. Indeed, the English edition of this book could not have come to fruition without the invaluable work of senior editor Helena Hurd, editorial assistant Katerina Lade, Turkish–English translator J. Zacharias Crist, and English proofreader Ayşegül Üstün. Again I am deeply grateful for all their earnest efforts. Finally, words cannot fully convey the amount of gratitude I feel for all the authors who wrote chapters for both editions of this book, namely, Halil Kürşad Aslan, Fatma Zehra Atıcı, Cihat Battaloğlu, Orhan Battır, Murat Çemrek, Clare Dalton, Michael David Clark, Alpaslan Durmuş, Fadi Farasin, Aygün Karakaş, Kerem Kınık, Mehmet Akif Kireçci, Christopher Lamb, Kaan Namlı, Hüseyin Oruç, Kaan Saner, Hugo Slim, Tore Svenning, İzzet Şahin, Segâh Tekin, Selen Turp, and Hakan Ünay.

I owe an immense debt of gratitude toward my mother, Hafiz Hikmet, my father, İsmail Hakkı, my husband, Özgür, and my two children, Ömer Faruk and Mehmet Oruç. They were an inexhaustible source of motivation and strength for me throughout this journey. Indeed, these extraordinary people deserve my deepest thanks.

Hafize Zehra Kavak

1   Humanitarianism, Philanthropy, and Humanitarian Diplomacy

Mehmet Akif Kireçci

By dint of its novelty, humanitarian diplomacy is, compared to its counterparts, a relatively lesser-studied facet of international relations. Recent years, however, have witnessed a remarkable upsurge in the amount of literature composed on this subject. Nevertheless, the historical, theological, and sociopolitical roots of humanitarian diplomacy have yet to be sufficiently discussed. Observing the practices in the field, we find that, on the one hand, humanitarian diplomacy overlaps with migration, war, crisis, and disasters and, on the other, is intertwined with classical diplomacy.

Humanitarian diplomacy encompasses all endeavors that one seeking to protect one's fellow man, to enshrine and safeguard human dignity, and to relieve suffering. It involves negotiations, sometimes with belligerent parties and at the risk of one's own life and limb, to ensure that aid reaches its intended destination. Since this emergent form of diplomacy significantly overlaps with humanism and humanitarianism, an undertaking into the epistemological underpinnings of these two concepts would be pertinent.

Concept and Historical Context

Helping people in need is as old as humanity itself (Spikins et al., 2010, pp. 303–325). According to Dr. Paul Brand, a student once asked anthropologist Margaret Mead what she considered to be the first sign of civilization in a culture (Brand and Yancey, 1980, p. 68). Mead's answer was not the myriad tools, pots, hunting devices, grinding stones, or religious artifacts that most of us would expect. On the contrary, she responded with a 15,000-year-old human femur that had healed after having been broken, arguing that it takes approximately six weeks for the femur, the longest bone in the body, to heal. Considering the conditions of the era in question, a person with a broken femur would be unable to escape from danger, move to find water or food, and therefore vulnerable to predator attacks. In other words, no one could survive long enough for his broken femur to heal without assistance. In Mead's eyes, this healed femur is evidence that someone *helped* the injured person, possibly bandaging the wound, transporting him to safety, and devoting time and resources to care for him while immobilized. It indicates that one person sacrificed his own

DOI: 10.4324/9781003503187-1

comfort and wellbeing to save another's life. This healed femur proves that an act of charity—a humanitarian act—had taken place, even before diplomacy itself had emerged.

Archeological findings demonstrate that our ancestors not only cared for the sick and infirm but also exhibited compassion and self-sacrifice. The human remains exhumed by archeologists in Shanidar Cave in Iraq dating back to between forty-five and seventy thousand years ago, for instance, are of a man who lived until the age of fifty despite clear signs of having experienced arm and leg fractures, partial blindness and deafness as a result of trauma to the head, and various bodily deformities (Solecki, 1972, p. 142). Experts explain that these injuries would have been fatal had the rest of the group not taken care of them.

Indeed, solidarity and mutual support are the foundation stones of civilization. Collaborating in times of hardship and creating complex societies requires a deep sense of fraternity. The transition from mobile hunter-gatherer communities to sedentary agrarian societies likewise required a more highly regulated division of labor and the will to take on greater social responsibilities. To state, therefore, that such sensitivities as fraternity and camaraderie are as old as human history itself is no exaggeration.

A plethora of answers can be provided to explain why one would help his fellow man. What is certain is that helping others benefits all of humanity, from ensuring the continuation of mankind to the creation of civilizations. Those who favor a biological explanation point to the fact that altruistic behaviors and compassion toward our fellow man cause the release of oxytocin, a hormone that causes one to feel pleasure, meaning that people help others to feel good. A utilitarian, however, would argue that these behaviors, once paramount for human survival, have become a cultural heirloom passed down from generation to generation, regarded now as how a respectable person is expected to act.

Helping people in need is considered a virtue in every society, religion, and belief system. While familial and ancestral bonds might explain displays of generosity toward one's family, tribe members, compatriots, and fellow citizens, they do not explain why one might aid a complete stranger or even an avowed enemy. Humanitarianism is the contemporary notion that one should lend a helping hand to those in need simply because they are human.

In order to gain a comprehensive understanding of humanitarianism, we must first delve into its origins and other related concepts. The Latin word *hūmānus*, meaning human, derives from a proto-Indo-European root meaning mortal or earthly (Online Etymology Dictionary, n.d.-a). The word humane from the same root means to have compassion, care, and closeness toward others, especially those who are suffering.

The origin of the word human in Turkish is based on the Arabic words *ins* and *insān*. In the Qur'ān, the word human is used eighty-three times in the singular and an additional 231 times in the plural. The Qur'ān holds mankind to be a unique creation with a unique story. While he can be both cruel and ignorant, he is similarly endowed with virtues. He can choose the path of righteousness and return to his hereditary abode—to Paradise—through a combination of merit and God's grace. Though his existence in this world is transient, an eternal life awaits him after death—one of boundless bliss for the righteous and perpetual punishment for the evil among man. Man's spatio-temporal existence is bound wholly to his Creator, whose power encompasses both life and death. More importantly, an entire chapter of the Qurʾān—*al-Insān*—is devoted to humankind. In this chapter, man is described as having been created from a droplet of sperm after material nothingness. Bestowed unto man, whose life in this world constitutes a journey to his final abode, are the powers of hearing and sight. The verses emphasizing human responsibility affirm that those righteous men and women, referred to as *abrār*—who use their God-given free will appropriately shall be rewarded abundantly in the hereafter. The righteous are further described as those who fulfill their promises, feed the poor, and act solely for the sake of God without seeking any worldly reward. Such people shall receive eternal bliss. By addressing all human beings and not simply those who identify as Muslims, this chapter highlights the universality of humanitarianism and philanthropy as fundamental to human existence.

Proclaimed in 632, the Prophet Muhammad's Farewell Sermon embodies the Islamic view of humanity:

> *All of mankind is from Adam and Eve. An Arab has no superiority over a non-Arab and a non-Arab has no superiority over an Arab. A White has no superiority over a Black and a Black has no superiority over a White—except by piety and good deed.*
>
> (Erul, 2012, pp. 591–593)

This declaration affirms in the Muslim psyche that all human beings descend from a single ancestral pair and are thus brothers and sisters with one another, thereby impelling them to live in fraternity. This principle demonstrates how Islam places humans in a cosmography extending to the very inception of their existence. Regardless of their social environment and other physical and ethnic markers, humans are humans. This is one of the cornerstones of humanitarian diplomacy: Lending a helping hand to one's fellow man out of a shared humanity.

The caliphate of ʿUmar b. al-Khaṭṭāb (634–644) deserves special attention for having pioneered humanitarian diplomacy practices in the Islamic tradition. His exemplary acts include exempting the Jews of Syria from paying *jizya*—a tax paid by non-Muslims living in an Islamic polity—because they could not afford it. More interestingly, he ordered that *zakāt*—alms obligatory upon Muslims only—be given to Christians with leprosy (Fayda, 2006, pp. 123–201). These two examples are noteworthy in showcasing how Islam encourages aid to be distributed to those who do not share the same cultural or religious identity.

Epistemological Background of the Concept

When discussing humanity and humanitarianism in the modern era, the literature in Western languages focuses primarily on philosophical discourse which
is deeply immersed, even if not always readily acknowledged, in Christianity
and its theology, or makes references to Christian epistemology. The concepts
and practices related to humanitarian aid born out of Sufi institutions and
awqāf (sing. *waqf*, perpetual philanthropic endowment) in the Islamic world
have yet to be fully acknowledged in modern philosophical discourse or the
social sciences. An examination of Western literature reveals that the term
humanitarian was first used during late eighteenth-century Christian theological debates to refer to one who affirmed the humanity of Christ whilst denying
his eternal and divine nature (Online Etymology Dictionary, n.d.-b). It then
took on a more secular meaning by the middle of the nineteenth century, referring to one who believed the most important moral duty of every human being
was to promote the welfare of the human race. During this early period, the
term also had connotations of naivety and radicalism: those seeking solutions
to social problems under the name of humanity were often faulted on being
too idealistic, detached from reality, excessively sentimental, and disingenuous
(Davies, 2012, pp. 3–4).

The first concept connected with humanitarianism is *humanism*. Its first
meaning dates back to the sixteenth century and refers to the body of schol-
arship on pre- and non-Christian philosophers and artists. It is also used to
denote a philosophical stance emphasizing the primacy and agency of human
beings over the divine. Kelly Oliver attributes the roots of humanitarianism to
Kantian humanism (Oliver, 2016). Kant suggests that most people help others
out of feelings of compassion and kindness, enjoying doing what they deem
to be good. According to Kant, actions arising from such personal motives
cannot be considered morally superior, even if they result in good. Therefore,
any act of assistance that derives from feelings of fear, remorse, or sympathy
is not of the same moral substance as one done solely out of a sense of duty
(Kraut, 2020).

Humanism holds that every human being is morally responsible to all of
humanity. In this respect, humanism is closely related to humanitarian philosophy in the theological sense. According to Kant, although Jesus was only a
human being, he had reached the zenith of moral development (Oliver, 2016).
As Kant states in *Religion within the Bounds of Bare Reason*, Jesus succeeded
in pleasing God despite—or perhaps as a result of—possessing carnal inclina-
tions, needs, and other base urges and despite suffering temptations similar to
those of an ordinary person (Kant, 1838, pp. 73–74). It is worth dwelling on
the causal relationship between the humanity of Jesus, that is, his ability to
achieve moral superiority as a mere human being, and his humanitarianism.
Man must recognize his transient, imperfect, and destitute nature before he
sees any reason to attempt to compensate for another's shortcomings. If Jesus
were wholly divine, however, neither the suffering and anguish he bore for

humanity, nor the degree of compassion and mercy he showed would be attainable for ordinary people. On the other hand, His human fragility, weakness, and lapses that come with being human make it possible for those who follow him to emulate him. It follows, therefore, that the prerequisite for attaining moral superiority is to be fallible.

The common ground between both definitions of humanitarianism, encompassing both its theological and humanist senses; was the effort to put forward a secular yet universal system of morality that is independent of the church and that encompassed all of humanity. So much so that the French philosopher Auguste Comte (1798–1857), lauded as the founder of positivism, even tried to build a religion based on humanist principles (Bourdeau, 2022).

Although the use of humanitarianism to describe messianic suffering caused by the world of the flesh continued well into the twentieth century, the word humanist gained its modern connotation of being humane, altruistic, and philanthropic in the middle of the nineteenth century. Perhaps by merging these two paradigmatically different concepts, humanitarianism came to be associated with situations in which people suffer severe and obvious bodily anguish similar to that of Jesus.

On one occasion, an expert in the law stood up to test Jesus. "Teacher," he asked, "what must I do to inherit eternal life?"

"What is written in the Law?" he replied. "How do you read it?"

He answered, "Love the Lord your God with all your heart and with all your soul and with all your strength and with all your mind; and, 'love your neighbor as yourself.'"

"You have answered correctly," Jesus replied. "Do this and you will live."

But he wanted to justify himself, so he asked Jesus, "And who is my neighbor?"

In reply Jesus said, "A man was going down from Jerusalem to Jericho, when he was attacked by robbers. They stripped him of his clothes, beat him and went away, leaving him half dead.

"A priest happened to be going down the same road, and when he saw the man, he passed by on the other side. So too, a Levite, when he came to the place and saw him, passed by on the other side. But a Samaritan, as he travelled, came where the man was; and when he saw him, he took pity on him. He went to him and bandaged his wounds, pouring on oil and wine. Then he put the man on his own donkey, brought him to an inn and took care of him. The next day he took out two denarii and gave them to the innkeeper. 'Look after him,' he said, 'and when I return, I will reimburse you for any extra expense you may have.'

"Which of these three do you think was a neighbor to the man who fell into the hands of robbers?"

The expert in the law replied, "The one who had mercy on him."

Jesus told him, "Go and do likewise."

(Luke 10: 25–37)

Interpreting this parable in a historical context helps clarify its relationship with humanitarian diplomacy. First, the road from Jerusalem to Jericho, where the story takes place, was known as the "Road of Blood" because of the "blood often spilled by thieves." This road was notorious for its danger and difficulty and therefore resembles insecure areas where humanitarian aid is most needed today. It is likewise interesting that the recipient of assistance is a Jew while the helper is a Samaritan given the ongoing hostility between these two groups at the time the story took place.

The contextual illustration of categorically aiding a known adversary in the story is often overlooked in contemporary discussions. Emphasizing this context, African-American rights activists such as Dr. Martin Luther King (d. 1968) interpreted the Samaritan as another race, highlighting the moral superiority of helping a disliked, hostile person. Beyond helping one's family, relatives, countrymen, and kin, helping a complete stranger or, more dramatically, an enemy under challenging circumstances is revered as the apex of moral maturity.

Similar to its underlying philosophy, the customs surrounding humanitarian aid are often linked to religious philanthropy. As a matter of fact, despite the efforts to connect humanitarian aid to a universal morality independent of religion, humanitarian aid today is perceived and practiced as a religious duty by many communities of different faiths.

Considering the historical background, the practice of humanitarian aid, like its philosophy, is deeply rooted in religious philanthropy. In the fourth century, the first Christian church in Cappadocia was renowned for distributing food to the poor and for engaging in myriad relief efforts (Placido, 2015). With the establishment of shelters, almshouses, nursing homes, and separate settlements for lepers in the twelfth century, philanthropy began to occupy an important place in Western Christianity (Brodman, 2009, p. 43).

Despite the efforts to connect humanitarian aid to a universal morality independent of religion, humanitarian aid today is perceived and practiced as a religious duty by many communities of different faiths. Examples abound of whom, how, any why to help in both Christianity and Islam.

Kindness, Charity, and Humanitarian Aid in Islamic Civilization

The Qurʾān and Sunnah—the compilation of verbal traditions and practices of the Prophet Muhammad—constitute the primary Islamic sources enjoining benevolence, doing good unto others, and looking after the needy. Beyond being a constantly emphasized virtue, giving one's earnings, possessions, and even loved ones to others is a religious obligation in the Qurʾān and Sunnah. So much so that it is incumbent upon every Muslim, both man and woman, who has reached a designated level of affluence to pay *zakāt*—2.5 percent of one's material wealth—to the needy after having covered one's own basic needs.

Beyond enjoining *zakāt* as an obligatory pillar of Islam, the Qurʾān emphasizes the voluntary giving of charity and the performance of good deeds. It further emphasizes what it calls *infāq*, or spending with the sole intent of earning God's pleasure, encompassing not only charity but also a much wider arena. The Qurʾān draws significant attention to *zakāt* and who constitute eligible recipients—the poor and needy, those employed to distribute *zakāt*, those whose hearts are attracted to Islam, travelers separated from their wealth, those in debt, and those who strive in Allah's cause, and slaves, specifically to secure their freedom (9:60). That *zakāt* is strictly prohibited from being given to one's immediate family—because one is required to provide for their needs regardless—implies that it is primarily to be used to see to the needs of society's most vulnerable. Furthermore, the fact that paying *zakāt* is an annual obligation upon affluent Muslims strongly emphasized in the religion's primary sources clearly indicates its role as a fundamental cornerstone in the greater Islamic socioeconomic system.

Sufi institutions and charitable *awqāf* that emerged during the early period of Islam constitute the most highly institutionalized, longest-running forms of humanitarian aid in Islamic civilization. *Awqāf*, as Robert D. McChensney explains, are where philanthropy is most effectively performed in the Islamic world (1995, pp. 6–8). According to Islamic law, a *waqf* is an endowment established by a living man or woman, designated specifically for the perpetual provision of one or more social services. Though in existence since the first years of Islam, *awqāf* played a central role in the social and economic lives of Muslim societies primarily between the twelfth and nineteenth centuries (Singer, 2012, p. 126). ʿUmar b. al-Khaṭṭāb established the first Islamic *waqf* under the direction of the Prophet Muhammad while he was still alive (McChesney, 1991: 8). Indeed, the Prophet Muhammad and each of the first four caliphs devoted the proceeds of their own personal estates to the public treasury, otherwise known as the *bayt al-māl* in Arabic (Günay, 2012, pp. 475–479).

Most scholars regard *awqāf* as preeminent institutions providing social services in the Islamic world especially before the emergence of the modern state (McChesney, 1991, p. 3). Buildings affiliated with *awqāf* include houses of worship, libraries, guesthouses, fountains, wells, bridges, caravanserais, and public graveyards open to the entire public or institutions such as soup kitchens, hospitals, clinics, and widows' houses that can only be used by the poor. The Ottoman Empire boasted near-countless *awqāf* devoted to serving the public and engagement in charitable activities, the details of which are so intricate that the contemporary chronicler would be left in astonishment upon even a cursory look into them. It would be helpful to mention some of these philanthropy models, as we have access to the deeds of thousands of Ottoman *awqāf*. In addition to those whose aim was to feed and clothe the needy in various localities, numerous *awqāf* were established to provide students with assistance in their academic endeavors, to shelter the poor and wayfarers, to feed stray animals living among the urban population, and to ensure the continuity of various artistries and businesses (Çizakça, 2006, pp. 19–31). Other *awqāf* mended injuries to storks left behind by their flocks during migration or, by transporting snow and ice from nearby mountains, provided cold water to workers in the heat of summer. The pride and joy of Islamic civil society, such institutions embodied and many continue to embody the spirit of philanthropy and altruism, performing many duties that would be the envy for modern humanitarian aid organizations.

In addition to the practices of *zakāt* and charity, both of which are essential means for instituting cooperation in Islamic societies, *awqāf* have ensured that philanthropic activities are made permanent under Islamic law. In this respect, *awqāf* elevate charitable activities from one-time donations to perpetual initiatives. Furthermore, although *awqāf* are themselves Islamic institutions, they are universal in terms of the services they provide. Nothing in Islamic law requires that a *waqf*'s beneficiaries be Muslims or even citizens of the Islamic state. The sole requirements are that property to be endowed be privately owned and not be allocated for a religiously impermissible activity. The endowment becomes public property and cannot be sold, bequeathed, or appropriated in any way thereafter. Finally, everyone, including other *awqāf* and people who do not receive *zakāt* or charity, should be able to benefit from the services provided. Similarly, society as a whole should be involved in their upkeep to the extent that their personal situation allows. In fact, Islamic law guarantees not only the sanctity of human and even animal life but also the maintenance of places of worship, urban facilities, the natural environment, and roads.

The Islamic landscape is dotted with copious amounts of philanthropic institutions founded by Sufis. Sufi organizations have, since the earliest centuries of Islam, provided some of the most sincere, long-standing examples of philanthropy (Schimmel, 1975). The charitable initiatives undertaken by Aḥmad Yasawī's disciples in Anatolia and the Balkans, the dervish lodges established by the Ottomans in these same lands, and the aid distributed among people of all ethnicities and faiths showcase the rich tradition of Sufi-driven philanthropy. Historical sources explain that the first dervish lodges—the structures in which Sufi philosophy was put into practice—were built during the eighth century either in the Palestinian district of Ramla or that of Abadan in modern-day Iran, after which they spread to cover a vast geographical area stretching from "Baghdad to Bukhara and from Cairo to Cordoba" (Kara, 2011, pp. 368–370). Established in areas populated by Muslim and non-Muslim alike, these lodges sought to internalize religious teachings and create *dhikr* (i.e., remembrance) circles while simultaneously feeding the local citizenry and working to bolster social solidarity. Dervish lodges and Sufi orders became renowned as civil institutions that helped the needy, the wayward traveler, and the homeless throughout the classical and pre-modern eras.

The Institutionalization of Humanitarian Aid in the Modern Age

Humanitarian initiatives have evolved almost exclusively out of the goal to ensure the health and wellbeing of armies, as commonly practiced by modern nation-states, and of providing protection and care to all citizens affected by conflict and social strife. The history of providing humanitarian aid during military conflict traces back to the French Revolution and the Napoleonic Wars of 1793 to 1814 (Aaslestad, 2019, pp. 171–192). It was during these wars that military medicine gained prominence. Henry Dunant, a Swiss business-man horrified by the near-total neglect of wounded soldiers by both the Italian-French alliance and the Austrian armies during the Battle of Solferino (1859), convened the nations of the world together to form the Red Cross and mobi-lized national units dedicated to the care of sick and wounded soldiers under an international umbrella organization (Dunant, 1986, p. 9). Dunant was also instrumental in the adoption of the first Geneva Convention in 1864, which protected prisoners of war, the sick, wounded, and civilians in conflict zones.

The efforts spearheaded by Dr. ʿAbdullāh Bey led to the Ottoman Empire's participation in said movement on 11 June 1868, on which date the humanitar-ian aid association known today as the Red Crescent was established under the name of the Ottoman Aid Society for Wounded and Sick Soldiers (Kızılay Tarih, 2016). After the Ottoman declaration of the First Constitutional Monarchy in 1876, the Red Crescent focused on providing housing and human-itarian aid for the victims of natural disasters, especially during the great chol-era epidemic in Istanbul (Kızılay, 2006). The foundation, renamed the ʿOsmānlı Hilāl-i Aḥmer Cemʿiyyeti (Ottoman Red Crescent Society) in 1877, the Türkiye Hilāl-i Aḥmer Cemʿiyyeti (Turkish Red Crescent Society) in 1923, the Türkiye Kızılay Cemiyeti (Turkish Red Crescent Society) in 1935, and finally the Türkiye Kızılay Derneği (Turkish Red Crescent Society) in 1947, played a leading role in caring for injured and sick soldiers on the battlefield. In addition to its involve-ment in disaster and emergency preparedness, response, and recovery efforts both domestically and internationally, the Turkish Red Crescent runs compre-hensive humanitarian aid projects, blood drives, and public health initiatives. As in the rest of the world, a wide array of non-governmental humanitarian organ-izations thrive in Türkiye. Unified around a set vision and mission, these organ-izations are keen to employ the latest technology to produce effective results in their specific spheres of activity, such as emergency and developmental aid.

Why Does Humanitarian Aid Need Diplomacy?

Humanitarian aid crossed what we would now call national and international borders in the pre-modern world. The caravanserais and hospitals established along the trade and pilgrimage routes running from Algeria to Istanbul and beyond, the constant flow of gold sent to support the poor of Mecca and Medina, and the pilgrims sojourning to Jerusalem and the Hejaz became the vehicle of Islamic humanitarianism (Hoexter, 2003, p. 151). The closer the phys-ical distance between benefactor and beneficiary, the more effectively they melted barriers between people who may hold mutually antagonistic identities. Sharing meals with one's neighbors, building a fountain for passers-by, feeding the stay animals living in one's neighborhood, and other acts of charity strength-ened the bonds of kinship essential for the survival of local communities (Singer,

2012, p. 126). As physical distances increased, it was customary that the benefactor and beneficiary had similar identities, most often being of the same religious community.

Increased transportation opportunities allowed the average person to gain a greater awareness of the daily lives and hardships faced by people living in far-off lands. Whereas long-distance travel had previously been the privilege of armies and emissaries, this infrastructure, coupled with loose borders and a widespread desire to aid travelers, facilitated the journeys of pilgrims, dervishes, and merchants, permitting them both to embark more frequently into the outside world and to interact with people of diverse walks of life. Yet, the eventual establishment of nation-states, the consolidation of national sovereignty, and the tightening of borders forced aid to require special permissions similar to commercial goods and political embassies in order to enter or pass through a territory. In short, increased cross-border interactions and the clear demarcation of borders created an environment where diplomatic efforts were required to ensure aid reached those in need.

The official history of humanitarian diplomacy ironically begins with the most violent form of cross-border interaction—war. The first successful act of humanitarian diplomacy is the affirmation that the lives of healthcare workers are sacrosanct. In other words, opposite sides agreed not to target hospitals in which doctors and medics cared for the sick, wounded, and injured. Although a few temporary bilateral agreements had been signed in the past to protect field medics and to send them back to their home countries should they have been caught, it was not until the middle of the nineteenth century that modern medical care became an integral part of armed conflict (Gross, 2007, pp. 718–721).

Humanitarian work began to advance once again during World War I when the importance of non-combatant and neutral countries in managing humanitarian aid emerged (Hitchcock, 2014, pp. 145–163). During the Nigerian Civil War of 1967–1970 between the Nigerian government and the separatist Biafra region, calls to stave off hunger and declarations of a humanitarian emergency broadcast on television were responded to by European and American communities and Catholic missionaries (Aaronson, 2013, pp. 176–196). These and similar initiatives served to shape subsequent humanitarian aid operations.

The ability of humanitarian organizations to act is severely curtailed where firm political decisions are absent. Moreover, dissonance between politics and humanitarian response efforts sets the stage for acute human tragedies to rear their ugly head. Over the years, the world's inability to field an appropriate response to major natural disasters and other egregious humanitarian crises have compelled the international community to identify and strengthen weak links in the humanitarian aid system.

Every humanitarian crisis since the second half of the twentieth century, such as the Nigerian Civil War mentioned above, has served as an incentive to identify and strengthen weak elements present in the humanitarian system.

Humanitarian organizations set out, for instance, to develop guidelines and medium-term strategies to deliver vital support to Cambodian refugees fleeing Pol Pot guerrillas on the Cambodia–Thailand border in the 1980s (Taithe, 2016, pp. 335–358). The Yugoslav War in the 1990s, however, demonstrated how utterly helpless humanitarian organizations were in the absence of firm political resolve. The subsequent genocide in Rwanda (April–July 1994) exposed the absolute necessity for politics and humanitarian interventions to be well coordinated. Likewise, major natural disasters in the last decade and a half, such as the 2010 Haiti Earthquake and the 2011 Japan Tsunami, have revealed that available humanitarian aid resources are woefully inadequate to mount appropriate relief operations.

The biggest humanitarian crisis after the Second World War, the civil war in Türkiye's neighbor Syria has raged on for more than a decade, producing a humanitarian crisis that has affected the very nature of international humanitarian aid policies and how they are implemented in the field (Kireçci, 2015, pp. 1–6). Consequently, the management of this extensive humanitarian crisis, the diplomatic intricacies associated with it, the allocation of resources, and the countries that have contributed aid, along with the motivations behind their assistance are the subject of many studies in a myriad of disciplines and will continue to be so for years to come.

The Evolution from Classic Diplomacy to Humanitarian Diplomacy

Diplomacy is the established method of influencing the decisions and behavior of foreign governments and peoples through dialogue, negotiation, and other nonmilitary means. Historically, diplomacy constituted the nonviolent apparatus used to establish and maintain official relations between sovereign states. Although modern diplomatic practices, like other universal norms and institutions of international relations, are a product of the post-Renaissance European nation-state order, it would be no exaggeration to state that diplomacy has been practiced in every part of the world and by every human community since the beginning of political organization (Black, 2010, pp. 1–2). With the diversification and deepening of international relations in the twentieth century, diplomacy has expanded from official bilateral relations to include multilateral meetings and organizations, parliamentary diplomacy, international activities of supranational and subnational actors, as well as informal international ties between nongovernmental actors.

Factors such as the spread of communication, the end of the Cold War, the acceleration of economic and social globalization, and the increase in cross-border issues and conflicts underlie this expansion and deepening of international relations. By eliminating the restrictions of the formal, relatively slow, bureaucratic nature of traditional interstate relations, modern international relations and diplomacy are shaped to offer a more robust response both to the opportunities and threats emerging as a result of transnational interests.

Diplomacy has changed in scope, levels, and goals, becoming a fast-paced field driven by technological developments and an increasing number of actors. Given its embrace of other tools, goals, and objectives, some argue that the emergence of the new multifaceted form of diplomacy goes beyond expansion, asserting it to be a break from the former, almost as if it were a different craft altogether (Cooper, Heine and Thakur, 2013, p. 3). Several experts refer to classical diplomacy as club diplomacy in which a small number of elected individuals negotiate important issues with specific parties face to face, classifying the complex multilateral practice carried out by a much wider array of actors through different channels as network diplomacy (Cooper et al., 2013, p. 3).

The emergence of public diplomacy can also be read as an extension of the recent intricate change in international relations. Public diplomacy is an attempt by states, traditionally accustomed to communicating with other sovereign states through well-defined structures, to involve non-state actors in diplomacy (Sevin, 2017). Public diplomacy is a foreign policy tool in which governments mobilize resources, culture, values, and policies to communicate with and influence the citizens as opposed to the governments of other countries (Nye, 2008, pp. 94–109).

Because of the actors involved and the issues it seeks to resolve, humanitarian diplomacy falls on the soft power side of the diplomacy spectrum, alongside public and cultural diplomacy. Nevertheless, humanitarian diplomacy often rubs up against and even extends into the realm of hard power as it deals with very high-risk issues arising from humanitarian crises, natural disasters, and armed conflict.

Developed in the early 1980s to describe different forms of communication in world politics, track-one and track-two diplomacy are two concepts related to humanitarian diplomacy. Whereas track-one diplomacy covers the communication channels professional diplomats use in classical diplomacy or club diplomacy (Davidson and Montville, 1981, pp. 145–157), taking place between governments and government-authorized bodies, track-two diplomacy describes the informal, unstructured interactions of non-state actors. The success of humanitarian diplomacy depends on the practical and coordinated implementation of both tracks of diplomacy, especially in times of crisis.

Among the new forms of diplomacy frequently associated with soft power, fields such as public diplomacy, back-channel (track-two) diplomacy, and science and education diplomacy are often interconnected with each other and work in a symbiotic, if not synergetic manner. Humanitarian diplomacy, on the other hand, in addition to boasting its own unique practices, serves as the glue binding the above fields together.

Humanitarian Diplomacy

The success of humanitarian diplomacy depends on the methodical and coordinated execution of track-one and track-two diplomacy. What this means in practice is that, especially during times of crisis, the government-authorized communication channels used by professional diplomats need to

be accessible to non-state actors and open to more informal, unstructured interactions between parties.

Although helping those in need is as old as man himself, the emergence of humanitarian diplomacy as a concept is relatively new. According to Régnier, despite the increasingly widespread use of humanitarian diplomacy both in academia and in the field, an internationally accepted definition and understanding of how it should be conducted has yet to be reached (Régnier, 2011, pp. 1211–1237).

According to the International Federation of Red Cross and Red Crescent Societies (IFRC), humanitarian diplomacy is defined as "persuading decision makers and opinion leaders to act, at all times, in the interests of vulnerable people, and with full respect for fundamental humanitarian principles" (IFRC, 2017). Humanitarian diplomacy activities include efforts such as ensuring their participation in regulating the presence of humanitarian organizations in a given country, negotiating access to the civilian population in need of assistance and protection, monitoring aid programs, promoting respect for international law and norms, advocating at various levels to support humanitarian causes, and supporting local individuals and institutions (Minear and Smith, 2007, p. 1). Some experts include international legal processes, such as international humanitarian law, among humanitarian diplomacy activities (Whitall, 2009, p. 38).

Improving access to humanitarian assistance in conflicts and complex emergencies has always been a significant concern for policymakers and humanitarian actors. Since, historically, humanitarian efforts have often been conducted under precarious and unstable political conditions to ensure civilian aid delivery and protection, it is imperative that a balance between the conflict at hand and diplomacy be struck if humanitarian diplomacy is to have any real effect. In any case, the aim of humanitarian diplomacy differs from its classical counterpart in that the former seeks to protect the interests of individuals and communities caught in the crossfire of conflicts or crises and to secure their basic health, shelter, food, and security needs whereas the latter prioritizes the national interests of the states involved. Accordingly, one might perceive a conflict of interests between classical and humanitarian diplomacy. However, the effective coordination of classical and humanitarian diplomacy is probably the only efficient method to achieve the results desired. This would require state-appointed diplomats charged with eliminating or improving the political conditions leading up to the crises to work hand-in-hand with humanitarians who work outside of the diplomatic apparatus to identify the needs and to collect and distribute the aid.

While international organizations, supranational and national NGOs, and humanitarian organizations take a leading role in humanitarian diplomacy, individual nations occasionally involve themselves in humanitarian operations and the surrounding diplomacy. That said, however, there exist profound differences between the humanitarian diplomacy engaged in by nation-states and that practiced by the aforementioned organizations, most often arising from practitioners' legal and official status. Certain activities are most naturally carried out by government-appointed diplomats responsible for humanitarian aid. Similarly, some conventional diplomats employed in foreign ministries, development aid and disaster management agencies, and public or private organizations specializing in security and defense are specialists in humanitarian work. Like all their counterparts, these diplomats have rights and responsibilities defined by traditions and international diplomatic and consular law that are rarely violated. In contrast, since humanitarian organizations do not usually employ humanitarian diplomats, staff members lacking any experience in diplomatic negotiations frequently find themselves in the very center of the diplomatic nexus (Régnier, 2011, p. 1217), operating outside of a well-established international legal framework and supported only by nebulous interpretations of international humanitarian law, human rights law, and refugee law. Moreover, except for employees of the International Committee of Red Cross (ICRC) and IFRC, aid volunteers lack diplomatic immunity (Minear, 2007, p. 9). Finally, since political and security interests sometimes take precedence over the fundamental human rights of afflicted populations, especially the right to life, when nations deliberate over the best course of diplomacy, humanitarian diplomats may find their ability to maneuver and deliver aid to those in need severely limited.

Given all the above, it is absolutely vital that parties observe several fundamental humanitarian principles while engaging in humanitarian diplomacy and relief operations, namely humanity, impartiality, neutrality, independence, voluntary service, unity, and universality (ICRC, 2015). These principles shape the humanitarian diplomacy activities of the entire International Red Cross and Red Crescent Movement—the ICRC, the IFRC, and the national Red Crescent and Red Cross societies of 192 countries—both in theory and practice.

Humanity, impartiality, neutrality, independence, voluntary service, unity, and universality are the core principles guiding all the decisions and activities of the national Red Crescent and Red Cross societies and their employees.

The principle of humanity articulates that humanitarian efforts work to prevent and alleviate human suffering, to protect their lives and health, and to respect all people regardless of any superficial differences. Neutrality requires humanitarians to work toward the alleviation of all human suffering without discriminating on the basis of nationality, race, religious belief, class, or political opinion, affording priority to the most urgent situations. Impartiality means not to take sides in hostilities and not to become embroiled in political, racial, religious, or ideological discussions. The principle of independence involves acting autonomously of governments. Voluntary service means that those involved do so solely out of a humanitarian impetus and not to acquire any worldly gain. The principle of unity means that each country has only one Red Cross or Red Crescent Society that is open to everyone residing within the country's borders. Universality stipulates that humanitarianism is a worldwide endeavor and that all organizations involved in humanitarian work have equal status and share equal responsibilities and duties in helping one another.

Although those involved in the humanitarian aid system embrace universal principles such as equality and impartiality, political involvement is inevitable, especially pertaining to questions of who is in need, what needs are to be prioritized, who should provide for these needs, and by what means they should be delivered. Terms used in humanitarian aid system such as protection and prevention, relief from pain, and rehabilitation, point to a series of politically ascertained objectives. Similarly, "development aid" implies a long-term political goal that goes beyond immediate needs of people, whereas "foreign aid" prioritizes foreign policy interests of the donors.

Utilization of legal terminology to describe the different types of aid arises from the imperative to legitimize the provision of aid. This often involves framing aid within the context of safeguarding or promoting human rights, providing basic civilian infrastructure, and contributing to global welfare. The concept of "humanitarian intervention" is frequently invoked in conditions where humanitarian aid can only be provisioned through use of military means, as seen in creation of "humanitarian corridors" amidst war zones (Paulmann, 2013, pp. 215–238). Given this, some argue that humanitarian diplomacy serves as a tool to extend state sovereignty, akin to the role of war (Oliver, 2016). Paradoxically, while nation-states rely on international humanitarian organizations to deal with mass displacement and refugees, their own armies may simultaneously engage in actions such as capturing, detaining, and controlling the movements of the same affected populations (Weizman, 2012). This complex interplay evokes a strange and indirect connection between aid and the perpetuation of violence (Lopez et al., 2015, pp. 2232–2239).

Institutionalization of practices embedded in the epistemological accumulations of different cultures through the concepts of humanitarianism and philanthropy came in as an effort to mitigate the detrimental effects of crises caused by war and natural disasters in the modern era. Humanitarian diplomacy, one of the newest subfields of the discipline of international relations, will assuredly be subject to further discussion within academia, especially in how it can be effectively wielded to resolve humanitarian crises. As scholars delve into the complexities of humanitarian diplomacy, the discussion will extend beyond the immediate operational challenges to the broader implications for international relations and diplomacy.

References

Aaronson, M. (2013). The Nigerian Civil War and humanitarian intervention. In Everill, B. & Kaplan, J. (Eds.). *The history and practice of humanitarian intervention and aid in Africa* (pp. 176–196). Palgrave Macmillan.

Aaslestad, K. B. (2019). Aid to the war distressed: Early transnational humanitarian exchange at the close of the Napoleonic Wars. *Annales Historiques de la Révolution Française*, *397*(3), 171–192.

Black, J. (2010). *A history of diplomacy*. Wiltshire: Reaktion Books.

Bourdeau, M. (2022). Auguste Comte. In *The Stanford encyclopedia of philosophy*. https://plato.stanford.edu/archives/spr2022/entries/comte/

Brand, P. & Yancey, P. (1980). *Fearfully and wonderfully made*. Zondervan Publishing Company.

Brodman, J. W. (2009). *Charity and religion in Medieval Europe*. The Catholic University Press.

Cooper, A. F., Heine, J. & Thakur, R. (2013). *The Oxford handbook of modern diplomacy*. Oxford University Press.

Çizakça, M. (2006). *Osmanlı dönemi vakıflarının tarihsel ve ekonomik boyutları, Türkiye'de hayırseverlik: Vatandaşlar, vakıflar ve sosyal adalet* (pp. 19–31). TÜSEV.

Davidson, W. D. & Montville, J. W. (1981). Foreign Policy According to Freud. *Foreign Policy*, *45*, 145–157.

Davies, K. (2012). *Continuity, change and contest: Meanings of 'humanitarian' from the 'religion of humanity' to the Kosovo War*. Overseas Development Institute. https://cdn.odi.org/media/documents/7769.pdf

Dunant, H. (1986). *A memory of Solferino*. Geneva: ICRC.

Erul, B. (2012). Veda Hutbesi. In *TDV İslam Ansiklopedisi* (vol. 42, pp. 591–593). https://islamansiklopedisi.org.tr/veda-hutbesi

Fayda, M. (2006). *Hz. Ömer zamanında gayr-ı müslimler*. Marmara İlahiyat Vakfı.

Gross, M. L. (2007). From medical neutrality to medical immunity. *Virtual Mentor*, *9*(10), 718–721. Doi: 10.1001/virtualmentor.2007.9.10.mhst1-0710

Günay, H. M. (2012). Vakıf. In *TDV İslam Ansiklopedisi* (vol. 42, pp. 475–479). https://islamansiklopedisi.org.tr/vakif#1

Hitchcock, W. I. (2014). World War I and the humanitarian impulse. *The Tocqueville review/La revue Tocqueville*, *35*(2), 145–163.

Hoexter, M. (2003). Charity, the poor, and distribution of alms in Ottoman Algiers. In Bonner, M., Ener, M. & Singer, A (Eds.). *Poverty and charity in Middle Eastern contexts* (pp. 145–164). SUNY Press.

Kant, I. (1838). *Religion within the boundary of pure reason*. Thomas Allan and Co.

Kara, M. (2011). Tekke. In *TDV İslam Ansiklopedisi* (vol. 40, pp. 368–370). https://islamansiklopedisi.org.tr/tekke#1

Kızılay Tarih Belge ve Arşiv Yönetimi Müdürlüğü. (2016). *Dünya'nın ilk Kızılay'ı, dünyaya hilali armağan eden Kızılay*. http://kizilaytarih.org/dosya001.html

Kızılay. (2006). *Hilal-i Ahmer'den Türk Kızılayı'na 148 yıllık yardım çınarı*. https://www.kizilay.org.tr/Haber/HaberDetay/2850

Kireçci, M. A. (2015). Humanitarian diplomacy in theory and practice. *Perceptions*, *20*(1), 1–6.

Kraut, R. (2020). Altruism. In *The Stanford Encyclopedia of Philosophy*. https://plato.stanford.edu/archives/fall2020/entries/altruism/

Lopez, P. J., Bhungalia, L. & Newhouse, L. (2015). Environment and planning A: Economy and space. *Geographies of Humanitarian Violence*, *47*(11), 2232–2239.

McChesney, R. (1991). *Waqf in Central Asia*. Princeton University Press.

Minear, L. (2007). The craft of humanitarian diplomacy. In Minear, L. & Smith, H. (Eds.). *Humanitarian diplomacy: Practitioners and their craft* (pp. 7–35). United Nations University Press.

Minear, L. & Smith, H. (2007). Introduction. In Minear, L. & Smith, H. (Eds.). *Humanitarian diplomacy: Practitioners and their craft* (pp. 1–4). United Nations University Press.

Nye, J. S. (2008). Public diplomacy and soft power. *The Annals of American Academy of Political and Social Science*, *616*(1), 94–109.

Oliver, K. (2016). *Carceral humanitarianism: Logics of refugee detention*. University of Minnesota Press.

Online Etymology Dictionary. (n.d.-a). *Human*. https://www.etymonline.com/word/human

Online Etymology Dictionary. (n.d.-b). *Humanitarian.* https://www.etymonline.com/word/human

Paulmann, J. (2013). Conjunctures in the history of international humanitarian aid during the twentieth century. *Humanity: An International Journal of Human Rights, Humanitarianism, and Development, 4*(2), 215–238.

Placido, N. (2015). *A history of charity and the church.* The North American Association of Christians in Social Work Convention. Grand Rapids.

Régnier, P. (2011). The emerging concept of humanitarian diplomacy: Identification of a community of practice and prospects for international recognition. *International Review of the Red Cross, 93*(884), 1211–1237. https://doi.org/10.1017/S1816383112000574

Schimmel, A. (1975). *Mystical dimensions of Islam.* North Carolina University Press.

Sevin, E. (2017). *Public diplomacy and the implementation of foreign policy in the US, Sweden and Turkey.* Palgrave Macmillan.

Singer, A. (2012). *İyilik yap denize at: Müslüman toplumlarda hayırseverlik.* Kitap Yayınevi.

Solecki, R. S. (1972). *Shanidar: The humanity of neanderthal man.* Allen Lane.

Spikins, P. A., Rutherford, H. E. & Needham, A. P. (2010). From homininity to humanity: Compassion from the earliest archaics to modern humans. *Time and Mind, 3*(3), 303–325.

Taithe, B. (2016). The cradle of the new humanitarian system? International work and European volunteers at the Cambodian border camps, 1979–1993. *Contemporary European History, 25*(2), 335–358.

The International Committee of the Red Cross (ICRC). (2015). *The fundamental principles of International Red Cross and Red Cresent Movement.* https://www.icrc.org/sites/default/files/topic/file_plus_list/4046-the_fundamental_principles_of_the_international_red_cross_and_red_crescent_movement.pdf

The International Federation of Red Cross and Red Crescent Societies (IFRC). (2017). *Humanitarian diplomacy policy.* https://www.ifrc.org/sites/default/files/Humanitarian-Diplomacy-Policy_EN.pdf

Weizman, E. (2012). *The least of all possible evils: Humanitarian violence from Arendt to Gaza.* Verso Books.

Whitall, J. (2009). 'It's like talking to a brick wall': Humanitarian diplomacy in the occupied Palestinian territory. *Progress in Development Studies, 9*(1), 37–53.

2 The Relationship between Classic and Humanitarian Diplomacy

Orhan Battır

In today's world, nation-states constitute the very cornerstone of the international system. Diplomacy is, in this current status quo, the single most effective tool that individual nation-states have at their disposal to structure and regulate their relations both with each other and supranational organizations. Yet, this has indeed been the case for all states and state-like entities throughout history, as primitive societies living in small groups have, even if not calling it by this name, engaged in some form of diplomacy in their dealings with neighboring communities.

Though their methods may differ or go by diverse names at different times of human history, it is thus possible to observe acts of diplomacy in the political apparatus of every human community that has existed—whether in the smallest of ancient communities, multiethnic empires spanning large swaths of geography, or modern nation-states. Despite these deep roots, however, it is only natural that diplomacy, just like every other political and administrative apparatus, would evolve in parallel with the changing status quo in order to fit political modus operandi and fulfill the needs of the societies that constitute them.

Old, otherwise known as classic or traditional diplomacy and *new* diplomacy, which includes a wide range of novel actors, practices, and other mechanisms that operate in the diplomatic process. While discussing the difference between new and old diplomacy, the literature differs between *ad hoc diplomacy*, essentially acts undertaken on a one-time basis in response to a specific issue, and the *continuous diplomacy* conducted during modern times by official emissaries and ambassadors (Tuncer, 2002). Similar to numerous concepts related to international politics, the very concept of diplomacy has undergone a fundamental transformation in the twenty-first century, thus giving birth to new strands of diplomacy featuring entirely new approaches and practices. What comes to mind when new diplomacy is discussed today are diplomatic practices based on dynamic interactions between new actors acting outside the authority of governmental bodies as opposed to practices that are bound to certain formal conditions and procedures executed by official diplomats employed in permanent diplomatic missions.

DOI: 10.4324/9781003503187-2

The bloc politics that emerged following WWII gave way to a new international system, which, in turn, gave rise to entirely new dimensions in international relations. Rapid globalization has likewise paved the way for unparalleled interaction not only between political and military actors, as had traditionally been the case, but also between financial, social, cultural, and other elements of societies. The diversity of issues finding themselves on the agenda of internal and external politics consequently increased with each passing year. As an integral part of the international policymaking and execution apparatus, diplomacy similarly underwent radical changes both in theory and practice, taking on new dimensions entirely. This multidimensional form of diplomacy, further characterized by an influx of diverse actors, has been dubbed *new diplomacy* in the literature. Given, on the other hand, their formal sedentary practices and relatively rigid rules, it would be more prudent to designate both continuous and ad hoc diplomacy as *classic diplomacy*.[1]

In order, thus, to fully understand the relationship and interplay between classic and humanitarian diplomacy, it is imperative that one keep in mind not only the aforementioned aspects of classic diplomacy but also the distinction between old and new diplomacy.

Conceptual and Theoretical Framework

To address the relationship between classic and humanitarian diplomacy essentially requires one to compare old and new diplomacy with one another. Such an analysis will naturally delve into how these two forms of diplomacy are framed and understood as well as how they manifest in practice. However, despite their having the same conceptual and functional foundations, even frequently serving as references for one another, the relationship between classic and humanitarian diplomacy is frequently misconstrued. Whereas relatively new concepts are sometimes overshadowed by classic concepts and thus fail to manifest their true value, old and new concepts are sometimes misunderstood to be alternatives or opposites to one another. We similarly observe new concepts in particular being evaluated outside of their original scope in the literature, something that stems mostly from concepts not having been clearly defined and developed. Yet when new concepts derived from classic concepts are correctly understood within their own framework, their positive sides—sides that reinforce, support, and enrich the old—shine through. With this understanding, we may are imbued with the ability to make informed comparisons between the old and new, to accurately define the relationship between them, and to identify where they overlap and oppose one another. Given this, it would be beneficial to examine the word's etymology and how, as a concept, it has developed over time. This, when combined with an awareness of the distinction between classic and new diplomacy, will allow us not only to grasp both what humanitarian diplomacy is and what it is not but also to conceptualize its relationship with classic diplomacy.

What is Diplomacy? Exploring its Etymology, Historical Development, and Definitions

Knowledge of the etymological roots of established and widely accepted words/concepts opens up a window into said words' historical development, as the names used to represent them are a natural byproduct of the social and/or geographical realities of the community in which they originate. The widely accepted view in the literature is that the word *diplomacy* finds its origins in the Greek *diplomeis*, which, in turn, gave birth to the Latin *diplōma*. The word diploma itself means *double* or *to fold into two*. Historically in the Roman Empire, two metal plates containing folded over the other were used as official documents and licenses by different segments of the population, including by officials sent into foreign lands as messengers and envoys. Called a *diplōma* based on their shape, these metal plates eventually evolved into documents made of other, non-metallic materials; however, the name diploma was retained. This was not only the case in the Ancient Roman Empire; indeed, Ancient Greek city-states similarly called government-issued documents and, more specifically, documents used between different states and communities diplomas because they consisted of two parts folded over the other (Meray, 1956, p. 81; Tuncer, 2002, p. 9). In fact, the information they contained was both protected and concealed from prying eyes while in transit by folding these documents. Folding was a physical act that demonstrated the importance afforded to documents' content and—perhaps more important for our specific purposes—to the notion of confidentiality, a principle that forms the basis of classic diplomacy.

Considering that at least one sense of the word *diploma* was used for practices or documents *official* in foreign affairs, international relations were governed by certain rules and principles during the Ancient Greek and Roman periods, which, although differing both in form and methodology from those espoused today, laid the very foundation for modern diplomacy. Still, even the most primitive of societies engaged in some sort of diplomacy—even if it went by a completely different name or none at all—that was dictated by specific conventions and rules during their interactions with others. Without a doubt, even the smallest and most basic communities were unable to survive without interacting with other human groups. In addition to engaging in trade to acquire necessary goods that they did not produce, communities would, at the very least, open and maintain communication channels to ward off potential threats. Such communication was undertaken directly by community leaders themselves or through representatives, envoys, or messengers who either spoke on behalf of the rulers or carried news, letters, and edicts between them.

States or similar political entities have throughout human history built and maintained relations with one another through representatives (what may be considered diplomats in modern parlance) and negotiations. These interactions constitute the bare minimum of diplomacy. Indeed, from something as small as land-sharing agreements between tribal communities partitioning hunting and farming areas to military, political, and economic negotiations between large empires, whether they be executed verbally or in writing, are all the end product or result of diplomatic endeavors. It would therefore appear not only that the history of diplomacy has deeper roots than of states themselves but that diplomacy has also served as a central tool in establishing and maintaining relations with *other* societies, thereby making it, so to speak, essential to external policy. Despite this, however, it would be impossible to assert that the way diplomacy is understood and diplomatic activities are conducted have remained unchanged till this day.

By virtue of its fundamental role in the creation and implementation of foreign policy throughout history, diplomacy has, in whatever form it may have manifested at a given time, naturally been afforded a place of primacy in statecraft. Until the nineteenth century, diplomacy was largely regarded as the use of subterfuge, lies, and intrigue to acquire what could not be attained through war (Tuncer, 2015, p. 253). In fact, we find several influential writers characterizing diplomacy in a negative ethical light. Among these are Ambrose Bierce, who, it ironic and otherwise sarcastic manner, describes diplomacy as "the patriotic art of lying for one's country," Charles Maurice de Talleyrand-Périgord, who equates it to "lying and denying," (Bierce, 2000, p. 57), Ludwig Börne, who likens it to "Diplomacy is to speak French, to speak nothing, and to speak falsehood," (Freeman, 1997, p. 73) and Zhou Enlai, who regards diplomacy as the "continuation of war by other means." Similarly, a Chinese proverb speaks of diplomacy as "the art of saying the nastiest things in the nicest way" (İskit, 2014, p. 3).

With the rise of nation-states and the international community's eventual espousal of relations being *among equals*, both the nature of diplomacy and its fundamental role in statecraft became ever more apparent. For in modern statecraft, diplomacy no longer deals simply with the rules and principles governing foreign relations and policy (Kürkçüoğlu, 2005, p. 312); it constitutes the entire apparatus by means of which the international community engages in discussions and negotiations with one another on the grand scale. Diplomacy thus directs policymakers in their decisions concerning bilateral and multilateral relations, trade agreements, peace treaties, and declarations of war. The Turkish Language Association (Türk Dil Kurumu, TDK) defines diplomacy as *(i)* "the entirety of agreements governing international relations," *(ii)* "the occupation and art of representing one's nation in a foreign nation and in international meetings," and *(iii)* "the profession of one employed in this capacity" (Türk Dil Kurumu, n.d.). The *Oxford Advanced Learner's Dictionary* defines diplomacy as *(i)* "the activity of managing relations between different countries; the skill in doing this" and *(ii)* "the skill in dealing with people in difficult situations without upsetting or offending them" (Oxford Learner's Dictionaries, n.d.). Being inherently related with international relations and foreign policy, diplomacy has also various different definitions and interpretations. According to Morgenthau, diplomacy is the art of peaceful protection of national interests, the conduct of international relations by peaceful means and methods (Morgenthau, 1946, p. 1068). Diplomacy also defined as "the conduct of relations between sovereign states through the medium of officials based at home or abroad" (Berridge and James, 2003, pp. 69–70), and "the process of transferring the opinions of thinkers and opinions of a government directly to the decision-makers of other governments" (Gönlübol, 1993, p. 116).

Diplomacy, having the highest level of acceptance in terms of international law and universal values, is an interaction and primary foreign policy tool in which the most appropriate options other than war are sought out.

It can be argued that of all the foreign policy tools at nations' disposal, diplomacy stands out in its affirmation of international law and espousal of universal values, which, in turns increases its legitimacy in the eyes of decision makers. Indeed, its constructive nature and aversion to war allows diplomats to arrive at the most appropriate course of action quickly and easily. In fact, diplomacy is, by its very nature, grounded in mutual interaction in which the interests of all parties, as opposed to those of a single member state, are served. That said, however, it would be a gross overstatement to assert that diplomacy always produces results beneficial to all parties involved or ensures the peaceful resolution of disagreements. Indeed, diplomatic negotiations have the potential to further aggravate ongoing conflicts and exhaust peaceful solutions. In addition to this, diplomacy can also shake up the power balance/imbalance between parties and exacerbate running conflicts of interests.

Distinction between Old (Classic) and New Diplomacy

The meaning attached to diplomacy has changed to fit the needs of whatever stage of development a nation or society finds itself in at the time. This change was intrinsically related to how nations were structurally organized, governed, and interactions. In absolute monarchies, for instance, diplomacy consisted of monarchs and the emissaries charged with carrying out their will and representing them abroad, with the most important characteristic of this form of diplomacy being confidentiality. As nation-states and democratic governments came to dominate the international system, diplomacy rose to become the most important policymaking tool and was able, at least partially, to be followed by the public as an indicator of increasing political involvement. However, transparency was only first codified as a central tenant of diplomacy in 1918 when US President Woodrow Wilson set down his Fourteen Points, which, as a consequence, gave rise to the concept of *open diplomacy*.[2]

The most visible change is in how diplomacy is executed on the practical level is the transition from ad hoc to continuous diplomacy. Dominant from the time that the first settled civilizations began to emerge until the fifteenth century, ad hoc diplomacy involved messengers or emissaries who would travel abroad to realize a single, defined objective or to perform a specific duty before immediately returning to their homeland. The Hittites, Ancient Egyptians, Greek city-states, Romans, Byzantines, and Ottomans all engaged in ad hoc diplomacy to resolve problems that arose between nations, to reach mutual agreements, and to communicate with other polities. As its unilateral and temporary nature began to respond increasingly less to nations' needs, ad hoc diplomacy would begin to give way to what may be considered as the first examples of modern diplomatic systems in Europe by the fifteenth century and in the Ottoman Empire toward the end of the eighteenth century. However, the progressive adoption and ubiquity of continuous diplomacy did not spell the complete end of ad hoc diplomacy. For even as permanent diplomatic missions gained greater clout on the wider international scene, ad hoc diplomacy continued in the form of official visits by heads of state, international conferences attended by ministers of foreign affairs or other ministers, and specialists sent abroad to conduct special negotiations or projects (Tuncer, 1984, pp. 51–56).

Overtime, modern nation-states would increasingly adopt continuous diplomacy and begin establishing permanent missions in each other's capital cities. This transition away from ad hoc diplomacy was indeed a watershed moment for diplomacy as it represented a shift away from unilateralist *modus operandi* and a move toward bilateral relations in which representatives of diplomatic missions and policymakers play a significantly more active role. Accordingly, it would certainly not be out of place to refer to continuous diplomacy as *new diplomacy* given the stark difference between it and ad hoc diplomacy. That said, however, since representatives of permanent missions were for all intents and purposes the effective agents of continuous diplomacy and acted in an official and formal capacity, it may be more prudent to refer to this form of diplomacy as *traditional/classic diplomacy*. This becomes even more clearer considering that diplomacy continued to evolve and take on ever-increasing roles and obligations toward the middle of the twentieth century—so much so that the term *new diplomacy* now evokes markedly different concepts and practices than what is described above. The international system underwent a fundamental restructuring in terms of how it functioned as the Cold War continued to loom on, thus forcing the concept of diplomacy to undergo major changes and policymaking to adopt new concepts and practices congruent with the emergent status quo. New forms of diplomacy characterized by the introduction of civilian organizations and actors began to materialize at increasing speeds, such as public diplomacy, digital diplomacy, cultural diplomacy, and humanitarian diplomacy.

One frequent change frequently encountered while exploring the conceptual and historical development of diplomacy is, beyond the means and methods employed while conducting international relations, the influx of new actors, stakeholders, and alternative arenas where parties can engage with one another that emerge in tandem with increased political participation and democratization. Contrary to classic diplomacy, the most apparent characteristic of the new forms of diplomacy that have cropped up is the active role that civilian entities play in the diplomatic process.

While individual nations and international organizations continue to constitute the most essential elements of the international system, various civilian entities, such as NGOs, multinational corporations, media organs, social media networks, think tanks, and opinion leaders, not only exert exceptional influence in the political arena but also play central roles in new diplomacy practices. Another important characteristic of new diplomacy practices is that, unlike classic diplomacy, new diplomacy does not seek solely to protect state interests and increase a state's power within the international community; it strives to advance humanitarian values, safeguard basic human rights, and promote global peace. Of all the new forms of diplomacy that have emerged in modern times, humanitarian diplomacy is certainly that which most strongly embraces a human-centric outlook.

Humanitarian Diplomacy

Adding the words *humanitarian* or *humanist* as qualifiers to a preexisting concept generally implies an effort to rectify and prevent infringements against human rights and values. These efforts are maintained by civilian initiatives and activism just as much as state authorities and the political elite. Humanitarian aid, humanitarian law, humanitarian security, humanitarian intervention, and humanitarian diplomacy are but a few examples of such concepts. The characteristic dominant shared by all of these concepts beyond the fact that they are all related either directly or indirectly to international policy is that they embrace a human-centric approach while endeavoring to prevent and solve problems and thus, by extension, prioritize human welfare over policies that seek to increase state power.

The humanitarian tragedies and human rights violations that would occur when, during political, military, economic, and legal interventions, the human component was either ignored entirely or afforded a position of secondary importance spurred civilian organizations into action, impelling them to work hand in hand with official actors in their diplomatic endeavors. The birth and evolution of humanitarian diplomacy was largely a consequence of this process

(See Figure 2.1). Humanitarian diplomacy was, in essence, born out of the genuine need to solve problems caused by increasingly brutal practices that ignored the human element during an era when international policy prioritized national security and survival over real political concerns. Similarly, humanitarian diplomacy is grounded in collective actions seeking to improve the situations of people who find themselves helpless in the face of natural and manmade disasters.

Since humanitarian diplomacy is relatively new compared to similar concepts used in the field, it is difficult to offer a universally agreed-upon definition for it. Since humanitarian diplomacy generally evokes humanitarian relief work, efforts undertaken against human rights violations, and humanitarian interventions, these concepts are sometimes misconstrued to be the same thing. That the humanitarian relief efforts and human rights advocacy undertaken by humanitarian relief organizations are both directly and indirectly associated with humanitarian diplomacy[3] has led the public to perceive it as such. Nevertheless, humanitarian relief organizations and non-governmental human rights advocacy groups are indeed the most important actors in humanitarian diplomacy. Likewise, the term humanitarian diplomacy first appeared in a paper entitled "Humanitarian Diplomacy of the United States" (Straus et al., 1912) presented at the annual meeting of the American Society of International Law. In this paper, Straus argues that at the foundation of American humanitarian aid lies polices seeking to intervene in the internal politics of nations less powerful than herself. Yet, this would appear to be closer to humanitarian intervention than actual humanitarian diplomacy.

Humanitarian diplomacy, however, adopts a human-centric approach and is more closely associated with on-the-ground work actively seeking resolutions to humanitarian issues; however, it is also much more than this (Battır, 2017, pp. 39–40). As one of the fundamental elements of public diplomacy, humanitarian diplomacy makes prolific use of what I shall call humanitarian negotiations that involve both official and civilian actors. The most important function of humanitarian negotiations is to imbue diplomacy with a humanitarian quality.

Definitions for humanitarian diplomacy are, for the most part, structured around humanitarian relief, basic human rights, official and civilian actors, and humanitarian negotiations. The International Federation of Red Cross and Red Crescent Societies (IFRC), for instance, defines humanitarian diplomacy as "persuading decision makes and opinion leaders to act, at all times, in the interests of vulnerable people, and with full respect for fundamental humanitarian principles" (IFRC, 2009). Founded in Türkiye, IHH Humanitarian Relief Foundation describes itself and its works as follows:

> *In addition to humanitarian relief work and human rights activities, IHH [carries] out humanitarian diplomacy and take[s] action where intergovernmental diplomacy fails in order to protect civilians, to find missing people, to rescue hostages, [and to] take steps to resolve the issues in conflict areas, areas hit by natural disaster, and warzones.*

(IHH, n.d.)

MILESTONES IN THE DEVELOPMENT OF HUMANITARIAN DIPLOMACY

1820's

Responsibility to Protect

Movement within state and civil society to address human suffering

1864

ICRC sends delegates

ICRC sent two delegates on a mission to approach the parties to conflict (the Danish and Austro-Prussians) who were fighting over the Duchies of Schleswig and Holstein.

1912

Humanitarian diplomacy policy

Straus introduces humanitarian diplomacy as foreign policy tool and calls it the "diplomacy of humanity".

1980

First book on humanitarian diplomacy

The first book that sees humanitarian diplomacy as a foreign policy tool of the state is published.

Farer, Tom J. Toward a Humanitarian Diplomacy: A Primer for Policy. New York: New York University Press, 1980.1984

ICRC founded

Dunant organizes diplomatic conference, appeals to state leaders.

1863

"Humanitarian Diplomacy" introduced

American Diplomat Oscar Straus introduces term into vernacular of foreign policy.

1891

Geneva Convention

ICRC status gives it unique access to diplomatic space.

1949

ICRC as primary actor

Gasser replaces the state with ICRC as primary practitioner of humanitarian diplomacy.

1984

MORAL IMPERATIVE: RESPONSIBILITY TO PROTECT

PRIMARY OBJECTIVE: PROTECTION (ACCESS ASSUMED)

1820 … 1980

1864 … 1984

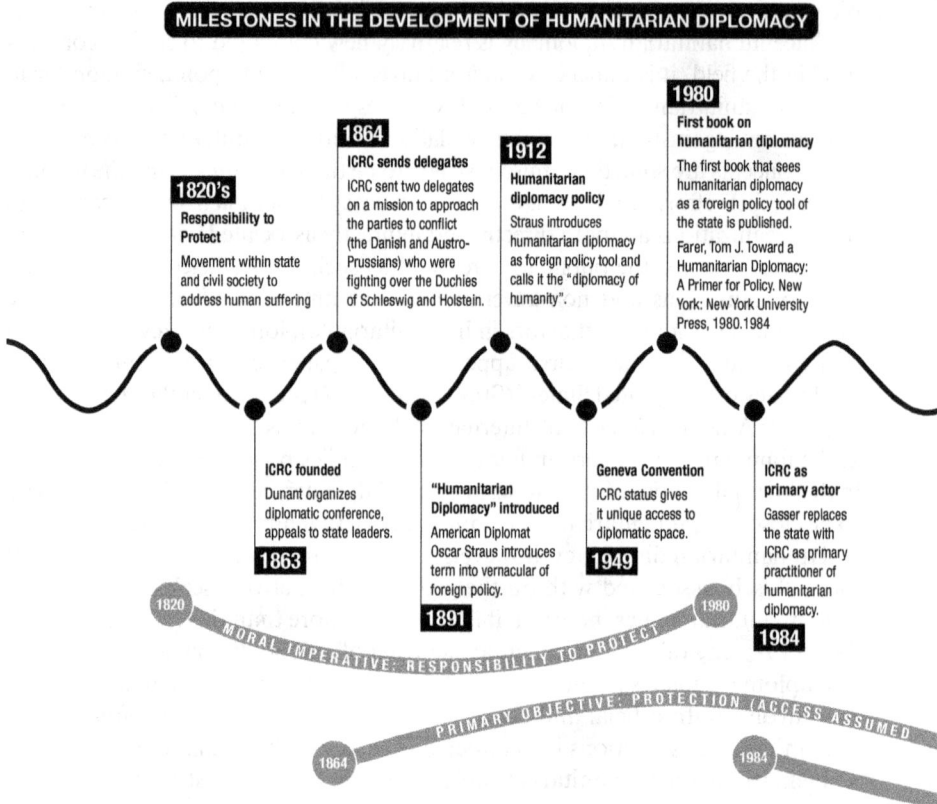

Timeline of humanitarian diplomacy. The idea and practice of humanitarian diplomacy has been shaped over time. The phrase was first introduced by a state actor in 1891, but today most commonly occurs in non-state actor discussions. The basis for practicing humanitarian diplomacy were moral grounds, but since 1949 the practice of humanitarian diplomacy is enshrined as a legal framework involving humanitarian law. Whereas until the 1990's humanitarian access was assumed as a prerequisite to practice humanitarian diplomacy, the focus of modern is to negotiate access in the first place.

Figure 2.1 "The milestones in the development of humanitarian diplomacy."

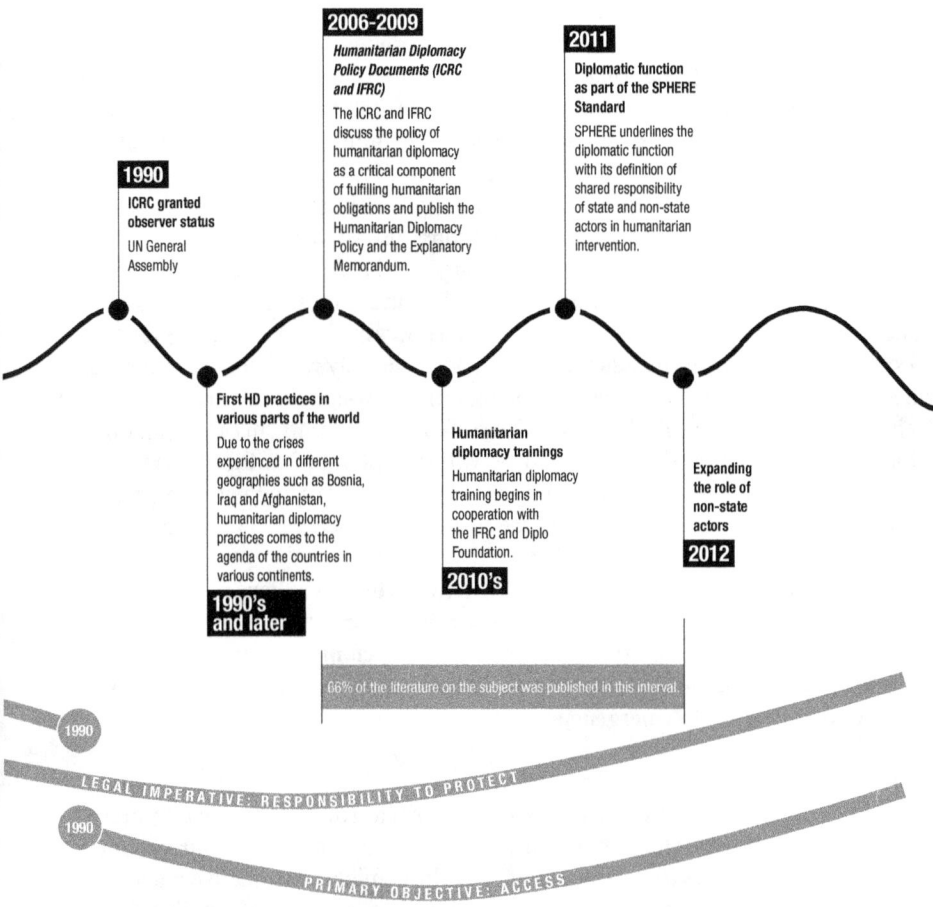

2006-2009

Humanitarian Diplomacy Policy Documents (ICRC and IFRC)

The ICRC and IFRC discuss the policy of humanitarian diplomacy as a critical component of fulfilling humanitarian obligations and publish the Humanitarian Diplomacy Policy and the Explanatory Memorandum.

2011

Diplomatic function as part of the SPHERE Standard

SPHERE underlines the diplomatic function with its definition of shared responsibility of state and non-state actors in humanitarian intervention.

1990

ICRC granted observer status

UN General Assembly

First HD practices in various parts of the world

Due to the crises experienced in different geographies such as Bosnia, Iraq and Afghanistan, humanitarian diplomacy practices comes to the agenda of the countries in various continents.

1990's and later

Humanitarian diplomacy trainings

Humanitarian diplomacy training begins in cooperation with the IFRC and Diplo Foundation.

2010's

Expanding the role of non-state actors

2012

66% of the literature on the subject was published in this interval.

1990

LEGAL IMPERATIVE: RESPONSIBILITY TO PROTECT

1990

PRIMARY OBJECTIVE: ACCESS

-ed: This image is derived from the doctoral thesis of Michael David Clark with his permission and has been enhanced by the editor. Michael David Clark, Humanitarian Multi-Track Diplomacy, University of Groningen, 2018, p. 60.

Whitall describes humanitarian diplomacy as "the use of International Law and the humanitarian imperative as complimentary levers to facilitate the delivery of assistance or to promote the protection of civilians in a complex political emergency" (Whitall, 2009, p. 38). As is the case elsewhere, this definition emphasizes humanitarian aid and a human-centered outlook. Finally, Minear and Smith point out that "humanitarian diplomacy involves activities carried out by humanitarian institutions and personnel, as distinct from diplomacy exercised by traditional diplomats" and "comprise[s] such efforts as arranging for the presence of international humanitarian organizations and personnel in a given country, negotiating access to civilian populations in need of assistance and protection, and monitoring assistance programmes, promoting respect for international law and norms" after having "obtain[ed] the space from political and military authorities within which to function with integrity." (2007, p. 1).

Based on the characteristics and definitions discussed above, humanitarian diplomacy differs from traditional diplomacy in that the former incorporates actions supportive of humanitarian work. Accordingly, humanitarian diplomacy makes up where traditional diplomacy falls short because it lacks practices tailored specifically to deal with the issues at hand and is severely restricted by numerous rules and conventions. The areas in which government-appointed diplomats may legitimately act are naturally limited to those areas the government of the nation in which they are employed considers to be within diplomats' authority. As such, diplomats are obligated to act according to the rules laid out by their own government and by the political authority of the country in which they are stationed.

Humanitarian diplomacy actors are, by virtue of being civilians themselves, bound by markedly fewer external restraints. This autonomy protects humanitarian diplomacy from the lethargic and clumsy nature of classic bureaucratic procedures and renders it more adept at providing quick and effective responses to emergencies.

Humanitarian diplomacy actors are, by virtue of being civilians themselves, bound by markedly fewer external restraints. This autonomy protects humanitarian diplomacy from the lethargic and clumsy nature of classic bureaucratic procedures and renders it more adept at providing quick and effective responses to emergencies. Indeed, the defining characteristic of humanitarian diplomacy is that it provides a platform for traditional and official entities to collaborate with civilian organizations.

Comparing Classic and Humanitarian Diplomacy: Their Actors, Goals, Approaches, and Tools

Classic and Humanitarian Diplomacy: A Comparison of Actors

Those involved in the creation and execution of international policy can be divided into two primary categories: *(i)* institutional-level actors and *(ii)* executive actors. The former consists of sovereign nations and the international organizations created by them. Diplomatic negotiations are invariably conducted between sovereign nations and various second-level organizations vested with official authority to act on their behalf abroad. Executive actors, on the other hand, are carefully selected to represent their nation abroad and consist of foreign affairs officials, representatives of diplomatic missions, and other individuals vested with some form of official authority.

Since diplomacy regulates international relations, it naturally falls under the auspices of the state apparatus. In short, diplomacy is the formal practice of putting international policies devised by decision makers into practice (Arı, 1997, p. 297). In lieu of conflict and attrition, diplomacy embraces more constructive means, such as counsel and negotiations. Given, furthermore, that diplomacy seeks to achieve national foreign policy goals and to ensure that certain red lines are not transgressed, diplomatic enterprises must be conducted with the utmost finesse by skilled state officials. These individuals naturally need to have mastered the diplomatic processes related to the foreign policy positions of their own nation and whatever specific objective they were vested with fulfilling. It was essential, furthermore, that they be well versed not only in the politics of the nations with which they were engaged but also in their linguistic peculiarities, cultural codes, and values. In addition to all this, diplomats need to be effective representatives and possess highly refined skills of persuasion in order to lead successful negotiations.

The above paragraph applies to classic formal diplomacy because the content each line describes ways to augment state power, prestige, and efficacy. Nevertheless, the last few decades have borne witness to the rise of new non-state actors, which has enacted a visible change in the *modus operandi* of the international system. The extraordinary interconnection and interaction precipitated by political and economic globalization marked the conclusion of an era where nation-states were the sole actors in international politics. The subsequent era has seen an unprecedented number of non-state entities with the power to influence and even direct the actions of decision makers. The most important characteristic of these new actors is—beyond the fact that they shoulder central roles in international politics and, by extension, diplomacy—their civilian character. The most apparent factor distinguishing humanitarian diplomacy from classic and new diplomacy is the character of the actors.

Consultation and negotiations between similar-ranking officials form the foundation of classic diplomacy both in theory and in practice. Given that strict protocol is followed during formal negotiations and international proceedings, the executive actors of classic diplomacy are not overly diverse and include heads of state, cabinet ministers, other governmental officials, representatives of permanent diplomat missions, and official diplomats. Even when the institutional and executive actors of classic diplomacy are taken together, humanitarian diplomacy actors exhibit a significantly greater diversity in terms of functions and roles.

Humanitarian diplomacy actors fall into two basic categories: Official and civilian actors. The former group includes the entirety of institutional and executive actors in classic diplomacy. In other words, the actors of classical diplomacy are also the official actors of humanitarian diplomacy. Civil actors, on the other hand include the staff, volunteers, and other individuals either working in or somehow affiliated with these organizations. Given all this, humanitarian diplomacy boasts a considerably more diverse typology of actors compared to classic diplomacy.

Classic and Humanitarian Diplomacy: Similarities and Differences in Goals, Methods, and Tools

Power struggles are endemic in the international system and international relations. All states seek out means to augment their power and ability to influence others either directly or indirectly. Throughout the twentieth century, power was conceived in the conventional sense—as military and economic superiority—whose increase was considered a policy goal. With increasingly advanced information, communication, and transportation technologies began to permeate into every facet of life, including international policymaking, decisionmakers, and societies at large were forced to reevaluate how they perceived of power.

More recently, power has acquired new conceptual and practical dimensions without ceding any of its original importance. As the traditional sources and axes of power have shifted in line with this new understanding, mutual cooperation between different actors has become the norm in international politics. While goals have remained the same, this has led not only to a change in how nations execute foreign policy and diplomatic processes but also to the diversification of the tools at their disposal. Table 2.1 above outlines the main characteristics of classic and humanitarian diplomacy.

The Evolution of Diplomacy: Changing Methods to Achieve Unchanging Goals

While power is the fundamental element of the international system, diplomacy acts as grease that keep the gears of the system turning, indicating a synergetic relationship between the two. Indeed, greater power allows nations to engage in diplomacy more effectively, as the party with the upper hand during negotiations is generally regarded in a more favorable light and thus better positioned to ensure that its interests are served. Likewise, greater diplomatic clout enhances the overall efficacy of power, which in turn helps nations leave negotiations having attained certain concessions from the other party.

The quality and use of power possessed by international system actors is just as important as its conceptual framework. Material and immaterial power can, depending on the situation at hand, manifest as either hard or soft power. Whereas hard power is the ability to coerce others to act in a certain way through, for instance, economic and military interventions and is thus more material in nature, soft power is the capacity to persuade others through more abstract means. Examples of hard power in international policymaking include military intervention and economic sanctions against a country to precipitate changes of behavior. Soft power, on the other hand, is when a nation achieves her political goals by shaping the preferences of other countries that hold her in high esteem or that covet welfare and the opportunities she offers, in such a way that persuades them to act in a desired manner (Nye, 2005, pp. 14–15). In other words, soft power is when a nation creates an alluring image of its material and cultural lifestyle in the collective psyche of other nations, so alluring, in fact, that it causes them to willfully behave in ways that advance its own political goals. Smart power, on the other hand, is when a nation adopts a political strategy that makes use of both hard and soft power in a synthesized manner (Nye, 2011, p. XIV). The use of smart power in international relations invariably involves signaling the ideal course of action to other nations but also implies a relatively superior foreign political capacity and the potential introduction of economic and military assets.

Driven forward by globalization and the information revolution, the use of power in international politics has undergone two fundamental changes during the modern era: *(i)* power transition, or the transfer of power from one state to another, and *(ii)* power diffusion, or the transfer of power from states to non-state actors (Nye, 2011, p. XV). The transfer of power from one nation to another has, throughout history, transpired as a result of war, geographical discoveries, scientific and industrial advances, and other similar developments that would have regional and sometimes even global repercussions. Just as such events have caused even the most powerful of states to lose their sources of power and shed their advantaged position, they have allowed weaker nations to grow and fill in the gap left by waning superpowers. Power diffusion, on the other hand, occurs in one of two manners. The first is when different nations, whose economic, political, military, and various other interests converge, come together to create supranational organizations vested with official authority. The second form of power diffusion occurs when civilian organizations increase in both quality and quantity to such a degree that they are able to influence traditional actors. Though civilian actors do not replace states in the literal sense, they are able to direct state power to achieve their own objectives. Over time, gaining public approval and the support of civilian initiatives has become the most effective means for nations to acquire greater power in the international arena.

As non-state actors gain enough clout to influence the behaviors of individual nations, or, more precisely, of the political elite of these nations, their presence is increasingly felt on the international stage and their ability to affect international policy becomes ever more apparent. With globalization and technological advances making information and of communications devices easier to access than ever before, individuals and societies alike demand and expect increasingly more from their governments. These demands center on democratization, or rather *free political participation*, and the expansion of human rights. Decision makers, unable to remain aloof to these demands, naturally began developing policies to meet their constituents' expectations. On the international level, the end of the Cold War was

Table 2.1 "Comparison chart between classical diplomacy and humanitarian diplomacy"

Type of Diplomacy	Actors		Goals	Methods	Instruments
Classic/ Traditional Diplomacy	*Institutional Actors* • International organizations representing state will, whether governmental or non-governmental • State organs and official institutions functioning diplomatically on behalf of the state	*Implementing Actors* • State and/or government heads • Ministers and other government officials • Representatives of established diplomatic missions and professionals authorized for official representation (diplomats)	• Developing policies and actions on behalf of the state in line with national interests	• Persuasion • Mediation • Collaboration • Negotiation • Bargaining/ Compromise • Pressure	• Negotiations • Agreements • Mediation efforts and issuing notes • Practices such as imposing certain sanctions, ultimatums, adjusting, suspending, or terminating diplomatic relations
Humanitarian Diplomacy	**Official Actors** • All of the institutional and implementing classic diplomacy actors • Interstate/ governmental organizations • Military actors	**Civilian Actors** • Humanitarian Aid Organizations • Civil Society Organizations • Think tanks • Multinational corporations • Volunteers • Opinion leaders • Religious leaders • Respected celebrities • Goodwill ambassadors	• To persuade decision-makers and opinion leaders to adopt attitudes and behaviors that consistently respect fundamental humanitarian principles in the interests of vulnerable individuals • To generate human-centered and sustainable solutions to humanitarian issues.	• Persuasion • Mediation • Collaboration • Negotiation • Advocacy • Bargaining/ Compromise • Pressure	• Humanitarian aid • Legal support • Advocacy/ public awareness • Mediation/ negotiation • Conflict resolution/ peacebuilding • Exchange • Evacuation • Transfer

Note: Prepared by Meryem Esra Varol

Beneficiaries	Legal Resources	Format	Target Location/ Geography	Level
• States • State institutions and organizations • Citizens • Transnational entities/beyond-national organizations	• International Law • International Customary Law	• Official • Confidential	• Official spaces structured within the sovereignty boundaries of mutually recognizing states • Legal entity spaces structured by intergovernmental organizations • Neutral areas mutually accepted by the participating states.	Official actors
• Those affected by war, occupation, conflict, genocide, massacre, etc. • Those affected by natural disasters • Vulnerable populations such as children, elderly, women, persons with disabilities, refugees, etc. • Populations that can be victimized or made vulnerable due to factors such as religion, language, race, gender, etc.	• International Humanitarian Law • International Human Rights Law • International Refugee Law • Disaster Law	• Official and unofficial • Confidential or public	• Areas experiencing hardships due to reasons such as war, occupation, conflict, genocide, massacre, etc. • Areas experiencing hardships due to natural disasters, climate change, epidemic diseases, etc. • Areas experiencing hardships due to poverty, deprivation, etc. • All geographical locations where humanitarian issues are encountered	Everyone, from those in the highest decision making authority to those on the ground

undoubtedly a watershed moment that precipitated a fundamental transformation in international policymaking.

Spurred on by increased collaboration with civilian elements, the espousal of human-centric practices in foreign policy has wrought profound changes in how nations view their role in the world and interact with one another.

We no longer live in a world where military superiority, striking power, and deep economic pockets—otherwise known as hard power—constitute the primary elements that afford nations an advantageous position in the international system. Since this is acknowledged by all those active in enacting policies and practices that prioritize humanitarian values, nations have amended their foreign political visions and methods of interacting with each other. This change in status quo has impelled nations not only to collaborate with non-state (i.e., civilian) elements but also to create and enact policies that take into consideration the human component in addition to simply national interests.

Although the practices and those vested with executing them have changed, both forms of diplomacy in essence seek to advance one's own national interests and the actors involved work, whether directly or indirectly, to increase states' power. During negotiations, nations naturally back propositions introduced by other governments and international organizations that either coincide with their own interests or, at the very least, do not act in opposition to them. Whether nations succeed in achieving this objective depends on one of two factors: *(i)* that they are militarily, economically, and politically more powerful than their interlocutor or *(ii)* that they possess some other means of garnering the unconditional support of the international community. The prevailing goal in diplomacy is to acquire auxiliary means of power and to gain the support of other actors in the international system through these means. In addition, it is important that the international community hold these sources of power to be legitimate and that they do not make a pariah out of any other nation or international organization. This being the case, human rights and universal humanitarian values constitute the true source of this type of power.

The way international actors understand and exert power in their relations with others has a direct impact on their foreign policy decisions and, by extension, the methods they adopt while enacting policies. It is, however, difficult to cite a steadfast rule for how nations perceive and exert power. Nevertheless, any nation desiring to have voice on the international stage will be required to collaborate increasingly with civilian actors, not only in diplomacy but in various other realms. In addition to increased collaboration, the continued rise of humanitarian diplomacy has, over the past years, greatly expanded the use of soft power—the most legitimate form of exerting influence over others—among members of the international community.

The Diverse Tools at Diplomacy's Disposal

In addition to negotiations, treaties, and more coercive methods authorized by international law (e.g., issuing memoranda, ultimata, and statements of censure), classic diplomacy has several practices that policymakers can employ during times of political or military tension (e.g., reevaluating, suspending, and terminating relations). Beyond these, classic diplomacy can make use of more indirect methods, such as acting as a neutral arbitrator between conflicting nations. Since nations that act as arbitrators in their region during times of conflict are at least tacitly regarded as being more powerful and in a position of relative superiority in relation to the others, leading arbitration hearings is highly valued by nations. Yet, the diversification of actors and the shift in how power is perceived in international policymaking have given rise to an order in which classic diplomacy practices are, by themselves, inadequate. This does not mean, however, that said practices should be wholly abandoned. Quite the contrary, they should be supported with human-centric policies and practices. Considering its characteristics discussed above while describing its conceptual framework and the ways in which nations interact with one another in the new global order, it is no longer a question as to whether one will adopt humanitarian diplomacy practices. Indeed, engaging in humanitarian diplomacy has, for all intents and purposes, become an obligation for all nations endeavoring to maintain relevance in the current international system.

Humanitarian diplomacy, instead of prioritizing the interests of a specific nation, seeks to create a global community in which the preservation of human rights and dignity is enshrined both in law and the cultural psyche. Among these rights include the right to life, to freedom from slavery and discrimination, to receive an education, to own property, to organize into social groups, and to participate in the political process.

Humanitarian diplomacy, instead of prioritizing the interests of a specific nation, seeks to create a global culture in which the preservation of human rights and dignity is enshrined both in law and the cultural psyche. Human rights advocacy is associated—especially on the practical level—with a wide array of different disciplines. With respect to human rights, these include the right to life, to freedom from slavery and discrimination, to receive an education, to own property, to organize into social groups, and to participate in the political process. While nearly all of these rights could be discussed at great length one by one in their own context, I have decided, since they are all tools employed by official and civilian actors involved in different capacities of humanitarian diplomacy, to divide them into two comprehensive groups—*(ii) international humanitarian relief*, which includes official development assistance, and (ii) *peacebuilding efforts*—and analyze them accordingly.

International humanitarian relief encompasses all forms of material aid and assistance campaigns undertaken by individual nations, governmental organizations, NGOs, and the larger private sector outside of their own national borders. During the modern age, and particularly following the end of the Cold War, civilian actors have become noticeably more visible in the field, providing increasingly larger quantities and more comprehensive forms of relief. This greater effectiveness and increased activism on the part of civilian actors was indeed instrumental in convincing political authorities that it was to their advantage to collaborate with them. An integral component of international relief, *official development assistance* is when governments provide concessional resources to other countries in need. Development assistance is invariably state-funded and seeks to promote medium- to long-term economic development in the recipient country. Nations eligible for development assistance tend to be underdeveloped and, as a result, find themselves in both socioeconomically and politically disadvantaged situations. In addition to contributing to the resolution of humanitarian problems occurring on local and regional levels, official development assistance helps humanitarian diplomacy achieve its long-term goals. Because of this, official development assistance should be counted among the various tools at humanitarian diplomacy's disposal.

Given that humanitarian relief efforts, by their very nature, seek to preserve human life and dignity, they constitute the most critical leg of humanitarian diplomacy. When faced with humanitarian tragedies, be they natural or human-induced, the first priority of humanitarian workers is to safeguard affected communities and ensure that they are able to obtain their basic survival needs. After this, priorities quickly shift to creating conditions that conform to human dignity (Battır, 2017, p. 88). Emergency humanitarian aid prioritizes the immediate provision of basic physiological needs, which include access to clean water and food, health services, and shelter. In addition to these are the medium- to long-term provision of education, health, agriculture, infrastructure services, and sustainable development assistance.

Emergency humanitarian relief efforts during times of humanitarian crises are the first and perhaps most important element of humanitarian diplomacy. Even if no previous trade, economic, political, cultural, or religious bond existed prior to the crisis, humanitarian aid serves as a means for the two countries to initiate formal relations with one another without needing to go through the normal rituals of classic diplomacy. Furthermore, humanitarian aid can inspirit a mutual feeling of good faith and sympathy both in the political elite and the populaces of two nations that may have otherwise maintained negative diplomatic relations. As a consequence, positive relations are reinforced and negative sentiments are either permanently or temporarily overlooked, which, in turn, allows for more constructive interactions to subsequently develop. In either case, these interactions advance the basic objectives of humanitarian diplomacy.

Peacebuilding efforts involve much more than putting an end to an ongoing conflict through the signing of a peace treaty by two antagonistic parties. Peacebuilding, in essence, seeks, on the one hand, to enshrine a culture of peace in individual societies and, on the other, to persuade all nations of the world to accept peace as a non-negotiable value. Whereas peace entails the prevention of or bringing an end to conflict, war, and other forms of violence, peacebuilding seeks to establish a stable, permanent, and orderly social balance in which disagreements do not, out of principle, escalate into violence and in which peaceful means to resolving disputes are institutionalized. Galtung dubs the first of these two concepts *negative peace* and the second *positive peace* (Galtung, 1996 pp. 1–3). Given this, the proliferation of positive peace is simultaneously a fundamental goal of humanitarian diplomacy and a means by which human-centric practices can be further propagated.

Peacebuilding efforts include *(i)* precipitating peace between separate nations, *(ii)* resolving conflicts arising between groups in the same nation, and *(iii)* combating terrorism (Battır, 2017, p. 120). Whatever the case may be, however, peacebuilding requires that conflicting or potentially belligerent parties remain in communication with one another. However, lasting peace between societies that have borne the brunt of widespread violence and perpetual conflict can only be sustained when the grievances and internal dynamics of each society involved are properly addressed. Efforts to create legitimate institutional structures that instill a culture of peace can be spearheaded by local, regional, and/or global bodies, such as the sending of goodwill ambassadors, arbitration, and, more importantly, all acts undertaken to persuade decision-makers and opinion leaders to actively work toward eliminating the political, military, economic, and other factors that perpetuate conflict.

General Assessment and Conclusion

The international system is indeed dynamic. The political, economic, and sociocultural developments that have transpired over history have impacted the organizational structure of the most prominent actors in the system—individual nations—as well as the decisions made by political regimes. These same developments have also been instrumental in defining how the various actors and stakeholders making up said system interact with one another. Diplomacy, by dint of its being the single most important tool in policymaking, allows parties to reach the most appropriate decisions without resorting to military intervention. As humanity has advanced through the ages, it is only natural that diplomacy has undergone profound changes in terms of structure and practice. The most important structural and operational change that has occurred was the transition from ad hoc to continuous diplomacy. Whereas the former is defined by unilateral, temporary representation of a monarch by envoys in foreign courts, the latter has given way to the establishment of permanent missions in foreign countries. The current status quo of international relations began to appear in the fifteenth century in Europe and the eighteenth century in the Ottoman Empire. Although the international community has wholly adopted continuous diplomacy as its diplomatic *modus operandi*, remnants of ad hoc diplomacy persist, such as when high-level state officials meet behind closed doors with a foreign counterpart to negotiate the details of bilateral agreements.

Increased globalization has led to a marked diversification in the types of actors influencing how the international system conducts its daily affairs. In addition to the traditional official organs, civilian actors have benefited greatly from their use of information communications technologies, increasing their clout enough to be able to sway decision makers in one direction or another. Given their pervasive influence in more than just international policy, civilian organizations shoulder important responsibilities in the development of new diplomatic practices—practices that, as we have seen, manifest through the exertion of soft power. Similar to the advances made in the field of human rights and democratization, civilian activism has proven instrumental in guiding the trajectory of humanitarian diplomacy and the development of human-centric policies.

Humanitarian diplomacy features an entirely different operative structure than traditional diplomacy and the practices associated with it. Humanitarian diplomacy is most plainly and thoroughly described as *the espousal of a human-centric approach while endeavoring to produce solutions to humanitarian problems plaguing the international community*. As such, now when humanitarian diplomacy is discussed, important concepts pertaining to international relations, such as humanitarian interventions and humanitarian rights advocacy, come to mind. Yet, although humanitarian diplomacy does, at least to a certain extent, address these concepts, it also includes a much more diverse range of practices.

Humanitarian diplomacy differs from its classic counterpart not only in terms of the actors involved in diplomatic processes but also in terms of the tools and methods employed to facilitate these processes. Whereas classic diplomacy involved only state-appointed actors, civilian actors assumed an active role in humanitarian diplomacy. Moreover, while civilian actors may appear to take on a secondary role compared to official organizations and institutions in the creation of international policy, their independent and autonomous status permits them to circumvent certain restrictions and thus be more effective in humanitarian relief efforts, human rights advocacy and activism, and increasing international awareness than official organs.

The fundamental objective of classic diplomacy is to amplify state power by implementing foreign policy that actively advances the interests of said nation. Similarly, the means nations use to increase and project their power have undergone significant changes in line with how the international community currently perceives power. Nations today have made it a priority to implement policies that will bolster their soft power, which is molded around basic human rights and universal humanitarian values, whereas they had previously striven to augment their hard power, which is measured by more tangible metrics, such as economic and military superiority. While classic diplomacy is grounded more firmly in hard power and makes use not only peaceful means but also embargos and even the threat of war to leverage other nations to, for want of a better phrase, fall in line. The same cannot be said for humanitarian diplomacy, however, as it eschews all forms of coercion and instead seeks to exert different forms of soft power. Given the primacy of human rights and values, humanitarian diplomacy seeks to accomplish to fundamental objectives: To promote universal values as well as nations' interests and to expand the sphere of influence within the international system.

Using negotiations, treaties, advocacy, memoranda, and ultimata—all of which are tools primarily associated with classic diplomacy—nations can reevaluate, suspend, or even terminate relations with other governments. Humanitarian diplomacy, on the other hand, seeks to devise and implement sustainable solutions to humanitarian crises that prioritize human life. In addition to this, humanitarian diplomacy mobilizes both official and civilian to spearhead humanitarian relief and peacebuilding efforts in order to pave the way for permanent recovery and reconstruction. Still, civilian actors also have access to several of the tools of classic diplomacy—persuasion, negotiation, and advocacy—which they can use to advance their philanthropic causes.

A human-centric approach very often requires policymakers to overlook political, economic, and even military disagreements between individual nations or communities. This allows conflicting parties to put aside their differences, if only temporarily, and sit down at the negotiating table to ensure that emergency aid is able to reach the civilian populations whose lives are under direct threat in the wake of humanitarian crises. This allows belligerents who, under normal circumstances, would wholly refrain from engaging in any form of positive communication with the other to meet in good faith for the good of the innocent bystanders caught in the crossfire. Here, humanitarian diplomacy shows off its effectiveness in reducing and, in some cases, completely eliminating the existing tension between conflicting parties, thus allowing for positive results that would otherwise remain elusive.

Humanitarian diplomacy excels in a great many areas where classic diplomacy, weighted down by cumbersome rules and formalities, falls painfully short largely because it prioritizes the promotion of human values over national interests. Indeed, in a world where the notion of power itself has witnessed a major upheaval within the international system, humanitarian diplomacy offers a framework that allows classic diplomacy to address modern developments. For while classic and humanitarian diplomacy do diverge from one another and follow a different path on specific issues, they certainly are not opposing *modi operandi*. Quite the contrary, they are two mutually complementary models of diplomacy that work hand in hand to produce the best policy possible.

Notes

1 Subsequent chapters will employ the terms old and new diplomacy in line with this division.
2 The first of these points reads as follows: "Open covenants of peace, openly arrived at, after which there shall be no private international understandings of any kind but diplomacy shall proceed always frankly and in the public view." See National Archives. President Woodrow Wilson's 14 Points (2022). Retrieved May 13, 2023, from https://www.archives.gov/milestone-documents/president-woodrow-wilsons-14-points.

3 See IHH Humanitarian Relief Foundation. (n.d.). Humanitarian Diplomacy. Retrieved May 13, 2023, from https://ihh.org.tr/en/humanitarian-diplomacy. Anadolu Agency. (2016). Türk Kızılayı "insani diplomasi"de güçlü aktör olacak. (Yeşim Sert Karaaslan. 23 Mar 2016). Retrieved August 28, 2021, from https://www. aa.com.tr/tr/turkiye/turk-kizilayi-insani-diplomaside-guclu-aktor-olacak/542328.

References

Arı, T. (1997). *Uluslararası ilişkiler ve dış politika*. Alfa Yayınevi.

Battır, O. (2017*)*. *İnsani diplomasi: Teoriden pratiğe Türk dış politikasının yeni aracı*. Çizgi Yayınları.

Berridge, G. & James, A. (2003). *A dictionary of diplomacy* (2nd ed.). Palgrave.

Bierce, A. (2000). *The Collected Fables of Ambrose Bierce*. Ohio State University Press.

Freeman, C. W. Jr. (1997). *The diplomat's dictionary*. US Institute of Peace Press.

Galtung, J. (1996). *Peace by peaceful means: Peace and conflict, development and civilization*. Sage Publications.

Gönlübol, M. (1993). *Uluslararası politika*. Attila Kitabevi.

IHH. (n.d.). *İnsani diplomasi*. https://www.ihh.org.tr/insani-diplomasi

İskit, T. (2014). *Diplomasi*. İstanbul Bilgi Üniversitesi Yayınları.

Kürkçüoğlu, Ö. (2005). Dış politika nedir? Türkiye'deki dünü ve bugünü. *Ankara Üniversitesi Siyasal Bilgiler Fakültesi Dergisi, 35*(1), 309–335.

Meray, S. L. (1956). Diplomasi temsilcilerinin hukuki statüsü. *Ankara Üniversitesi Sosyal Bilimler Enstitüsü Dergisi, 11*(3), 79–117.

Minear, L. & Smith, H. (Eds.). (2007). *Humanitarian diplomacy: Practitioners and their craft*. United Nations University Press.

Morgenthau, H. J. (1946). Diplomacy. *The Yale Law Journal, 55*(5), 1067–1080.

Nye, J. S. (2005). *Yumuşak güç: Dünya siyasetinde başarının yolu*. (R. İ. Aydın, Trans.). Ankara: Elips Kitap.

Nye, J. S. (2011). *The future of power*. Public Affairs.

Oxford Learner's Dictionaries. (n.d.). *Diplomacy*. https://www.oxfordlearnersdictionaries. com/definition/english/diplomacy?q=diplomacy

Straus, O., Wheeler, E., Ion, T., Lange, C., Marburg, T. & Wheless, J. (1912). Humanitarian diplomacy of the United States. *Proceedings of the American Society of International Law At its Annual Meeting (1907–1917), 6*(Nisan 25–27, 1912), 45–59.

The International Federation of Red Cross and Red Crescent (IFRC). (2009). *Humanitarian diplomacy policy*. https://www.ifrc.org/sites/default/files/Humanitarian-Diplomacy-Policy_EN.pdf

Tuncer, H. (1984). Tarihte ve günümüzde ad-hoc diplomasi. *Milletlerarası Hukuk ve Milletlerarası Özel Hukuk Bülteni, 4*(1), 50–57.

Tuncer, H. (2002). *Eski ve yeni diplomasi*. Ümit Yayıncılık.

Tuncer, H. (2015). Eski ve yeni diplomasi (Doktora Tezi Özeti). *Ankara Üniversitesi SBF Dergisi, 37*(1), 251–257. https://dergipark.org.tr/tr/pub/ausbf/issue/3233/45055

Türk Dil Kurumu. (n.d.). Diplomasi. In *Güncel Türkçe Sözlük*. https://sozluk.gov.tr

Whitall, J. (2009). 'It's like talking to a brick wall': Humanitarian diplomacy in the occupied Palestinian territory. *Progress in Development Studies, 9*(1), 37–53.

3 The Normative and Ethical Framework of Humanitarian Diplomacy

Kaan Saner

Though now encompassing a much wider spectrum that includes both natural and human-induced disasters, *humanitarian relief* was originally regarded simply as medical aid delivered during armed conflicts. Henry Dunant, upon witnessing the carnage that transpired during the Battle of Solferino in 1859 established the Red Cross in 1863 together with a cadre of volunteers charged with alleviating the suffering of sick and wounded soldiers. Then in 1864, Dunant lobbied for the signing of the First Geneva Convention for the Amelioration of the Condition of the Wounded in Armies in the Field, which would be amended in 1906 to reflect evolving realities. The Geneva Conventions institutionalized the retrieval, treatment, and care of sick and wounded soldiers during armed conflict.

Whereas the *Law of Geneva* deals with the rights of non-combatants and those no longer fit to fight, *Law of the Hague* lays out the rules governing how belligerent parties may conduct themselves during armed conflicts. As part of the Law of the Hague, the St. Petersburg Declaration of 1868 prohibited the use of certain small explosives and incendiary devices. The laws and customs of war were then formally compiled at the Hague Conventions of 1899 and 1907. The same conventions also saw the acceptance of agreements stipulating the rules for land and naval warfare. These regulations, however, are not always adequate, at least by themselves, to bring about the outcomes they intend to achieve. As a result, pressure from other parties, public backlash, and emphasizing certain moral obligations may be necessary to see the requirements of these regulations be put in practice. With respect to the Law of Geneva, several issues were brought up between the First and Second World Wars, including the amelioration of sick and wounded military personnel in war zones, the amelioration of wounded, sick, and shipwrecked naval personnel, the treatment of prisoners of war, and the protection of civilians during hostilities. Then, with the signing of the Fourth Geneva Conventions in 1949, a consensus on international protocols was reached (Shaw, 2018, pp. 854–5). Two additional protocols aptly named Protocol Additional II and III were subsequently adopted in 1997 and 2005 to these conventions, the latter of which recognized a third emblem to the existing Red Cross and Red Crescent.

DOI: 10.4324/9781003503187-3

The International Court of Justice points out that although The Hague and Geneva Conventions are separate currents, they are closely related, interact with one another, and constitute a single, elaborate system known as *international humanitarian law* (Shaw, 2018, p. 855, as cited in International Court of Justice, 8 July 1996).

International law regulates how parties may conduct themselves in ongoing conflicts (i.e., *jus in bello*), thus addressing not only the treatment of prisoners of war, the sick and wounded, and civilians but also the legality of specific weapons and military techniques. The names used to refer to this concept have changed over times—known first as the law of war, then as the law of armed conflict, and finally as international humanitarian law (henceforth IHL). Although IHL evolved out of a series of international agreements and was one of the most developed facets of international law, a portion of the rules that would make up part of it were either completely or partially found in customary international law. It could even be argued, in fact, that since warring nations will appeal to customary international law if they are not party to a specific international agreement, many principles of customary law are held in higher regard than the rules laid out in international agreements (Shaw, 2018, p. 853).

The principles delineated in the first agreement laying out the foundations for IHL would eventually evolve into the basic philosophy underlying humanitarianism. The International Red Cross and Red Crescent Movement officially accepted *humanity, neutrality, impartiality*, and *independence* as binding institutional principles in 1965 at the XXth International Conference of the Red Cross in Vienna.[1] As time passed, these principles were later espoused by other humanitarian actors and the wider international community, culminating in the adoption of the Code of Conduct of the International Red Cross and Red Crescent Movement and NGOs in Disaster Relief in 1994. Beyond principles, quality control measures, such as *Core Humanitarian Standards, Sphere Standards*, and *Humanitarian Accountability Partnership*, grew into essential standards in the humanitarian sector. The UN General Assembly endorsed humanity, neutrality, impartiality, and independence as humanitarian principles with Resolution 46/182 in 1991 and Resolution 58/114 in 2004.

Overview of the Principles and Ethical Framework of the Humanitarian Field

Humanity

Born out of human necessity, the principle of *humanity* seeks to alleviate human suffering wherever it is found, protect human life and health, and instill respect for human dignity regardless of nationality, race, religion, class, or political ideology. Similarly, humanitarian assistance focuses on the human condition and provides relief solely for humanity's sake. In other words, this principle asserts that all people deserve to be treated humanely and with dignity irrespective of their current condition or the various political, military, religious, and ethnic elements that make up their identity.

Humanitarian works are considered to be faithful to the principle of humanity when they identify and analyze the specific needs of affected communities objectively. Since it is possible to determine whether a particular situation necessitates humanitarian intervention only after ascertaining the severity and urgency of a community's needs, it is imperative that objective measures be used to evaluate the conditions of all the territories controlled by combatant parties. Humanitarian diplomacy actors can be accused of harboring ulterior motives for various reasons, such as when objective standards are not employed while assessing the degree of communities' needs, when the delivery of necessary items in delayed, and when the wrong items are sent. For instance, one may question whether an aid organization truly values the principle of humanity if it limits its operations to a select few areas of a country in which the majority of the population suffers from food insecurity and extended periods of drought. When, however, the needs of one group affected by a conflict are more urgent than those of another's, prioritizing the first group over the latter is in fact a principled act. The use of humanitarian aid is used for ulterior purposes, on the other hand, does indeed constitute a genuine violation of said principle and causes humanitarian work to be regarded with suspicion.

Care should be taken to prevent individual nations from restricting the work performed by humanitarian organizations or from using the environment created by humanitarian organizations as a means to further their political goals. During the Darfur Crisis, for instance, humanitarian organizations provided the basic needs of displaced persons at camps set up at various locations. After some time, however, it began to be questioned whether these camps facilitated a specific policy seeking to change the ethnic makeup of the region. A similar situation occurred in Myanmar with the Rohingya Muslims, an ethnic group denied citizenship in their own home country. The transfer of Rohingya Muslims to camps established in exclusion zones where their basic needs were met after their homes had been destroyed does indeed appear to be a humanitarian solution at first glance. However, the question was eventually raised as to whether this uprooted the Rohingya people from their ancestral lands and created the circumstances that would expedite their expulsion from Myanmar.

Regardless of how political debates pan out, humanitarian actors are obliged to act in ways befitting to the principle of *humanity*. One particularly salient example showcasing such principled adherence is that although the Taliban administration failed to gain international recognition after having taken control of Afghanistan on 30 August 2021 following US withdrawal from the country, the International Committee of the Red Cross, the World Food Programme, and the Turkish Red Crescent remained in contact with local powers in order to continue their humanitarian work.

Neutrality

Maintaining neutrality and not exhibiting a hostile demeanor or bias toward a specific political, racial, religious, or ideological group are vital if humanitarian relief organizations are to be trusted and not to be perceived as a threat or alternative form of intervention by belligerent parties. It is imperative that humanitarian relief organizations and workers neither become embroiled in political, religious, ethnic, and ideological disputes nor exhibit a penchant toward either side while employed in the field, as failing to do so places workers and the communities they seek to aid at risk. Nevertheless, since humanitarian relief organizations' neutral stance may be misperceived in certain environments, such as in areas where relief efforts coincide with ongoing political programs, military operations, and/or developmental projects, utmost care should be taken to prevent parties from regarding aid workers with contempt.

> A study examining the Somali Red Crescent Society found that the principle of neutrality was instrumental in allowing the organization to continue to play an active role in Somalia despite the exceptionally high number of operational risks in the country (O'Callghan & Backhurst, 2013).

Common Article 3 of the Geneva Conventions permits impartial organizations, such as the International Red Cross Committee, to offer their services to belligerent parties. Although the term "belligerent parties" used in Article 3 is noticeably vague, convention holds it to comprise both the armed forces of signatory nations and non-state armed factions involved militarily in international and national conflicts. Given this, humanitarian organizations may interact with all parties involved in armed conflicts.

Impartiality

Impartiality means that the most essential forms of aid should be prioritized and distributed to the communities in need of them without discrimination and was first enshrined in Article 6 of the First Geneva Conventions (1864). Common Article 3 of the Geneva Conventions of 1949 obligates humanitarian organizations to offer their services to belligerent parties in an impartial manner.

In the Shadow of "Just Wars": Violence, Politics and Humanitarian Action, a collection of essays published by Médecins Sans Frontières (MSF), describes how Western pacifists attempted to stop MSF from working with Hamas, regarding it as a terrorist organization. It was argued, however, that if humanitarian organizations wanted to operate in Gaza, they were required to collaborate with Hamas, as they were the sole political authority in region (Weismann, 2004).

The principle of impartiality obligates that humanitarian relief be provided on the basis of need to where they are most urgently required without discriminating based on nationality, ethnic origin, sex, religion, class, or political ideology. Jean Pictet (1914–2002), one of the authors of the Geneva Conventions of 1949, regarded impartiality as being an aspect of neutrality more than a separate guiding principle, as humanitarian organizations may render their services in an impartial manner only as long as they maintain their neutrality during ongoing conflicts and political disagreements. There are no good or bad victims in combat zones; humanitarian organizations pay no import to the identities, affiliations, or rationales of victims.

Médecins Sans Frontières argues that regarding others as being either "with us or against us" while attempting to root out terror poses serious risks to humanitarian principles and gravely undermines the effectiveness of relief efforts. As we have seen in Syria and Nigeria, national laws and international regulations restrict populations deemed, whether legitimately or otherwise, to be supporters of terrorism from receiving humanitarian aid. Likewise, the fear of being taken captive either by the government or rogue individuals deters relief workers from operating in Afghanistan, Pakistan, Mali, and Somalia. MSF relates that the situation is even more critical for them, as the only form of humanitarian relief they offer, whether to civilians and combatants, is medical aid, arguing that the right and responsibility of medical workers to treat anyone in need of medical assistance without discrimination has come into question (MSF, 2019).

By employing ambulance workers from every segment of society, the Lebanese Red Cross is able to maintain communications with and deliver aid to all eighteen of the country's different political and demographical groups in their own areas.

Maintaining impartiality in today's world requires organizations to adopt a more confrontational stance because delivering aid to zones under the control of political authorities that international community either regards as illegitimate or refuses to recognize altogether can result in accusations of organizations' providing services to seditious groups operating in areas outside of state control during civil wars or supporting hostile groups in nations under international embargo. Humanitarian efforts may be put on hold in certain situations. Humanitarian organizations may hesitate to provide aid to communities residing in areas under the control of terrorist organizations or armed groups declared illegal by central governments when doing so places them at the risk of legal or extra-judicial repercussions.

Independence

Independence requires that humanitarian work be allowed to be conducted autonomously, unbeholden to any external political, military, or economic objective. This means that humanitarian organizations should not be subject to any form of manipulation or imposition during either the decision-making process or the implementation of relief efforts.

While conflicts were still ongoing between Sudan and the SPLM–N (Sudan People's Liberation Movement–North), several civilian-led humanitarian organizations stated that in order to avoid being subjected malevolent and otherwise questionable acts committed by Sudanese state authorities, they operated in zones under the firm control of the Sudanese government. This led organizations to forgo the deliverance of aid to refugee camps located in the Blue Nile and South Kordofan regions altogether out of fear that they would be accused of supporting the SPLM–N for doing so as said group was in control of these two areas (Grace, 2015, p. 3).

Both national and rogue military forces may attempt to leverage humanitarian relief organizations so that they can gain control of humanitarian aid, funnel it into areas that will advance their interests, or impede its delivery altogether. Unfortunately, this can sometimes happen with donors—be they nations or private institutions—that impose conditions to aid that hinder humanitarian organizations' ability to act independently. Indeed, humanitarian relief organizations often find their hands tied and unable to operate freely when their activities are incorporated into programs engaged in nation-building, strengthening governance, brokering peace, and establishing the supremacy of law.

The US government notoriously refused to donate to relief efforts led by the Action Against Hunger (ACF) in Palestine because it supported only one of the two combatants. In a similar vein, however, the French-based ACF refused to engage in humanitarian operations in areas of Afghanistan where the French Armed Forces were actively deployed (Dyukova and Chetcuti, 2013).

The Principles of IHL

IHL holds an important place among the normative guidelines that humanitarian diplomacy practitioners follow during their negotiations. IHL regulates the conduct of war by limiting the weapons and techniques that may be employed during international and internal armed conflicts and by guaranteeing the protection of certain categories of people and property affected by said conflicts. The categories of people protected include sick and injured soldiers *hors de combat*, civilian non-combatants, prisoners of war, medical and religious personnel, and humanitarian aid workers.

Understanding that on which the fundamental principles of IHL guaranteeing the protection of the aforementioned categories of people are based will help foster a deeper appreciation of the protection regime reinforced by these rules. The principles of *humanity, impartiality, necessity, proportionality*, and *humane treatment* allow us to interpret IHL rules and, as a result, to develop arguments to be used during humanitarian negotiations. Since the rules derived from these principles—given their grounding in humanitarian exigencies—are themselves regarded as embodying rules of customary international law, they are binding on all nations whether or not they are party to the Hague and Geneva Conventions.[2]

Signed on 18 October 1907, the Hague Conventions respecting the Laws and Customs of War on Land articulates that the right of belligerents to adopt means of injuring the enemy is not unlimited (Article 22). The principles of humanity, impartiality, necessity, proportionality, and humane treatment thus seek to minimize the amount of damage that may be caused during armed conflict.

Humanity

The principle of *humanity* appears in the preamble of the Martens Clause in the 1899 Hague Convention II—Laws and Customs of War on Land[3] following efforts to expand the people protected by IHL. Given that armed civilian resistance groups operating in occupied lands were not considered prisoners of war, this rule endeavored to clarify the protections that such civilians should be afforded. In addition to foreseeing that both native populations and combatants should be protected in cases not covered by the regulations adopted by the high contracting parties until humanitarian law was fully codified, this rule asserts that international conventions, humanitarian principles, and the demands of the public conscience for the basis for providing protection.

Impartiality

A core value in IHL, the principle of *impartiality* requires that all parties distinguish between protected persons and combatants while conducting their operations. Article 48 of Protocol Additional I further obligates that parties limit their operations to military objectives and target neither civilians—defined as those not directly involved in armed conflicts—nor civilian objects. Indiscriminate attacks in which both civilians and combatants are simultaneously targeted may very well constitute *war crimes*. Similar to Article 48 of Protocol Additional I, Rules 1 and 7 of the ICRC's *Customary International Humanitarian Law*, first published in 2005, further reinforce the notion that attacks should be restricted to military targets.

Attacks that are not directed at a specific military objective or that employ a method or means of combat that, by its very nature, cannot be used in a discriminatory manner as required by IHL are considered indiscriminate attacks. Article 51 of Protocol Additional I and Rules 11 and 12 of the ICRC's *Customary International Humanitarian Law* prohibit such attacks.

Although enemy military personnel may occupy heavily populated areas, subjecting the civilian population to aerial bombardment, artillery fire, or chemical and biological attacks in order to strike military targets constitutes an indiscriminate use of force. Furthermore, because airburst munitions have a wide area of affect that can last for an extended period of time, thus having a high likelihood to cause civilian casualties and damage to civilian objects, their use in such circumstances is judged similarly.

Necessity

The principle of *necessity* permits only the degree and kind of force required to eliminate the enemy during a legitimate military purpose not otherwise prohibited by IHL. The only legitimate military purpose is to weaken the military capacity of the other parties to the conflict. Methods and means that inflict excessive human suffering are expressly prohibited.

Barrel bombs, by their very nature, have a widespread affect. The damage they cause, especially when dropped from a high altitude by fast-moving aircraft, extends over an area much greater than their intended target. Resolution 2139 adopted by the UN Security Council in 2014 and Resolution A/RES/70/234 adopted by the UN General Assembly in 2015 express serious reservations about the indiscriminate use of barrel bombs. On 14 December 2015, the Under-Secretary-General of the UN Office for the Coordination of Humanitarian Affairs condemned the aerial attacks that struck a school and resulted in the death of at least one child (UN OCHA, 2015).

In his work *Perpetual Peace: A Philosophical Sketch* (1795), Immanuel Kant argues that since the total annihilation of one's enemy and the methods used to achieve this will not secure perpetual peace, total annihilation should be prohibited (Kant, 2020/1795). Similarly, by stating that "war is the continuation of policy by other means" in his book *On War* (1832), Carl von Clausewitz drew a link between war and political objectives. Per von Clausewitz, the goal of war is to harm one's enemy until he is rendered militarily impotent (Von Clausewitz, 1975/1832). These philosophies continued to gain increasing credence among members of the international community, eventually culminating in the endorsement and promulgation of the Lieber Code (1863) during the American Civil War. The Lieber Code defines military necessity as the "measures which are indispensable for securing the ends of the war" and considers "all direct destruction of life or limb of armed enemies, and of other persons whose destruction is incidentally unavoidable in the armed contests of the war" to be lawful. Article 16 of the Lieber Code

> Military necessity does not admit of cruelty – that is, the infliction of suffering for the sake of suffering or for revenge [...]; and, in general, military necessity does not include any act of hostility which makes the return to peace unnecessarily difficult.

We observe several parallels between the Lieber Code (1863) and the Declaration of Saint Petersburg (1868), the first formal agreement prohibiting the use of certain weapons of war. This declaration emphasizes that the necessities of war ought to yield to the requirements of humanity, that force should be directed not against the entire population but against enemy military forces, and that to win a war it is sufficient to weaken the enemy force by disabling the greatest possible number of soldiers. While Article 23 of The Hague Convention IV and its Annex prohibits the destruction of property unless demanded by the necessities of war, Article 27 of the same convention enjoins the protection of buildings dedicated to religion, art, science, or charitable purposes, historic monuments, hospitals, and places where the sick and wounded are collected, provided they are not being used at the time for military purposes.

Proportionality

The principle of *proportionality* requires that incidental loss of civilian life and damage to civilian objects be kept to a minimum while engaging in military operations. While Article 51 of the 1977 Protocol Additional I related to the Protection of Victims of International Armed Conflicts prohibits attacks that may be expected to cause incidental loss of civilian life, injury to civilians, damage to civilian objects, or a combination thereof, which would be excessive in relation to the concrete and direct military advantage anticipated, Article 85 rules such attacks to constitute serious breaches of the aforementioned protocol.

In its 2010 observations, the Committee on the Rights of the Child expressed its concerns in relation to the ongoing civil war in Colombia, namely, that schools were being used by armed groups and that military operations were being executed in close proximity to schools. Highlighting that the presence of military forces near schools increases children's risk of being caught in the crossfire during skirmishes and/or acts of reprisal committed by illegal armed forces, party nations requested that and end be put to schools being used for military purposes (the United Nations, 2010).

Armed groups often embed themselves among civilians and in heavily populated areas as a means to protect their weapons, military personal, and equipment. When military personnel or weapons planted in schools, hospitals, places of worship, and factories are targeted during an otherwise legitimate operation, civilian casualties and injury to civilians are inevitable.

Humane Treatment

The principle of *humane treatment* requires that any individual captured by an enemy force be treated in such a way that respects his dignity as a human being. Sick and wounded persons *hors de combat*, prisoners of war, and civilians must be treated humanely. Common Article 3 of the Geneva Convention (III) relative to the Treatment of Prisoners of War prohibits violence to life and person, murder, mutilation, cruel treatment, torture, hostage-taking, outrages upon personal dignity, humiliating and degrading treatment, and the passing of sentences and the carrying out of executions without previous judgment pronounced by a regularly constituted court against any individual who has surrendered his weapons or who is sick, wounded, detained, or otherwise *hors de combat*. Indeed, multiple articles of the Geneva Conventions of 12 August 1949 are devoted to humane treatment.[4]

[The report found that since the beginning of the civil war on 30 December 2013,] most of the atrocities were carried out against civilian populations taking no active part in the hostilities. Churches, mosques, and hospitals were attacked, humanitarian assistance was impeded, towns pillaged and destroyed, places of protection were attacked. Unlawful killings of civilians or soldiers who were believed to be *hors de combat* (no longer taking part in hostilities) were committed by elements of the security forces of the Government. The evidence also leads the Commission to conclude that war crimes of rape and torture were committed against civilians in and around Juba (African Union Commission of Inquiry on South Sudan, 2014).

The principles of *humanity, impartiality, necessity, proportionality,* and *humane treatment* seek to limit how power can be exerted in war and armed conflict. It is absolutely critical that all actors abide by these limitations to ensure the protection of the civilian population. As such, humanitarian negotiations help protect civilians *(i)* by identifying where civilians and civilian objects are located, thus distinguishing them from military elements, *(ii)* by seeking to limit combat techniques to those that minimize civilian casualties, injuries to civilians, and damage to civilian objects, *(iii)* by warning, as much as conditions permit, civilian populations of impending attacks by telephone, leaflets, radio broadcast, or other forms of communication, and *(iv)* preventing combatants and their equipment from occupying the same areas as civilians and their property.

Providing Protection to Vulnerable Persons under International Humanitarian Law

While IHL endeavors to provide protection to the greater number of people as possible, a sharp distinction must be made between combatants and those *hors de combat* (Shaw, 2018, pp. 855–6). It is thus important to gain a grounded understanding of the protection regime offered by IHL and to know who it does and does not cover, as such knowledge will allow those involved in humanitarian negotiations to develop robust, cogent arguments that they can then use to advocate for human rights.

The ICRC formulated the following principles as a guide to understand the relevant statutory rules:

1 *Persons taking no active part in the hostilities, including members of armed forces who have laid down their arms and those placed hors de combat are entitled to respect for their lives, including their physical and psychological integrity, be respected and shall in all circumstances be treated humanely, without being subject to any form of adverse distinction.*
2 *It is prohibited to kill or injure an enemy who has surrendered or who is hors de combat.*
3 *The sick and wounded shall be collected and cared for by the detaining party. Protection covers medical personnel, facilities, vehicles, and equipment. The Red Cross (Red Crescent, Red Lion and Sun) emblem symbolizes this protection and must be respected.*
4 *Captured combatants and civilians under the authority of an adverse party are entitled to respect for their lives, dignity, personal rights, and convictions. Such persons are protected from all forms of violence and reprisal. They are entitled to contact their families and receive support.*
5 *All persons are entitled to benefit from basic judicial guarantees. No one shall be held responsible for an act that he did not commit. No one shall be subject to physical or mental torture, corporal punishment, or treated in a way that is cruel, inhumane, or degrading.*
6 *Parties to a conflict and members of their military forces are not entitled to the unrestricted use of whatever military methods and means they choose. It is prohibited to use weapons or methods of warfare that cause superfluous injury or unnecessary casualties.*
7 *Parties to a conflict shall, in all circumstances, distinguish between the civilian population and combatants in order to spare the civilian population and their properties. Neither the civilian population as such nor civilian persons shall be the object of attack. Attacks shall be directed solely against military objects.*
(International Review of the Red Cross, September–October 1989, p. 404, as cited in Shaw, 2018, p. 882)

Civilians

Inspired by the Hague Regulations (Hague Convention (IV) respecting the Laws and Customs of War on Land and its annex: Regulations concerning the Laws and Customs of War on Land, 1907), the Fourth Geneva Convention wartime addresses the protection of civilians during wartime. An extension of the rules in place prior to 1949, the Fourth Geneva Convention stipulates that

> "persons protected by the Convention are those who, at a given moment and in any manner whatsoever, find themselves, in case of a conflict or occupation, in the hands of a party to the conflict or occupying power of which they are not nationals".
>
> (Article 4)

The same convention regards the protection of civilians in occupied territories within the same scope.

Protocol Additional (I) relating to the Protection of Victims of International Armed Conflicts designated important criteria concerning the protection of civilians: Civilians shall not be the object of attack, attacks that are not directed at a specific military objective are prohibited, attacks on areas containing dense civilian populations are prohibited, attacks against the civilian population or individual civilians by way of reprisal are prohibited, attacks shall not be executed against cultural heritage sites or the natural environment, starving civilians as a war tactic is prohibited, military elements shall not be stationed in or near areas with high concentrations of civilians, nor shall works or installations containing dangerous forces, namely dams, dykes and nuclear electrical generating be attacked (Protocol Additional I to the Geneva Conventions, Articles 50–58, 1977).

Protocol Additional II relating to the Protection of Victims of Non-International Armed Conflicts stipulates that:

- The civilian population and individual civilians shall enjoy protection against the dangers arising from military operations. The civilian population as such, as well as individual civilians, shall not be the object of attack. Acts or threats of violence the primary purpose of which is to spread terror among the civilian population are prohibited.
- Civilians shall enjoy the protection afforded by this Part, unless and for such time as they take a direct part in hostilities.
- Starvation of civilians as a method of combat is prohibited. It is therefore prohibited to attack, destroy, remove, or render useless, for that purpose, objects indispensable to the survival of the civilian population, such as foodstuffs, agricultural areas for the production of foodstuffs, crops, livestock, drinking water installations and supplies and irrigation works.
- Works or installations containing dangerous forces, namely dams, dykes, and nuclear electrical generating stations, shall not be made the object of

attack, even where these objects are military objectives, if such attack may cause the release of dangerous forces and consequent severe losses among the civilian population.

- It is prohibited to commit any acts of hostility directed against historic monuments, works of art or places of worship which constitute the cultural or spiritual heritage of peoples, and to use them in support of the military effort.
- The displacement of the civilian population shall not be ordered for reasons related to the conflict unless the security of the civilians involved or imperative military reasons so demand.
- Should such displacements have to be carried out, all possible measures shall be taken in order that the civilian population may be received under satisfactory conditions of shelter, hygiene, health, safety, and nutrition. Civilians shall not be compelled to leave their own territory for reasons connected with the conflict (Protocol Additional II to the Geneva Conventions, Articles 13–17, 1977).

Sick and Wounded

The First Geneva Convention, in addition to addressing the care of wounded and sick military personnel in the field, governs medical units and institutions, the protected afforded to medical personnel, and recognized emblems (e.g., red cross, red crescent). The Second Geneva Convention deals with the conditions of wounded, sick, and shipwrecked armed forces at sea. Albeit containing similar rulings to the First Convention, the Second Convention stipulates that hospital ships shall not, under any circumstances, be subject to attack or capture, and shall instead be respected and protected. Parts I and II of Protocol Additional I, adopted in 1977, reaffirmed the rulings in both conventions and amended them where needed. Protocol Additional II, on the other hand, stipulates that the sick and wounded receive, to the fullest extent practicable and with the least possible delay, the medical care and attention required by their condition (Geneva Conventions, Articles 15, 16, and 18, 1949; Protocol Additional II to the Geneva Conventions, Articles 7–8, 1977; Customary IHL, Rule 111). Suitable conditions can be interpreted to mean the existence of appropriate conditional, equipment, supplies, and infrastructure. Required medical care means that sick and wounded individuals are afforded whatever treatment is necessary for their specific medical situation, without being subject to any form of adverse distinction (Protocol Additional II to the Geneva Conventions, Article 12, 1949; Protocol Additional II to the Geneva Conventions, Article 7, 1977; International IHL, Rule 110 *see* Hencaerts & Doswald-Beck, 2005 "Kural 110"). The sole grounds for distinction are medical in nature, such as when the severity and urgency of a specific case requires prioritization. While transporting a wounded soldier off the field and to a medical unit or fully functioning hospital, priority is thus afforded not on whether said soldier is a friend or enemy but on the degree of medical urgency.

Prisoners of War

Adopted in 1949, the Third Geneva Convention pertains to prisoners of war and is based on the imperative to treat prisoners humanely in every circumstance and delineates several comprehensive behavioral principles. Article 4 below is important for prisoners of war, as it constitutes a detailed explanation of their status as combatants.

A Prisoners of war, in the sense of the present Convention, are persons belonging to one of the following categories, who have fallen into the power of the enemy:

1 *Members of the armed forces of a Party to the conflict as well as members of militias or volunteer corps forming part of such armed forces.*
2 *Members of other militias and members of other volunteer corps, including those of organized resistance movements, belonging to a Party to the conflict and operating in or outside their own territory, even if this territory is occupied, provided that such militias or volunteer corps, including such organized resistance movements, fulfill the following conditions:*

   a *that of being commanded by a person responsible for his subordinates;*
   b *that of having a fixed distinctive sign recognizable at a distance;*
   c *that of carrying arms openly;*
   d *that of conducting their operations in accordance with the laws and customs of war.*

3 *Members of regular armed forces who profess allegiance to a government or an authority not recognized by the Detaining Power.*
4 *Persons who accompany the armed forces without actually being members thereof, such as civilian members of military aircraft crews, war correspondents, supply contractors, members of labor units or of services responsible for the welfare of the armed forces, provided that they have received authorization from the armed forces which they accompany, who shall provide them for that purpose with an identity card similar to the annexed model.*
5 *Members of crews, including masters, pilots and apprentices, of the merchant marine and the crews of civil aircraft of the Parties to the conflict, who do not benefit by more favorable treatment under any other provisions of international law.*
6 *Inhabitants of a non-occupied territory, who on the approach of the enemy spontaneously take up arms to resist the invading forces, without having had time to form themselves into regular armed units, provided they carry arms openly and respect the laws and customs of war.*

B *The following shall likewise be treated as prisoners of war under the present Convention:*

1 *Persons belonging, or having belonged, to the armed forces of the occupied country, if the occupying Power considers it necessary by reason of such*

allegiance to intern them, even though it has originally liberated them while hostilities were going on outside the territory it occupies, in particular where such persons have made an unsuccessful attempt to rejoin the armed forces to which they belong and which are engaged in combat, or where they fail to comply with a summons made to them with a view to internment.

2 *The persons belonging to one of the categories enumerated in the present Article, who have been received by neutral or non-belligerent Powers on their territory and whom these Powers are required to intern under international law, without prejudice to any more favorable treatment which these Powers may choose to give and with the exception of Articles 8, 10, 15, 30, fifth paragraph, 58–67, 92, 126 and, where diplomatic relations exist between the Parties to the conflict and the neutral or non-belligerent Power concerned, those Articles concerning the Protecting Power. Where such diplomatic relations exist, the Parties to a conflict on whom these persons depend shall be allowed to perform towards them the functions of a Protecting Power as provided in the present Convention, without prejudice to the functions which these Parties normally exercise in conformity with diplomatic and consular usage and treaties.*

C *This Article shall in no way affect the status of medical personnel and chaplains as provided for in Article 33 of the present Convention.* (ICRC, (n.d.)., Article 4.)

As from July 1974, ICRC delegates in Cyprus and Turkey have made regular visits to soldiers and civilians who have been granted prisoner-of-war status by the authorities on either side. On the eve of resumed hostilities, they were distributed as follows: 3,268 Turkish Cypriots interned in eight camps in Cyprus; 63 Greek Cypriots in Saray Hospital, in the Turkish part of Nicosia, and 385 Greek Cypriots in a camp in Turkey. As fighting in August resulted in further captures, the ICRC requested permission to visit existing and new prisoners on either side. Visits were made to 3,336 Turkish Cypriot prisoners in four camps in the south. A total of 2,432 Greek Cypriot prisoners were first visited in transit camps in Cyprus, and then in three camps in Turkey. The agreement reached by the ICRC, Clerides, and Denktash resulted in the repatriation of 1,200 Turkish and 880 Greeks between 20 September and 3 October. Those repatriated were wounded and sick students and teachers (Keser, 2010, vol. 1, p. 581).

Regular and Irregular Armed Forces

In today's world, where armed conflicts are much more likely than before to transpire in densely populated civilian areas, knowing how to distinguish regular and irregular (e.g., militiae, volunteer corps) combatants from the civilian population is essential. Distinguishing between these two groups, however, is made difficult now that internal (i.e., non-international) combat has increased, civilians engage more frequently in hostilities, armed forces receive material support from external sources, combatants share the same areas with and use the same facilities as civilians, and armed forces often eschew military uniforms for civilian clothing.

National laws and regulations define which individuals are considered bona fide members of nations' armed forces in international armed conflicts. The regular armed forces of a nation that follow a distinct chain of command are defined in IHL as combatants. Militiae, volunteer corps, and organized resistance movements that, despite being independent from regular military forces, are under the command of a specific authority, carry distinctive markings recognizable from a certain distance, and act in accordance to the laws and customs governing armed conflict are considered irregular forces, not civilians. Similarly, persons in a *levée en masse*—a concept that traces back to the French Revolution—are also not considered civilians. In IHL, a *levée en masse* refers to when the inhabitants of a non-occupied country take up arms to defend against an approaching enemy force.

Members of non-state organized armed groups differ from civilians who take up arms in a spontaneous, sporadic, and unorganized manner, who fill an administrative or political role, or who provide logistical support for non-military purposes. Similarly, individuals who join such an armed group, receive basic training, and subsequently leave said group are considered civilians until they return to active duty. In non-international armed conflict, persons who assume *permanent combatant function* include those who are part of an organized armed group engaged in hostilities and those who prepare, lead, or command military operations. Such individuals are considered members of an armed group and forfeit their protection from being targeted during military operations for as long as they remain active members.

Civilians Involved in Hostilities

Civilians who are not directly involved in armed conflict are protected under IHL.[5] Only when civilians participate directly in hostilities do they forfeit the protection afforded to them. Accordingly, knowing what constitutes direct participation in hostilities is vital. While no formal definition exists in IHL, the ICRC has developed the following criteria to determine what qualifies as direct participation in hostilities:

- The act in question must be likely to adversely affect the military operations or military capacity of a party to the conflict or, alternatively, to inflict death, injury or destruction on persons or objects not under the effective control of the acting individual, and
- there must be a direct casual link between the act in question, or a concrete and coordinated military operation of which it constitutes an integral part, and the aforementioned consequences, and

- the act in question must be specifically designed to bring about the afore-mentioned consequences in support of a party to the conflict and to the detriment of another.

In order to determine whether civilians working in a factory that produces or repairs weapons located outside of the immediate combat zone constitute legitimate targets in an armed conflict, we need to determine whether there exists a direct causal relationship between the production of these weapons and the harm they cause on the field. Since a direct causal relationship cannot be established, the civilians working in said factories cannot be considered to be direct participants to hostilities. The same cannot be said, however, for a civilian driver transporting weapons to a combat zone or the frontlines of an armed conflict. Indeed, transporting weapons to combat zones is an integral part of combat preparations and deployment. As such, a direct causal link can be drawn between the driver and combatants. On the other hand, however, civilians who do not participate in armed attacks carried out by an organized armed group in a non-international armed conflict but who are involved in spreading propaganda, rallying morale, education, or politics cannot, given the required threshold of harm, be deemed direct participants to hostilities.

Humanitarian Assistance

The Geneva Conventions and their Additional Protocols require the expressed consent of belligerent parties in all but one case for humanitarian assistance to be provided during armed conflicts. Consent, however, does not grant unlimited discretionary authority. In both national and international armed conflicts, belligerent parties are responsible for ensuring that the population under their control is provided their basic needs.

Article 70 of Protocol Additional I of the Geneva Conventions relating to the Protection of Victims of International Armed Conflicts states that if the civilian population of any territory under the control of a party to the conflict is not adequately provided clothing, bedding, means of shelter, other supplies essential to its survival, relief actions shall, subject to the agreement of the parties concerned, be implemented without delay. Such actions shall not be regarded as interference in the armed conflict or as unfriendly acts. The relief actions in question shall likewise be humanitarian and impartial in character and undertaken without any adverse distinction.

As Protocol Additional I to the Geneva Conventions relating to the Protection of Victims of International Armed Conflicts accords privileged treatment or special protection to children, infants, expecting mothers, maternity cases, and nursing mothers, they shall be given priority in the distribution of relief.

The term "parties concerned" used in Protocol Additional II relating to the Protection of Victims of Non-International Armed Conflicts encompasses, in addition to belligerent parties, neighboring states through whose territory relief passes, nations who intend to provide humanitarian relief without taking part in the armed conflict, and neutral states designated as protecting powers by belligerent states to safeguard their interests.

The principle of impartiality dictates that beneficiaries of relief be determined without consideration to their religion, language, race, nationality, sex, or political convictions. If relief is indeed to have a humanitarian character, beneficiaries are to be identified based strictly on their degree of need and vulnerability.

In armed conflicts in which invasion takes place by one or more of the parties to the conflict, Articles 55 and 56 of the Geneva Convention (IV) relative to the Protection of Civilian Persons in Time of War require the occupying power to ensure that the population in occupied territories have sufficient food, medical supplies, hospital establishments and services, public health services, and hygienic services. Protocol Additional I expands occupying powers' duties to include the provision of bedding, means of shelter, and other supplies essential to the population's survival.

If sufficient supplies of these materials cannot be provided to the population living in the occupied territory, the occupying power is required to accept assistance. This assistance shall be provided in an impartial manner by other nations and/or humanitarian organizations such as the ICRC and shall prioritize consignments containing food, medical equipment, and clothing.

If the occupying power is, as a result of exercising its discretionary authority, unable to provide for the civilian population either partially or wholly, humanitarian relief organizations shall not be required to obtain consent of the occupying power as long as they abide by the basic humanitarian principles are there exists no security risk.

There is a larger grey area in non-international conflicts with respect to the provision of humanitarian assistance. Article 3 of the Geneva Conventions of 12 August 1949 states that the obligation to act in a humane manner includes not fostering conditions that would leave people deprived of their basic human needs.

Article 18 of Protocol Additional I of the Geneva Convention relating to the Protection of Victims of Non-International Armed Conflicts articulates that local relief societies such as the Red Cross and Red Crescent organizations may offer their services to the civilian population. The same article then stipulates that if the civilian population is suffering undue hardship owing to a lack of the supplies essential for its survival, such as foodstuffs and medical supplies, relief actions for the civilian population that are of an exclusively humanitarian and impartial nature and that are conducted without any adverse distinction shall be undertaken subject to the consent of the high contracting party concerned. Here the term "high contracting party concerned" refers to the state in which the conflict is taking place. Although there exists no legal obligation to obtain the consent of non-state armed groups involved in the conflict, it would be operationally impossible to conduct relief efforts without having done so.

Common Article 3 of the Geneva Conventions states that an impartial humanitarian body, such as the International Committee of the Red Cross, may offer its services to the parties to the conflict. In cases where the basic needs of the civilian population are not met, medical services are not provided, and/or there exists the threat of starvation in the territory controlled by any party to the conflict, both the state and non-state armed groups may request the services of humanitarian relief organizations.

Having access to humanitarian relief is vital. Article 30 of the Geneva Convention (IV) relative to the Protection of Civilian Persons in Time of War states that protected persons shall have every facility for making application to the protecting powers [e.g., international and national organizations]. Article 62 of the same convention states that protected persons in occupied territories shall be permitted to receive the individual relief consignments sent to them. While prisoners of war and interned individuals are widely thought to be included among protected persons, considering that protection covers is limited to civilians in occupied territories and other international combat zones are protected, the rights enumerated in these articles are similarly restricted to the general civilian population. IHL also addresses humanitarian assistance. After having received consent from participant parties, Articles 23, 31, and 61 of the same convention lay out regulations for relief operations. Foodstuff, clothing, and tonics intended for expecting mothers, children under the age of fifteen, infants shall be permitted to pass freely. However, permission is possible only after having received credible assurance that consignments will not be sent except to locations where they are needed nor will they be used for military purposes.

Relief materials may, however, be sent to another location in which they are in urgent need as long as they are used in a way that does not contravene their intended purpose. Occupying powers shall expedite the free passage and swift distribution of consignments and may not impose taxes on relief materials or require a fee for their passage unless it benefits the local economy or is used for the benefit of the occupied territory. Parties shall, as much as conditions permit, facilitate humanitarian organizations in carrying out their humanitarian functions.

Article 8(2)(b)(iii) of the Rome Statute of the International Criminal Court considers intentional attacks against personnel, installations, material, units, or vehicles involved in humanitarian assistance, whether during international or non-international armed conflicts, to constitute war crimes. It is imperative that humanitarian relief personnel know the legal foundations and principles underpinning IHL when they establish communications or enter into negotiations with the parties to an armed conflict while carrying out their humanitarian duties. Likewise, humanitarian organizations should take full advantage of the opportunities granted to them by these laws and regulations in order to safeguard the communities they serve, their own personnel, and their operations. Several factors, such as the desire to establish authority over the population in the territory under their control, to prove their political legitimacy and compliance with civil rights requirements, and to portray themselves in a positive light in the eyes of the international community, impact how belligerent parties regard humanitarian norms. Similarly, belligerents' power and their capacity to exert this power affect how their rapport with these norms. Whereas humanitarian relief workers remind belligerent parties of their responsibilities, they may at times be required to use their discretion as to when, given the risks of their specific circumstances, they are to make concessions while still ensuring that certain red lines are not transgressed.

> Published on 13 May 2016, the *Report of the Secretary-General on the Protection of Civilians in Armed Conflicts* (S/2016/447) articulates that between August and December of 2015, Houthi authorities persistently denied approval for the delivery of humanitarian supplies to 175,000 civilians in an enclave of the city of Ta'izz in Yemen. Whereas sieges are a legitimate method of warfare in international humanitarian law, their legality depends on how they are run (The UNSC, 2016).

Medical Services

Hospitals

Medical units are defined as all establishments, whether military or civilian, that are used for medical purposes or that provide health services. Medical purposes include the location, collection, diagnosis, and treatment of sick, injured, incapacitated, and pregnant persons. For instance, depositories containing medical equipment and supplies are considered medical units.

Civilian hospitals charged with caring for sick, injured, incapacitated, and pregnant persons may, under absolutely no circumstances, be made a target of attack and must be both respected and protected by all belligerent parties (Geneva Conventions, Article 18, 1949). Party nations are obligated to provide civilian hospitals with documentation showing that they are indeed civilian hospitals and that the buildings they occupy are not being used for any purpose that will cause them to lose their protected status.

Belligerent parties shall, to the extent that military considerations permit, endeavor to mark civilian hospitals with distinctive emblems easily visible to hostile land, air, and naval forces that identify their civilian and medical status in order to eliminate the possibility of their being the target of enemy aggression.

The protection afforded to civilian hospitals shall not cease unless they are not used to commit, outside their humanitarian function, acts harmful to the enemy (Geneva Conventions, Article 13, 1949). Protection may, however, cease only after a warning has been given setting, whenever appropriate, a reasonable time-limit, and after such warning has remained unheeded.

Treating sick or wounded members of the armed forces in these hospitals or the possession of small arms and ammunition taken from the wounded or sick that have yet to be handed over to the proper service unit shall not be considered acts harmful to the enemy.

Personnel in charge of the administration and operations of civilian hospitals shall, as laid out in Article 38, be respected, protected, and vested with the authority to issue distinctive emblems during the performance of their duties. The capacity in which they are employed shall be marked on their identity cards. The administration of every hospital shall, at all times, have at hand an up-to-date list of personnel that they can present to national or occupying authorities upon demand.

Vehicles used to carry sick and wounded individuals

IHL requires that belligerent parties take measure to expedite the search for and collection of sick and wounded individuals (Geneva Conventions, Articles 15–18, 1949; Protocol Addition II to the Geneva Conventions, Article 8, 1977; Customary IHL 109 *see* Hencaerts & Doswald-Beck, 2005 "Kural 109"). These measures require that medical personnel and vehicles be granted unhindered access to sick and wounded individuals so that any necessary medical care may be administered wherever and whenever they are essential and that sick and wounded individuals be granted access to medical facilities. While ambulances may be stopped and searched at control points, search procedures must not be so invasive or lengthy so as to have a detrimental impact on the health of sick and wounded passengers or to impede the ambulance from performing its duties.

Land vehicles, hospital train consignments, and specially designated hospital ships carrying wounded and sick civilians, incapacitated individuals, expecting mothers, and infants shall be afforded the same respect and protection. These vehicles are permitted to use the distinctive emblems described in the Amelioration of the Condition of the Wounded and Sick in Armed Forces in the Field Article 38 of the Geneva Conventions of 12 August 1949 (Geneva Conventions, Article 21, 1949).

Aircraft used exclusively to carry medical personnel and equipment, sick and wounded civilians, incapacitated individuals, expecting mothers, and infants shall not be subject to attack. Belligerent parties shall respect such aircraft in areas they physically control while flying at the altitude, time, and route agreed upon beforehand (Geneva Conventions, Article 22, 1949).

Medical personnel

Article 15 of Protocol Additional I to the Geneva Conventions of 1949 relating to the Protection of Victims of International Armed Conflict emphasizes the following points:

- *Civilian medical personnel shall be respected and protected.*
- *Civilian medical personnel shall be provided with all available forms of assistance in areas where civilian medical services personnel have been interrupted as a result of armed conflict.*

- *Occupying nations shall provide all forms of assistance to the civilian medical personnel in the areas under occupation so that humanitarian workers may perform their duties to the best of their ability. Occupying nations may not require that, in the performance of those functions, medical personnel shall give priority to the treatment of any person except on medical grounds nor shall they compel medical personnel to carry out them to perform any task incompatible to their humanitarian mission.*
- *Civilian medical personnel shall have access to any place where their services are essential, subject to such supervisory and safety measures as the relevant Party to the conflict may deem necessary.*
- *Civilian religious personnel shall be respected and protected. The provisions of the Conventions and of this Protocol concerning the protection and identification of medical personnel shall apply equally to such persons.*

Attacks on medical personnel during armed conflicts are grounds for serious concern. In September and October of 2018, Boko Haram executed two medical workers that they had been holding hostage for several months in northern Nigeria (ICRC, 2018).

Implementing the principle of impartiality is bound to ethical restrictions and IHL requires that medical personnel act ethically appropriate. As a result, medical personnel cannot be punished for any medical activity as long as it is compatible to medical ethics (Additional Protocol I to the Geneva Conventions, Article 16, 1977; Additional Protocol II to the Geneva Conventions, Article 10, 1977; Geneva Conventions Article 18, 1949; Customary IHL Rule 26 *see* Hencaerts & Doswald-Beck, 2005 "Kural 26"). Moreover, parties cannot legally prosecute medical experts for acting in a way compatible to medical ethics (Protocol Additional I to the Geneva Conventions, Article 6, 1977; Protocol Additional II, Article 10 (1), (2); Customary IHL 26 *see* Hencaerts & Doswald-Beck, 2005 "Kural 26").

Medical personnel working to prevent the spread of disease and/or search for, collect, transport, and care of the sick and wounded, individuals administrating medical units and institutions, and the religious personnel of armed forces shall be respected and protected under all circumstances (Geneva Conventions, Article 24, 1949). All personnel involved with the search for, transport, and care of sick and wounded civilians, incapacitated individuals, expecting mothers, and infants shall also be respected and protected (Geneva Conventions, Article 20, 1949).

Hospital ships, their crew, and the various personnel aboard are protected. Civilians carried by these ships shall not be forced to surrender to any party that is not their own nor shall they be subject to capture at sea (Geneva Conventions, Article 22, 1949).

Personnel in charge of the administration and operations of civilian hospitals shall be respected, protected, and vested with the authority to issue distinctive emblems during the performance of their duties. The capacity in which they are employed shall be marked on their ID cards. While carrying out their duties in occupied lands and military zones, the aforementioned personnel shall wear embossed photo identification issued and stamped by the competent authority certifying their status in water-resistant card armlets affixed to their left arm. This armlet shall carry the relevant distinctive emblem described in Article 38 of the Convention I for the Amelioration of the Condition of the Wounded and Sick in Armed Forces in the Field. The administration of every hospital shall, at all times, have at hand an up-to-date list of personnel that they can present to national or occupying authorities upon demand.

This protection is extended to *(i)* the military medical personnel of belligerent parties, civilian medical personnel, medical personnel assigned to tasks of civil defense, medical personnel authorized by the Red Cross or Red Crescent organizations, and medical personnel of authorized by other national aid societies; *(ii)* medical personnel made available by a neutral or other state that is not a party to the conflict and medical or by a recognized and authorized aid society of such state; and *(iii)* the medical personnel provided by an impartial international humanitarian organization.

Medical personnel lose the protection to which they are entitled when they participate in hostilities outside of their exclusively assigned medical duties, when they carry weapons and equipment other than small arms to defend themselves and their patients that can be used in military assaults, and when they use their medical services or protective emblem for perfidious reasons, such as to conceal military operations. Even in such cases where medical personnel forfeit their protection, the sick and wounded under their care retain their protected status.

Contact between Family Members

All persons in the territory of a Party to the conflict, or in territory occupied by it, shall be enabled to give news of a strictly personal nature to members of their families, wherever they may be, and to receive news from them (Geneva Conventions, Article 25, 1949). Such correspondence shall be delivered expediently and without being subject to arbitrary delays.

If extant conditions render it difficult or impossible to correspond through conventional postal services, the relevant party or parties shall have access to a neutral organ, such as a Central Information Agency described in Article 140 of the 1949 Geneva Convention Relative to the Protection of Civilian Persons in Time of War. Parties shall consult with national Red Cross and Red Crescent societies to determine how to best coordinate their efforts to come up with the best working solution possible. If belligerent parties deem it necessary to restrict correspondence, they may do so provided that they permit individuals to write their family members once a month using a standard form containing twenty-five freely chosen words.

Each party to the conflict shall facilitate enquiries made by members dispersed owing to the war, with the object of renewing contact with one another and of meeting, if possible (Geneva Conventions, Article 26, 1949). Belligerent parties shall encourage the work of humanitarian organizations working toward this goal on condition that they act in accordance with the provisions laid out in the Geneva Conventions and abide by the security regulations put in place.

Article 25 of the Geneva Convention IV guarantees everyone residing in armed combat zones or territories occupied by a belligerent party the right to be informed of the whereabouts of their family members when such information is available. Article 136 of the same convention enjoins belligerent parties to establish official information bureaus responsible for receiving and transmitting information concerning the protected persons residing in areas under their control. This way, families may obtain information about their children or other members who have been kept in custody for an excess of two weeks, subjected to assigned residence, or interned. These bureaus must keep records of deaths, births, releases, repatriations, escapes, and hospital admittances. Article 74 of Protocol Additional II requires that both high contracting and belligerent parties facilitate the reunification of families dispersed as a result of international armed conflicts.

> In line with the Geneva Conventions ratified by the Grand National Assembly of Türkiye on 21 January 1953, a National Intelligence Bureau was established [by the government of Türkiye] to allow prisoners of war captured during the Cyprus Peace Operation to communicate with the outside world (Keser 2010, vol. 2, p. 210).

International Human Rights Law

In addition to the limits imposed and rights recognized by IHL, international human rights law plays an important role in ensuring that individuals be treated humanely during armed conflicts and in protecting their physical and mental integrity. Non-derogable rights—those rights that cannot be suspended even during emergency circumstances—ensure that this protection regime shall continue at all times. For instance, Article 1 of the Universal Declaration of Human Rights states that all human beings are born free and equal in dignity and rights; Article 3 that everyone has the right to life, liberty, and the security of person; and Article 5 that no one shall be subjected to cruel, inhuman, or degrading treatment or punishment.

After the international community approved and adopted the Universal Declaration of Human Rights on 10 December 1948, the UN General Assembly, in order to render these standards binding on signatory nations, adopted the International Covenant on Civil and Political Rights on 16 December 1966. Coming into force on 23 March 1976, this multilateral treaty commits party states to ensure that the rights recognized therein be ensured to all individuals without distinction of any kind, such as race, skin color, sex, language, religion, political or other convictions, national or social origin, property, birth, or other status. Article 6 of this treaty affirms that every human being has the inherent right to life, that this right shall be protected by law, and that no one shall be arbitrarily deprived of his life.

Combatants are entitled to use lethal force against enemy forces to render them incapacitated. That said, however, the use of lethal force against persons who are not involved directly in hostilities; who have laid down their arms or have surrendered; who are *hors de combat* because of sickness, injury, or disability; who are prisoners of war; and who have been detained by one of the parties to the combat violates not only IHL but also international human rights law for not respecting non-combatants' right to life.

Parties to an armed conflict are responsible for maintaining public order in the territories they control. Acts that do not contribute directly to hostilities, such as public demonstrations, instances of societal violence, and acts related to public security are subject to the local legal system and international human rights law. While responding to such incidents, authorities may not employ direct lethal force against armed demonstrators or individuals participating in violent movements in the same way that they do against combatants. Instead, they are expected to use proportional force against civilians and take into consideration instances of legitimate self-defense in order to ensure that no human rights violations are committed.

Article 7 of the International Covenant on Civil and Political Rights affirms that no one shall be subjected to torture or to cruel, inhuman or degrading treatment or punishment. In particular, no one shall be subjected without his free consent to medical or scientific experimentation. This specific article is of vital importance for arrested, detained, and interned persons, as it complements Common Article 3 of the Geneva Conventions of 1949, which delineates the minimum protection standards necessary during non-international armed conflicts. From the purview of both humanitarian and human rights law, it is imperative that the conditions under which detainees are to be held, the practices followed in detainment camps, and the disciplinary measures used against detainees not jeopardize their physical and mental health. Article 8 of the same covenant states that no one shall be held in slavery and prohibits slavery and the slave-trade in all their forms. Articles 15, 16, and 18 state that everyone shall have the right to recognition everywhere as a person before the law, that no one shall be held guilty of any criminal offence on account of any act or omission which did not constitute a criminal offence, and that everyone shall have the right to freedom of thought, conscience and religion. IHL further stipulates that hunger shall not be used as a weapon of war, that objects necessary for human survival shall not be targeted, that sick and wounded individuals shall be protected along with the medical personnel transporting and/or caring for them, and that infrastructure shall not be intentionally targeted.

Articles 11, 12, and 13 of the International Covenant on Economic, Social and Cultural Rights, ratified by the UN General Assembly Resolution 2200A (XXI) of 16 December 1966 and entering into force on 3 January 1975, recognize every person's right to a standard of living adequate for the well-being of himself and of his family, including food, clothing, and housing; the right to be free from hunger; the right to the enjoyment of the highest attainable standard of physical and mental health standards; and the right to education. Nations involved in an international armed conflict, occupying states, and non-governmental armed groups responsible for maintaining public order in the territories under their control during international and non-international armed conflicts shall take the necessary measures to ensure that the aforementioned rights may be enjoyed, to remove any obstacles impeding their enjoyment, and to prevent third parties from violating these rights. Whereas the suspension or restriction of certain social, economic, and cultural rights is permitted in certain circumstances, the protection of one's right to life—which cannot be suspended or infringed upon even in times of war or emergency—is possible only by safeguarding said person's access to the basic necessities ensuring his continued survival and health. A party that intentionally targets food sources during an armed conflict runs the risk not only of being accused of using hunger as a weapon under humanitarian law but of having committed a human rights violation by rendering it impossible for a population to access the resources necessary for its survival, thereby depriving said population of its right to life.

Conclusion

The foundational documents of IHL and the principles of humanity, impartiality, necessity, proportionality, and humane treatment enshrined in these documents regulate armed conflict by specifying the limits placed on the use of violence during hostilities and the sanctions imposed on parties that transgress these limits. The principles of humanity, neutrality, impartiality, and independence defined by the main actors of the humanitarian aid ecosystem furnish an ethical approach that humanitarians can use in their efforts to protect human life, guarantee basic human rights, and the basic human needs of aggrieved persons during armed conflict and other crisis situations.

By taking advantage of the resources provided by international law, humanitarian actors and diplomats can develop a viable diplomatic approach to armed conflicts. By collaborating with civilian groups, state actors, and humanitarian organizations, protecting powers are able to ensure the transport of civilians to hospitals and other safe zones. Such collaboration also enables protecting powers to promote communication between belligerent parties and lead negotiations to establish neutral areas, to expedite the provision of necessary medical care and humanitarian services, to ensure that prisoners of war are treated humanely, to bring up instances where ethical rules have been violated, and to facilitate communication between family members separated by the conflict. Humanitarian diplomacy actors may appeal to international human rights law in areas where IHL is either vague or silent, such as the right to life, security, housing, food, health, education, and a standard of living adequate for the well-being of himself and of his family. Nevertheless, IHL and international human rights law collectively provide a robust framework protecting both aggrieved individuals and the humanitarian workers serving them, thus allowing humanitarian diplomacy actors to operate in combat and crisis zones.

Notes

1 The humanitarian principles accepted by the International Red Cross and Red Crescent Movement are currently articulated as the *7 Fundamental Principles*, namely, humanity, impartiality, neutrality, independence, volunteer service, unity, and universality.
2 For instance, the International Court of Justice, at the request of the UN General Assembly, issued an advisory opinion on the legality of threat or use of nuclear weapons, ruling that in light of the United Nations Charter, the available corpora of law on armed conflict, international customary law, and humanitarian law, states do not process absolute freedom in choosing the weapons they use. See International Court of Justice, 8 July 1996.
3 The Martens Clause was first introduced into the preamble of the 1899 Hague Convention II – Laws and Customs of War on Land. It reads:

Until a more complete code of the laws of war is issued, the High Contracting Parties think it right to declare that in cases not included in the Regulations adopted by them, populations and belligerents remain under the protection and empire of the principles of international law, as they result from the usages established between civilized nations, from the laws of humanity and the requirements of the public conscience.

(The International Committee of the Red Cross (ICRC), n.d.). The Martens Clause and the Laws of Armed Conflict, https://www.icrc.org/en/doc/ resources/documents/article/other/57jnhy.htm).

4 See Article 12 of the 1949 Geneva Convention I for the Amelioration of the Conditions of the Wounded and Sick in Armed Forces; Article 12 of the 1949 Geneva Convention II for the Amelioration of the Conditions of the Wounded, Sick and Shipwrecked Members of Armed Forces at Sea; Article 13 of the 1949 Geneva Convention III Relative to the Treatment of Prisoners of War; Articles 5, 27, and 127 of the 1949 Geneva Convention IV Relative to the Protection of Civilian Persons in Time of War; Articles 10 and 75 of Protocol Additional I relating to the Protection of Victims of International Armed Conflicts; Articles 4, 5 and 7 of the Protocol Additional II relating to the Protection of Victims of Non-International Armed Conflicts; Article 87 of Customary IHL.
5 See Article 3 of the 12 August 1949 Geneva Convention (I) for the Amelioration of the Condition of the Wounded and Sick in Armed Forces in the Field; Article 3 of the 12 August 1949 Geneva Convention (II) on Wounded, Sick and Shipwrecked of Armed Forces at Sea; Article 3 of the 12 August 1949 Geneva Convention (III) on Prisoners of War; Article 3 of the Geneva Convention (IV) on Civilians; Article 51 of Protocol Additional (I) relating to the Protection of Victims of International Armed Conflicts; Article 31 of Protocol Additional (II) relating to the Protection of Victims of Non-International Armed Conflicts; and Rule 6 of Customary IHL, ICRC.

References

African Union South Sudan Commission of Inquiry. (2014). *Final report of the African Union Commission of Inquiry on South Sudan*. http://www.peaceau.org/uploads/auciss.final.report.pdf

Dyukova, Y. & Chetcuti, P. (2013). Humanitarian principles in conflict. *ACF-International*. https://knowledgeagainsthunger.org/technical/humanitarian-principles-in-conflict/

Grace, R. (2015). *Humanitarian negotiation: Key challenges and lessons learned in an emerging field*. ATHA White Paper Series. https://hhi.harvard.edu/files/humanitarianinitiative/files/humanitarian_negotiation_-_key_challenges_and_lessons_learned_in_an_emerging_field.pdf?m=1610651653

Hencaerts, J. M. & Doswald-Beck, L. (2005). Kural 26, 109, 110. In *Uluslararası insancıl teamül (örf-âdet) hukuku. v. 1: Kurallar*. Galatasaray Üniversitesi Hukuk Fakültesi Yayınları. https://www.icrc.org/en/doc/home/languages/turkish/files/uluslararasi-insancil-teamul-orfadet-hukuku-customary-ihl-vol1.pdf

Kant, I. (2020/1795). *Ebedî barış üzerine felsefi bir tasarı (Zum ewigen Frieden, Ein philosophischer Entwurf, 1795)*. (C. Yeşilçayır, Trans). Fol Yayınları.

Keser, U. (2010). *Kızılay belgeleri ışığında Kıbrıs 1963–1974 (c. 1–2)*. Türkiye Kızılay Derneği Yayınları. http://kizilaytarih.org/yayinlar/10-kizilay-belgeleri-isiginda-kibris-1963-1974-profdrulvi-keser.pdf

Medecins Sans Frontieres. (2019). *Medical humanitarian needs in a changing political and aid environment*. https://msf-analysis.org/medical-humanitarian-needs-changing-political-aid-environment/

O'Callghan & Backhurst. (2013). *Principles in action in Somalia*. https://library.alnap.org/help-library/principles-in-action-in-somalia

Protocol Additional to the Geneva Conventions of 12 August 1949, and relating to the protection of victims of non-international armed conflicts (protocol I). (1977). https://ihl-databases.icrc.org/en/ihl-treaties/api-1977

Protocol Additional to the Geneva Conventions of 12 August 1949, and relating to the protection of victims of non-international armed conflicts (protocol II). (1977). https://ihl-databases.icrc.org/applic/ihl/ihl.nsf/INTRO/475

Shaw, M. N. (2018). *Uluslararası hukuk* (Y. Acer, İ. Kaya, M. T. Demirtepe, & G. E. Şimşek, Trans.). TÜBA.

The Geneva Conventions and their commentaries. (1949). https://www.icrc.org/en/war-and-law/treaties-customary-law/geneva-conventions

The ICRC. (2018). *Nigeria: Health worker Hauwa Mohammed Liman executed in captivity*. https://www.icrc.org/en/document/nigeria-health-worker-hauwa-mohammed-liman-executed-captivity#:~:text=The%20International%20Committee%20of%20the,murdered%20in%20the%20last%20month

The International Committee of the Red Cross (ICRC). (n.d.). *Convention (III) relative to the Treatment of Prisoners of War. Geneva, 12 August 1949. Article 4 - Prisoners of war*. https://ihl-d4?at4?ab4?ases.icrc.org/en/ihl-tre4?aties/gciii-1949/4?article-4?4?activeT4?ab=1949GCs-APs-4?and-comment4?aries

The United Nations. (2010). *CRC/C/OPAC/COL/CO/1*. https://undocs.org/Home/Mobile?FinalSymbol=CRC%2FC%2FOPAC%2FCOL%2FCO%2F1&Language=E&DeviceType=Desktop&LangRequested=False

The UNSC. (2016). *The Report of the Secretary-General on the Protection of Civilians in Armed Conflicts* (S/2016/447). https://www.securitycouncilreport.org/atf/cf/%7B65BFCF9B-6D27-4E9C-8CD3-CF6E4FF96FF9%7D/s_2016_447.pdf

UN OCHA. (2015). *Statement to the press on Syria*. http://www.unocha.org/node/207361

Von Clausewitz, C. (1975/1832). *Savaş üzerine* [Vom Kriege, 1832]. (Ş. Yalçın, Trans.). May Yayınları.

Weismann, F. (Ed.). (2004). *In the Shadow of "Just Wars": Violence, Politics and Humanitarian Action*. Cornell University Press.

4 Globalization and Humanitarian Diplomacy

Case Study of Türkiye

Hakan Ünay and Murat Çemrek

Given its profound impact on how people go about their daily lives, globalization has stimulated debates on nearly every facet of human life, including the place of many societal values, fundamental concepts, academic disciplines, and workplace procedures. As a consequence of the resulting symbiotic relationship, daily realities and the concepts used to interpret them have been imbued with a new, globalized character. This has, in turn, provoked mankind to reevaluate these realities and concepts, which has brought about various, sometimes radical structural changes and influenced the trajectory of globalization itself.

Globalization has similarly forced diplomacy to evolve, causing it to expand into arenas from which it had previously been excluded. So much so, in fact, that modern diplomacy has outgrown its traditional restraints and now incorporates economic, cultural, health, education, political, and technological dimensions into its *modus operandi*. Accordingly, humanitarian diplomacy has emerged as a potent force effective in dealing with the increasingly severe conflicts and crises that have come to characterize the twenty-first century.

Humanitarian diplomacy activities seek to resolve active humanitarian crises by alleviating the underlying crisis situation and include all activities that are reconciliatory in nature and that prioritize humanitarian relief. Just as these activities may pertain directly to the distribution of humanitarian relief to vulnerable populations in crisis zones, so too may they encourage or even compel international organs to consult or negotiate with one another to bring an end to the crisis at head. Türkiye, the case under examination in this chapter, has devised policies seeking to see that these two facets of humanitarian diplomacy are properly carried out and has recently made cooperation with two organizations in particularly—AFAD (i.e., Disaster and Emergency Management Presidency) and the Turkish Red Crescent (henceforth TRC)—a central part of her foreign policy initiatives in this vein (Güder et al., 2020, pp. 124–125).

Understanding Globalization and its Transformative Effect

Globalization has been a driving force behind the transformation of nearly every aspect of life, including individuals, nation-states, international organizations, and supranational entities. Everything that was solid—local, national,

DOI: 10.4324/9781003503187-4

regional, international, and global borders—has since "evaporated" and become global. Inspired by the notion that "war is peace, freedom is slavery, [and] ignorance is power" put forward in George Orwell's *1984*, we can comfortably assert that the local is global and the global is local. With exponentially more advanced and affordable communication and transportation technologies, globalization has brought about a revolution of astronomical proportions that, by destroying the traditional barriers of the physical world, has rendered David Harvey's notion of time-space compression a reality (2010, p. 270). As a meta-concept, globalization may be amalgamated with virtually any existing concept to produce an entirely new term altogether.

A firm grasp of the conditions leading up to its initial rise and growth allows us to understand how globalization has succeeded in permeating into every aspect of our daily life. Indeed, this multidimensional character has precipitated debate on when globalization began, its justifications, its real and potential outcomes, and its consequences on today's modus vivendi. As such, addressing the changes brought about by globalization is essential to lay the very foundation of our study.

The most celebrated outcome brought about by globalization is that national boundaries, despite being so idolized by nation-states, have lost a significant amount their former importance. This has in turn permitted individuals, knowledge, money, property, and just about anything the mind can conceive, whether of benefit or detriment to mankind, to travel previously unfathomable distances more quickly and easily than ever before in human history (Battır, 2019, p. 155). As modernity has increasingly shifted from solid to liquid, thus acquiring a viscous nature, (Ritzer and Dean, 2019) it has simultaneously become more flexible. One concrete, yet paradoxical example of this change is how, despite the walls and advanced electronic surveillance equipment guarding them, national borders have become increasingly more porous. A more abstract example is how the clear ideological distinctions between right and left have all but dissipated, forcing both sides to reevaluate their positions and to be less effective at determining policies.

Globalization naturally has many proponents, opponents, and skeptics who debate with one another on all sorts of both central and peripheral issues. Its conceptual formation cannot similarly be regarded in a vacuum, especially one that ignores the realities of those who coined this term and the theoretical paradigms they espoused as a result. Discussions on globalization are inevitably shaped by the specific area and questions/problems under scrutiny. Whereas skeptics prefer the terms *internationalization* and *regionalization*, proponents, often referred to as *hyperglobalists*, emphasize that we live in a truly globalized world. While speaking of the globalizing world, this latter group describe the world as being molded by highly enmeshed relationships, rapidly evolving currents, movements, and networks that cut across regions and continents (Held and McGrew, 2008, p. 52).

The impact that globalization has had on different concepts and values is yet another area of dispute between globalists and skeptics. Whereas skeptics assert that power remains in the hands of the nation-state, whose rules are thus valid, globalists maintain that since sovereignty, autonomy, and legitimacy in the Westphalian sense have waned, the monopoly of power formerly enjoyed by nation-states has been dispersed among international organizations, non-governmental organizations (NGOs), multinational corporations (MNCs), and even individuals. In parallel to this, advocates of globalization underline that the economy has taken on a supranational character, which they refer to as *global information capitalism*. Skeptics, on the other hand, hold that nation-states maintain their authority over the economy and that, with the exception of select regional economy blocks, it is still too early to speak of a supranational or even global economy. While skeptics likewise insist that nation-states retain their dominance over the cultural flow, globalists argue the complete opposite to be true, namely, that a global popular culture has taken root the world over (Held and McGrew, 2008, p. 52).

In addition to proponents, skeptics, and opponents is a fourth group known as the transformationalists. Adopting a slightly more moderated approach, transformationalists have added their own input into the ongoing debates on globalization.

While the literature lacks a consensus on the exact date that globalization became a force in the world, it is clear that it has, for better or for worse, played a central role in our lives for a significant period of time. This raises the question as to whether globalization is indeed a new phenomenon. The different parties to the debate naturally have diverging opinions on this matter. Whereas hyperglobalists argue that the world has indeed entered a new global age, opponents and skeptics focus more on globalization's economic and geographic impact, asserting that what is actually new here is the existence of trade blocks and the erosion of the nation-state's Westphalian sovereignty. Transformationalists, on the other hand, emphasize a deep-rooted mutual dependency (Bülbül, 2009, p. 141). Here, all groups at least agree that globalization has produced certain novelties in the world. It should be underlined, moreover, that globalization's greatest effect is the transformative effect of the concept itself.

The subject of this study, diplomacy, was similarly forced to diversify and undergo a massive transformation as a result of globalization. This transformation would give rise to, among numerous other outcomes, the rise of humanitarian diplomacy. As globalization has continued to spawn new globalizations in diverse areas (Berger and Huntington, 2012), it is only natural that humanitarian diplomacy and all of its actors have, as its very essence would require, risen to become a sought-after value in their own right.

Globalization and Humanitarian Diplomacy

Globalization, in addition to being host to a plethora of values and a phenomenon that has left a lasting impression on every aspect of modern life, remains an ongoing process. Globalization has, in so far as we have hitherto experienced it, succeeded in refining the notion of human that had gained currency during the Enlightenment—perhaps its most important outcome. The word humanitarian is added to security, law, development, aid activities, international organizations, and diplomacy, thus turning each one into a human-centric version of itself. This transformation, Özlük argues, can be described as a humanitarian renaissance (2016, pp. 1–2) and is an extension of the transformative effect of globalization, one of the theses of this study.

It is difficult to arrive on a mutually agreed upon definition for most concepts in the social sciences. It is no different for such a novel concept as humanitarian diplomacy. The definition put forward by the International Federation of Red Cross and Red Crescent Societies asserting that humanitarian diplomacy is "persuading decision makers and opinion leaders to act, at all times, in the interests of vulnerable people, and with full respect for fundamental humanitarian principles" is merely one of several definitions (IFRC, 2009). According to this definition, vulnerable people are the focus of humanitarian diplomacy whereas the effective parties are opinion leaders and decision makers. This illustrates that nation-states, despite being the main actors of international relations, no longer have a monopoly on diplomacy. This shift is indisputably an outcome of globalization.

Globalization's impact on the evolution of diplomacy first manifested in the negative developments that triggered the emergence of humanitarian diplomacy. Albeit somewhat controversial, it is largely accepted in the literature that globalization began its ascendency during the Cold War Era. Diplomacy, like so many other things during this period, underwent a radical transformation. Following the end of the Cold War, nation-states began to develop new modes of combat that involved non-state actors fighting within the borders of a single nation-state instead of warring against one another with cumbersome armies and classic methods that had become largely obsolete in this new age of rapid change (Dülger, 2017, p. 2). While neo-legionnaires, essentially private military companies comprised of paramilitary forces and mercenaries, have gained growing representation as a result of globalization, humanitarian diplomacy has simultaneously been the subject of more and more discussions. However, humanitarian diplomacy is still a very new concept and area of research (Lauri, 2018, p. 3). In fact, the first book to include humanitarian diplomacy in its title—*Humanitarian Diplomacy: Practitioners and Their Craft*—was published only at early as 2007 (Minear and Smith, 2007). Interestingly, we find ourselves in a world that is in ever increasing need of humanitarian diplomacy, despite its relative novelty. The types of armed conflict and natural disasters that have rendered humanitarian diplomacy necessary are a result of globalization and continue to become more frequent and intense as time passes. This epitomizes not only how globalization has increased the need of humanitarian diplomacy but also that these two phenomena are mutually and directly related to one another.

As articulated above, globalization has not only spawned numerous crisis environments in need of humanitarian diplomacy but has also, as a result of the profound transformations that have occurred in the field of diplomacy, paved the way for the emergence of humanitarian diplomacy itself. This is but one of many manifestations of globalization's curiously paradoxical makeup. In essence, while it is true that globalization has spurred more meaningful interaction between and greater personal awareness of diverse individuals, societies, and institutions, thus increasing the number of worldwide philanthropic activities, it has simultaneously led to an increased number of crises and, by natural extension, crisis-induced anxiety. Looking at the subject with a critical and inquisitive eye reveals that globalization has not had strictly positive or negative outcomes. On the contrary, we observe globalization to display a host of contradictory, conflicting, and even reconciliatory characteristics (Bülbül, 2009, p. 14). These seemingly paradoxical facets of globalization were rendered ever more apparent when humanitarian diplomacy arrived on the international scene. Nevertheless, the existence of two crisis scenarios, namely, armed conflict and humanitarian crises triggered by natural disasters, sparked humanitarian diplomacy into existence (Veuthey, 2012, p. 198). It is possible to observe the paradoxical effects of globalization in both of these crisis scenarios. On the one hand, globalization laid the groundwork for the mass communication and transportation network required to spread and promote the values it embraced, namely, democracy, equality, human rights, and world peace. On the other hand, however, these values have been progressively eroded away as humanitarian crises, themselves a result of globalization, increasingly reared their ugly head. These crises could only be solved through humanitarian diplomacy. Likewise, both this increased environmental awareness and the fact that ecology has moved beyond being an academic research field and found a place on the worldwide political agenda are a direct result of globalization. The world is now a veritable field of competition in every possible sense imaginable, which has precipitated a massive upsurge in environmental problems; so much so, in fact, that the current global climate crisis can no longer go unnoticed by any rational observer. The same process of globalization that has made it possible for us to watch with eyes wide open the now unignorable number of natural disasters whether on traditional or social media channels has been the very impetus for the emergence and ascendance humanitarian diplomacy.

Whereas globalization has played a crucial role in making humanitarian diplomacy into a viable and practical form of diplomacy, humanitarian diplomacy has likewise caused globalization to rise to new heights. This, in turn, has disclosed an oddly symbiotic relationship between the two. In fact, not only has globalization forced diplomacy to undergo such a radical transformation and set into motion unprecedented humanitarian crises, it has also even made it easier for such crises to occur in parts of the world that they would otherwise not have. While humanitarian diplomacy activities have increased in quantity and become more entrenched, their diversification has caused the very mechanisms that coordinate and control these activities to be stripped of their local, national, regional, and even international character, thus paving the way for their globalization. After emerging as one of the more prominent nations in the field of humanitarian diplomacy in the 2000s, Türkiye has only increased her involvement in humanitarianism—so much so, in fact, that she is now one of the foremost actors in the field.

Türkiye's Humanitarian Diplomacy in a Globalized World

Globalization has both transformed the international system and diversified the actors involved in this same system. While these new actors very often forge relationships with nation-states, even rivaling them in terms of effectiveness, they act in several spheres still under the strict authority of nation-states. The interplay between globalization and nation-states cannot be denied here. However, those who would argue that globalization and nation-states are diametrically opposed or even antagonistic to one another, overlook the fact that nation-states, having served as the dominant political unit for nearly five hundred years, are the product of globalization.[1] On the contrary, the phenomenon of nation-states and the process of globalization nurtured one another's growth. That said, however, this symbiotic relationship, as is the case with every relationship, has led to mutual friction.

Globalization's interaction with nation-states and their mutual support for one another is, where humanitarian diplomacy is concerned, upheld by non-state actors. The stagnant bureaucratic apparatus in which policymaking, decision-making, and policy execution are, at least in today's context, severely hampered has rendered the ascendency of non-state actors a necessity. Here, NGOs have emerged as the most important humanitarian diplomacy actors. As will be discussed in greater detail below, Türkiye engages in humanitarian diplomacy through the numerous public institutions and NGOs based within her borders, of which TRC and AFAD are at the fore. Similarly, globalization has had an irrefutable effect on Türkiye's humanitarian diplomacy activities and NGOs exert extraordinary influence on Turkish foreign policy. Whereas Türkiye continues to globalize as a result of these actors and her vision of humanitarian diplomacy, one that is completely synthesized with her foreign policy, she has simultaneously become one of the major powers directing the trajectory of globalization itself, even while questioning the potential repercussions of doing so. In short, the very nations that have used globalization as a catalyst to increase the horizontal and vertical interactions of individuals, communities, and societies also find themselves as actors in this process.

Humanitarian diplomacy activities intertwined with the foreign policy understanding of a nation-state form the cornerstone of the active foreign policy apparatus in Türkiye. Here, Türkiye has developed new foreign policy instruments to complement the active foreign policy strategy she espoused in the 1990s following the end of the Cold War (Kardaş and Erdağ, 2014, p. 170). The 2000s were of particular importance for Turkish foreign policy and Türkiye's integrated vision of humanitarian diplomacy. During this decade, Türkiye was able to reach numerous countries on the African continent, the most important of which being Somalia, and implement a foreign policy that put humans before all other interests both in Palestine and Syria. Türkiye was selected as the "most generous nation" in a 2018 report published by UK-based Development Initiatives (DI) for allocating 8.07 billion USD, equivalent to 0.85% of her GDP, to humanitarian assistance (Anadolu Agency, 2018). That this assistance was provided not only to those nations with whom Türkiye shares ethnolinguistic and/or religio-sectarian links but to the entire world was indeed a major reason for being awarded this honor (Çemrek and Yılmaz, 2021, p. 52).

As humanitarian diplomacy constitutes the most important aspect of her foreign policy vision, Türkiye conducts humanitarian diplomacy activities with diverse actors, of which TRC and AFAD play major roles, in a multitude of areas (Güder et al. 2020, p. 124). The more prominent of these two organizations, TRC, seeks "to prevent and alleviate human suffering, to safeguard human life and health, to promote respect for every individual, and to promote mutual understanding, friendship, respect, cooperation, and permanent peace among men" and strives to be an "organization that is held up as a model in humanitarian aid service in Türkiye and the world, supporting people at their most difficult hour" (Kızılay, 2021).

TRC has provided humanitarian assistance to and taken steps to ensure the lasting welfare in Afghanistan, Azerbaijan, Bangladesh, Bosnia and Herzegovina, Bulgaria, Indonesia, Palestine, South Sudan, Iraq, Kyrgyzstan, the Turkish Republic of Northern Cyprus, Myanmar, Pakistan, Senegal, Somalia, Sudan, and Yemen through the permanent delegations established in these seventeen countries. TRC provided humanitarian assistance, mostly in the form of disaster intervention, in fifty-one countries spanning three continents in the year 2021 alone, reaching 8.5 million individuals abroad and 38.5 million at home (Kızılay, 2022, pp. 12, 15, 26; Kızılay 2022a, p. 50; also see Figure 4.1).

TRC has run successive humanitarian assistance campaigns in response to the mass migration of refugees into Türkiye over the course of the Syrian Civil War. Having participated in the majority of activities related to humanitarian assistance for migrants, TRC has played a major role in Türkiye's diplomatic negotiations with the EU, using EU-funded projects to expand its sphere of influence and reach considerably more people in need. TRC has enhanced its worldwide network through collaboration with various entities in different parts of the globe. In addition to promoting Türkiye's foreign policy vision of humanitarian diplomacy, TRC has become a global asset through the philanthropic work it has conducted in various countries.

The cultural dimension of TRC's humanitarian works reinforces Türkiye's vision of cultural diplomacy. Remaining true to its historical mission and background, TRC has been the primary driving force behind Türkiye's rise to a position among the top international humanitarian aid donors. Regarded favorably throughout the world and even becoming a global name in the humanitarian relief field, TRC is a godsend for Türkiye with the amount of

☐ Beneficiaries   ▮ Countries

Year	Beneficiaries	Countries
2020	8,250,000	57
2019	7,250,000	71
2018	7,000,000	53
2017	6,850,000	38
2016	5,650,000	28

0   1,000,000 2,000,000 3,000,000 4,000,000 5,000,000 6,000,000 7,000,000 8,000,000 9,000,000

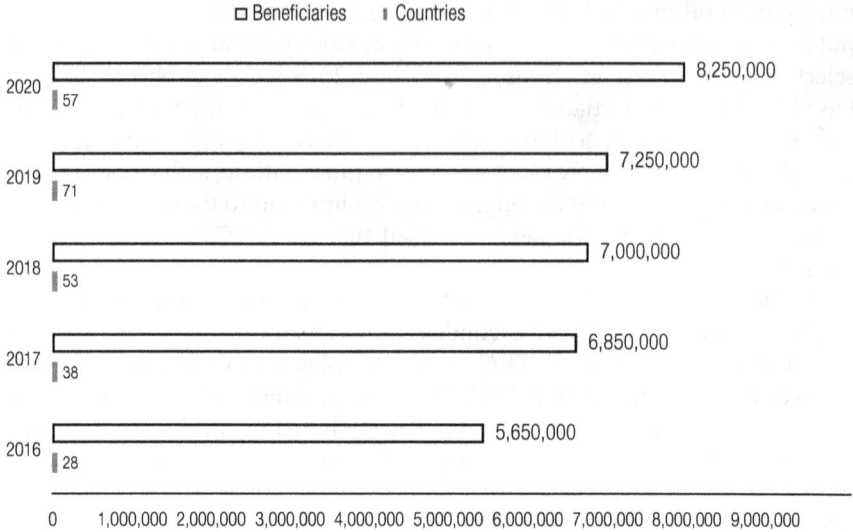

Created by the authors by analyzing the 2016-2021 annual activity reports of the Red Crescent.

Figure 4.1 Number of countries and beneficiaries where the Red Crescent operates (2016–2020).

Source: The Author.

experience in traditional diplomatic relations that the organization has accumulated over its lifetime. Through TRC, Türkiye has been able to ensure that relief materials reach areas in need without delay, thereby improving her global visibility level and strengthening her public diplomacy activities (Güder et al., 2020, pp. 125–126).

Formed in 2009, AFAD is another keystone in driving Türkiye's globalization process and vision of humanitarian diplomacy. This organization is responsible for preventing natural disasters, conducting post-disaster reconstruction, and coordinating disaster relief efforts run by different organizations. AFAD is engaged in humanitarian work both at home and abroad, including in such countries as Haïti, Japan, Chile, and Myanmar. It has led evacuation operations and humanitarian relief programs in Libya, Tunisia, Egypt, and Syria. Türkiye's sensitivity toward and ability to respond to global problems are put into practice through the various campaigns spearheaded by AFAD, thus ensuring that the necessary assistance is provided to areas where it is needed.

Türkiye has hosted roughly 3.5 million refugees fleeing from the Syrian Civil War that erupted in 2011, which has only worked to further solidify AFAD's importance on both the national and international levels. The myriad refuge centers and tent cities, health and educational, and facilities responding to the physical, social, and psychological needs of refugees established by AFAD have offered Syrian refugees the opportunity to build a new life in a new land. AFAD has also participated in Türkiye's cross-border operations to create safe living areas for and provide needed humanitarian aid to civilians. In fact, the UN awarded AFAD with a Public Service Award in 2015 for Improving the Delivery of Public Services with its Sheltering Centre Management System (AFKEN). Bolstered by this achievement, AFAD has gone far to promote Türkiye's vision of humanitarian diplomacy by participating in humanitarian activities in more than fifty countries on five continents over the past six years. Accordingly, AFAD, has emerged as yet another powerful element in advancing Türkiye's vision of humanitarian diplomacy, has skillfully demonstrated how public diplomacy can be used effectively in a globalized world. A nation's ability to exercise soft and smart power accumulates over time. As a result of her humanitarian diplomacy practices, Türkiye will augment her capacity to exercise soft and smart power and eventually grow from a regional to a global power.

TRC and AFAD engage in work aiming to provide people in need with humanitarian assistance during crisis situations, especially humanitarian crises that result from armed conflicts and natural disasters. Accordingly, these two organizations, by embodying the fundamental dynamics of Türkiye's humanitarian diplomacy vision, have transformed into the very backbone of the nation's humanitarian diplomatic regime. There are numerous national NGOs, large and small, working diligently to propagate Türkiye's understanding of humanitarian diplomacy among people in need of assistance in various parts of the world. While we have refrained from going into excessive detail on the organizations and foundations in question so as not to go beyond the scope of this study, it is essential that we recognize the important contributions they have made to Türkiye's globalization by putting her vision of humanitarian diplomacy into practice.

The humanitarian diplomacy actors of Türkiye and the activities they spearhead have made Türkiye "the most generous country in the world." This is clearly seen in reports published on the global level. The annual *Global Humanitarian Assistance Report* published by Development Initiatives has found Türkiye to donate the most humanitarian assistance in proportion to national income. Figure 4.2 shows Türkiye's yearly humanitarian assistance expenditures by national income from 2016 to 2020 (Development Initiatives, 2021, p. 51).

Türkiye has joined the US as one of the most prolific donors of humanitarian relief. After ranking third worldwide in the amount of humanitarian aid donated in proportion to GDP for three consecutive years from 2013 to 2015, Türkiye upped her humanitarian diplomacy endeavors, thus propelling her into the top two donors during the subsequent years (See Figure 4.3). These figures are much more than mere statistical data; they serve as indicators of Türkiye's growth and transformation into a nation able to devote a portion of her budget to foreign aid.

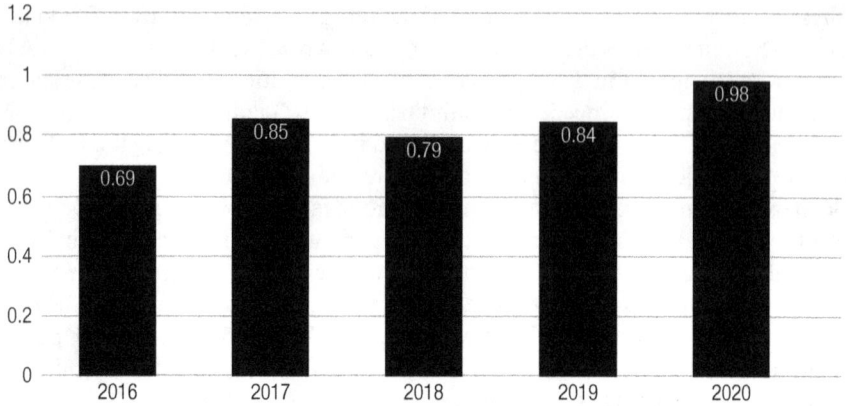

Created by the authors by analysing the 2016-2021 reports of the Global Humanitarian Assistance Report.

Figure 4.2 Ratio of Türkiye's Humanitarian Aid to GNP (2016–2020).

Source: The Authors.

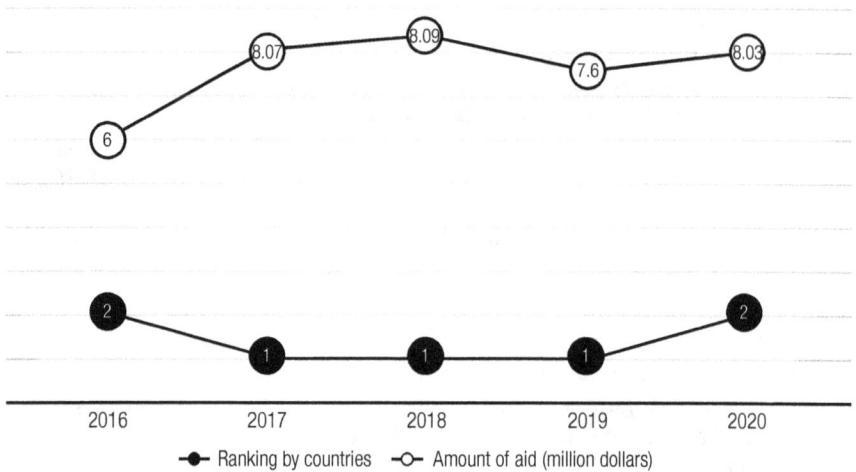

Created by the authors by analyzing the 2016-2021 annual activity reports of the Red Crescent.

Figure 4.3 Amount of aid provided by Türkiye and Ranking of top donor countries by GNP.

Source: The Authors.

Figures from 2016 to 2022 demonstrate that Türkiye has succeeded in realizing her vision of humanitarian diplomacy more efficaciously with each passing year, transforming herself into a globally recognized brand in the humanitarian field. Globalization is anticipated to become increasingly associated with humanitarian diplomacy in forthcoming years. The Credit Suisse Research Institute, for instance, predicts that the greatest challenges to global governance will be geopolitical military conflicts and climate disasters, perhaps even leading to the end of globalization (2015, p. 6). Since these two phenomena have proven true in today's world, it is only natural that the relationship between humanitarian diplomacy, which was developed to respond directly to these two issues, and globalization continue to gain strength. It would be no exaggeration to state that Türkiye has played a critical role in strengthening this relationship. For indeed Türkiye has spearheaded humanitarian diplomacy initiatives, emerged as a leader in this regard through the various humanitarian actors based within her borders, thus turning humanitarian diplomacy into a global value, and not only embraced by also popularized the values espoused by globalization.

Today's world is blighted by myriad international and internal conflicts that either result of or are greatly aggravated by geopolitical disagreements. Such conflicts are inevitable in a world where environmental problems have, despite years' worth of warnings, reached unprecedented heights and where natural disasters have become such common occurrences that they now threaten the infrastructures of even the most developed nations. Governments that have turned a blind eye to the numerous warnings of the impending dangers of global warming, namely, desertification and flooding, find themselves increasingly powerless as these predictions gradually become a reality. Apart from environmental disasters, civil disorder, and other similar problems, more complicated issues, such as food security, appear with increasing frequency in the news. Nation-states struggling to deal with these challenges have inclined toward cooperating with their neighbors and beyond, as it has become abundantly clear that they are incapable of enduring, let alone redressing, such wide scale problems by themselves. In short, while problems are global, proposed solutions that are regional, national, or local in nature fail to adequately address them. As broken windows theory proposes, problems, and especially those of a civil or criminal nature, that are not immediately addressed become entrenched into the social fabric and breed further, often significantly more serious problems. Moreover, the simplest and most cost effective method to redress problems is to prevent them from rearing their head in the first place. This may be accomplished by taking such precautionary measures as implementing preventative healthcare and other similar services. Otherwise, devising and implementing solutions after problems have fully matured will be exponentially more costly. Taking all of this into consideration, nations like Türkiye that have the necessary diplomatic tools and actors to come up with solutions for humanitarian crises in our globalizing world will continue to increase over time and other nations are anticipated to follow a similar trajectory.

Note

1   Discussions on the antagonism between globalization and the nation-state generally argue that the dominant nation-state paradigm has reached its shelf life. For similar studies, see Hankiss, 1999; Held and McGrew, 1998; Ohmae, 1995; Strange, 1997; Wolf, 2001.

References

Anadolu Agency. (2018). *Küresel insani yardım raporu: Dünyanın 'en cömert ülkesi' Türkiye.* https://www.aa.com.tr/tr/dunya/kuresel-insani-yardim-raporu-dunyanin-en-comert-ulkesi-turkiye/1180618

Battır, O. (2019). Küreselleşme çağında bir yumuşak güç unsuru olarak sağlık diplomasisi. *Anemon Muş Alparslan Üniversitesi Sosyal Bilimler Dergisi, 7*(5), 151–161. https://doi.org/10.18506/anemon.552103

Berger, P. L. & Huntington, S. P. (2012). *Bir küre bin bir küreselleşme* (A. Ortaç, Trans.). Kitabevi Yayınları.

Bülbül, K. (2009). *Küreselleşme, temel metinler - ekonomi, siyaset, kimlik, kültür, medeniyet.* Orion Kitabevi.

Credit Suisse Research Institute. (2015). *The end of globalization or a more multipolar world?* https://www.credit-suisse.com/about-us/en/reports-research/studies-publications.html

Çemrek, M. & Yılmaz, B. (2021). Türkiye'nin 2020 yurt dışı insani yardımları: Pandemi ve ötesi. In Kesgin, S. S. & Durmuş, A. (Eds.) *Türkiye İnsani Çalışmalar Yıllığı 2020* (pp. 51–53). Kızılay Akademi.

Development Initiatives. (2021). *Global humanitarian assistance 2021.* https://devinit.org/resources/global-humanitarian-assistance-report-2021/

Dülger, K. (2017). Etkinliği giderek artan yeni bir kavram olarak insani diplomasi ve bu alanda örnek teşkil eden Türkiye'nin insani diplomasi anlayışı. *Uluslararası Politik Araştırmalar Dergisi, 3*(2), 1–20.

Güder, S., Çemrek, M. & Mercan, M. H. (2020). *Geleceğin Türkiye'sinde dış politika.* İlke İlim Kültür Eğitim Vakfı. https://ilke.org.tr/images/dis_politika_rapor_ozeti_online.pdf

Harvey, D. (2010). *Postmodernliğin durumu* (S. Savran, Trans.). Metis Yayınları.

Held, D. & McGrew, A. G. (2008). *Küresel dönüşümler: Büyük küreselleşme tartışması* (A. R. Güngen, Trans.). Phoenix Yayınevi.

Kardaş, T. & Erdağ, R. (2014). Bir dış politika aracı olarak TİKA. *Akademik İncelemeler Dergisi (AID), 7*(1), 167–194.

Kızılay. (2021). *Misyonumuz ve vizyonumuz.* https://www.kizilay.org.tr/kurumsal/misyonumuz-vizyonumuz

Kızılay. (2022). *Türk Kızılay 2019–20–21 konsolide faaliyet raporu.* https://www.kizilay.org.tr/Upload/Dokuman/Dosya/turk-kizilay-2019-20-21-konsolide-faaliyet-raporu-13-05-2022-38119111.pdf

Kızılay. (2022a). *2021 faaliyet raporu.* https://www.kizilay.org.tr/Upload/Dokuman/Dosya/turk-kizilay-2021-faaliyet-raporu-11-05-2022-98842565.pdf

Lauri, A. (2018). *Humanitarian diplomacy: A new research agenda.* CMI Brief No: 04. https://www.cmi.no/publications/6536-humanitarian-diplomacy-a-new-research-agenda

Minear, L. & Smith, H. (Eds.). (2007). *Humanitarian diplomacy: Practitioners and their craft.* United Nations University Press

Özlük, E. (2016). İnsani diplomasinin insan(i) boyutu. In E. Akıllı (Ed.), *Türkiye'de ve dünyada dış yardımlar* (pp. 1–33). Nobel Akademik Yayıncılık.

Ritzer, G. & Dean, P. (2019). *Küreselleşme: Bir temel metin* (M. Çemrek & Y. Sayın, Trans.). Orion Yayınları.

The International Federation of Red Cross and Red Crescent (IFRC). (2009). *Humanitarian diplomacy policy*. https://www.ifrc.org/sites/default/files/Humanitarian-Diplomacy-Policy_EN.pdf

Veuthey, M. (2012). Humanitarian diplomacy: Saving it when it is most needed. In A. Vautravers & Y. Fox (Eds.). *Humanitarian space. Webster University Geneva 16th Humanitarian Conference* (pp. 195–208). Webster University.

Hankiss, E. (1999). Globalization and the end of the nation state? *World Futures, 53*(2), 135–147.

Held, D., & McGrew, A. (1998). The end of the old order? Globalization and the prospects for world order. *Review of International Studies, 24*(5), 219–245. https://doi.org/10.1017/S0260210598002198

Ohmae, K. (1995). *The end of the nation state: The rise of regional economies.* Simon and Schuster Inc.

Strange, S. (1997). The erosion of the state. *Current History, 96*(113), 365–369.

Wolf, M. (2001). Will the nation-state survive globalization? *Foreign Affairs, 80*(1), 178–190. https://doi.org/10.2307/20050051

5 Humanitarian Diplomacy in Complex and Protracted Crises

Segâh Tekin

While examples of practices that would fall under the contemporary definition of humanitarian diplomacy can be found as far back as the nineteenth century, the term itself was only coined during the 2000s in response to the specific needs of our era. United Nations (UN) figures reveal that the number of people in need of emergency humanitarian assistance has, at 132 million, reached its highest point since World War II (UN OCHA, 2021). The upsurge in number of protracted crises beginning during the second half of the twentieth century was indeed instrumental in driving humanitarian diplomacy's coinage as an academic term and subsequent conceptual development, its increase in currency in today's global political apparatus, and its growth into a vibrant discipline within academia. As these crises have brought to light the urgency of humanitarian aid in today's world, they are just as much the subject of policy debate as they are the topic of countless studies in the growing corpus of academic literature.

While several systems of classification have been developed to help compartmentalize these crises, the complexity of factors—some of which being the devastating armed conflicts, natural disasters, and human-induced calamities accompanying crises—has rendered it all the more difficult to recommend a general categorization (HPG, 2016, p. 22). Despite, moreover, the diversity of definitions surrounding them, protracted crises are host to specific characteristics that distinguish them from other types of crises. Such crises are those that are perpetuated over extended periods of time, that are difficult to root out, and whose unstable nature gives birth to ever-changing needs (ICRC, 2016, p. 9). Protracted crises are those in which "a significant proportion of the population is acutely vulnerable to death, disease, and disruption of their livelihoods" and are further frustrated by governments' inability or, more tragically, disinterest in responding to them (Macrae and Harmer, 2004, p. 1). The most important aspect distinguishing protracted crises from natural disasters and famine is that their "causes and effects [...] are often structural and long-lasting" (EU and UN FAO, 2008, p. 1). There are, however, no hard lines differentiating urgent and long-term needs from one another. For instance, resilience-building and the creation of sustainable sources of livelihood—two facets of development assistance—cause the provision of emergency aid to

DOI: 10.4324/9781003503187-5

morph into a much more complex and entangled endeavor. As such, there is significant overlap between development assistance initiatives and the activities run by aid organizations (Carbonnier, 2021).

The food insecurity crisis that plagued Africa during the second half of the twentieth century, when combined with subsequent failed policies and interventions, led to increased instances of internal violence. Though this constituted the predominant understanding of protracted crises for several decades, this perception has undergone a marked change in more recent years. The end of the Cold War triggered the reorganization of regional and global powers, which resulted in major power balance shifts. Developments occurring in different continents—such as the breakup of Yugoslavia; the invasions of Afghanistan and Iraq; armed conflict in Yemen, Myanmar, Syria, Venezuela, and Haiti; natural disasters; and political instability—not only were instrumental in remolding how protracted crises were perceived but also brought previously obscure dimensions of theirs to the public eye. Advances in transportation and communications technologies allowed the public to be more informed of the humanitarian emergencies afflicting crisis zones than ever before. These technological advances have similarly made it easier for people to escape crisis zones, creating a situation where the number of displaced persons has reached record proportions never before seen in human history. Waves of irregular migration made up of individuals fleeing crisis zones have, in turn, precipitated separate regional and global crises involving asylum seekers and refugee populations.

One of the main objectives of humanitarian diplomacy is to engage in efforts working to resolve lurking problems that, if left to fester, have the potential to lead to armed conflict or a humanitarian crisis and, by extension, to support individuals affected caught in the wake of such inauspicious events.

Humanitarian diplomacy seeks, on the one hand, to solve problems that, when left unaddressed, have the potential to lead to armed conflict and humanitarian crises and, on the other, to help affected individuals cope with these problems (UN OCHA, 2017, p. 5). The resolution of problems caused by protracted crises requires the confluence of several complementary factors, such as economic power, diplomatic vigor, the ability to identify problems and their solutions, various forms of expertise, and security while conducting fieldwork. This, in turn, requires relief organizations and individual nations to cooperate with one another (Régnier, 2011, p. 1212). Actors involved in humanitarian diplomacy include international organizations, the most important of which being UN organizations, nation-states, non-governmental organizations (NGOs), hybrid organizations operating on the international level, such as Red Cross and Red Crescent Societies,[1] and myriad independent entities. Commercial enterprises, foundations, and individuals contribute to humanitarian diplomacy through various means, the most significant of which being monetary donations (UN CERF, n.d.). United around a shared vision and purpose, these actors strive to reduce affected individuals' risk of suffering loss or damage as a consequence of crises (UN OCHA, 2019, p. 10). In addition, the diversity of actors and of the objectives they seek to achieve is visible in the types of activities in which they engage (Lauri, 2018, pp. 3–4). When the entirety of humanitarian action is taken together as a whole, it is this diversity that differentiates humanitarian diplomacy from its classic, more nation-state heavy counterpart.

The high population density of armed conflict and crisis zones, coupled with the complex and protracted nature of crises, necessitates that a multitude of actors closely collaborate with one another while conducting humanitarian works. While UN and hybrid organizations play a leadership role in these situations, NGOs, nation-states, and other actors play a supporting role. Since the complex nature of humanitarian crises requires that a wide range of services be provided, of which include food aid, road construction, educational and health services, legal support, and access to clean water, the international community is keen to work hand in hand with various organizations that specialize in dealing with a specific task.

Although the ultimate aim of humanitarian diplomacy is to bring a definitive end to such crises, its ability to effectuate change is still somewhat limited. As such, it would be unreasonable to consider solutions to crises as disconnected from traditional diplomacy or political, social, and economic reconstruction efforts. With respect to protracted crises, humanitarian diplomacy seeks first and foremost to ensure that all necessary relief materials are provided to those in need of them and to eliminate or alleviate as much as possible the hardships faced by affected communities. Consequently, I shall prioritize my discussion to revolve around the specific characteristics of protracted crises that distinguish them from other types of crisis situations, focusing specifically on their conceptual and historical peculiarities. Thereafter, I intend to identify the steps necessary to assure the effective management of such crises while simultaneously drawing attention to certain model humanitarian diplomacy practices.

Complex and Protracted Crises

Similar to how humanitarian diplomacy has only recently entered into the vernacular of academia, literature on the definition of complex and protracted crises—most of which is based on the experiences of aid providers—is still in its nascent phases. As such, writers often differ in the metrics and definitions they use as well as the criteria they use to identify crisis zones. For instance, while the Food and Agriculture Organization of the United Nations (FAO) maintains that the majority of protracted crisis zones are found in assorted African countries, all of which are suffering from food crises (FAO and WFP, 2010, p. 53), other scholars include long-term political and military crises (Leader, 2001, p. 4), such as the Israeli–Palestinian conflict (Macrae and

Harmer, 2004, p. 1), the ongoing crises in Afghanistan and Ukraine, and the Syrian Civil War (ICRC, 2016, p. 4). Although the bulk of protracted crises do not materialize within the borders of a single country, addressing crises on the national level will allow us to devise analysis parameters more easily. Such crises are more common in fragile and failed states (Maxwell et al., 2012, p. 12321). In these countries, inadequate state institutions and power vacuums, combined with efforts by local powers to seize resources and/or territory, result in crisis situations (EU and UN FAO, 2008, p. 2).

Depending on the underlying causes and subsequent consequences of crises, diverse assessment criteria (e.g., famine, armed conflict, displacement, refugee emergencies) exist to identify countries suffering protracted crises. The UNICEF cites Afghanistan, Burkina Faso, Cameroon, the Central African Republic, Chad, the Democratic Republic of the Congo (DRC), Ethiopia, Iraq, Libya, Mali, Myanmar, Somalia, South Sudan, Sudan, Syria, and Yemen as countries dealing with protracted crises, which, although not exhaustive, is a comprehensive list of extant crisis centers (UNICEF, 2019). Several countries can be added to this list, including *(i)* Bangladesh because of the refugee crisis the country currently faces as a result of the massive influx of refugees from neighboring Myanmar, *(ii)* Syria's neighbors, who have had to deal with crisis-level conditions brought about by hosting displaced Syrian refugees for such extended periods of time, *(iii)* Colombia, who has had to deal with an upsurge of Venezuelan refugees in addition to the displacement of her own citizens, and *(iv)* Haiti. Though the majority of countries on this list are located in Africa, similar crises currently blight Asia, the Middle East, and Latin America.

The terms *complex* and *protracted* have their origins in a 1978 description of the Israeli–Palestinian conflict, referred to as a "complex and protracted social conflict" (Policinski and Kuzmanovic, 2019, p. 966; Azar et al., 1978). Since the initial expulsion of native Palestinians from their ancestral lands in 1948, for instance, the UN, international aid organizations, and various other entities have led diverse humanitarian diplomacy activities to ameliorate the consequences of the ongoing policy of eviction and apartheid against the Palestinian people. These activities include advocacy, the encouragement of peace talks, and the distribution of relief materials to refugees and displaced persons (Minear and Smith, 2007, p. 25; ICRC, 2016, pp. 4–9). Although protracted crises are characterized by their enduring nature, the detrimental effects they have on affected populations, and their propensity to morph into armed conflicts, it is impossible to cite a single reason or cause for their emergence (Maxwell et al., 2012, p. 12321). We do, however, encounter the notion of *complex emergencies* in the literature—a term originally used to describe a number of humanitarian crises that emerged in Africa in the 1980s, each of which for different reasons (Duffield, 1994, p. 44). Thereafter, the terms *chronic conflict* and *political instability* began to be used to characterize the enduring nature of such crises (Schafer, 2002, p. 2; Harvey, 1997, p. 14). Humanitarian aid is tailored to respond to three distinct crisis categories: *(i)* emergencies, *(ii)* recurrent crises, and *(iii)* protracted crises. The term *complex and protracted* has thus evolved into an umbrella term describing crises that, despite having different underlying causes, persist over extended periods of time and whose negative impact on affected populations extends over generations.

Protracted crises can refer to long-term conflicts, chronic economic problems, political and social unrest, famine and food deficiencies, and similar humanitarian crises. Given this, conflicts that fall into this definition should not be regarded as occurring during a specific period of time but as a *conflict process* (Azar et al., 1978, p. 50). While protracted crises differ in terms of their underlying causes, they resemble each other in that they involve armed conflict that engulfs a specific area—be it an entire country, region, or specific area within a single country—disruptions in administration and the provision of public services, the depreciation of living standards, an inability to safeguard food security, an increase in violence, and the collapse of legal or traditional protection mechanisms (FAO and WFP, 2010, p. 12; UN OCHA, 2018, p. 25). These factors exacerbate the already arduous living conditions borne by affected populations during protracted crises. It is furthermore often the case that governments struggle to consolidate their authority during periods of armed conflict or natural disasters. While this may often lead to long-term crisis periods requiring emergency relief, such as during the 2010 Haiti Earthquake, protracted crises can beget their own case-specific quagmires. One example would be how certain parts of Syria have faced the risk of severe famine following the onset of the 2011 civil war.

While protracted crises differ in terms of their underlying causes, they resemble each other in that they involve armed conflict that engulfs a specific area—be it an entire country, region, or specific area within a single country—disruptions in administration and the provision of public services, the depreciation of living standards, an inability to safeguard food security, an increase in violence, and the collapse of legal or traditional protection mechanisms.

The international community began discussing, on both the theoretical and practical levels, how to best deal with protracted crises in the 1990s after having witnessed major crises that struck serious blows to several African countries in the 1980s (Duffield, 1994, p. 44) and an explosion of internal conflicts and small-scale skirmishes as the Cold War slowly came to an end (Jones, 2004, pp. 14–15). Since crises were most frequently encountered in fragile and failed states, initiatives addressing famine and malnutrition were prioritized. Over time, however, projects addressing political and security problems either triggered or further inflamed by crises gained importance (Maxwell et al., 2012, p. 12324). Whereas initially, the majority of protracted crises involved African nations, other countries such as Syria and Afghanistan found themselves dealing with long-term crises as years passed. The difference, however, is that while conflicts were the result of food insecurity in Africa, they caused it in later contexts.

Crises in today's world are characterized by "a systemic collapse in the [crisis] area" that encompasses healthcare, education, infrastructure, and food supply chains as opposed to short-term disruptions to the normal flow of life or temporary hiccups in the provision of public services (Maurer, 2014). Nations suffering from protracted crises are the recipients of the lion's share of humanitarian aid (EU and UN FAO, 2008, p. 1). Beyond the fact that they endure significantly longer, modern humanitarian crises differ from those of the past in that urban populations are more severely affected than people living in rural areas (ICRC, 2016, p. 5), are not always the consequence of direct conflict between nations, and are followed by an international audience as communications technologies advance. People living in war-torn cities find themselves deprived of basic public services and facing looming death at every turn. Should, on the other hand, they elect to relocate to safer lands, they often find themselves forced to leave all their memories and possessions behind for years on end without any guarantee that they will even be able to return home. As an added complexity, children born and raised in crisis zones are often completely unaware of what life is like outside of such environments (Policinski and Kuzmanovic, 2019, p. 966). In any case, to recap, protracted crises frequently involve *(i)* the weakening or complete collapse of the social institutions and networks that provide security and ensure the continuance of daily life activities, *(ii)* the inability or lack of adequate resources on the part of the government to exert its authority in such an environment, *(iii)* the decline of perceived governmental legitimacy by third parties, *(iv)* the growth of an off-the-record economy, *(v)* the exposure or immediate danger of being exposed to violence, poverty, famine, malnourishment, the deprivation of basic rights, the discontinuance public services, and the inability to earn a living among at least certain segments of the society (Schafer, 2002).

Protracted crises necessitate the coordination and simultaneous execution of humanitarian aid distribution, development assistance, and peacebuilding/ peacekeeping efforts.

Protracted crises necessitate the coordination and simultaneous execution of humanitarian aid distribution, development assistance, and peacebuilding/ peacekeeping efforts. This has required changes to be made to traditional humanitarian relief initiatives (Policinski and Kuzmanovic, 2019, p. 968). There is a growing consensus that humanitarian aid and development assistance should be applied in a coordinated manner, which has, for certain political reasons, caused peacebuilding/peacekeeping missions to be relegated to a position of secondary importance. In short, development assistance and humanitarian aid programs need to be executed together and in concert with local actors in order to achieve *sustainable humanitarian impact* (Carbonnier, 2021). Accordingly, the humanitarian diplomacy practices discussed in this chapter, among these being food or education support, will be examined under the presumption that they constitute integral steps needed to be taken to resolve crises and not as simple footnotes. These steps include *(i)* long-term planning, *(ii)* development assistance, *(iii)* interinstitutional collaboration, *(iv)* partnerships with local actors, and *(v)* the delivery of aid materials to people in real need of them. Since, however, humanitarian needs often go hand in hand with one another in the field, these steps need not be executed in sequential order.

Humanitarian Diplomacy and Problem Resolution

Long-term Planning

As the problems that, when left unaddressed, are known to lead to protracted crises become more deeply entrenched and complicated, thereby inhibiting people from going about their daily routines, the environment becomes a breeding ground for new short- and/or long-term crises. This, in turn, renders immediate and short-term aid inadequate (UN OCHA, 2019, p. 80). It was not until protracted crises finally became a field of study that discussions on how to plan for the long-term provision of aid began to even be had. After such deliberations, it was concluded that immediate/short-term initiatives needed to be conducted in conjunction with sustainable long-term development strategies that involved local actors in order to be effective (Russo et al., 2008, pp. 3–4). Short-term plans for the delivery of aid materials were found to overlook the underlying causes of problems and could, in the long term, lead to material deficiencies and other negative repercussions.

Protracted crises, by their very nature, require long-term humanitarian aid. The number, severity, and magnitude of such crises have increased, which has led to larger numbers of affected individuals. Consequently, the global budget allocated to humanitarian aid has grown to unprecedented proportions. The amount of total humanitarian aid available, however, falls short of the demand for it, and this gap continues to expand overtime.

When traditional diplomacy fails to reduce the severity of a specific crisis or to solve the problems that result from it, humanitarian diplomacy likewise loses much of its own potency. The resulting situation forces aid organizations to try to manage a seemingly irresolvable crisis that nonetheless requires continued assistance. The inability of traditional diplomacy to settle refugees into a third country, for instance, requires aid organizations to deal with a situation of permanent displacement (Minear and Smith, 2007, p. 25). The prolonged length and underlying complications of such crises can cause actors who are otherwise able to provide assistance to hesitate to do so, thus rendering it even more difficult to resolve an ongoing crisis (Maxwell et al., 2012, p. 12321). A further compounding factor is that protracted crises necessitate long-term humanitarian relief and, despite the largest budget available to humanitarian aid in human history, the number of people affected by increasingly more severe humanitarian crises continues to multiply at an ever-accelerating pace. In short, statistics for humanitarian crises reveal that the gap between the amount of humanitarian aid available and those in need of this aid has only grown bigger over time and is, given current predictors, anticipated to worsen in the foreseeable future (HPG, 2016, p. 59).

The famine and malnutrition that accompany protracted crises further exacerbate an already dire situation, rendering their swift resolution ever more unlikely. Famine and malnutrition in war and conflict zones frequently mushroom into structural problems, especially in the case of protracted crises. Beyond this, other issues such as social inequality, poor economic administration, and natural disasters (e.g., drought, earthquakes, and floods) can further aggravate instances of famine and malnutrition:

> *The United Nations Food and Agriculture Organization used three criteria to identify countries in complex and protracted crisis: first, the number of years in crisis, i.e., countries reporting a crisis requiring external assistance in at least 8 of the past 10 years; second, composition of external assistance, i.e., countries receiving 10% or more of official development assistance as humanitarian aid since 2000; and third, basic economic and food security information, i.e., only low-income, food deficit countries were included.*
>
> (Maxwell et al., 2012, p. 12321)

The adverse effects that harsh living conditions, acute weather events, and the COVID-19 pandemic have on the economy further compound food security problems, thus worsening the situation in which people living in crisis zones find themselves. The lack of access to safe, nutritious, and adequate food is unfortunately expected to intensify. Projections for 2021, for instance, aroused the fear that food insecurity in Syria, South Sudan, and the Central African Republic may deteriorate into famine (UNHCR, 2021, p. 9; Carbonnier, 2021).

Solutions to famine and food insecurity differ depending on whether they pertain to emergency situations or protracted crises. We even observe certain cases where humanitarian relief aimed at short-term recovery exerts undue pressure on natural resources or causes financial resources to be spent on non-essential areas, thereby triggering new food security issues. For instance, aid organizations operating in Somalia distributed free seeds to the local population despite their being no difficulty finding affordable alternatives. A similar mishap occurred in the DRC when the fishing equipment distributed to the local population was used in excess, eventually causing shortages in Lake Edward's fish population and paving the way for larger problems in the long term (EU and UN FAO, 2008, p. 3).

While ensuring continued agricultural production is indeed an important component to alleviating famine and malnutrition, its primary goal should be to uproot poverty and its underlying causes. Accordingly, it is of vital importance that needs be accurately identified, that education on how to use the right farming technology for the right job be provided, that the planting of alternative products offering advantages to local farmers be encouraged, and that support impoverished producers (Longley, 2001, pp. 6–8). The goal here is to ensure that both emergency and long-term food security assistance are provided simultaneously. (EU and UN FAO, 2008, p. 5). It should be remembered, nonetheless, that protracted crises eventually produce their own systems of order and economies. For instance, material aid can fall into the hands of certain power centers, black marketeers, and looters who either make use of these items themselves or sell them to a third party. In other words, certain individuals seek to use the crisis and resulting environment for their own personal advantage, especially in areas suffering from ongoing food insecurity (Bubna, 2010, p. 8).

The Syrian Civil War has given birth to the most severe humanitarian crisis of our era and is unfortunately plagued by numerous problems, including widespread famine and malnutrition (UN OCHA, 2018, p. 5). Multiple actors are actively working both independently and in collaboration with others to put an end or at least to alleviate these problems as much as humanly possible. However, after an excess of ten years, families who elected to remain in Syria have exhausted their savings and face dire economic conditions in the forthcoming years (UN News, 2021). As seen in the case of Syria, prolonged food security crises eventually morph into ever-growing, seemingly endless problems. When, despite the concerted efforts by myriad humanitarian diplomacy practitioners, viable political solutions cannot be found to crises, an air of uncertainty reigns dominant. Since this causes the food crisis to be viewed through the lens of perpetual urgency, proposed solutions prioritize the immediate provision of edible goods instead of building sustainable food security.

Development Assistance

As crises linger on, humanitarian aid can metamorphose into long-term assistance. Since this can lead not only to difficulties in finding sources to finance continued aid but also to dependency and agricultural decline, instituting programs that support development is important because they prevent such problems from arising in the first place and ensure that sustainable economic systems can thrive.

As humanitarian relief works have become increasingly institutionalized during the twenty-first century, it has become increasingly more apparent that they do not exhibit the same effectiveness over the long term as they do over the short. As crises linger on, humanitarian aid can metamorphose into long-term assistance. This can lead to difficulties in finding sources to finance continued aid, dependency, agricultural decline, and even the pillaging of aid materials, which, in turn, breed new problems altogether, such as famine, disruptions in the delivery of public services, and poverty (Grunewald, 2001, p. 3). Consequently, instituting programs that support development is important because they prevent such problems from arising in the first place and ensure that sustainable economic systems can thrive. As articulated above, the enmeshment of urgent and long-term development needs—as well as the problems that trigger these needs—is what distinguishes protracted crises from other emergencies. Nevertheless, development assistance requires long-term, comprehensive programs and generous funding, the likes of which generally exceed the objectives, scope, and budgets of both hybrid and other humanitarian relief organizations. In short, actors need to be intimately involved in the *mobilization, coordination*, and *distribution of resources* so that these crises may be alleviated (Macrae and Harmer, 2004, p. 1). As such, protracted crises plaguing today's world necessitate more permanent, long-term solutions. Aid organizations alone cannot handle all of the logistics required to identify needs, deliver relief items, conduct negotiations with diverse actors, and plan long-term development assistance programs; this requires the collaboration of diverse stakeholders and important obligations fall onto the shoulders of intergovernmental organizations and nations.

Until very recently, the dominant trend was for humanitarian aid to be delivered at the onset of a crisis and then, once it became apparent that the crisis would persist over an extended period of time, to development assistance. However, experience has shown that humanitarian and development assistance should not be provided independent of one another during crisis situations and that qualified organizations of both fields should, despite the differences in their objectives and means of achieving these objectives, work together if there is to be any hope to putting an end to such crises (World Bank, 2017, p. 2).

Development assistance programs prioritize efforts to revive the job market and facilitate the delivery of social support services. These seek to increase job opportunities and increase employment qualifications among vulnerable populations living under crisis conditions and, in the shorter term, to ensure that their day-to-day needs are adequately met (World Bank, 2017, p. 74). Since damaged infrastructure hinders, among other things, access to clean water and food security, efforts to rebuild damaged infrastructure are of vital importance. As has been the case throughout history, restricting access to water sources is used in war to weaken the resolve of one's enemy. In addition to this, urban warfare and the shelling of residential areas have more detrimental effects on civilian populations, cause greater damage to infrastructure, and limit access to clean water for drinking and sanitation needs (UNICEF, 2021). Protracted crises have pernicious consequences for public healthcare institutions, reducing the total number of healthcare workers and thus curtailing their capacity to operate effectively and provide needed services. For example, the ongoing civil war in Syria has had the effect of diminishing the number of healthcare institutions working at full capacity to half of what it had been prior to the war, effectively paralyzing the country's healthcare system. This has led to a visible increase in the number of polio cases in children that, had healthcare services functioning at normal capacity, would have been prevented by routine vaccination (UN OCHA, 2018, p. 5). Generally speaking, modern crises are increasingly marked by urban warfare, natural disasters, and terrorist attacks. Communication, transportation, energy infrastructure, water distribution networks, hospitals, schools, and various other public services all suffer damage during crises as a result. Repairing damaged infrastructure and superstructure will help reduce interruptions to education, bolster available healthcare services, prevent the spread of infectious diseases, and safeguard food security. That said, however, the repair or complete reconstruction of damaged buildings and systems invariably requires third-party assistance (ALNAP, 2018). The need for such support is not limited to the countries suffering the brunt of crises; the countries in which displaced persons are resettled also need material assistance, as the influx of refugees places increased strain on educational and healthcare services, energy and water distribution networks, sewage systems, and other public services. With this in mind, host countries whose own financial situations are shaky or who realize that refugees will not return to their country of origin after having settled into their new homes may drag their feet in this regard (World Bank, 2017, p. 7).

A central goal of development support is to increase *resilience* among populations living in crisis zones. A core component of crisis resolution, resilience building prioritizes the development of long-term, sustainable solutions. Actions taken to protect sources of livelihood are of vital importance, as this allows people "not just to survive crises, but also to protect themselves in advance and to recover afterwards" (HPG, 2016, pp. 28–46). By their very nature, however, resilience-building efforts do little, if anything, to ameliorate the conditions produced by armed conflict and rampant human rights violations. They are, however, significantly more effective in reducing the damage wrought on communities by natural disasters, both in the short and long run, as they constitute preventative measures counter the immediate destructive effects of natural phenomena and bolster the long-term sustainability of livelihood sources.

Building resilience is prioritized because of its emphasis on sustainability. With regard to Yemen, described in the literature as "the world's worst humanitarian crisis" (IDMC and NRC, 2021, p. 35), the severe dangers posed to aid workers prompted many organizations to cease operations in the country. One such example is that the facilities established to deal with a cholera epidemic that had engulfed the country stopped receiving funding from the countries that had financed them once the epidemic was brought under control. New funding will consequently be needed to reopen these facilities in the likely event that new epidemics emerge. Reopening closed facilities not only requires the transfer of larger amounts of funds but results in the loss of precious time that could have been avoided had they remained in continuous operation (ALNAP, 2018).

Natural disasters can lead to conditions similar to those of protracted crises. Although they may at first be perceived as simple short-term crises that can be resolved by emergency aid, the resulting destruction of homes and sources of livelihood can lead to long-term economic crises in disaster zones or cause inhabitants to relocate to other areas, essentially becoming displaced persons. The climatic conditions of certain regions in the Americas, East Asia, and South Asia, and especially of those countries along the Pacific coast, leave many people exposed to severe hurricanes and flooding. Fueled by climate change, extreme weather events are expected to trigger, among other complications, even more intense conflicts and waves of migration in the future. Natural disasters aggravate the already-difficult conditions faced by refugees and IDPs. The floods, fires, and drought that wrought Bangladesh, Yemen, Syria, and Somalia, for instance, had detrimental effects on many of the refugees and internally displaced persons (IDPs) living in these countries, causing new crises altogether to materialize (UNHCR, 2021, p. 26; IDMC and NRC, 2021, pp. 10, 35–37, 78). This cycle reveals the importance of including neighboring countries and regions into development assistance planning, as they also find themselves forced to bear the effects of crises spilling over national and internal borders with the influx of refugees and IDPs.

Interinstitutional Collaboration

Ongoing disputes between belligerent parties are not the sole cause for the wars and internal conflicts that breed long-term humanitarian crises to continue without resolution. Groups may attempt to take advantage of power vacuums to gain control over raw materials and natural resources (Grunewald, 2001, p. 2) while prolonged conflict keeps the market for arms and ammunition sales open. Likewise, third-party nations, individuals, and commercial enterprises are often obstacles to a peaceful resolution of conflicts. Another important factor hindering aid from being delivered to conflict zones in a timely manner is the concern among governmental authorities that aid materials may be used to strengthen certain groups politically. In addition to preventing certain groups from receiving the aid they need (DARA, 2011, p. 32), this can inflame tensions between conflicting parties, thus causing conflicts to continue and even intensify.

Turning our attention to the South Asian country of Myanmar, numerous humanitarian diplomacy actors have come together to attempt ameliorate the conditions of crisis zones within the country, and the success of these efforts demonstrates the importance of interinstitutional collaboration. Official statements by the government reveal that Myanmar is composed of 135 different ethnic groups speaking an excess of one hundred languages and dialects. Unfortunately, however, these groups do not live in perfect harmony with one another, as the country is plagued by internal violence and suffers from frequent natural disasters as a result of its climatic conditions (IFRC, n.d., pp. 5–6). Whereas the majority of Myanmar's population is Buddhist, more than one million Muslims, known as the Rohingya people, reside in Rakhine State. The Rohingya have for decades been subjected to persecution both by the national government and the country's Buddhist population (Council on Foreign Relations, 2024). While there are Muslims communities of other ethnicities living in Myanmar, the Rohingya have been regarded as a separatist group by the country's administration since the 1950s. When military rule was established following the Burmese coup d'état in 1962, the Rohingya were slowly deprived of their civil and social rights (Swazo, 2021, p. 14). The exclusionary policies of the 1960s resulted in many ethnic and religious groups to suffer undue persecution or, in the case of the Chinese and Indians, to be expatriated from the country altogether. The constitution of 1982 granted citizenship based on ethnic origin, leaving the Rohingya deprived of citizenship (Haque, 2021, p. 57). Tensions rose until 2012, when the Rohingya began to be subjected to systematic violence and forced expulsion, resulting in the deaths of thousands of individuals, the destruction of countless homes and workplaces, and the displacement of hundreds of thousands of individuals. As a result of the influx of more than one million Rohingya refugees from Myanmar, the situation in neighboring Bangladesh has likewise devolved into a protracted crisis of its own (Council on Foreign Relations, 2024). As a result, the Bengali government is actively seeking ways to repatriate the Rohingya refugees in her country (Kurlantzick, 2019). As these problems in Myanmar remained unresolved, the situation was further exacerbated with the 2021 military coup d'état. Some of the other countries in the region hosting refugees from Myanmar, such as Bangladesh and Malaysia, had either descended into or found themselves on the precipice of a truly cataclysmic crisis. Since many, if not all of these nations are not signatories to international agreements on the protection of refugees, whose asylum policies do not recognize refugees' rights and instead prioritize repatriation, an air of crisis increasingly eclipsed the region (Khairi et al., 2018, p. 194). Finding their situation utterly unbearable in both Bangladesh and Myanmar, hundreds of Rohingya boarded rudimentary boats and embarked for Indonesia, Malaysia, and Thailand. Unfortunately, however, a significant portion of these migrants perished before reaching their intended destination. That said, however, the aforementioned South Asian countries were not overly enthusiastic to host these refugees in the first place (Aljazeera, 2021). In such an atmosphere, it is of vital importance that humanitarian aid be delivered to those groups most in need, and this is only possible through collaboration between multiple institutions. While the 2021 military putsch and its aftermath made it more difficult for humanitarian diplomacy to be put into practice effectively in Myanmar, progress was made in this regard in Bangladesh, leading to greatly improved conditions for refugees in the country. The IFRC, various individual National Red Cross and Red Crescent Societies, and the Bangladesh Red Crescent have led numerous initiatives to improve the situation of the Rohingya living in Bangladesh, to ensure that their rights are protected, and to ease the lives of both refugees and the native populations of the areas in which they have been resettled. These works receive support from UN organizations and local NGOs (Atallah, 2019).

Indonesia has followed a different course of action with regard to the Rohingya, opting to move forward following an approach that synthesizes classic and humanitarian diplomacy. Through collaboration with the

Association of Southeast Asian Nations (ASEAN), Indonesia has received permission from the Myanmar government to deliver humanitarian aid to the Rohingya living within Myanmar's borders and cooperates with the governments of other nations and the ICRC to ensure that aid materials are delivered to their intended destinations and may be accessed by those who are in need of them. The Indonesian civilian population has likewise established eleven humanitarian relief organizations to support the Rohingya people and formed the Indonesia Humanitarian Alliance for Myanmar (IHA/AKIM) to provide educational, health, emergency aid, and economic support. The Indonesian government maintains works hand in hand with these NGOs, forwarding the Myanmar government plans for the projects these NGOs wish to conduct in the country. Several governmental ministries and civil institutions support Indonesia's humanitarian diplomacy efforts in Myanmar (Setiawan and Hamka, 2019, pp. 10–11). In contrast to other countries, Indonesia opts to engage in what is called *quiet diplomacy* instead of imposing sanctions against or suspending diplomatic relations with Myanmar in response to instances of human rights violations. This allows Indonesia to focus on delivering aid to the Rohingya without embroiling itself in Myanmar's internal affairs. In addition to allowing Rohingya refugees fleeing oppression to enter the country and helping these refugees settle into their new conditions, Indonesia has obtained permission from the Myanmar government authorizing Indonesian organizations to run relief programs for the Rohingya still living in Myanmar (Smith and Williams, 2021, p. 182). Similarly, the Myanmar Red Cross, in line with its goal to deliver relief materials to more destitute and remote parts of the country, collaborates with the IFRC, the Chinese Red Cross, the Myanmar government, and various volunteers to distribute assistance to communities negatively affected by armed conflict and natural disasters (IFRC, n.d.).

Partnerships with Local Actors

Although collaboration with local actors was often neglected in the past, building partnerships with native organizations has gained greater importance in recent years. Nevertheless, while the importance of cooperating with local organizations when national institutions are no longer able to ensure public safety and the continuance of public services is heavily emphasized, international actors are often criticized for not displaying the necessary diligence required to effectuate such partnerships (FAO and WFP, 2010, p. 24). It must be remembered, however, that working with local actors is, more often than not, rarely a choice that one can simply discount without deep consideration. Quite the contrary, the circumstances on the ground often require such collaboration. Humanitarian aid arrives at port cities and large population centers during protracted crises perpetuated by ongoing armed conflict. Aid workers then work diligently to transport aid materials from these collection centers to affected populations most in need of them, often putting their own lives on the line attempting to deliver them further inland (Lauri, 2018, p. 2). Yet, while securing the cooperation of local groups is imperative to ensure that aid materials arrive at their intended destinations, this can lead to undesired consequences, especially when conflict constantly looms overhead and corruption is rife. As such, working in concert with local actors, despite being necessary, requires extreme caution. Accordingly, humanitarian diplomacy actors are apt to conduct their own intricate analyses of local groups with whom they may potentially work. These analyses look into the backgrounds, priorities, desire to find a viable solution, and several other factors of potential partners. In Somalia, for instance, several organizations involved in humanitarian aid and development rushed to build partnerships with a number of local actors. Unbeknownst to them, however, was that these groups did not represent individuals who were in need of assistance. These organizations naively found themselves working with armed factions. Indeed, it becomes increasingly difficult to find trustworthy local partners when institutional mechanisms within the country have collapsed under the weight of the ongoing crisis and is only further exacerbated during civil wars, when local organizations and governments openly take part in the conflict (EU and UN FAO, 2008, pp. 3–5). Despite all the potential risks involved, however, forging partnerships and collaborating with local actors are of vital importance, especially when such crises occur in failed states.

Populations inhabiting the inner parts of a country are often the hardest hit and most deprived groups during protracted crises. As such, collaboration with local groups while delivering aid materials is vital not only to overcome these hardships but also to protect the lives of aid workers themselves. Before establishing any such partnerships, however, humanitarian diplomacy actors must do their due diligence and scrutinize the backgrounds of potential local partners as well as their priorities and desire to find a viable solution to the conflict.

To continue with the example of Somalia, the long-term humanitarian crisis plaguing the nation—one greatly aggravated by Somalia's status as a failed state—initially drew aid organizations from around the globe to assist affected populations. The lack of security and generally unsafe conditions, however, forced many of these actors to halt operations and leave the country altogether. One of the larger organizations that continued to operate in Somalia despite these risks was the UN World Food Programme (WFP). Established to maintain global food security and known for its effective work in humanitarian diplomacy, the WFP was at times forced to compromise on its founding principles and collaborate with local powers, knowing full well that they engaged in violent acts, to identify what food products were needed in each respective crisis zone and to organize the delivery, distribution, and continued security of relief materials. WFP workers were the target of sometimes fatal violent attacks and kidnappings; ships carrying food relief were attacked by pirates; several food distribution centers were pillaged; and the organization was sometimes forced to pay bribes in order to ensure that relief items reached the more inner parts of the country. The situation was so dire, in fact, that the US Navy was sometimes enlisted to protect WFP ships carrying food consignments into the country. While many of the WFP's efforts were successful, such as in working with military actors to ensure that humanitarian aid reached its intended destination, Somalia showcases, despite all efforts, humanitarian diplomacy's limitations in dealing with crises in failed states (Bubna, 2010, pp. 1–7).

Reaching People in Real Need

Since development assistance requires long-term, high-cost financing, it is essential that those in real need be correctly identified. Here, humanitarian diplomacy can help determine truly disenfranchised individuals and the specific type of assistance they need during protracted crises.

Since development assistance requires long-term, high-cost financing, it is essential that those in real need be correctly identified. Here, humanitarian diplomacy can help determine truly disenfranchised individuals and the specific type of assistance they need during protracted crises (World Bank, 2017, p. 7). However, as it is impossible to know which emergencies will morph into long-term crises, the identification of people in need occurs as the situation continues to develop. Moreover, conflicting interests among humanitarian diplomacy actors can, at times, frustrate the delivery of aid items to people in need and delay the crisis from being resolved. For instance, nations may harbor ulterior motives for engaging in humanitarian diplomacy beyond simply contributing to lasting global and region peace and security. Nations may simply want to bring an end to crises without having to become involved militarily (Setiawan and Hamka, 2019, p. 3), to prevent a localized conflict from spreading into neighboring countries, or to avert potential waves of migration.

Every individual affected by a crisis is, for all intents and purposes, a person in need. However, the consequences of crises—poverty, inadequate health services, the destruction of infrastructure, and the collapse of the job market—affect certain vulnerable populations more severely than others. With respect to protracted crises, vulnerable groups include women, children, disabled people, older adults, displaced individuals, and refugees. Under such onerous conditions, moreover, critically wounded and sick individuals may be categorized as vulnerable groups. Of these groups, however, disabled people face greater hardships in seeing to their daily needs, accessing basic public services, and fleeing conflict zones. Similarly, the difficulties faced by women, children, and older adults are, given that they are more likely to be the target of discrimination or violence, greatly exacerbated while living in and attempting to escape crisis zones (Policinski and Kuzmanovic, 2019, p. 972). Since such individuals generally lack the means to request assistance or to vacate crisis zones—two things made even more difficult when both formal and informal mechanisms of support have collapsed—the delivery of aid materials requires a concerted and deliberate effort on the part of those involved.

Since members of vulnerable groups face different problems and have different needs than other individuals, humanitarian diplomacy has developed a wide variety of practices tailored to each vulnerable group. It is of particular note that efforts geared specifically toward children, women, displaced individuals, and refugees—those groups hardest hit by protracted crises—have witnessed such a manifest increase. Not only do women and children form the two most vulnerable populations in crisis situations, they suffer unique, often significantly more destructive and severe effects, stress, and anxiety than other populations (UN OCHA, 2017, p. 6).

UNICEF data reveals that children caught in conflict zones are three times more likely to die from diseases linked to limited access to clean drinking water and sanitation than to violent acts committed during the conflict (UNICEF, 2019). Gender-based violence is one of the greatest threats to women and female children in the actual conflict zone, while attempting to flee to safer areas, and after having arrived in a new, unfamiliar location. Rape and sexual abuse are two of the primary reasons that drive women to flee their homes not only in Syria and Afghanistan, but also in all crisis zones throughout the world, including Nepal, Somalia, the DRC, and the Central African Republic. Conflict exposes women and girls to violence committed by militants, soldiers, human traffickers, and camp workers. The psychological stress of armed conflict and flight can also trigger an upsurge in domestic violence to degrees much higher than during normal, more peaceful times (World Bank, 2017, p. 84). Emergency situations and protracted crises greatly hinder the education of children and young people, often forcing students either to receive a subpar education or to drop out of school entirely. Women and girls suffer significantly more detrimental effects to their education than their male counterparts during protracted crises (Council of the European Union, 2018, pp. 2–4). Still, however, the longevity of crises forces aid and assistance targeting vulnerable and marginal groups to be used to respond to more pressing, daily needs. Similarly, since groups made up of IDPs and/or refugees frequently include individuals from other vulnerable and marginal segments of society, displacement and refugee crises have themselves turned into an area of activity for humanitarian diplomacy in their own right.

One of the longest-lasting humanitarian crises facing the modern world is the expulsion of the Palestinian people from their native lands, leading to both their internal displacement and refugee status in many countries. Wrought by armed conflict, the construction of Jewish settlements, and continued displacement, the conditions in which Palestinians live both in Gaza and the West Bank continue to deteriorate by the day (UN OCHA, 2017, p. 6). Europe similarly witnessed her refugee crisis in recent history when, during the breakup of Yugoslavia, thousands of people were displaced or turned into refugees as a result of successive armed conflicts, provoking a prolonged refugee crisis the likes of which had not been seen in Europe since World War II (Robinson, 2011). Brought on increasingly by internal conflict and/or political failure following the end of the Cold War, refugee crises remain in today's global headlines as a result of the waves of migrants originating from Syria and Venezuela. The marked increase in asylum and migration cases around the world has forced the literature on international law to evolve accordingly, spurring the UN High Commissioner for Refugees (UNHCR) to coin the term *protracted refugee situation* in 2001 (Khairi et al., 2018, p. 194). As per the UNHCR:

> *Protracted refugee situations those in which at least 25,000 refugees from the same country have been living in exile for more than five consecutive years. Refugees in these situations often find themselves trapped in a state of limbo: while it is not safe for them to return home, they also have not been granted permanent residence to stay in another country either.*
>
> (UNHCR, 2020)

Globally speaking, displacement (encompassing both refugees and IDPs) is, after the expulsion of the Palestinian people from their native lands, the second largest form of human migration since World War II. The majority of such people are citizens of low- or middle-income-earning countries; 94% of whom reside outside of refugee camps, generally interspersed among the local population in urban areas (World Bank, 2017, pp. 3–15). Similarly, 86% of refugees relocated to developing countries and a total of 6.7 million currently reside in the most underdeveloped countries (UNHCR, 2021, p. 11). As of 2020, the ten countries with the highest number of IDPs are, in descending order, Colombia, Syria, the DRC, Yemen, Somalia, Afghanistan, Ethiopia, Nigeria, Sudan, and South Sudan. Whereas Colombia is home to 8.3 million IDPs, South Sudan hosts 1.6 million. As in the cases of Yemen and the DRC, IDPs seeking refuge in other parts of their country after having fled internal fighting may still be subject to various acts of violence by armed groups as conflict zones branch outward and into new residential areas. Accordingly, crisis zones can experience what is dubbed multiple relocation. The UNHCR collaborates with political and bureaucratic institutions in different countries to provide humanitarian and legal assistance to IDPs and, more specifically, to devise and execute durable solutions for ongoing crises. For instance, the UNHCR has developed legal regulations that, once fully implemented, will allow IDPs in Colombia, El Salvador, Honduras, Mali, Mexico, Mozambique, the Philippines, South Sudan, and Ukraine access to legal and technical assistance (UNHCR, 2021, pp. 24–25).

Among the reasons causing refugee situations to cascade into full-blown crises include the enduring nature of the conditions that drove refugees to seek asylum in another country, policies of the host country (e.g., not issuing work permits, failure to recognize refugee status), and prolonged periods of residence in refugee camps. According to the UNHCR, the short-term nature of planning and financing are among the causes driving an emergency situation to deteriorate into a protracted crisis (UNHCR, 2004, Art. 4). In such cases, asylum seekers face three possibilities: *(i)* repatriation, *(ii)* resettlement in a third country, or *(iii)* resettlement in the country they initially applied for asylum. Resettlement is realized when asylum seekers are granted legal resident status or citizenship. Beyond the economic burden they exert on the education, healthcare, infrastructural, and residential systems, as well as the job market, of the countries in which they are resettled, resettled refugees often find themselves in need of programs to help them adapt to their new society (UNHCR, 2021, p. 48).

The majority of asylum seekers who are not considered refugees in the legal sense are deprived of basic rights, freedoms, and access to public services (UNHCR, 2020). These include the Bhutanese living in refugee camps in Nepal since 1989, successive waves of Afghan asylum seekers living in various parts of the world, many Somali and Syrian asylum seekers primarily in African countries but also in Europe and the rest of the world (UNHCR, 2004, Art. 4), and Haitians scattered throughout North and South America. After forty years of invasion and internal conflict that began with the Soviet invasion of Afghanistan in 1979, for instance, the number of Afghans living in refugee camps in Iran and Pakistan currently exceeds 2.4 million. UNHCR data from 2018 lists, in descending order, the ten largest refugee groups as Afghans, Syrians, South Sudanese, Rohingya, Somalis, Sudanese, Congolese, Central Africans, Eritreans, and Burundians. The total number of worldwide refugees as a result of protracted crises surpassed sixteen million in 2019 and is antici- pated to increase with each consecutive year (UNHCR, 2020).

In addition to refugee situations, protracted crises can also result in internal displacement, which can be further divided into *short-term*, *prolonged*, and *multiple* internal displacement (UN OCHA, 2018, p. 37). While the primary causes for internal displacement include natural disasters, armed conflict, and eco- nomic hardships, individual cases of internal displacement generally occur because of a confluence of more than one factor (IDMC and NRC, 2021, p. 35). Currently, IDPs number well into the millions worldwide (UNHCR, 2021, p. 7).

Colombia constitutes a unique case in this regard, as the country has had to deal with her own IDPs following decades of terrorist attacks coupled with a more recent influx of Venezuelan refugees numbering into the millions since 2014. The Colombian government is collaborating with international organizations—particularly UN organizations—and relief organizations to ameliorate current conditions. Widespread terrorism in rural areas has forced a massive influx of individuals to abandon their homes and relocate into newly constructed urban ghettos. The UNHCR and NGOs are working hand in hand with Colombian state organizations to ensure that IDPs have access to public services and are able to their exercise their rights (UNHCR, 2021, p. 24).

Prolonged refugee situations breed conditions that make it difficult for indi- viduals to earn a living. IDPs often struggle to provide diplomas, hospital records, documents proving their identity, and other official documentation (UN OCHA, 2018, p. 9). As a result, children are frequently deprived of a formal education, compelled to drop out of school, forced to receive military training and participate in armed conflicts, required to work outside the home, and pressured into early marriage (World Bank, 2020, p. 134).

The UNHCR and UN Development Programme (UNDP) have developed a roadmap containing strategies seeking to protect and see to the diverse needs of refugees and IDPs, to redress problems faced by countries hosting refugees and asylum seekers, to bring an end to ongoing crises in source countries, and to facilitate IDPs' safe return to their countries of origins. These two organizations continue their work to develop durable solutions for the ongoing global refugee crisis, specifically for the millions of Syrians who have suffered forced displacement since 2015, and have begun collaborating with both Lebanon and Jordan to this end (World Bank 2017, p. 103).

IDPs and refugees suffer, in addition to other hardships and deprivations, varying degrees of stress, trauma, and psychological disorders (UN OCHA, 2018, p. 58). Although the World Bank has funded studies examining the psychological effects of living in crisis zones, such as in Azerbaijan and Syria, relevant support services remain severely limited. While psychological problems lead to significantly diminished personal well-being, which, in turn, can trigger various psychological disorders that affect family members and even future generations, psychological support services are seldom provided to individuals during protracted crises and, even when they are provided, are often inadequate. That said, however, the lack of treatment opportunities is closely associated with a reluctance to share their experiences with others (World Bank, 2017, p. 84).

Long-term refugee status has profound effects on how individuals regard their lives, future, and sources of livelihood. As their worldview is largely molded by the trauma they have experienced, such individuals often struggle to secure socially and economically viable living conditions. Since it takes a certain amount of time before the realities of displacement set in, IDPs often believe their situations to be temporary and that they will return to their homes after a short period of time. This naturally influences IDPs' financial and social decisions. For instance, studies conducted by the UNHCR have found that most Syrian families arriving in Türkiye over the course of the civil war were under the impression that the situation would return to normal and that they would be able to return after only a short period of time. As a result, many of these families did not deem it necessary for their children to learn Turkish or to attend Turkish schools. However, as the crisis situation failed to improve the realization that they would not be able to return to Syria began to set in. As a result, countless children were deprived not only of an education but also of the opportunity to integrate into Turkish society more quickly. People living in crisis zones in Colombia, Afghanistan, and Uganda or who find themselves forced to relocate to rural regions tend to gravitate toward farming and livestock herding, as doing so offers quick returns. On the other hand, they tend to eschew long-term investments, despite the prospect of greater and more secure returns, out of the fear that they will lose everything or be forced to relocate once again should the crisis further deteriorate (World Bank, 2017, pp. 83–90). As the above makes abundantly clear, it is only through the collaboration of numerous actors that humanitarian aid needs can be properly identified and psychological support, health, and development services provided to affected populations. Since, moreover, the hardships related to prolonged displacement affect multiple dimensions, IDPs need continued material and psychological support to help them understand what they have gone through and how to best move ahead with their lives.

Conclusion

A portion of the complex and protracted crises in which the international community has involved itself existed long before humanitarian diplomacy was coined as a term in the literature. Nevertheless, humanitarian diplomacy remains a rapidly developing field, both in theory and in practice, that differs from classic diplomacy by virtue of its actors, objectives, and practices—the latter of which include arbitration, the evacuation of injured persons from conflict zones, collaboration with local actors to ensure that aid materials are successfully distributed, and psychological support services. Humanitarian diplomacy practices are, collectively speaking, but one tool in the larger diplomatic toolbox, and are most effective when used in conjunction with classic diplomacy, humanitarian aid, development assistance, and military interventions. Consequently, certain principles guide executive actors as they engage in humanitarian diplomacy during protracted crises. It is therefore necessary for theoretical discussions to be based in practice (Lauri, 2018, p. 1) and for both scholars and practitioners to continue to develop new principles that respond to the changing needs of crises. Slowly unfolding since the 1970s, this transformation reflects a deeper change not only in the number of crises and their internal dynamics but also in the humanitarian diplomacy practices employed in the field. The dominant perception of protracted crises until the 1990s was that they involved failed states, international disputes, separatist movements, and internal ethno-sectarian conflicts. Whereas the UN declared only ten unresolved *complex emergency situations* in the 1960s, this figure reached fifty by 1993 (Harvey, 1997, p. 14). At the time, the UN predicted that these crises would, given their multiple causes and grave human repercussions, need to be addressed in a more systemic manner (Duffield, 1994, p. 44). Crisis resolution involves the simultaneous coordination of traditional diplomacy, humanitarian diplomacy, and humanitarian interventions. In this context, humanitarian diplomacy can be employed to prevent human rights violations and violence, to deliver aid materials to people in need, and to build a robust state apparatus able to endure over the long term.

It was believed, albeit somewhat naïvely, that crises could be eliminated through a combination of military and humanitarian interventions in the 1990s. This same level of optimism, however, is lacking in today's world, especially after having borne witness to the human atrocities that took place during and following the breakup of Yugoslavia and the ethno-sectarian violence that fraught both Rwanda and Somalia in Africa. This has likewise begotten a new era entirely—one in which political solutions that involve military interventions are regarded separately from humanitarian aid initiatives (Duffield, 1994, p. 47). The ascendency of humanitarian diplomacy is but one extension of this process. Likewise, both the internal dynamics of complex and protracted crises and how the international community—and, more specifically UN organizations—perceive crises have changed, which has, in turn, led to a diversification in humanitarian diplomacy practices. As such, the older approach that sought to address crises on the systemic level has given way to a newer approach that employs humanitarian diplomacy to alleviate humanitarian suffering arising from crisis situations. Aid organizations and institutions devoted to providing development assistance work in unison with the UN, individual nations, multinational enterprises, municipalities, international NGOs, and unofficial volunteer organizations to meet the diverse needs of people living in crisis conditions. This plurality of actors demonstrates the profound impact that specialized aid can have for people in crisis zones. In the meantime, efforts to come up with political solutions have been demoted to a position of secondary importance.

As has been clearly demonstrated, responding to protracted crises is a multifaceted and multistage endeavor. The delivery of humanitarian aid and those activities supporting the successful execution thereof are of vital importance to resolving or, at the very least, mitigating the detrimental effects of protracted crises and alleviating the human suffering surrounding them. Viable solutions can be proffered only after the necessary political will has been mustered and properly channeled into eliminating the underlying catalysts of crises and redressing the damage caused as a result (IRRC, 2019, p. 987). Accordingly, the primary objective of humanitarian diplomacy is not to solve the problems set into motion by crises but to address the ancillary problems accompanying them. As such, humanitarian diplomacy is, despite all the benefits that it affords, not the be-all and end-all when it comes to crisis resolution. Lasting, comprehensive solutions are only possible when political authorities and international organizations mobilize all the resources, including humanitarian diplomacy, available to them.

Note

1 Members of the Red Cross and Red Crescent Movement are dubbed hybrid organizations because they are neither governmental institutions nor wholly independent NGOs and play an auxiliary role in diplomacy (Berridge, 2015, p. 86).

References

Aljazeera. (2021). *2020 was 'deadliest' year ever for Rohingya sea journeys: UNHCR.* https://www.aljazeera.com/news/2021/8/20/rohingya-sea-journeys-un
ALNAP. (2018). *Yemen: Life-saving assistance and beyond, state of the humanitarian system.* https://sohs.alnap.org/blogs/yemen-life-saving-assistance-and-beyond
Atallah, Y. (2019). *How humanitarian diplomacy helps in complex emergencies?* Canadian Red Cross Blog. https://www.redcross.ca/blog/2019/2/how-humanitarian-diplomacy-helps-in-complex-emergencies

Azar, E., Jureidini, P. & McLaurin, R. (1978). Protracted social conflict: Theory and practice in the Middle East. *Journal of Palestine Studies, 8*(1), 41–60.

Berridge, G.R. (2015). *Diplomacy: Theory and practice* (5th ed.). Palgrave Macmillan.

Bubna, M. (2010). *Humanitarian diplomacy and failed states: Case study of the WFP operations in Somalia.* IDSA Issue Brief. https://www.files.ethz.ch/isn/137975/IB_WFPOperationsinSomalia_mayank.pdf

Carbonnier, G. (2021). *Humanitarian economics: ICRC Vice President on how it can better address protracted conflicts.* https://www.icrc.org/en/document/humanitarian-economics-icrc-vice-president-how-it-can-better-address-protracted-conflicts

Council of the European Union. (2018). *Education in emergencies and protracted crises-council conclusions.* https://data.consilium.europa.eu/doc/document/ST-14719-2018-INIT/en/pdf

Council on Foreign Relations. (2024). *Rohingya crisis in Myanmar.* https://www.cfr.org/global-conflict-tracker/conflict/rohingya-crisis-myanmar

DARA. (2011). *The humanitarian response index 2011: Addressing the gender challenge.* https://daraint.org/wp-content/uploads/2012/03/HRI_2011_Complete_Report.pdf

Duffield, M. (1994). Complex emergencies and the crisis of developmentalism. *IDS Bulletin, 25*(4) https://www.ids.ac.uk/download.php?file=files/dmfile/duffield254.pdf

European Union (EU) & Food and Agriculture Organization of the United Nations (UN FAO). (2008). *Food security in protracted crises: What can be done?* Food Security Information Action, Policy Brief. https://reliefweb.int/sites/reliefweb.int/files/resources/4CA8F144CBB5A0B24925762D001C696E-Full_Report.pdf

Food and Agriculture Organization of the United Nations (FAO) & World Food Programme (WFP). (2010). *The state of food insecurity in the world: Addressing food insecurity in protracted crises.* Roma: FAO http://www.fao.org/docrep/013/i1683e/i1683e.pdf

Grunewald, F. (2001). Responding to long-term crises. *Humanitarian Exchange*, no: 18, 2–3. https://odihpn.org/wp-content/uploads/2003/06/humanitarianexchange018.pdf

Haque, Md. M., (2021). The Rohingya Crisis and Geopolitics: A Public Policy Conundrum. In Swazo, N. K., Haque, Sk. T. M., Haque, Md. M. & Nower, T. (Eds.) *The Rohingya crisis: A moral, ethnographic, and policy assessment* (pp. 34–51). Routledge.

Harvey, P. (1997). *Rehabilitation in complex political emergencies: Is rebuilding civil society the answer?* IDS Working Paper 6. https://opendocs.ids.ac.uk/opendocs/handle/20.500.12413/3364

Humanitarian Policy Group (HPG). (2016). *Planning from the future: Is the humanitarian system fit for purpose?* Humanitarian Policy Group, King's College, London and Tufts University. https://fic.tufts.edu/wp-content/uploads/pff_report_uk.pdf

Internal Displacement Monitoring Center (IDMC) & Norwegian Refugee Council (NRC). (2021). *GRID 2021: Internal displacement in a changing climate.* https://www.internal-displacement.org/global-report/grid2021

International Review of the Red Cross (IRRC). (2019). Stretched: Protracted conflicts and the people living in the midst of it all. *Voices and Perspectives, International Review of the Red Cross, 101*(912). https://international-review.icrc.org/articles/stretched-protracted-conflicts-people-living-in-midst-ir912

Jones, B. D. (2004). The changing role of UN political and development actors in situations of protracted crisis. In Harmer, A. & Macrae, J. (Eds.). *Beyond the continuum: The changing role of aid policy in protracted crises* (pp. 14–27). HPG Report 18. Overseas Development Institute.

Khairi, A., Askandar, K. & Wahab, A. (2018). From Myanmar to Malaysia: Protracted refugee situations of Rohingya people. *International Journal of Engineering and Technology, 7*, 192–196. Doi: 10.14419/ijet.v7i3.25.17545

Kurlantzick, J. (2019). Rohingya refugees risk going back to another genocide in Myanmar. *World Politics Review.* https://www.worldpoliticsreview.com/articles/28219/rohingya-refugees-risk-going-back-to-another-genocide-in-myanmar

Lauri, A. (2018). *Humanitarian diplomacy: A new research agenda.* CMI Brief No: 04. https://www.cmi.no/publications/6536-humanitarian-diplomacy-a-new-research-agenda

Leader, N. (2001). Donor governments and capacity-building in Afghanistan. *Humanitarian Exchange*, no: 18. https://odihpn.org/publication/donor-governments-and-capacity-building-in-afghanistan/

Longley, K. (2001). Beyond seeds and tools: Opportunities and challenges for alternative interventions in protracted emergencies. *Humanitarian Exchange*, no: 18. https://odihpn.org/wp-content/uploads/2003/06/humanitarianexchange018.pdf

Macrae, J. & Harmer, A. (2004). *Beyond the continuum: Aid policy in protracted crises* (pp. 1–12). HPG Report 18. Overseas Development Institute.

Maurer, P. (2014). Speech given by Mr Peter Maurer, President of the International Committee of the Red Cross, OSCE Parliamentary Assembly. In *New security challenges and the ICRC.* https://www.oscepa.org/en/documents/autumn-meetings/2014-geneva/speeches-13/2646-speech-by-peter-maurer-president-of-the-international-committee-of-the-red-cross-5-oct-2014/file

Maxwell, D., Russo, L. & Alinovi, L. (2012). Constraints to addressing food insecurity in protracted crises. *Proceedings of the National Academy of Sciences of the United States of America, 109*(31), 12321–12325.

Minear, L. & Smith, H. (Eds.). (2007). *Humanitarian diplomacy: Practitioners and their craft.* United Nations University Press.

Policinski, E. & Kuzmanovic, J. (2019). Protracted conflicts: The enduring legacy of endless war. *International Review of the Red Cross, 101*(912), 965–976.

Régnier, P. (2011). The emerging concept of humanitarian diplomacy: Identification of a community of practice and prospects for international recognition. *International Review of the Red Cross, 93*(884), 1211–1237. https://doi.org/10.1017/S1816383112 000574

Robinson, D. M. (2011). *Humanitarian diplomacy in the Balkans.* U.S. Department of State, Bureau of Population, Refugees, and Migration. https://2009-2017.state.gov/j/prm/releases/letters/2011/181127.htm

Russo, L., Hemrich, G., Alinovi, L. & Melvin, D. (2008). Food security in protracted crisis situations: Issues and challenges. In Alinovi, L., Hemrich, G. & Russo, L. (Eds.). *Beyond relief: Food security in protracted crises* (pp. 1–11). FAO.

Schafer, J. (2002). *Supporting livelihoods in situations of chronic conflict and political instability: Overview of conceptual issues.* HPG Working Paper 183. Overseas Development Institute. https://www.files.ethz.ch/isn/100520/wp183.pdf

Setiawan, A. & Hamka, H. (2019). Role of Indonesian humanitarian diplomacy toward Rohingya crisis in Myanmar. *Proceedings of the 2nd International Conference on Social Sciences.* ICSS Jakarta.

Smith, C. Q. & Williams, S. G. (2021). Why Indonesia adopted 'quiet diplomacy' over R2P in the Rohingya crisis: The roles of Islamic humanitarianism, Civil–Military Relations and Asean. *Global Responsibility to Protect, 13*(2–3), 158–185.

Swazo, N. (2021). The Rohingya crisis: A moral-philosophical assessment. In Swazo, N. K., Haque, Sk. T. M., Haque, Md. M., & Nower, T. (Eds.) *The Rohingya crisis: A moral, ethnographic, and policy assessment* (pp. 1–33). Routledge.

The International Committee of the Red Cross (ICRC). (2016). *Protracted conflict and humanitarian action: Some recent ICRC experiences.* ICRC.

The International Federation of Red Cross and Red Crescent Societies (IFRC). (n.d.). *Myanmar Red Cross Society: Humanitarian diplomacy in action.* https://www.rcrc-resilience-southeastasia.org/wp-content/uploads/2016/07/Myanmar_Humanitarian-Diplomacy-in-action_WEB.pdf

UN CERF. (n.d.). *Who we are.* https://cerf.un.org/about-us/who-we-are

UN News. (2021). *Food insecurity in Syria reaches record levels: WFP.* https://news.un.org/en/story/2021/02/1084972

UN OCHA. (2017). *Humanitarian response strategy: January-December 2018, humanitarian response plan.* https://www.humanitarianresponse.info/sites/www. humanitarianresponse.info/files/documents/files/2017_hrp_draft5_20_12_2017_v2.pdf

UN OCHA. (2018). *Humanitarian response plan, January-December 2018. Syrian Arab Republic.* https://reliefweb.int/sites/reliefweb.int/files/resources/2018_2018_hrp_syria.pdf

UN OCHA. (2019). Sustaining the ambition: Delivering change. *Agenda for Humanity Annual Synthesis Report 2019.* http://agendaforhumanity.org/system/files/asr/2019/ Dec/AfH%20Synthesis%20Report%202019_Executive%20Summary_0.pdf

UN OCHA. (2021). *Agenda for humanity.* https://www.unocha.org/about-us/agenda-humanity

UNHCR. (2004). *Protracted refugee situations.* Executive Committee of the High Commissioner's Programme. EC/54/SC/CRP.14. https://www.unhcr.org/excom/ standcom/40c982172/protracted-refugee-situations.html

UNHCR. (2020). *Protracted refugee situations explained.* https://www.unrefugees.org/ news/protracted-refugee-situations-explained/

UNHCR. (2021). *Global trends: Forced displacement in 2020.* https://www.unhcr.org/ 60b638e37/unhcr-global-trends-2020

UNICEF. (2019). *Children living in protracted conflicts are three times more likely to die from water related diseases than from violence.* https://www.unicef.org/press-releases/ children-living-protracted-conflicts-are-three-times-more-likely-die-water-related

UNICEF. (2021). *UNICEF's water under fire change agenda.* https://www.unicef.org/ stories/water-under-fire?utm_campaign=world-water-day-2019&utm_medium=pr& utm_source=medi

World Bank. (2017). *Forcibly displaced: Toward a development approach supporting refugees, the internally displaced and their hosts.* World Bank.

World Bank. (2020). *The mobility of displaced Syrians: An economic and social analysis.* World Bank Group.

6   Humanitarian Diplomacy Ecosystem

Halil Kürşad Aslan and Selen Turp

In this chapter, we aim to explore what we have come to dub the humanitarian diplomacy ecosystem. As we embark on our journey, we must first discuss three key terms that underpin this concept, namely, humanitarian aid, humanitarianism, and humanitarian diplomacy (henceforth HD). Only after having completed this step can we engage in a coherent conversation on the fundamental principles, prominent participants, structural characteristics, procedures, and other aspects of this ecosystem.

Humanitarian relief refers to the food, shelter, clean water, and security provided to people affected by natural and human-induced disasters. Humanitarianism, on the other hand, concerns the collective policies beyond first-tier humanitarian aid efforts, essentially "encapsulat[ing] a broader concept and application area in the context of international law, solidarity, social justice, and the creation of aid policies" (Özerdem, 2016, p. 130). Humanitarianism has been molded and refined for more than a century in response to the great wars and natural disasters that beleaguered twentieth-century man. Over time humanitarianism would act as the impetus for the growth of transnational organizations and institutions (Rush et al., 2021, p. 1). Somewhat of an amalgamation of the two previous concepts, though simultaneously more comprehensive in scope, HD encompasses the various diplomatic initiatives led to alleviate humanitarian crises. That said, however, no universal consensus has been reached on the definition of HD.

An upsurge in conflict and violence after the culmination of the Cold War has opened new wounds in world politics. The ensuing crises that would engulf Somalia, Rwanda, and Bosnia combined with a toothless international political system and disproportionate application of international law set off alarms in the global humanitarian aid system. These developments were a watershed moment in the humanitarian aid sector and precipitated existential inquiries and transformation.

An upsurge in conflict and violence after the culmination of the Cold War has opened new wounds in world politics. The ensuing crises that would engulf Somalia, Rwanda, and Bosnia combined with a toothless international

DOI: 10.4324/9781003503187-6

political system and disproportionate application of international law set off alarms in the global humanitarian aid system. These developments were a watershed moment for the humanitarian aid sector and precipitated existential inquiries and transformation. After such a severe blow to their morale, leading humanitarian actors began to discuss the most effective ways to institute internal reform and improve the efficacy of the greater humanitarian aid system (Barnett and Walker, 2015, p. 132).

Analysts take many factors into account while examining where humanitarian initiatives fall short. These include fractures in global governance, divergent interests, and asymmetric values (Barnett & Walker, 2015, p. 131). Still, despite the limited funding allocated to humanitarian aid, personnel of such organizations as the United Nations (UN), the International Organization for Migration (IOM), and the UN High Commissioner for Refugees (UNHCR) are often seen driving expensive vehicles in disaster areas. This obviously plants the notion of wasted resources in the minds of the general public and affected individuals, causing local populations to regard humanitarian organizations with apathy and even ire (Barnett and Walker, 2015, p. 134). The authors of a research project funded by Sweden (Binder et al., 2010, p. 4) underlined that Westerners maintained a monopoly over the mechanisms governing the vast majority of humanitarian organizations, with in turn allowed them to form their own closed system. Aid organizations, such as the OECD's Development Assistance Committee (OECD DAC), do not allow China, Russia, Saudi Arabia, or Brazil to set the agenda or to participate in deliberations and decision-making despite their recent increased clout in the field of humanitarian aid. Aside from the United Nations' General Assembly and the Economic and Social Council (ECOSOC), there exists no other widely recognized platform where prominent participants in the global aid system can convene to discuss reform possibilities or the future of the aid system, let alone craft a collective reform agendum.

The 9.1-magnitude earthquake and subsequent tsunami that rocked the Indian Ocean and killed 225,000 people on 26 December 2004 were among the most catastrophic disasters in recorded history. Fourteen countries, including Indonesia, Sri Lanka, India, the Maldives, and Thailand, suffered extensive damage and, in some cases, wholesale destruction. Official sources reported that an excess of three hundred thousand people perished in the 2010 Haiti earthquake, which registered a catastrophic 7.0 on the Richter scale. These two disasters, coupled with the 2011 earthquake and tsunami that triggered a major nuclear disaster in Japan, reveal just how vulnerable all countries—regardless of their level of development—are to natural disasters. Likewise, these disasters demonstrated the paramount importance of coordinated international assistance in quickly and effectively relieving problems plaguing disaster victims. Though national governments often lead humanitarian operations following a catastrophe within their own borders, these efforts may be co-opted by one or more international aid organizations whose knowledge, experience, and resources can greatly expedite operations (Kunz and Reiner, 2012, p. 116).

Each of the aforementioned disasters served to amplify the voices calling for global governance reform and institutional reshuffling, especially where it pertained to the ability of the humanitarian aid sector to run successful humanitarian aid initiatives.

The humanitarian aid community has faced criticism for its shortcomings, as studies from the UN and other organizations have emphasized the necessity for more robust reforms. Although aid groups have increased in competency, coordination, and professionalism, they continue to face criticism for their perceived detachment from local populations. Furthermore, budget constrictions have forced aid organizations to compete with one another for supplementary funds and resources. Indeed, the reform literature identifies several key challenges to institution any real change; these include inadequate planning, the absence of standards, uncoordinated responses in crisis zones, confusion arising from conflicting objectives, and the sector's overly cumbersome nature (Barnett and Walker, 2015, p. 132).

The partial changes made to the global humanitarian aid system in the 1990s and early 2000s were the precursor to more extensive reforms in 2005, after which subsequent experiences would lead the UN to adopt the Transformative Agenda in 2011. One characteristic of the UN reforms pertains to the revamped funding system that seeks to consolidate assistance requests from multiple UN agencies under a single roof. The new Central Emergency Response Fund (CERF) pools resources and secures rapid funding not only to shorten emergency response time (Barnett and Walker, 2015, p. 133) but also to ensure that urgently needed humanitarian aid reaches people quickly during crises. Established by the UN General Assembly in 2005, CERF ensures that the humanitarian response ecosystem delivers an adequate amount of lifesaving assistance in the shortest time possible. The convening of the 2016 World Humanitarian Summit that took place in Istanbul on 23–24 May of said year and the agenda items discussed at this event are themselves the clearest indicators of the need for additional, more effective reforms (Cook, 2021). Leading donors and humanitarian aid organizations present at this summit signed a mutual agreement known as the Grand Bargain (IASC, 2023). This agreement codified signatories' commitment not only to implementing measures to alleviate the suffering of disaster victims and people in need but also to increase the overall efficacy of humanitarian efforts (Development Initiatives, 2021). Several resolutions, collectively known as the International Aid Transparency Initiative (IATI), were similarly adopted at the summit as part of the Grand Bargain.

Aid organizations should prioritize coordination, embrace new technologies like drone-assisted damage assessment, adopt disaster-management techniques employed in the private sector, and incorporate technological and managerial innovations. They should also implement operational and structural reforms, refine logistics, enhance contribution management, and uphold guiding values. By embracing innovative approaches, aid organizations can help usher in a more inclusive and efficient humanitarian system (Betts and Bloom, 2014, p. 5; Rush et al., 2014, p. 28).

Transformations in Global Politics and Humanitarian Diplomacy

Recent years have witnessed mounting polarization between the US, the EU, and BRICS countries that has been greatly exacerbated by increasing competition and, perhaps more strikingly, intense conflicts of interests and values among dominant powers and country blocs. This was articulated very clearly, when, in 2011, the American neoclassical realist scholar Randall Schweller argued that America's hegemonic role in world politics had embarked on an irreversible decline.

Without a clear hegemonic power, the global political system is expected to experience further dissolution in the forthcoming years. What is clear is that the previous two decades have seen increasing challenges to American hegemony, thus complicating world politics to an unprecedented degree. This is further aggravating by an emboldened China and Russia, the proliferation of nuclear weapons by Iran and North Korea, climate change, the rise of far-right movements and authoritarianism, transnational terrorism, migration waves, hybrid wars, social inequality, populism, and Islamophobia. In short, modern-day international relations are both more informal and more multipolar while simultaneously being significantly less multilateral (Parlar-Dal, 2018, p. 12).

The pessimistic attitude prevailing throughout the twenty-first century has only served to increase diplomacy's currency in global politics. Given the turmoil embroiling the global political order and the clear inadequacies of global governance, a plethora of diplomatic tools and channels have emerged to fill in the gaps, especially those pertaining to preliminary agreements. This has transformed diplomacy into the most powerful tool in the intricate world of global politics. Yolanda Kemp Spies characterizes diplomacy as a "constant effort to build a bridge. It aims to connect entities that are different from each other, disconnected from each other, conflicting but in need of each other" (2019, p. 3). While once the exclusive realm of a few elite state officials, diplomacy has evolved into a multi-actor, multi-layered field of quasi-public action today (Berridge, 2015; Seib, 2016; Kemp Spies, 2019). Hedley Bull, one of the most renowned names in international relations, describes diplomacy as one of the most important institutions within the international community, emphasizing that it serves primarily to bring an air of order and stability to global politics. In other words, the nations of the world, after having embraced a shared set of values and intellect, have used diplomacy to develop specific techniques to facilitate reconciliation between antagonistic parties so as to ensure that global politics might run as smoothly as possible (Bull and Watson, 1984). This reconciliatory role is frequently discussed alongside its role in influencing the trajectory of international political discourse.

Considering the dire situation in which global politics is currently entangled, it would be fruitful to discuss how humanitarian aid and diplomacy can help ameliorate the status quo. Humanitarian aid comprises the food resources, water, shelter, and other basic human needs delivered in the wake of a disaster. HD, on the other hand, covers not only state behavior, but also the support activities engaged in by domestic and international non-governmental actors, including the private sector. Reflecting a commitment to taking institutional measures to address and devise solutions to problems that concern humanity as a whole, HD employs awareness-raising, resource mobilization, negotiations, and other methods to influence policies and their potential outcomes (Regnier, 2011, p. 1213).

Although a consensus has yet to be reached on HD's exact definition, the IFRC emphasizes the importance of persuading decision-makers to alleviate the suffering of stricken individuals. In the first systematic study conducted on HD, Minear and Smith discuss both a narrow and broad reading of HD (2007, p. 21). Whereas the narrow definition focuses more on civilian humanitarian organizations, the authors elaborate the more comprehensive and abstract activities humanitarian diplomats (henceforth HDiplomats) engage in to resolve human grievances. One of the reasons why a common conceptual framework has yet to be put forward is related to the extensive scope of its activities, a challenge further exacerbated by the diversity of actors making up the ecosystem. More recent literature, however, defines HD as the amalgamation of all humanitarian activities carried out by civilian, semi-public, public, and international organizations (Slim, 2019; Rousseau and Pende, 2020). The ICRC identifies four fundamental characteristics of HD:

i   A diverse array of both governmental and non-governmental entities,
ii A concentration on all aspects of humanitarian efforts, encompassing but not restricted to peacebuilding missions,
iii Autonomy that, while acknowledging government support, remains shielded from external influence,
iv The role of representation is crucial for humanitarian objectives, necessitating the mobilization of influential networks to accomplish primary goals (Cook, 2021, p. 5).

The importance of non-state actors and, more specifically, of non-state networks has increased exponentially in recent decades (McClory and Harvey, 2016). Social media, mobile communications, sports associations, youth groups, religious communities, philosophical social clubs, and cross-border networks bolster HDiplomats' abilities to devise viable solutions to problems.

Civil and governmental actors collaborate with one another to produce solutions to protect and improve the day-to-day lives of people affected by natural and human-induced disasters. These efforts include procedures that facilitate aid workers' operations, such as removing travel barriers, facilitating visa approval, ensuring worker safety, increasing financial and logistical support, and negotiating for effective humanitarian responses co-opted by civilian and military authorities, intergovernmental organizations, UN aid agencies, the media, and human rights organizations. In addition, "risk reduction in natural and man-made disasters, climate change, environmental protection, access to water, food security, migration and refugee policies, health, education, poverty alleviation, development, democracy, and human rights are the main focuses of humanitarian diplomacy" (Kınık & Aslan, 2020, p. 363).

The UN equates HD with negotiations in which solutions to humanitarian problems are discussed and devised. Since the focus here is for member states to convene and deliberate with one another, the UN prefers to use the term humanitarian negotiations in lieu of humanitarian diplomacy. In fact, the organization's political implications and close association with statecraft has led United Nations officials to avoid using the term HD altogether (IHH, 8 May 2018). Nevertheless, other international civil society actors embrace this term wholeheartedly, contending that diplomacy encompasses negotiations in which, humanitarian workers play a crucial role. Mediation between antagonistic parties, during which negotiations are of paramount importance, falls squarely within the scope of HD. Nevertheless, given the relative novelty of humanitarianism, humanitarian aid, and HD in academia, their meanings and nuances have yet to be fully fleshed out. In fact, that these terms are often used interchangeably sometimes leads to unintentional misunderstandings. Since, however, our primary focus in this chapter is to build a case for the humanitarian ecosystem, no unnecessary confusion will result from the synonymous use of these terms.

What is the Humanitarian Diplomacy Ecosystem?

Annual global humanitarian reports issued since 2000 provide a comprehensive assessment of the status of humanitarian assistance worldwide. The GHA Report 2020 illustrates how existing systemic and structural vulnerabilities have worsened at both the global and national levels during the COVID-19 pandemic (Development Initiatives, 2021).

Humanitarian Aid as an Ecosystem

Drawing on concepts that emphasize networking and interaction, ecosystem literature focuses on specific dynamics and characteristics reminiscent of real ecosystems, including complexity, interdependence, the coexistence of competition and cooperation, keystone actors, resource flows, and growth.

Order within the ecosystem is not established by a central authority's imposition of a macroplan. Rather it is a decentralized, self-organizing system that relies on the actions of interdependent agents. These decentralized actions are informed by the knowledge and experience of local individuals who constantly adapt their responses based on the feedback they receive by constituents of the ecosystem (Rush et al., 2021, p. 4). Ecosystem literature focuses primarily on networks and places a strong emphasis on different combinations of main actors' interaction styles.

Common features of the ecology metaphor, itself forming the basis of ecosystems literature, are (i) complexity, (ii) interdependence, (iii) the coexistence of competition and cooperation, (iv) keystone actor(s), and (v) resource flows (Rush et al., 2021, p. 4).

Complexity: The global humanitarian aid system has continued to grow in resources, actors, and the scope of its activities (Weiss, 2016, p. 185). New methodologies have been developed to analyze activities falling within the humanitarian aid regime—a area that has continues to grow in complexity as a result of technological advancements, innovations driven by economic globalization, and the unique challenges of the twenty-first century. Since the behaviors and procedures guiding the humanitarian aid regime frequently entail diverse interactions, it is often characterized as "non-linear, dynamic, and unpredictable" in nature (Rush et al., 2014, p. 4).

Interdependence: According to Dijkzeul and Sandvik (2019, p. 97), "[b]efore the 1990s, humanitarian organizations were rather decentralized, because headquarters was not able to quickly understand and react to the situation 'on the ground'." The rise in both frequency and severity of disasters over the past twenty-five years has compelled humanitarian organizations to make gradual yet significant improvements to their decision-making and response mechanisms. Likewise, the challenges and complexity of the field necessitate ongoing innovation and procedural refinement, which therefore compels all humanitarian actors to improve upon their own operational performance across several domains. States, humanitarian organizations, and non-state actors coexist within an intricate ecosystem of diverse hierarchies, networks, and economic realities that collectively uphold the global governance of the humanitarian regime. Bound by a shared destiny, each organization making up the ecosystem experiences the same fate as the whole, mirroring the interconnectedness inherent in biological ecosystems (Rush et al., 2021, p.4).

Coexistence of competition and cooperation: Symbiotic competition and cooperation among different subpopulations and actor groups are commonly observed in biological ecosystems, such as in the competitive relationship between lions and gazelles. As highlighted above, "business and innovation ecosystems involve varying combinations of competition and cooperation between participants" (Rush et al., 2021, p. 4).

Keystone actor(s): Similar to keystone species in natural ecologies, the removal of any constituent of the humanitarian ecosystem would result in significant disturbances (Rush et al., 2021, p. 4). Just as the demise of a queen bee results in the complete collapse of the colony's ecosystem, the absence of any critical or interconnected element of a social ecosystem will likely yield comparable outcomes. One salient real-life example is the UN, which, despite receiving significant criticism, fulfills an indispensable role in the global aid regime—so vital a role, in fact, that the dissolution of the UN would spell the end of global humanitarian aid for the foreseeable future.

Resource flows: "[B]iological ecosystems are fundamentally shaped by their energy dynamics, involving complex flows of materials and nutrients through the system" (Rush et al., 2021, p. 4). Human capital corresponds to energy and food resources in social ecosystems. Similarly, resources such as human skills, finance, knowledge management, physical assets, technologies, network location, and time manifest in different forms. Their interest in and impact on the ecosystem are contingent on their origin—how they were created, by whom and what means they are distributed, and for what purpose they were designed (Rush et al., 2021, p. 4).

While food security has been a global priority since the 2000s, concerns over food safety have recently intensified. The 2021-GHA Report found that COVID-19 had detrimental effects on global food insecurity, with poverty-stricken populations bearing the brunt of the impact. Over 80 percent of people experiencing severe food insecurity live below the international poverty line. Additionally, a staggering 243.8 million people worldwide are in need of humanitarian assistance. Among them, 82.1 million have experienced forced displacement, with half being internally displaced persons forced to leave their homes for other regions within their own countries (Aslan and Durmuş, 2021; Development Initiatives, 2021).

Global humanitarian aid financing witnessed an annual increase of twelve between 2012 and 2018, reaching 30.9 billion USD in 2020. However, 2019 was marked by a five- percent decrease, which was followed by a notable decline in contributions from the UK, UAE, and Saudi Arabia between 2019 and 2020. This situation was further exacerbated by the global coronavirus pandemic, which increased demand for assistance while simultaneously constricting human, physical, and financial resources.

In recent years, many different types of actors, including civil and governmental institutions and individuals have taken place in various humanitarian crises. The humanitarian field has diversified rapidly, and we are now talking about a very colorful humanitarian ecosystem.

The disparity between supply and demand has grown wider with the increasing frequency and severity of humanitarian disasters. To make matters worse, several major donors have likewise scaled back their contributions to the global aid pool. The recent conflicts in Afghanistan, Yemen, and Syria underscore the glaring inadequacy of the international community's ability to address complex humanitarian crises. The international community's response to the COVID-19 pandemic countries' inability to cooperate on even the most basic of operations, as they were unable to deliver aid to the most impoverished and therefore most vulnerable regions of the world. This has caused many to raise concerns about the international community's ability to deal with future crises. Global climate change has amplified the destructiveness of natural disasters, which, when coupled with rapid urbanization and increased cross-border migration, has greatly exacerbated the human toll of humanitarian crises (Barnett and Walker, 2015, p. 130). Given the growing gravity of the situation, there is mounting pressure to find solutions to the systemic problems that have long plagued the humanitarian aid sector. Yet, the greatest obstacle to reforming the humanitarian aid sector is its adoption of a market-like logic, which, while not fully embodying a purely capitalism market, does exhibit traits akin to a quasi-market. Since this system is not demand oriented as is the case in completely free markets, however, it is mired by "dysfunctional competition and fragmentation in aid efforts" and by "clear limits placed on innovations" (Rush et al., 2014, p. 37). What donors, UN agencies, and NGOs within the system demand is not a traditional coordination mechanism, but a functional ecosystem in which actors can work collaboratively.

Several scholars seeking to reform the humanitarian aid system have proposed regarding it as an ecosystem. These scholars emphasize the complex, open, and adaptive nature of ecosystems (ALNAP, 2018, p. 31). Regarding the humanitarian aid system as an ecosystem affirms its complex nature, multi-actor structure, diverse value sets, and capacity for adaptation (ALNAP, 2018). While building resilience is one of the most important goals sought to be achieved by providing humanitarian aid, "[it] is not something that is pursued or fostered, but an unplanned-for or unintentional attribute that arises from the complex interactions of system components" (Matyas and Pelling, 2015, p. 5).

One study examining innovation in the humanitarian aid sector emphasized the need to develop a comprehensive framework, doing so by highlighting three main systemic factors. The first being the growing problems facing the humanitarian sector, the second being that only partial improvements have been achieved through innovation while a comprehensive solution remains elusive, and the third being the belief that an ecosystem-based approach to innovation will foster a clearer understanding of the complexities and interrelationships within the humanitarian sector (Rush et al., 2021, p. 12). An alternative interpretation posits that risk management, resilience, and critical reflexivity in the humanitarian ecosystem imply an inherent capacity for self-learning, transformation, and growth (Matyas and Pelling, 2015, p. 14).

"Knowledge generation of ecosystems should be explicitly integrated with management practice and evolve with the institutional and organizational aspects of management" (Olsson et al., 2004, p.75). Collective management depends on the collaboration of diverse actors operating at different levels, including members of the local community, municipal bodies, national institutions, and international organizations. Ecosystems are based on interactions at the local and macro levels that support one another through feedback loops. They are complex, adaptive, and well-integrated systems (Olsson et al., 2004, p. 76). Knowledge is crucial for effectively managing unforeseen consequences in the ecosystem, understanding the internal dynamics of actors, and facilitating adaptation. Gaining knowledge about the entire environment requires comprehending social memory. The knowledge system fuses into social learning processes that aim to address the challenges posed by the ecosystem's own internal dynamics (Olsson et al., 2004, p. 77). Put simply, the authors argue that our limited understanding of the intricate and interrelated nature of eco-systems requires management strategies to be adaptable and to include a mechanism that allows us to use policy experiments to gain knowledge about ecosystem dynamics (Olsson et al., 2004, p. 86). Moreover, trust plays a pivotal role in the self-regulating mechanisms of ecosystem management within the social ecosystem. Without trust, nurturing the enduring relationships that foster collective governance is indeed an arduous endeavor. As such, the lack of trust indirectly prevents the reciprocal advantages inherent in this form of governance from taking root.

Being able to understand the long-term ramifications of the decisions and policies enacted by executive actors within the ecosystem is of paramount importance. It is likewise imperative to measure the long-term impact that these decisions have on the humanitarian services offered to affected communities (Obaze, 2019). These services aim to foster societal development by increasing overall welfare, creating collective value, and imbuing community members with relevant skills. This way, people's basic needs are met and the groundwork is laid for a sustainable system that will improve their lives over the long term. To ensure this, however, good planning and effective governance mechanisms must be put into place.

Recent studies have highlighted the importance of discovering under-served communities receiving desperately inadequate amounts of humanitarian aid where many disenfranchised individuals live in the same region or country, such as Yemen, Sudan, and Syria (Obaze, 2019, p. 412). These shortcomings are often due to the nature of humanitarian aid work. "Relief workers often rush" because they know little "about the lay of the land, local customs, and the cultural traits that might determine a community's ability to survive and recover" (Barnett & Walker, 2015, p.134). In areas where humanitarian aid is provided, foreign relief workers often lack sufficient knowledge of local social relationships, cultural codes, ethnic differences, and sectarian dynamics. This, in turn, may lead to misperceptions, negative thoughts, and resentment during aid operations (Kınık and Aslan, 2020, p. 369).

Local knowledge is often just as vital as food and water, and small local groups are often the only ones able to provide it. The response to the 2014–2016 West African Ebola virus epidemic "could not have ultimately succeeded without the active involvement of local community health workers, village elders, and teachers, who helped convince the families of victims to forgo traditional burial rituals in order to contain the spread of infection" (Barnett & Walker, 2015, p. 134). The response to the April 2015 Nepal earthquake, during which the local nomadic Sherpa community and truck drivers transported aid "to remote villages at great personal risk," is yet another salient example of how local knowledge can expedite the delivery of humanitarian aid (Barnett and Walker, 2015, p. 134).

Early warning messages are one of the most important components of Disaster Risk Reduction (DRR). However, as is often the case in this field, events can unfold very differently than planned. The empirical methodologies used in social science research on disaster risks do not always align seamlessly with the conditions found in the field. Risk-related rationales vary and individuals' judgments are impacted by social networks and sociocultural norms (Ayeb-Karlsson et al., 2019). The distrust propagated by opponents to COVID-19 vaccinations, the vast majority of whom gained prominence on social media, exemplifies this problem.

Perceptions of what causes disasters are strongly linked to cultural, religious, and social understanding of the world. After Cyclone Nargis, in which over eighty thousand people died, devastated Myanmar in 2008, neighboring countries and regional organizations conducted effective humanitarian operations. Cultural proximity, combined with the existing networks and connections of neighboring countries and regional organizations—especially the Association of Southeast Asian Nations (ASEAN)—played a crucial role in ensuring the success of the humanitarian response (Betts and Bloom, 2014, p. 25). Likewise, despite early warning messages sent to the local population prior to Typhoon Haiyan that struck the Philippines on 8 November 2013, the early warning system—hindered by social inequalities, societal mistrust, and miscommunication between social groups—failed to work as expected. In short, the "local government did not trust the information it received from the meteorological experts, and people did not trust the local government's knowledge." The population's lack of familiarity with technical vocabulary used in warnings, particularly regarding meteorological terms, significantly contributed to the distrust that permeated throughout society (Ayeb-Karlsson et al., 2019, p. 759). Hurricane Soudelor, which struck Saipan on 1 August 2015, is yet another example. While the storm was not initially expected to inflict serious damage, it was upgraded to a typhoon just hours before it struck the Saipan's coast, making it one of the most formidable storms to hit Saipan in nearly thirty years. When asked why people failed to seek refuge in designated shelters, one young man responded as follows: "It's our culture. We live together with our elders. When the storms come, we don't rush." In sum, many people remained at home for cultural and religious reasons despite having received timely warnings (Ayeb-Karlsson et al., 2019, p. 760).

A diverse array of actors, including civil and governmental organizations, individuals, and the private sector, have played an active role in responding to more recent humanitarian crises. This has given rise to a humanitarian ecosystem in which different actors spontaneously harmonize with one another as opposed to operating within a well-organized centralized system. This ecosystem includes Gulf countries, Türkiye, China, and India—all new donors—as well as more established organizations like the World Bank. "Militaries, peacekeepers, private military and security companies, other businesses, diaspora organizations, faith-based organizations, and regional organizations, such as the Organisation of Islamic Cooperation or the Association of Southeast Asian Nations" are also part of this ecosystem (Dijkzeul and Sandvik, 2019, p. 94). New technologies, the internet, and social media have imbued the humanitarian ecosystem with a range of transformative capabilities. In its 2014 report, USAID discussed the impact of framing humanitarian policies within an ecosystem approach, introducing what it has dubbed the 5R framework (i.e., resources, roles, relationships, rules, and results).

It is crucial to understand the components and complex network of relations making up the humanitarian aid ecosystem. To this end, Obaze (2019, p. 411) has posited a managerial nexus that oversees supply chains, logistics, and donations to ensure the smooth delivery of humanitarian services. Like all ecosystems, the humanitarian ecosystem is governed by certain rules and customs that shape how actors interact with each other. Launched in 1997 by a group of humanitarian aid workers, the Sphere Movement sought to enhance the quality of disaster responses efforts by creating a set of standards and behavioral norms. This initiative would lead to the signing of the Humanitarian Charter and formalization of the Sphere Standards. Originally developed by the Red Cross and Red Crescent Movement and affiliated organizations, the Sphere Standards have become the primary reference for national and international NGOs, volunteers, UN agencies, governments, donors, the private sector, and other actors. Today, the Sphere Movement has grown into a worldwide community that brings together various actors and empowers them to improve the quality not only of humanitarian aid but also of the accountability mechanisms that govern it. In addition to setting specific metrics for humanitarian efforts, such as minimum per capita nutrition and clean water requirements and shelter construction standards, the 2020 Sphere Standards establishes baseline requirements for each major sub-sector.

The humanitarian space seeks primarily to save lives and meet the urgent food, shelter, and heating needs of disaster-stricken communities. However, the scope of its activities has gradually expanded to include addressing the root causes of conflicts through appeals to human rights and democracy as well as socioeconomic development and state-building initiatives.

Humanitarian agencies must ensure that their aid services are both well structured and sustainable. Aid delivery services should be conceived as an integral part of a broader ecosystem in which representatives of recipient groups play an active role in the governance and planning of aid initiatives. By involving local actors as partners in humanitarian operations, agencies empower them to realize their potential to create value within the ecosystem and to foster social change. Ultimately, whether or not successful outcomes are achieved hinges on bilateral participation in which all stakeholders are able to contribute in a meaningful manner (Obaze, 2019, p. 411).

An example of this can be seen in the Syrians living in Turkey. Different sectors in this community receive different levels of support from both public and private international organizations as well as from the Turkish government and Turkish NGOs. If relief services for Syrian families in Istanbul were to be imagined as an ecosystem, the first line of business would be to improve coordination between humanitarian agencies. This would entail formulating approaches that enable marginalized populations to attain self-sufficiency within a period of five to ten years, thus reducing wasted aid resources. Furthermore, specific standards evaluating different levels of need would need to be developed.

Prior to the early 2000s, the humanitarian aid system relied on camps established outside urban centers. Though effective during its own era, this approach has since been recognized as insufficient for addressing contemporary crises, as such camps were specifically designed for rural environments and short-term relief efforts. A 2014 UNHCR survey found that refugees remain displaced for an average of seventeen years, with more than fifty percent of refugees residing in urban areas (Betts and Bloom, 2014, p. 6). Refugees face unique hardships in metropolitan environments, including difficulties forming social networks and accessing information beyond how to secure their basic necessities like food and shelter. As such, the evolving and growing needs of the modern age necessitate an overhaul of the humanitarian ecosystem, with disaster management mechanisms receiving particular attention.

Given the above, humanitarian organizations must acknowledge the necessity of creating supply channels that extend beyond the provision of minimum daily needs by guaranteeing access to long-term care, education, economic opportunities, and human rights. For this reason, aid organizations have begun to emphasize promoting an adherence to human rights alongside their traditional activities (Barnett, 2017, p. 327). To summarize, it would be more accurate to conceptualize humanitarian space as an ecosystem that takes into account life's realities and that is able to adapt to changes in the global system. By virtue of ecosystems' self-renewing nature, interventions that will pave the way for sustainable and resilience-based transformations will be desirable.

Humanitarian Diplomacy Actors and Inter-Actor Relations

Developing a framework to understand the identities, worldviews, and roles of actors in the global humanitarian ecosystem is essential. HD actors can be categorized into three groups: (i) humanitarian diplomats, (ii) counterparts, and (iii) beneficiaries.

Key actors contributing to humanitarian diplomacy beyond those specializing solely in humanitarian aid include:

i The International Red Cross and Red Crescent Movement, particularly the ICRC, the IFRC, and National Societies,

ii International humanitarian organizations such as Doctors Without Borders (known commonly by its French acronym MSF), IHH Humanitarian Relief Foundation, and Doctors Worldwide Türkiye,

iii Human rights NGOs such as Human Rights Watch and Amnesty International,

iv Intergovernmental organizations like the International Criminal Court,

v UN agencies like UN OCHA, the World Food Programme, WHO, UNHCR, and UNICEF,

vi Prominent international figures including celebrities, goodwill ambassadors, and representatives from the arts and sports, and

vii Locally and nationally influential individuals (Kınık and Aslan, 2020, p. 365–366).

Humanitarian Diplomacy Activities of International Organizations, States, and Bureaucratic Structures

The 1950s saw growing momentum to institutionalize the global humanitarian aid regime. Discussions on how rich countries would provide aid to poor countries in a systematic manner were had by the UN and other influential platforms throughout the 1960s. The Development Assistance Group (DAG) was established on 23 July 1960 as a platform where donor nations could consult with one another on providing aid to developing countries. Along with the US and EU—the two leaders in the global humanitarian aid sector—several UN agencies and the OECD's Development Assistance Committee (DAC) dominated the system. Later, alternative aid initiatives began to emerge in China, India, Türkiye, Brazil, and Saudi Arabia, all of whom have likewise emerged as prominent HD actors.

By helping to form the field's normative structure, the UN and its affiliates have played a central role in HD. The UN is also the principal provider of emergency and humanitarian aid. Specialized UN agencies facilitate the delivery of emergency aid to disaster-stricken individuals while simultaneously developing strategies to prevent such disasters from occurring in the first place. In 2020, for instance, nine specialized UN agencies were authorized to allocate 3.3 billion USD to enhance their rapid response capabilities (Development Initiatives, 2021).

UN OCHA and OECD-DAC are the two leading agencies in the global humanitarian system, functioning as coordination centers for development and humanitarian aid agencies, international aid organizations, and NGOs to report their aid operations. In other words, these two organizations store and coordinate information on different actors' global aid operations. As of

January 2024, the OECD-DAC network boasts thirty-two members including all EU countries.

Most of the funds (15.8 billion USD) transferred to the humanitarian pool from public (i.e., state or international organizations) actors are ultimately distributed to final recipients by public actors such as UN agencies. Data collected from nine UN agencies showed a significant increase in unallocated funds, rising by 535 million USD between 2016 and 2020 and then peaking at 3.3 billion USD in 2020. The UNHCR received the lion's share of this (1.3 billion USD) in 2020. Notably, the WHO witnessed a substantial rise in funding from 98 million USD in 2019 to 699 million USD in 2020, reflecting a sevenfold increase to combat the Covid-19 pandemic. Additionally, DAC donor governments contributed the majority of funds (85%, 1.7 billion USD) to the ICRC in 2019 (Development Initiatives, 2021).

Global fund distribution procedures align with the Grand Bargain targets set at the 2016 World Humanitarian Summit. Moreover, the International Aid Transparency Initiative (IATI) implements "development finance tracking with detailed, real-time data published by many donors" (Development Initiatives, 2021), which has led to an increase in the publication of more comprehensive data on humanitarian activity.

A division of the UN Secretariat, OCHA focuses on coordinating humanitarian organizations to field an effective response to emerging crises. It is tasked to address obstacles that hinder access to humanitarian aid by mobilizing and coordinating resources effectively. To achieve this, OCHA has bolstered its capabilities in international reporting, analysis, and data assessment by employing advanced data collection systems to track outcomes and enhance reporting methods, thereby promoting greater transparency and accountability. OCHA created the Financial Tracking Service (FTS) to document international humanitarian assistance and to allocate funds equitably. While OCHA does not engage directly in humanitarian activities, it emphasizes the role of trustworthy actors, influencers, and advocates. It further oversees information and communication services, assesses global field operations, and supports capacity-building initiatives and networks through its regional and national offices.

OCHA's objective is to create efficient decision-making procedures that facilitate coordination among different actors, including the Inter-Agency Standing Committee (IASC), the United Nations Disaster Assessment and Coordination (UNDAC) system, and the International Search and Rescue Advisory Group (INSARAG). These mechanisms are governed by OCHA and were designed to facilitate rapid and effective decision-making. For instance, OCHA utilizes the Humanitarian Program Cycle (HPC) to devise the strategies and mechanisms necessary to coordinate inter-agency responses to humanitarian crises that prioritize needs over projects. The cycle involves five consecutive stages: (i) a needs analysis, (ii) strategic response planning, (iii) resource mobilization, (iv) execution and monitoring, and (v) a post-response evaluation.

Delivering aid to millions of people facing trauma is fraught with challenges, especially in the absence of careful supervision. Michael Barnett likens the OECD-DAC-based Western humanitarian aid system to an elite club—an oligopolistic market-like structure with significant barriers to entry (Barnett and Walker, 2015, pp. 136–137; Lewis et al., 2021). The most important club member is Washington DC, represented by the US Agency for International Development (USAID). Other influential club members include the British government, represented by the Department for International Development (DFID), and the European Civil Protection and Humanitarian Aid Operations (ECHO). "Club membership yields useful privileges: a seat at the planning table, an invitation to field coordination meetings, and UN credentials" (Barnett & Walker, 2015, p. 137). Additionally, the club's unwavering insistence on using English is often cited as a barrier preventing small communities and local associations in crisis areas from collaborating. A dozen or so NGOs occupy the club's front lines, including CARE International, MSF, Caritas Internationalis, Save the Children, OXFAM International, and World Vision International, all of whom receive the majority of their funds from major Western donors (Barnett and Walker, 2015, p. 136).

Based on OCHA's FTS database, eight non-OECD-DAC donor countries provided an average of 6 percent of worldwide humanitarian aid between 2000 and 2008 (Binder et al., 2010, p. 7). Another source reports OECD members accounted for around ninety percent of government donations to the global humanitarian pool between 2007 and 2012. The bulk of the funds pooled by OECD-DAC were allocated to UN agencies and needy regions through leading international NGOs (Barnett and Walker, 2015, p. 136). Recent statistics suggest a large increase in new donor countries (Kınık and Aslan, 2020, p. 374). The literature on humanitarian relief is replete with figures on the donations made by non-OECD-DAC organizations. Contributions by new donors ranged from 11 to 41.7 billion USD per year during the first decade of the new millennium, representing between 8 and 31 percent of total global official development assistance (Walz and Ramachandran, 2011, p. 1). These figures have only likely risen in the last decade. Moreover, a number of previous recipient countries have become donors themselves, such as India, South Korea, Brazil, China, various Gulf countries, Iran, Russia, and several Eastern European countries. Each of these countries has its own reasons for offering aid and employs diverse approaches to do so. Alongside the introduction of new donor countries, recently established international NGOs employ innovative techniques to guarantee that aid is delivered to its intended recipients (Oloruntoba and Kovács, 2015, p. 709).

The financial contributions of new donors have outpaced their traditional counterparts every year. The recent economic slowdown in many Western countries suggests that this trend will most likely persist into the future (Barnett and Walker, 2015, p. 138). In his 2013 report to ECOSOC, former Secretary-General of the UN Ban Ki-moon stated that "as new actors emerge, the current system has not adapted quickly and flexibly enough to meet the new realities. There is a need to build a more inclusive global humanitarian system, with stronger relationships at the global, regional and national levels" (Betts and Bloom, 2014, p. 6). However, the literature raises concerns about the greater potential for new actors to politicize humanitarian aid compared to traditional donor countries. China's strategy of using debt as a diplomatic tool and debt-trapping has been criticized by many. Barnett affirms the validity of this critique, citing several instances where humanitarian aid has been utilized as a geopolitical tool to further countries' national objectives (Barnett and Walker, 2015, p. 138).

Humanitarian Diplomacy and International NGOs

As world politics and global disputes become increasingly complex, traditional diplomatic and aid approaches are no longer sufficient to address newly emerging realities. HD seeks to fill in this void in two ways; first, by employing peaceful and preventive diplomacy strategies that prioritize human rights, humanitarian law, and humanitarian ethics; second, by persuading nations, non-state actors, policymakers, and practitioners to mobilize the public to empathize with and aid disaster-stricken individuals (Kınık and Aslan, 2020, p. 357). IHH, a humanitarian organization based in Türkiye, defines HD as (i) saving lives, (ii) defending rights, (iii) protecting and upholding human dignity, and (iv) opening dialog channels. IHH also considers all the steps taken to alleviate human suffering as part of HD (IHH, 8 May 2018).

Former MSF president Rony Brauman was the first to coin the term humanitarian space, defining it as an area where aid workers can freely assess people's needs, monitor the distribution and use of aid, and communicate with beneficiaries (Çalışkan Ciğer, 2016, p. 22). Freedom in this context means that politics do not interfere in the distribution or the relationship between donors and recipients. In short, relief workers must have the autonomy to carry out their mandate effectively. Political pressure, in addition to going against the very fundamentals of humanitarian aid, undermines the quality of humanitarianism. Common activities in which humanitarians are engaged include regulating the terms and conditions that must be fulfilled to establish humanitarian organizations in a given country, negotiating access to aggrieved civilian populations, monitoring aid programs, promoting respect for international law and norms, supporting local individuals and institutions, and advocating for the fulfillment of humanitarian objectives (IHH, 8 May 2018). Two of IHH's recent HD initiatives in Syria include reaching towns closed off by the central government or paramilitary groups in an attempt to prevent humanitarian aid from entering and dialoguing with different groups to resolve instances of kidnapping and detention, both of which are quite common in Syria (IHH, 8 May 2018).

While organizations dependent on government support cannot be considered completely autonomous, NGOs that finance their activities through their own means remain largely, if not completely, independent. Since government interference in the decision-making processes of self-sufficient organizations is a non-issue, a strong civil society facilitates autonomy in humanitarian space. Civil organizations have both the freedom to act independently of the government and, perhaps more importantly, the flexibility to carry out activities that the government cannot do for legal reasons (Kınık and Aslan, 2020, p. 362).

As world politics grapple with increasingly complex conflicts, traditional methods have proven to be inadequate in achieving desired results. Traditional diplomatic actors find themselves increasingly incapable of solving modern problems. This has paved the way for NGOs to step up and bridge the ever-widening gap. This shift has in turn granted them greater power and influence in world politics.

According to Joseph Nye (2011), world politics has been characterized by a significant megatrend over the past fifty years. Non-state actors exert greater influence than state actors do in the global power structure. This megatrend, known as power diffusion, also impacts the global humanitarian aid regime. Diaspora groups, businesses, and local emergency response units serve a unique function within the international humanitarian ecosystem. The support that diaspora groups send to their countries of origin has the potential to precipitate great changes. Remittances sent by workers abroad exceed the amount of official development assistance by three fold globally and some of this money is used to fund local humanitarian activities (Barnett and Walker, 2015, p. 139). The IOM estimates that there are a total of 169 million migrant workers worldwide whose remittances amount to approximately 702 billion USD—a figure that excludes both informal and in-kind transfers (McAuliffe and Triandafyllidou, 2021; Aslan, 2022).

International NGOs with seemingly unending budgets that work with the UN for humanitarian purposes play an ever-increasing role in the humanitarian ecosystem. Such NGOs have recently gained notoriety at the local, national, and international levels for their work in humanitarian aid and development. Whereas post-earthquake relief efforts used to be limited to the provision of tents and food, humanitarian organizations now engage in a much broader range of activities that includes economic development and post-crisis reconstruction. Several NGOs now serve as active partners in HD, where they work hand in hand with other organization in emergency response efforts, democratic development, conflict resolution, human rights, cultural protection, environmental activism, policy analysis, research, and information dissemination.

Though a minority of NGOs receive substantial state funding and resemble large public bureaucracies in structure, the majority consists of more informal outfits that operate on a smaller scale. Larger NGOs are, for all intents and purposes, highly professionalized organizations that, similar to private for-profit businesses, have strong institutional identities (Lewis et al., 2021, p. 4). While some NGOs boast multimillion-dollar budgets that support professional staff and thousands of employees, others rely heavily on volunteers, organization members, and sponsors for funding and manpower (Lewis et al., 2021, p. 4).

International NGOs can be categorized by their function, such as how MSF focuses on healthcare provision, or by the regions in which they operate. "Some have provided enduring services for decades (e.g., Oxfam), while others exist only for the duration of a specific emergency" (Oloruntoba and Kovács, 2015, p. 709). A growing number of religious and faith-based organizations have propped up alongside secular ones (Lewis et al., 2021, p. 4). Though some NGOs endorse UN-sanctioned international military interventions to support humanitarian efforts, others oppose such actions, citing the international aid community's commitment to the principles of neutrality and impartiality (Oloruntoba and Kovács, 2015, p. 709).

According to the latest data published by the Union of International Associations (UIA), more than 41,000 active and 32,000 inactive associations exist worldwide, with around 1,200 new associations added to the register every year. The number of international associations increased from 6,000 in 1990 to more than 50,000 in 2006, reaching approximately 73,000 today (Union of International Associations, 2021).

NGOs seek to effectuate enduring social change in disaster and poverty-stricken areas through the aid projects they finance (Heyse, 2016, p. 19). With closer ties to local populations than the government, NGOs are more readily positioned to reach marginalized, disadvantaged, and afflicted populations. As a result, they are considerably more adept at encouraging the average person to participate in relief efforts, meaning that much of the real work needing to be done crisis response efforts falls on the shoulders of local NGOs.

NGOs are sometimes criticized for being self-serving organizations. There is a perception that NGO staff—particularly those in poor countries—enjoy generous salaries and lead more luxurious lifestyles. Several scholars point to NGOs' role in expanding and sustaining neo-colonial relations in Africa. These points of criticism, coupled with increased resource flows in the NGO sector, have led to calls for greater transparency and accountability.

NGOs exist because they are believed not only to outperform state and market actors but also to complement public-market spheres (Heyse, 2016, p. 20). Just as neoliberalism, the prevailing ideology in the global political economy throughout the 1980s and '90s, paved the way for the private sector to supplant inefficient public institutions, it similarly allowed NGO initiatives to assume a more dominant role in the civilian sphere. During the aforementioned two decades, the cumbersome, overly statist model was subject to heavy criticism. NGOs were in vogue among Western donors both for their greater potential to garner local support and grassroots participation and because they offered alternative, more flexible funding channels. Today, NGOs compensate for market and government failures by complementing, substituting, or balancing the roles played by state and market organizations.

Viewed by many as an alternative form of networking to increase efficiency in the humanitarian ecosystem, the public–private partnership model has gained importance in recent years. *A World in Turmoil: Governing Risk, Establishing Order in Humanitarian Crises*, a report co-published by OCHA and the World Economic Forum in 2008, marked a turning point in the humanitarian ecosystem (Dijkzeul and Sandvik, 2019, pp. 97–98). While the private sector has long been a major contributor to humanitarian action, with large national, regional, and multinational companies supporting humanitarian objectives, it has become a more influential and visible player on various humanitarian fronts in the last decade.

At the World Humanitarian Summit 2016, the Connecting Business Initiative (CBI) was launched to formalize public–private partnerships. A joint initiative of OCHA and UNDP, CBI seeks (i) to involve the private sector in humanitarian, development, and peace initiatives, (ii) to strengthen the private sector's strategic engagement in disaster risk reduction, emergency preparedness, and response and recovery efforts at the community, sector, and company levels, and (iii) to bolster the private sector's role in coordinating national, regional, and international humanitarian efforts by supporting and collaborating with global private sector networks (UN OCHA, 2021).

According to the 2020 GHA Report (Development Initiatives, 2021), private companies and foundations contributed 6.7 billion USD of funds to humanitarian aid in 2020. The second largest donor of the private sector—the IKEA Foundation—donated 56 million USD in humanitarian aid in 2019. Since they seek to avoid involvement in protracted political crises and conflicts, private sector organizations allocate the majority of their humanitarian contributions to natural disaster preparedness programs.

Relations between Civil Society and Political Structures

Interactor relations within the humanitarian ecosystem have a profound impact on HD initiatives. Formal and semi-formal legal arrangements between nations and other political structures invariably influence humanitarian organizations. The importance of governments' capacity to govern and mobilize non-state actors cannot be understated. Civil society actors must recognize that the government has many tools at its disposal that they are also in need of. When a nation or UN organization formally declares a group active in a crisis zone to be a terrorist organization, it becomes impossible for humanitarian organizations to provide assistance to that group without violating humanitarian principles. Given this, the realities of the world have an undeniable impact on humanitarian action (IHH, 8 May 2018). Areas under the control of terrorist-listed armed groups lack humanitarian access, sometimes to the point of being entirely cut off from aid. Aid organizations that provide medical care to all injured individuals are sometimes targeted by a country's armed forced once a combatant group has been declared a terrorist organization (IHH, 8 May 2018). International news reports detailing Russian and Syrian forces targeting hospitals and civilian medical support units in Syria between 2015 and 2020 are bloody testaments to this grim reality, as is the Israeli army's wanton destruction of Gaza's entire healthcare and educational apparatus in Occupied Palestine both prior and subsequent to 7 October 2023.

Several logistical problems plague the humanitarian field. Among the factors that can force actors to compromise on humanitarian principles are hurdles to the delivery of humanitarian aid, the lack of coordination among stakeholders, the absence of comprehensive aid policies, and situations requiring cooperation between the government, civilian population, and military. The principle of doing no harm to others is brought up frequently when violations to it occur in the sector. Critics argue that humanitarian action sometimes fails to benefit people in need and occasionally does more harm than good. This is because the humanitarian aid ecosystem has begun to ignore, if not wholly eschew, fundamental humanitarian principles. In fact, aid workers have been accused of taking sides in conflicts, directing resources in such a way so as to strengthen their side and weaken the other. Some humanitarian organizations receive funding from the very nations fueling the war in the countries they are providing aid, thus leaving these countries broken and destitute. This contravenes all the principles espoused by humanitarian organizations. It is also a move that negatively affects their ability to act independently and impartially. This irony is tragically embodied in how the United States would distribute food aid through USAID, its humanitarian arm, while its air force simultaneously raining bombs upon Afghanistan's civilian population beginning in 2002 (Özerdem, 2016, p. 134).

The evolving nature of humanitarian crises, coupled with increasingly difficult global challenges, has compelled humanitarian organizations to become more bureaucratic and professionalized (Barnett, 2005, p. 725). Over the last quarter century, the humanitarian ecosystem has seen significant infrastructural improvements, including the implementation of higher standards, more robust codes of conduct, evidence-based programs, and more sophisticated metrics for measuring effectiveness (Barnett, 2017, p. 328). Yet, this same centralization has resulted in there being a greater distance between donors and recipients. Surveys conducted with disaster victims emphasize that aid organizations are so out of touch with afflicted populations that they are completely unaware of their day-to-day realities and needs (Barnett and Walker, 2015, p. 134). When responding to a disaster, humanitarian organizations must go the extra mile to properly document and report their activities to sponsors. If, for instance, a speedboat is necessary to deliver aid in the event of flooding, field workers must consider donors' sensitivities and ensure that they have not imposed a ban on purchasing one (Barnett, 2005). In short, although reforms seeking to foster closer coordination and more stringent regulations within the humanitarian aid system have succeeded in centralizing efforts under a defined hierarchy, they have not been without their pitfalls. While these measures have compelled agencies to implement more robust standards, they have simultaneously caused aid workers to prioritize the sensitivities of large donor states over the needs of beneficiaries (Barnett and Walker, 2015, p. 137). Disaster-stricken people need more than a blanket to keep their bodies warm; they need to be embraced by real human compassion. Though humanitarian organizations are formal structures, they should also demonstrate to those seeking assistance that their activities are grounded in love, compassion, and empathy.

One of the most critical needs of the humanitarian world is the training of skilled professionals. Amateurs, volunteers, and locals, though well intentioned, can unwittingly cause more harm than good. Highly trained professionals are needed at all levels, from managing minor disasters in small villages to global governance. The growing demand for certification in the humanitarian sector has likewise prompted Western countries to develop graduate programs to train supply chain specialists, project managers, coordinators, monitoring and evaluation specialists, and security experts. Ultimately, it has become increasingly important to develop strategies that address the requirements of the field and that enhance the overall effectiveness of the humanitarian ecosystem (Barnett and Walker, 2015).

Conclusion

The increasing frequency and severity of humanitarian crises over the past fifty years highlight the need for fundamental changes to be made to the aid system. The UN, OECD, and other Western organizations have faced growing criticism for their lackluster responses to disasters. All elements of the system require comprehensive reform and reintegration so that it may be transformed into a symbiotic ecosystem capable of responding to the evolving needs of modern crises. International bodies, NGOs, and donors demand traditional arrangements for coordination and an efficient governance structure rooted in interactor cooperation, thereby mirroring the dynamics of a real, biological ecosystem. This governance must prioritize accountability, close ties with local actors, and sustainable partnerships. Poor planning, the absence of standards, conflicting interests, incongruous working methods, cumbersomeness, and criticism surrounding UN funding for humanitarian aid should all be addressed while reorganizing the system.

The growing importance of non-state actors and networks represents one of the major transformations of recent years. Social media, mobile communications, sports and youth networks, religious communities, and philosophical groups have demonstrated their effectiveness in helping diplomats solve existing and potential problems. Likewise, the experience and knowhow of different sectors can be leveraged to diversify communication and negotiation strategies. Systemic arrangements, the use of new technologies, the participation of national and international actors, and a common vernacular will help humanitarian actors develop solutions to problems. Humanitarian organizations should adopt a holistic approach to humanitarian innovation that draws on ecosystem, systems management, and private sector to foster systemic adaptation and recovery (Betts and Bloom, 2014, p. 5).

Actors, their positions, functions and activities, and value judgments are constantly changing at the global level. The growing importance of private-sector and civil-society actors in humanitarian aid activities has increased their influence in the logistics of delivering humanitarian aid. This had led some to rightfully question whether they are indeed able to act as effective humanitarian diplomacy actors. To establish a more inclusive and effective humanitarian aid system, aid agencies must rethink their *modus operandi* and mindsets.

This transformation will therefore require aid agencies to completely restructure their operations to effectively respond to new duties and responsibilities. Beyond this, aid agencies must advocate for these changes to be adopted globally so as to facilitate large-scale and multilateral humanitarian initiatives, something that can be expedited by a mutual sharing of knowledge and experiences across various venues and networks.

References

ALNAP. (2018). *The state of the humanitarian system.* ALNAP Study. ALNAP/ODI.

Aslan, H. K. & Durmuş, K. T. (2021). *Arap ayaklanmalarının politik ekonomisi: Mısır ve Tunus örnekleri.* ORSAM Rapor, No: 29. https://www.orsam.org.tr/d_hbanaliz/arap-ayaklanmalarinin-politik-ekonomisi-misir-ve-tunus-ornekleri.pdf

Aslan, H. K. (2022). Körfez bölgesinde emek göçü dinamikleri. *Ortadoğu Analiz 13,* (109), 34–37.

Ayeb-Karlsson, S. et al. (2019). I will not go, I can not go: Cultural and social limitations of disaster preparedness in Asia, Africa, and Oceania. *Disasters, 43*(4), 752–770.

Barnett, M. (2005). Humanitarianism Transformed. *Perspectives on Politics, 3* (4), 723–740.

Barnett, M. (2017). Introduction. In Barnett, M. *Paternalism beyond borders.* Cambridge University Press. https://doi.org/10.1177/1464993418786399

Barnett, M. & Walker, P. (2015). Regime change for humanitarian aid. *Foreign Affairs, 94*(4), 130–141.

Berridge, G. R. (2015). *Diplomacy: Theory and practice* (5th ed.). Palgrave Macmillan.

Betts, A. & Bloom, L. (2014). *Humanitarian innovation: The state of the art.* UN OCHA.

Binder, A., Meier, C. & Steets, J. (2010). *Humanitarian assistance: Truly universal. A mapping study of non-Western donors.* Global Public Policy Institute, Research Paper, no: 12. https://www.gppi.net/media/Binder_Meier_Steets_2010_Truly_Universal_-_Mapping_Study._GPPi_RP_12.pdf

Bull, H., & Watson, A. (1984). The expansion of International Society. *Foreign Affairs, 63*, 411.

Cook, A. D. (2021). Humanitarian diplomacy in ASEAN. *Asian Journal of Comparative Politics, 6*(3), 188–201.

Çalışkan Ciğer, S. (2016). *DWW's humanitarian space in Turkish foreign policy* [Unpublished master's thesis. Sabancı Üniversitesi].

Development Initiatives. (2021). *Global humanitarian assistance 2021.* https://devinit.org/resources/global-humanitarian-assistance-report-2021/

Dijkzeul, D. & Sandvik, K. B. (2019). A world in turmoil: Governing risk, establishing order in humanitarian crises. *Disasters, 43*(2), 85–108.

Heyse, L. (2016). *Choosing the lesser evil: Understanding decision making in humanitarian aid NGOs.* Routledge.

IHH. (2018). *Istanbul Humanitarian Diplomacy Roundtable Report – June 2018.* Proffessional Roundtable: The Emerging Concept of Humanitarian Diplomacy and its conduct within the Syria Crisis (The Roundtable was conducted under Chattham House rules) - 8 May 2018, Eresin Otel.

IASC. (2023). *Inter-Agency Standing Committee.* https://interagencystandingcommittee.org/

Kemp-Spies, Y. (2019). *Global diplomacy and international society/ global south perspectives on diplomacy.* Palgrave.

Kınık, K. & Aslan, H. K., (2020). İnsani Diplomasi. In Usul, A. R., & Yaylacı, İ. (Eds.), *Dönüşen diplomasi ve Türkiye* (pp. 353–393). Küre Yayınları.

Kunz, N. & Reiner, G. (2012). A meta-analysis of humanitarian logistics research. *Journal of Humanitarian Logistics and Supply Chain Management,* 116–147. Doi: 10.1108/20426741211260723

Lewis, D., Kanji, N. & Themudo, N. S. (2021). *Non-governmental organizations and development*. Routledge.

Matyas, D. & Pelling, M. (2015). Positioning resilience for 2015: The role of resistance, incremental adjustment and transformation in disaster risk management policy. *Disasters, 39*(1), 1–18

McAuliffe, M. & Triandafyllidou, A. (Eds.). (2021). *World migration report 2022.* International Organization for Migration.

McClory, J. & Harvey, O. (2016). The Soft Power 30: Getting to Grips with the Measurement Challenge. *Global Affairs, 2*(3), 309–319. https://doi.org/10.1080/23340460.2016.1239379

Minear, L. & Smith, H. (Eds.). (2007). *Humanitarian diplomacy: Practitioners and their craft.* United Nations University Press.

Nye, J. S. (2011). *The future of power.* Public Affairs.

Obaze, Y. (2019). The transformative community-based humanitarian service ecosystem. *Journal of Humanitarian Logistics and Supply Chain Management, 9*(3), 410–437.

Oloruntoba, R. & Kovács, G. (2015). A commentary on agility in humanitarian aid supply chains. *Supply Chain Management: An International Journal, 20*(6), 708–716.

Olsson, P., Carl, F. & Berkes, F. (2004). Adaptive comanagement for building resilience in social–ecological systems. *Environmental Management, 34*(1), 75–90.

Özerdem, A. (2016). İnsaniyetçilik ve Türk dış politikası. *Uluslararası İlişkiler Dergisi, 13*(52), 129–149.

Parlar-Dal, E. (Ed.). (2018). *Middle powers in global governance: The rise of Turkey.* Springer.

Régnier, P. (2011). The emerging concept of humanitarian diplomacy: Identification of a community of practice and prospects for international recognition. *International Review of the Red Cross, 93*(884), 1211–1237. https://doi.org/10.1017/S1816383112000574

Rush, H., Marshall, N., Hoffman, K. & Gray, B. (2014). *Innovation management, innovation ecosystems and humanitarian innovation* (pp. 1–42). Literature Review for the Humanitarian Innovation Ecosystem Research Project.

Rousseau, E. & Pende, A.S. (2020). Humanitarian diplomacy. In *Global Diplomacy*, 253–266. Doi:10.1007/978-3-030-28786-3_18.

Rush, H., Marshall, N., Bessant, J. & Ramalingam, B. (2021, April). Applying an ecosystems approach to humanitarian innovation. *Technological Forecasting and Social Change, 165*, 120529. https://doi.org/10.1016/j.techfore.2020.120529

Seib, P. (2016). *The future of diplomacy.* Polity Press.

Slim, H. (2019). Humanitarian diplomacy: The ICRC's neutral and impartial advocacy in armed conflicts. *Ethics and International Affairs, 33*(1), 67–77.

UN OCHA. (2021). Connecting business initiative. In *Engagement with the private sector*. https://www.unocha.org/es/themes/engagement-private-sector

Union of International Associations. (2021). *Yearbook of International Organizations 2021-2022, Volumes 1A & 1B (SET).* Brill.

Walz, J. & Ramachandran, V. (2011). *Brave new world: A literature review of emerging donors and the changing nature of foreign assistance.* Center for Global Development Working Paper 273. https://www.cgdev.org/sites/default/files/1425691_file_Walz_Ramachandran_Brave_New_World_FINAL.pdf

Weiss, T. G. (2016). *Humanitarian intervention.* Polity Press.

7 ICRC in the field of Humanitarian Diplomacy

Tore Svenning

Introduction

The International Committee of the Red Cross (ICRC) is itself an organization whose foundation is based on humanitarian diplomacy. The ICRC's core mandate[1] requires the organization to work closely with government agencies, both military and civilian. One important element expediting the implementation of its mandates in real time the ICRC's efforts to persuade governments and other armed entities to adhere to their commitment to conduct military operations in accordance with international law.

This largely resembles the definition put forward by the International Federation of Red Cross and Red Crescent Societies (IFRC), which describes humanitarian diplomacy (HD) as persuading decision makers and opinion leaders to act, at all times, in the interests of the vulnerable people, and with full respect for fundamental humanitarian principles (IFRC, 2017). In other words, HD—regardless of the term used to refer to it—is central to ICRC's work.

This chapter will present an overview of the myriad venues in which the ICRC engages in HD. While I shall provide several illustrative examples under each heading, I must admit that neither is it possible, given how rapidly changing nature of the world, to cover every aspect of HD nor is it my aim to do so. For those of a more analytical penchant, an article by Marion Harroff-Tavel, "The Humanitarian Diplomacy of the International Committee of the Red Cross," should suffice as a proper introduction (Tavel, 2005).

Humanitarian Diplomacy—The Term

HD is a relatively new term, one which may have been used in various—sometimes ironic—meanings for the past few decades. As a result, a universally agreed-upon definition for HD has hitherto remained elusive. However, with the adoption of IFRC's policy for the field, the creation of a formal academic training course, and the wider adoption of this definition by other institutions, the degree of ambiguity has been largely abated (Diplo Foundation, 2021). One example of this is how the Norwegian research body Christian Michelsen's Institute uses this

DOI: 10.4324/9781003503187-7

same definition in the article "Humanitarian Diplomacy: A New Research Agenda" without indicating its source (Lauri, 2018 p. 4) Perhaps this is a sign that IFRC's definition is rapidly on its way to gaining universal acceptance.

Henry Dunant at Solferino—Humanitarian action followed by HD

The story is well told by Henry Dunant himself in his book *A Memory of Solferino* published in 1862 (Dunant, 1862). In it, he recounts how he, a businessman, had ventured to Solferino to appeal to the French emperor Napoléon III to acquire certain land and water rights in land that he had been granted in Algeria. At the time, France was at war with Austria, her army stationed in Lombardy, and Napoléon III had established his headquarters at Solferino. As such, this is where Dunant arrived, in the evening of 24 June 1859, bearing witness to the immediate aftermath of the battle.

> **Henry Dunant's efforts to persuade political and military figures to act for the benefit of vulnerable people, followed by his convening of the Geneva platform, are among the first and most striking examples of humanitarian diplomacy.**

What he found was thousands of wounded, dying, and dead men, with little attempt to provide even the most basic of care to those who had survived. In response, Dunant rallied the civilian population, particularly women and girls, to provide relief. He purchased the necessary materials and constructed improvised hospitals. One of his first acts of HD occurred in this context: He persuaded the French to release the Austrian doctors they had captured so that they could put their skills and knowledge to use in the relief effort. Three years later, after Dunant had written and published his book at his own expense, he mailed it to leading political and military figures that he judged might be interested in his idea of a neutral organization charged with caring for wounded soldiers. Dunant's attempt to persuade political and military figures to aid vulnerable individuals and his convening the representatives of countries from around the world in Geneva are, in addition to constituting crucial turning points in the history of humanitarianism, striking examples of HD.

Dunant's call and aforementioned efforts propelled the Geneva Society for Public Welfare to pursue the establishment of a neutral organization for wounded soldiers. A committee created to this end met on 17 February 1863, a date later commemorated as the ICRC's founding date. Working at remarkable speed, this committee managed to convene a meeting with representatives of fourteen states in October of the same year, leading, one year later, the Swiss authorities to organize a diplomatic conference where the First Geneva Convention would be adopted. Therefore, both the ICRC and wider Red Movement were born out of such kind of a HD action.

On the other hand, an interesting article on the ICRC's website traces HD even further back, describing the work of the seventeenth-century Catholic priest Vincent de Paul. It is outside the scope of this article to spend much space on him, but a limited quote may serve as an illustration:

> *Humanitarian Diplomacy*
> *Major political events shaped the environment in which Vincent de Paul worked, in a period marked by clashes of ideology and religious wars. Faced with the disintegration of a weakened political power, a strongly divided Royal Court, an anomic society full of all forms of misery, he chose to commit himself to charitable work with an underlying political motive—"to soften the impact of the military occupation, to position France as the saviour, and to win the hearts and minds of the people [...]."*
> *His vision of humanitarianism was closely correlated with a mediation role aimed at curbing the conflict that prevailed and shaping a space for constructive discussion. For instance, in 1640 he asked for an audience with Cardinal Richelieu to convince him of the imperative need to restore peace in France. In 1649, he took a similar approach with Queen Anne of Austria (the spouse of Louis XIII) and Cardinal Jules Mazarin (the King's chief minister). He continually called for moderation in the treatment of Protestants, his efforts guided by a desire for impartiality and reconciliation.*
>
> (Irbah, 2019)

As this anecdote makes clear, the practice of HD has deep historical roots; what is new is the actual coinage of the term itself.

Humanitarian Diplomats: Specialists and Generalists

The ICRC's work, whose establishment and presence in the field of HD we mentioned above, is very wide-ranging, not only geographically and temporally but also thematically and in terms of technical specializations involved. The ICRC has been involved, as its mandate requires, in nearly all conflicts after the Second World War with both short-term and longer-term interventions and measures. Their efforts include everything from the provision of educational materials to highly specialized medical assistance and from the delivery of water and sanitation equipment to the identification of war victims. They advise on legal matters—both what the law *is* in situations of armed conflict and how it *ought* to be understood and, on occasion, constructed.

Based on the definition of humanitarian diplomacy and the function of delegates within the organization, it can be said that ICRC delegates in the field act as humanitarian diplomats due to the negotiations they conduct.

To conduct all of these tasks with the same effectiveness, the ICRC employs a wide array of specialists who, while perhaps spending most of their time on their technical duties, sometimes interact with government officials and other authority figures and thus need to be prepared to engage in minimal forms of HD. Explicit HD, however, is more often carried out by generalists in the ICRC's Geneva headquarters, in delegations in the field, in the offices of international organizations of interest, and in capitals of especially important countries.

Although those involved in HD have very different working days depending on their specific location, a delegate in the ICRC context refers, at least for recruitment purposes, to the staff in various parts of the world who, on the one hand, contribute to the mandate and mission of the institution and who, on the other, offer protection and assistance to vulnerable individuals, such as victims of armed conflict and violence. Delegates' responsibilities vary based on their position and can evolve rapidly as changing operational needs on the ground dictate (ICRC, 2017).

It would, given these inherent complexities, be advantageous to survey the functions that delegates are expected to fulfill. Delegates, first and foremost, contribute to the analysis of the general situation and the identification of humanitarian needs. They coordinate closely with relevant ICRC branches to provide economic stability, health services, and protection while simultaneously taking part in the defining, planning, and implementation of ICRC projects that fall within their specific sphere of responsibility. Moreover, delegates handle crucial tasks that, when managed correctly, help expand the delegation's contact pool and ability to network with those involved in the penitentiary system, thereby allowing them to follow up on the status of detainees and offer them assistance, whether legal or otherwise, during any trials, appeals, or detention while also respecting their rights to confidentiality. By virtue of the aforementioned and myriad other roles stated in official ICRC documents, delegates represent and promote the ICRC mandate and its activities (Troyon and Palmieri, 2007). For a more thorough look at what a delegate is, I recommend that readers read Troyon and Palmieri's 2007 article "The ICRC delegate: an exceptional humanitarian player?" and the transcript of Koichi Oi's interview "International humanitarian law: There's theory – and then there's practice" (ICRC, n.d.), both of which may be found on the ICRC's website. Depending on how one defines HD and places the function within an organization, the ICRC's delegates in the field, insofar as they follow negotiations, may very well be regarded as humanitarian diplomats.

Where the ICRC's HD Takes Place

While an element of persuasion is present in virtually all contacts and communications, thereby making HD a universal endeavor, my immediate focus is the deliberate use of persuasion in more clearly defined locations. What follows is not an exhaustive list, but one of examples, accompanied by selected topics and methods to help illuminate the point.

The ICRC in the Field

All Red Cross and Red Crescent units are "in the field" in the sense that they are active in locations in which vulnerable populations or people in need are found. Serving such individuals is, in essence, the *raison d'être* of every Red Society. Given the ICRC's mandate, this frequently entails working in live conflict zones, often in the midst of or, at the very least, in close proximity to ongoing hostilities. Conflicts give rise to a wide array of needs, as wounded people require varying degrees of care. On the wider scale, conflicts cause suffering among civilians caught in the crossfire of warring parties: Farmers find themselves unable to tend to their fields, roads to village and markets are rendered too risky to travel, and access to hospitals is largely impeded. The ICRC exerts considerable energy and resources to reach such populations.

Albeit trivial, one of the problems with powerful people is that they have power. To provide assistance to the victims of war, the ICRC needs the permission, at least tacitly, of the men holding the guns to do so. This means that the ICRC maintains open channels with the warring parties out of necessity to communicate, educate, and negotiate with them. While this sometimes means that highly specialized personnel are involved, negotiations much more often take place at a fairly low level, such as, for instance, when the leader of a small relief convoy seeking permission to cross a local checkpoint. This implies the need for personnel with knowledge, experience, training, and an amenable attitude—one of polite respect for the other, even when everything the other stands for is repugnant. Such people do simply not wander into an organization from off the streets; they are molded through training, culture, mentoring, and experience.

With Armed Forces

The term *dissemination* is closely associated with the version of HD in which the ICRC and many national societies engage while dealing with military forces and other armed groups. While nothing can make war a safe or pleasant experience, there are, as the ICRC and others are well aware, rules governing how hostilities may be conducted. The first step toward compliance with such rules is, naturally, being aware of them.

That is why the ICRC actively seeks contact with the armed forces of the world, to help educate officers and soldiers in the basics of International Humanitarian Law (IHL). In an ideal world, those manning the checkpoint mentioned above would have already been well abreast of the existence of the laws of war, acquainted with the ICRC and its role, and receptive to the idea of allowing a relief convoy to pass unhindered. In the less-than-perfect world that most inhabit, this is seldom the case. Still, as a result of earlier dissemination, someone up the chain of command does know, and is willing to be persuaded to allow the convoy to go ahead in the interest of vulnerable people, confident that the fundamental principles will be observed.

In Capital Cities

The ICRC is present in several capital cities of countries where it maintains limited operational activities because—and although this varies—the country is, in and of itself, important on the world stage. The more important of these include Beijing, London, Moscow, Paris, and Washington DC, though the ICRC is present in several other important countries not included here for reasons of space.

ICRC's direct access to influential figures is crucial in securing support for neutral, independent, and impartial humanitarian action.

Beijing

The capital of the People's Republic of China, Beijing, hosts the ICRC's Regional Delegation for East Asia, which covers, apart from China herself, the Democratic People's Republic of Korea (North Korea/DPRK), the Republic of Korea (South Korea/ROK), and Mongolia.

This delegation's focus, aim, and approach to humanitarian issues clearly identify the role it plays in relation to HD. The delegation seeks to promote awareness about IHL, to encourage its implementation, and to maintain a legal framework to minimize human suffering caused by war. The delegation's rapport with HD is visible in its efforts to familiarize governments, experts, National Red Cross Societies, and civil society with the ICRC's humanitarian work and emergency response initiatives around the world. In addition in this geography, in both China and the DPRK, the ICRC and National Red Cross Societies collaborate in physical rehabilitation projects geared to vulnerable groups (ICRC, 2018).

Separately, the delegation has set out its main areas of activity in a leaflet that can be summarized into six groups:

1 Domestic implementation of IHL through dialogue with national governments.
2 IHL integration by the armed forces—supporting IHL in military doctrine, education, training, weapons review, and sanctions systems.
3 Teaching of and research into IHL at universities.
4 A humanitarian education program tailored to young people aged 13–18 and carried out in cooperation with the Red Cross of China and her Ministry of Education.
5 Dialogue on humanitarian issues with authorities and think tanks—both civilian and military. Here the delegation maintains contact with numerous think tanks and other similar institutions. Giving particular importance to the protection of and provision of assistance to vulnerable individuals, the ICRC delegation is actively engaged in consultation and the exchange of ideas with stakeholders in such evolving conflict environments.

6 Cooperating with the International Red Cross and Red Crescent Movement partners to strengthen the humanitarian voice and advance a common vision. The ICRC cooperates with National Societies and helps build their capacity to, among other things, promote the principles underpinning humanitarian action. (ICRC, 2018).

In other words, while the ICRC surely does more and has other tasks than outlined here, the Beijing delegation has laid out a roadmap in which each element may be regarded as a unique form of HD encompassed by the definition put forward in this chapter. In addition to these activities, I should note that most renowned international organizations are present in Beijing, and some others, such as the Shanghai Cooperation Organization, are even headquartered in China. Taken together with the numerous nations represented in Beijing, the city offers rich opportunities for diplomatic activities, including that of the humanitarian sort.

London

"Why does the International Committee of the Red Cross need an office in London?" asked the ICRC in 2013, after which this question received an answer from the highest echelon—from then-president of ICRC, Dr. Peter Maurer (Maurer, 2014). In a separate Q&A paper, the ICRC describes a portion of their rationale for residing in London and gives a brief descriptions of the activities in which they are part (ICRC, 2018a).

The main reason for the presence, states said paper, is the strong voice of the United Kingdom (UK) in international affairs, not least through the permanent seat at the UN Security Council. It is absolutely integral that the ICRC have direct access to those with influence in order to build support for neutral, independent, and impartial humanitarian action.

The paper cites two additional reasons for the ICRC being in London. The city is a significant media hub, thus making it possible to connect with organizations with the ability to broadcast information across the word. Furthermore, the UK and the Republic of Ireland host a wide variety of organizations, think tanks, and internationally oriented academic institutions able to enrich the debate on humanitarian needs in light of the ever-changing nature of crises and conflicts.

In addition to allowing the organization to maintain ties with the Government of the UK, London offers the ICRC the ability to network with other international organizations present or headquartered there. Three of these are of particular interest: Amnesty International, the International Maritime Organization, and the Commonwealth of Nations. Of these, the Commonwealth offers the ICRC a venue in which it may dialogue with a host of countries from around the world should the need arise. Amnesty International is, like the ICRC, involved in its own humanitarian activities. While the International Maritime Organization, a UN agency, is not a humanitarian organization per se, commercial vessels find themselves engaging in humanitarian action at previously unseen rates as migrant flows become increasingly seaborne. Finally, by being present in London, the ICRC is in a position to maintain close, ongoing dialogue with the British and Irish Red Cross Societies—two invaluable facilities for all concerned.

Moscow

In brief, the ICRC Moscow delegation not only discusses humanitarian- and IHL-related issues with the Russian government but also supports the Red Cross Societies of the Russian Federation, Belarus, and Moldova. Present in Moscow since 2005, the ICRC has undergone compositional and operational changes over the course of Russia's history, meaning that the nature and composition of ICRC activities have likewise changed to reflect new realities on the ground.

One particular description, though a few years old as of the writing of this chapter, paints a reasonable picture of the ICRC's key concerns and priorities. Russia's fundamental role in both humanitarian affairs and the implementation of IHL at the regional and international levels is underlined in the aforementioned description. The ICRC cooperates with various stakeholders within the region in humanitarian affairs, such as ministries of foreign affairs, justice, and emergency response, as well as with regional organizations like the Commonwealth of Independent States (CIS), the Inter-Parliamentary Assembly (IPA), the Secretariat of the Council of Defense Ministers of the CIS, and the Collective Security Treaty Organization. In addition to these stakeholders, the ICRC maintains ties with the Russian academic community, thereby allowing it to devise talking points on both IHL-related topics and the promotion of international law.

In addition to Russia-focused work, Moscow serves as a springboard that, by providing advice, assistance, and venues for dialogue across most of the former Soviet Union, supports successor states' national societies. Moscow enjoys relations with a large number of nations, meaning that, as a result, the city boasts a rich diplomatic life that includes representatives from most UN organizations and agencies of interest from a humanitarian standpoint. Moreover, Moscow—and indeed Russia—is home to numerous academic institutions, universities, think tanks, and research institutes that afford both the ICRC and the wider humanitarian community opportunities for collaboration and exchange on issues of interest.

The ICRC engages with the Russian authorities at all echelons, including the highest, such as when then-ICRC President, Dr. Peter Maurer visited Moscow in November 2020 to meet with the Russian Minister of Foreign Affairs, Sergey Lavrov (ICRC, 2020a). Preparations for such a meeting are a major diplomatic undertaking that must have involved significant numbers of ICRC staff in Moscow, Geneva, and elsewhere before these two men met and talked with one another about humanitarian issues within Russia, armed conflict outside of Russia, COVID-19, and the importance of IHL.

Paris

Like London and Moscow, Paris is the capital of a country with a permanent seat on the UN Security Council and, hence, of importance to the ICRC and its mandate. An essential HD actor, the ICRC delegation in France maintains communications with the French government, military, and diplomatic officials to promote IHL and to facilitate the ICRC's humanitarian operations. As a member of the Security Council and a prominent figure in international relations, France is an important arena for those seeking to promote humanitarian business. The ICRC's Paris delegation therefore matters tremendously for humanitarian affairs (ICRC, 2010).

France is, of course, a major world power with considerable influence on humanitarian matters like those undertaken by the ICRC and the wider movement. Apart from France's position in the UN, Paris hosts several international organizations of interest to the ICRC.

One such is the United Nations Educational, Scientific and Cultural Organization (UNESCO), with whom ICRC signed a partnership agreement in 2016 that paved the way for the two organizations to undertake joint projects seeking to enhance the protection of cultural heritage sites during armed conflicts (UNESCO, 2016). A similar agreement was signed with the Blue Shield, an NGO pursuing similar goals (ICRC, 2020c). The following link refers to the ICRC's webpage on the protection of cultural property in armed conflict, including to the aforementioned 2016 agreement signed with UNESCO. While protecting cultural heritage sites has not always ranked high on most humanitarians' list of priorities, these agreements are indeed an expression of ICRC-led HD that simultaneously showcase successful examples of negotiations and persuasion (ICRC, 2016).

Washington DC

The ICRC has maintained a presence in Washington DC since the mid-1990s. One description of the office from a few years ago, though still on the ICRC website, reads as follows:

> *Established in 1995, the Washington regional delegation engages in a regular dialogue on IHL and issues of humanitarian concern with government officials and bodies, academic institutions and other interested groups in Canada and the United States of America. The delegation heightens awareness of the ICRC's mandate and priorities within the OAS [i.e., Organization of American States]. It mobilizes political and financial support for ICRC activities and secures support for IHL implementation. It visits people held at the US internment facility at Guantanamo Bay Naval Station in Cuba. It works closely with the American Red Cross and the Canadian Red Cross Society.*

(Refworld, 2015)

The context of the ICRC's work in Washington DC, the access the organization needs to American political, judicial, and military institutions as well as the large diplomatic community affiliated with embassies and other organizations make DC a major operational and diplomatic hub for Americas and beyond. The ICRC's 2020 annual report for the Americas mentions several significant areas of work during the year (ICRC, 2020b). One of these areas was the following up of detainees in Guantanamo Bay. The ICRC made visits, which were sometimes converted to video-calls that year because of the ongoing pandemic, both to the facility and to many other locations where people caught up in armed conflict had been detained, maintaining a running dialogue with relevant authorities. The delegation also communicates more broadly with American and Canadian authorities on conflict-related humanitarian issues, especially those relating to situations where military personnel from these two countries are involved.

The year 2020 saw continuing efforts to address migration-related issues, partly through keeping authorities abreast of their field observations, persuading them to design responses to the pandemic that take into account migrants' need for protection, seeking to improve responses to missing migrants, and discussing the possibility of gaining access to immigration detentions facilities.

Other lines of activity included coordinated projects with two national societies, the organization of several IHL awareness-building programs, and fundraisers for the Movement's activities. The ICRC worked with the American Red Cross to broker the implementation of the Safer Access Framework. These two organizations continued to explore areas for cooperation, including fundraising, digital innovation, and the Health Care in Danger initiative. Similarly, the Canadian Red Cross and the ICRC conducted joint initiatives to improve healthcare provision in environments affected by ongoing or previous armed conflicts.

Humanitarian Diplomacy at Global Fora

International Conferences of the Red Cross and Red Crescent

While several other conferences contend with the quadrennial International Conferences of the Red Cross and Red Crescent to be dubbed the most important humanitarian forum in the world, its significance is unrivalled within the Red Cross and Red Crescent Movement. The movement's statutes define the International Conference as follows:

SECTION III: STATUTORY BODIES

The International Conference of the Red Cross and Red Crescent

ARTICLE 8

Definition

The International Conference is the supreme deliberative body for the Movement. At the International Conference, representatives of the

components of the Movement meet with representatives of the States Parties to the Geneva Conventions, the latter in exercise of their responsibilities under those Conventions and in support of the overall work of the Movement in terms of Article 2. Together they examine and decide upon humanitarian matters of common interest and any other related matter.

(25th International Conference of the Red Cross, 1986, p. 13)

The International Conference touches upon all elements of HD emphasized by the IFRC. Decision-makers and their representatives are addressed, all issues brought up are humanitarian in nature, the interests of the most vulnerable are prioritized, persuasion is at the core of plenary and drafting committees, in meetings over coffee, and in venues' myriad corridors. Moreover, the framework informing all of these is predicated on adherence to the Fundamental Principles.

While this is not the place to offer a comprehensive review of the International Conference, a brief survey of the decisions reached during the early conferences showcases how core humanitarian and practical issues have been pursued by the ICRC since its inception. The 1869 conference in Berlin, for instance, articulated the desire for material donations to be thoroughly inspected to determine how national societies can put them to use in times of war whereas the 1887 conference in Karlsruhe dealt with the dissemination of both the IHL and Geneva Conventions. Similarly, the Congress of Peace in Geneva meeting in 1889–90 asserted that cooperating with women was indispensable for Red Cross work.

Soon thereafter in 1892, nations met in Rome to discuss expanding the protections afforded by the Geneva Conventions to cover maritime conflicts. Then in 1902, they gathered in Saint Petersburg, where they debated the perennial question concerning the implementation of resolutions reached at the International Conference.

Statutes, operational issues, law, the Movement's principles, and intra-ICRC relations have long been debated in these conferences, with the ICRC being the dominant actor until the creation of the League (the precursor to the IFRC). Still, even following the creation of this body, the ICRC has continued to set much of the tone and agenda.

The most recent—at least at the time of writing this chapter—Geneva Conference held in 2019 was no exception. During this conference members adopted a series of resolutions on (*i*) the implementation of IHL at the national level, (*ii*) the mental health of people affected by armed conflict, disasters, and other emergencies, (*iii*) actions to be taken during epidemics and pandemics, (*iv*) restoring family links, (*v*) women and leadership in the movement, and (*vi*) disaster law, which stipulates that no one is to be left behind (33rd International Conference of the Red Cross and Red Crescent, 2019). Each of these resolutions—all of which share the same underlying goal of benefitting those whom the Movement was created to serve—is the fruit of engagement and negotiation with multiple nations. In preparation for the following conference scheduled for October of 2024, the ICRC has already begun talking with its contacts, conducting research and analyses, and honing its HD skills to be better able to leverage and broker agreements for vulnerable groups of people.

UN General Assembly and Subordinate Bodies

The architects of the UN envisioned that the General Assembly would act as the world's supreme deliberative forum—a purpose that it has, to a large extent, served. There are few other fora where virtually all nations may come together to discuss such a wide gamut of issues for such a long time. It is therefore of utmost importance to follow and to seek to influence debates had and decisions reached both in this body and in those subordinate to it, such as the Economic and Social Council. Decisions reached in these bodies are of great significance for constituents of the Movement and, not least, for the ICRC.

Other aspects of the General Assembly make engaging with it inevitable. This is especially true during the high-level segment held at the beginning of each conference where various heads of state gather in New York City to allow civil actors and humanitarian diplomats an informal venue to interact with them. As such, HD takes on several diverse forms in relations to the General Assembly and, in a similar vein, in other global fora. These include:

- Being present and visible to the other participants,
- Consulting with others in advance and participating in the shaping the proposals to be made,
- Intervening in debates on issues deemed important,
- Sharing and gathering information,
- Following up and reporting, and
- Looking forward to the next round.

For a flavor of the formal debates in the UN, an example is the ICRC's statement in the Sixth Committee on Item 83, "Status of the Protocols additional to the Geneva Conventions of 1949 and relating to the protection of victims of armed conflicts" (ICRC, 2020e). The statement links the agenda item to the COVID-19 pandemic, to the increased needs it has given rise to, and to those caught in the crossfire of armed conflict. The ICRC then went on to report on what steps it had taken toward the implementation of and the garnering of support for the instruments in question before addressing Resolution 1 of the previous year's International Conference, "Bringing IHL Home."

Further on, the ICRC congratulated nations that had created national IHL committees as well as the fifty nations that had ratified the Treaty on the Prohibition of Nuclear Weapons, thus achieving the requisite number of ratifications to enter into force on 22 January of the following year. The ICRC will continue to work toward convincing as many nations as possible to adhere to the treaty (ICRC, 2020e). Finally, the ICRC proclaimed that it had continued to revise the Commentary on the 1949 Conventions, before concluding by drawing attention to the advisory services it offers on IHL.

UN Security Council

The Security Council is different from all other UN bodies; it is the only one to have permanent members and the only body able to make decisions binding upon member states (Wikipedia, n.d.-a, n.d.-b).

Other

The ICRC engages in HD in, among other venues, global fora, specialized agencies, regional bodies, international institutions of law, and the headquarters of military alliances. The list is too long to put here. While the subjects and objectives of HD vary from one setting to another, the methods and approaches suggested above remain similar, albeit with slight variations depending on the setting, culture, and nature of the institution in question.

Specialized agencies—a term most often applied to organizations comprising the UN family—are numerous, more so than one might initially assume. The UN itself lists six *funds and programs*, fifteen *specialized agencies*, nine *other entities and bodies*, and seven *related organizations*—ample evidence that the UN is less a result of deliberate design and more a patchwork organization cobbled together piecemeal (UN). The Universal Postal Union and UN Women are not considered entirely natural bedfellows—perhaps with the exception of lady philatelists.

While the term *regional organization* lacks a universally accepted definition, most onlookers can intuit what it might refer to upon first glance. This explains why Wikipedia maintains a list of forty-five so-called regional organizations ranging from the Association of Eastern Caribbean States with a combined population of 615,000 to the Asia Cooperation Dialogue with 4.5 billion (Wikipedia, n.d.-a). A particularly salient example of a regional organization with which the ICRC collaborates extensively with other entities of interest is the African Union (AU), headquartered in Addis Ababa, the capital of Ethiopia. In fact, the Federal Democratic Republic of Ethiopia, to use the country's full official name, hosts several institutions of interest to the ICRC. A useful list of international organizations present there—including the ICRC—can be found in Ethiopia's business directory (List of regional organizations by population, n.d.).

Of those international organizations and institutions, the most important one—and the reason for the presence of many others—is the AU. Established in 2002, the AU was largely built upon the structures of its predecessor, the Organization of African Unity. That said, however, the AU is by no means a clone of its forebear, as it did abolish certain moribund aspects of it. The Constitutive Act of the Union articulates the purpose, structure, operating principles, and other aspects necessary for it to function effectively as an international organization. Article 3 of this act, for instance, outlines the AU's objectives in fourteen points, one of which being to "(f) promote peace, security, and stability on the continent" (African Union, n.d.). While an institution that comprises most of the governments of Africa is indeed important enough, both as an actor and a forum, to be of interest to the ICRC in and of itself, this specific objective places AU close to the center of the ICRC's core concerns. This is why the ICRC has for years maintained a delegation in Addis Ababa specifically for the AU in addition to and separate from its operational office in Ethiopia. The ICRC describes said delegation as follows:

> *The ICRC delegation to the AU, based in Addis Ababa, works with the AU to draw attention to humanitarian issues, promote implementation of international humanitarian law throughout Africa and raise awareness of the ICRC's role and activities on the continent. Under the cooperation agreement signed in 1992 between the ICRC and the Organization of African Unity, predecessor of the African Union, the ICRC delegation to the AU works closely with the Commission and Member States of the AU, sharing experiences and views on humanitarian consequences arising from conflict. The ICRC delegation to the AU has observer status.*

(ICRC, 2014)

Interaction with the AU occurs on many levels. As is the case with other institutions of this nature, the delegation communicates daily and exchanges information with the AU's secretariat on various issues of interest. The delegation also maintains relations with representatives of AU member states and keeps tabs on their actions in formal meetings hosted by that organization and among themselves. At one end of the spectrum, the ICRC interacts with the AU at the highest level, such as when ICRC president, Dr. Peter Maurer, visited in early 2020 to meet with AU leaders—including officials from Ethiopia—and address the African Union Peace and Security Council and the African Union Partners Group. Dr. Maurer summarized the visit as follows:

> *The visit was an opportunity to pursue our dialogue with Ethiopian authorities as well as with the AU and its specialized organs and partners, on how to better respond to humanitarian challenges in Ethiopia and on the continent, and to strengthen respect of IHL. IHL compliance and support are amongst cornerstones of global governance to which the AU is engaged. Not only can IHL contribute to stabilization, it can also contribute to development. With its long-lasting humanitarian experience and its expertise in IHL, the ICRC can make a unique contribution to the AU's regional and global governance endeavor.*

(ICRC, 2020d)

With regard to day-to-day affairs, Bruce Mokaya, head of the ICRC Delegation to the African Union (ADO), described the delegation's role in a late-2020 interview. ICRC monitors, Mokaya related, assist and protect communities in need and work to influence member states to do more for vulnerable groups, such as migrants, detainees, and internally displaced persons. Additionally, Mokaya pointed out that the ADO informs AU members of humanitarian issues and the implementation of IHL. During the interview, Mokaya emphasized ADO's role in garnering the attention of decision makers about the dangers African communities face from violence and conflict. Since the ADO negotiates and coordinates with stakeholders to advance humanitarian interests, the ICRC's rapport with AU member states constitutes a palpable example of HD (ICRC, 2020f).

Courts and Military Alliances

A number of international courts exist, many with a focus on trade and other areas of dispute with relatively weak links to the realm of humanitarian affairs. A few, however, are of direct interest to humanitarians, including the ICRC. These include the International Criminal Court, the Special Court for Sierra Leone, and the Special Tribunal for Lebanon. Courts are normally not appropriate "targets" of persuasion by diplomats, but their work contributes to the establishment of norms informing the interactions of the ICRC and others organizations in *other* contexts, including in HD, such as policy development.

Military alliances are more numerous than one would be led to believe. They vary in scope, from the somewhat minimalistic Treaty of Friendship between the Government of New Zealand and the Government of Western Samoa to the North Atlantic Treaty Organization, or NATO, as it is more often known. Military alliances are possible "targets" for ICRC's HD for the same reason that it works with individual armed forces—to embed IHL in the consciousness of those who make and carryout military decisions.

Campaigns

It can sometimes be difficult to draw a clear distinction between HD and advocacy, as the ICRC occasionally initiates public campaigns on issues they pursue more quietly through diplomacy. Examples of such ICRC-led campaigns include one initiated on Mothers' Day 2021 to help mothers in conflict zones, "Not a Target" to strengthen the protections afforded to health workers and institutions, and the campaign against landmines (ICRC, 2021).

Conclusion

For generations, HD has occupied the core of the ICRC's work. By virtue of its unwavering adherence to its foundational values and ideals, the ICRC is a reliable partner for governments and others with whom it comes into contact—one whose stances may be readily anticipated. In a world in which fluidity and volatility is the norm, this makes the ICRC a major force for the good of the most downtrodden, disenfranchised, and vulnerable among us.

Note

1   The ICRC defines itself as an independent, neutral organization whose mandate is to "ensur[e] humanitarian protection and assistance for victims of armed conflict and other situations of violence. It takes action in response to emergencies and at the same time promotes respect for international humanitarian law and its implementation in national law." ICRC. (n.d.). *Mandate and Mission.* Retrieved June 05, 2021, from https://www.icrc.org/en/who-we-are/mandate.

References

25th International Conference of the Red Cross. (1986). *Statutes of the International Red Cross and Red Crescent Movement.* https://standcom.ch/download/stat/Statutes-EN-A5.pdf

33rd International Conference of the Red Cross and Red Crescent. (2019). *9–12 December 2019 in Geneva 33rd International Conference.* https://rcrconference.org/about/33rd-international-conference/

African Union. (n.d.). *Constitutive act of the African Union.* https://au.int/sites/default/files/pages/34873-file-constitutiveact_en.pdf

Diplo Foundation. (2021). *Humanitarian diplomacy.* https://www.diplomacy.edu/course/humanitarian/

Dunant, H. (1950–1990/1862). *Un souvenir de Solférino Comité International de la Croix-Rouge.* https://www.icrc.org/fr/doc/assets/files/publications/icrc-001-0361.pdf

International Federation of Red Cross and Red Crescent Societies (IFRC). (2017). *Humanitarian diplomacy policy.* https://web.archive.org/web/20210819081229/http://www.ifrc.org/Global/Governance/Policies/Humanitarian_Diplomacy_Policy.pdf

Irbah, K. (2019). *Vincent de Paul: A groundbreaking Humanitarian.* https://blogs.icrc.org/law-and-policy/2019/08/14/vincent-de-paul-groundbreaking-humanitarian/

Lauri, A. (2018). *Humanitarian diplomacy: A new research agenda.* CMI Brief No: 04. https://www.cmi.no/publications/6536-humanitarian-diplomacy-a-new-research-agenda

Maurer, P. (2014). Speech given by Mr Peter Maurer, President of the International Committee of the Red Cross, OSCE Parliamentary Assembly. In *New security challenges and the ICRC.* https://www.oscepa.org/en/documents/autumn-meetings/2014-geneva/speeches-13/2646-speech-by-peter-maurer-president-of-the-international-committee-of-the-red-cross-5-oct-2014/file

Refworld. (2015). *Annual Report 2015 - Washington (regional).* https://www.refworld.org/reference/annualreport/icrc/2016/en/112824

Tavel, M. H. (2005). The humanitarian diplomacy of the International Committee of the Red Cross. *Relations Internationales, 121*(1), 1–16.

The International Committee of the Red Cross (ICRC). (2010). *The ICRC delegation in Paris.* https://www.icrc.org/en/doc/where-we-work/europe-central-asia/france/overview-france.htm

The International Committee of the Red Cross (ICRC). (2014). *ICRC delegation to the African Union.* https://www.icrc.org/en/document/icrc-delegation-african-union

The International Committee of the Red Cross (ICRC). (2016). *Agreement between the ICRC and UNESCO on the protection of cultural property - Q&A.* https://www.icrc.org/en/document/cultural-property-protected-in-armed-conflict

The International Committee of the Red Cross (ICRC). (2017). *Profile of an ICRC delegate - What we are looking for.* https://www.icrc.org/en/document/profile-icrc-delegate-what-we-are-looking

The International Committee of the Red Cross (ICRC). (2018). *Regional delegation for East Asia.* https://www.icrc.org/en/document/regional-delegation-for-east-asia-leaflet

The International Committee of the Red Cross (ICRC). (2018a). *UK and Ireland Q&A: What we're doing and why.* https://www.icrc.org/en/document/what-does-icrc-do-uk-and-ireland

The International Committee of the Red Cross (ICRC). (2020a). *High level humanitarian dialogue with the Russian Federation.* https://www.icrc.org/en/document/high-level-humanitarian-dialogue-russian-federation

The International Committee of the Red Cross (ICRC) (2020b). *Annual report 2020.* https://www.icrc.org/en/document/annual-report-2020

The International Committee of the Red Cross (ICRC). (2020c). *The ICRC and the Blue Shield signed a Memorandum of understanding.* https://www.icrc.org/en/document/icrc-and-blue-shield-signed-memorandum-understanding

The International Committee of the Red Cross (ICRC). (2020d). *Addis Ababa: ICRC President urges more respect of IHL by AU member states for effective "Silencing the guns in Africa by 2020".* https://www.icrc.org/en/document/addis-ababa-icrc-president-urges-more-respect-ihl-au-member-states-effective-silencing-guns

The International Committee of the Red Cross (ICRC). (2020e). *ICRC statement to 75th session of UN General Assembly, sixth committee.* https://www.icrc.org/en/document/icrc-statement-75th-session-un-general-assembly-sixth-committee

The International Committee of the Red Cross (ICRC). (2020f). *African Union: Reflections on ICRC African Union Delegation activities.* https://www.icrc.org/en/document/reflections-on-delegation-to-the-au-activities

The International Committee of the Red Cross (ICRC). (2021). *ICRC launches a new campaign to help the world's mothers caught in war.* https://www.icrc.org/en/document/icrc-help-mothers-caught-war

The International Committee of the Red Cross (ICRC). (n.d.). *Stories from field: International humanitarian law: There's theory – and then there's practice.* https://careers.icrc.org/content/Interview-with-Koichi-Oi/?locale=en_GB

Troyon, B. & Palmieri, D. (2007). *The ICRC delegate: An exceptional humanitarian player?* https://international-review.icrc.org/sites/default/files/irrc-865-5.pdf

UNESCO. (2016). *UNESCO and ICRC partner on the protection of culture heritage in the event of armed conflict.* https://whc.unesco.org/en/news/1454#:~:text=UNESCO%20Director%2DGeneral%20Irina%20Bokova,the%20event%20of%20armed%20conflict.

Wikipedia. (n.d.-a). *List of regional organizations by population.* https://en.wikipedia.org/wiki/List_of_regional_organizations_by_population

Wikipedia. (n.d.-b). *United Nations Security Council.* https://en.wikipedia.org/wiki/United_Nations_Security_Council

8 What Makes a Good Humanitarian Diplomat?

Hugo Slim

Introduction

The growth of Turkish humanitarianism has been one of the most important humanitarian developments of the last decade. British humanitarians such as myself have always regarded the Turks as world leaders in earthquake relief. The Syrian war that would shake the entire world in 2011 showed how Turkish humanitarianism rose to the occasion in its response to the greatest conflict the twenty-first century had thus far seen. Turkey's display of generosity and expertise in handling the Syrian crisis on her southern border proves that Turkish humanitarians excel in extreme crisis situations brought about by war and displacement. In 2016, the Turkish government, its diplomats, and the Turkish Red Crescent (TRC) hosted the World Humanitarian Summit (WHS). This monumental event saw Turkish humanitarian diplomacy supervising the world's largest-ever multi-stakeholder conference on humanitarian aid. As such, Turkey has achieved a humanitarian hat trick by setting new standards in disaster response, wartime emergency, and humanitarian diplomacy.

My purpose in writing this chapter is to focus on the soft skills involved in successful humanitarian diplomacy—the kind of attitudes, behaviors, and personal skills that make a good humanitarian diplomat. I embark on this journey with the recognition that an embrace of political realism is a prerequisite for engagement in humanitarian diplomacy. I then emphasize interpersonal communication like listening, sensing, talking, perspective taking, networking, relationship-building, and meeting management before moving to more conceptual skills like objective setting, framing and narrative building, and the ability to deploy evidence, experience, and expertise. In all this, I examine the importance of synthesizing emotion and reason in diplomacy and the essential role of trust and distrust. I then put forward six distinct character virtues that I believe are paramount for humanitarian diplomats to cultivate in their professional lives. While most of the attributes I shall discuss are common to all forms of diplomacy and to most other professions, a few are unique to humanitarian diplomacy. These soft skills apply equally to the operational diplomat engaged in a fast-moving humanitarian response and to the academic diplomat working on humanitarian policy leading up to and during staged

DOI: 10.4324/9781003503187-8

diplomatic events like the WHS. Finally, before concluding my chapter, I offer several of my own suggestions regarding the rapidly growing field of humanitarian diplomacy.

I must make it absolutely clear at the outset that I have written this chapter as a reflective practitioner and not as a scholar who boasts significant academic expertise in diplomacy. As such, I do not claim to have mastered what I recommend herein. Realistically, very few will be able to master all of the skills and virtues that I touch upon in this chapter and most will inevitably be better at some things than others. This natural diversity between individuals means that humanitarian diplomacy is best pursued as a team endeavor. Only in a truly diverse team that combines different personalities, perspectives, and abilities will a foreign ministry, humanitarian organization, social movement, affected community group, or business achieve optimal diplomatic impact. Humanitarian diplomacy, like all forms of diplomacy, is best conducted in teams.

Diplomacy: An Art and Craft

A focus on soft skills implicitly acknowledges that diplomacy is, beyond an empirical science, an art and a craft. Indeed, diplomacy is a political art as old as human civilization itself, whose roots traces back long before being formalized into the conglomeration of ambassadors, embassies, protocols, and procedures that modern states use to interact with one another. Although as a term, humanitarian diplomacy has begun to receive widespread currency only recently, it too has roots in the ancient world. In the modern world, humanitarian diplomacy is practiced formally by state representatives and informally by everyday citizens, religious institutions, and civil society organizations (CSOs).

Wars, massacres, plagues, and other disasters have always elicited calls for compassion and aid, whether made directly by those affected, their governments, or third parties acting on their behalf. Throughout human history, formal messengers and envoys have been sent to negotiate or, should the circumstances require, plead for the lifting of sieges, the safe passage of certain groups, the release of prisoners, and truces (Benham, 2017). In modern times, humanitarian diplomacy has shined in several outstanding individuals. In the nineteenth century, for instance, the great Algerian freedom fighter, Emir Abdelkader, established clear rules mandating the humane treatment of the invading French. Later, while in exile, Abdelkader saved thousands of lives through humanitarian mediation and rescue operations during Syria's sectarian pogroms. Around the same time, Henry Dunant, the founder of the Red Cross and Red Crescent Movement, called representatives of several European nations to Geneva, where they wrote into law legal protections for wounded soldiers. A few decades later in 1899, Tsar Nicholas II of Russia convened several nations and CSOs from around the world in The Hague to negotiate humanitarian limits on military conduct and which weapons should be prohibited in armed conflict. The cruelty of the British military and the concentration camps they operated during the Boer War in South Africa were subjected to intense scrutiny and condemnation by Emily Hobhouse, an English humanitarian activist who had worked in several concentration camps holding Boer women and children. Hobhouse's advocacy galvanized the public and impelled David Lloyd-George and others in the British Parliament to support wider political action (Hall, 2008, pp. 64–117). While working as a mining executive in London in 1914 at the onset of WWI, the great American humanitarian and later president, Herbert Hoover, launched industrial-scale food aid operations.

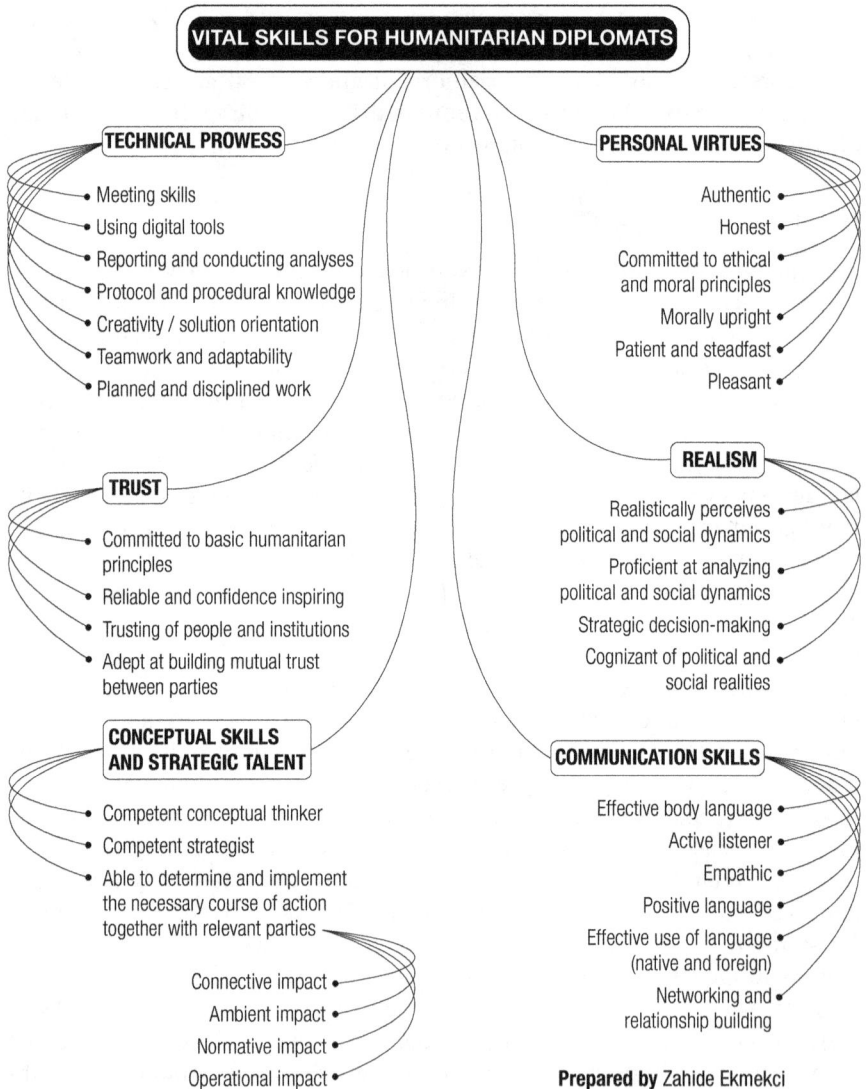

VITAL SKILLS FOR HUMANITARIAN DIPLOMATS

TECHNICAL PROWESS
- Meeting skills
- Using digital tools
- Reporting and conducting analyses
- Protocol and procedural knowledge
- Creativity / solution orientation
- Teamwork and adaptability
- Planned and disciplined work

TRUST
- Committed to basic humanitarian principles
- Reliable and confidence inspiring
- Trusting of people and institutions
- Adept at building mutual trust between parties

CONCEPTUAL SKILLS AND STRATEGIC TALENT
- Competent conceptual thinker
- Competent strategist
- Able to determine and implement the necessary course of action together with relevant parties
- Connective impact
- Ambient impact
- Normative impact
- Operational impact

PERSONAL VIRTUES
- Authentic
- Honest
- Committed to ethical and moral principles
- Morally upright
- Patient and steadfast
- Pleasant

REALISM
- Realistically perceives political and social dynamics
- Proficient at analyzing political and social dynamics
- Strategic decision-making
- Cognizant of political and social realities

COMMUNICATION SKILLS
- Effective body language
- Active listener
- Empathic
- Positive language
- Effective use of language (native and foreign)
- Networking and relationship building

Prepared by Zahide Ekmekci

Figure 8.1 Vital Skills for Humanitarian Diplomats.

Hoover shuttled between London, Berlin, Paris, and Brussels to allow his Belgian Relief program access into occupied Belgium and France for humanitarian purposes, something that he repeated during the Russian Civil War (Whyte, 2017). Several foreign missions in Istanbul were engaged in humanitarian diplomacy with the Ottoman Empire, seeking, first and foremost, to alleviate the tragic events that had befallen the Armenian population. Likewise, Ottoman governors and other state officials worked with church congregations, individual citizens, and the Ottoman Hilâl-i Aḥmer Society—the Red Crescent of the time—to protect the Armenian population and relieve their suffering. These individuals employed a host of soft skills while simultaneously attempting to use whatever means were available to them to leverage hard power.

The importance of humanitarian diplomacy, in both its formal and informal iterations, continues to grow in the modern world. Though certainly not new in and of itself, humanitarian diplomacy has gained currency among contemporary governments and humanitarian organizations. This then raises the question as to what soft skills should guide parties interested in practicing humanitarian diplomacy. I shall explore a range of attitudes, behaviors, and skills that, after years of experience in the field, I have found to be integral for humanitarian diplomacy. To help readers navigate the intricacies that invariably accompany such an endeavor, I have grouped said skills into five distinct categories: Political realism, interpersonal communication, trust, conceptual skills, and personal virtues.

A Sense of Reality

Attaining a clear sense of reality requires that humanitarian diplomats afford the utmost attention to two key components: (i) the conditions and needs of affected people and (ii) political actors' concerns, interests, needs, characters, and maneuvering room.

Indeed, it is of absolute imperative that humanitarian diplomats maintain a strong sense of political reality. While a humanitarian diplomat may very well be an idealist determined to bring about urgent humanitarian change or shape new humanitarian norms, the opportunity to realize his idealist aspirations will perpetually evade him should he remain aloof to the political situation on the ground and the powerful players in charge. Though ethical ideals can certainly constitute the motivation for one's engagement in humanitarian diplomacy, these ideals must always be informed and guided by astute political realism. Attaining a clear sense of reality requires that humanitarian diplomats afford the utmost attention to two key components: (*i*) the conditions and needs of affected people and (*ii*) political actors' concerns, interests, needs, characters, and maneuvering room.

A realistic sense of people's suffering is the first step. Humanitarian diplomats must understand the suffering and conditions of people whose lives they aim to save and improve. To be convincing and to begin their diplomatic efforts on the right foot, humanitarian diplomats need to be able to convey the real-life experiences of suffering people and what concrete actions will improve lives both in the short and medium term. A firm grasp of people's reality requires facts and, ideally, a first-hand appreciation of conditions. More than this, realism requires emotional honesty. Faced with such egregious images of human suffering, many people opt either to exaggerate the reality on the ground or to deny it altogether. It is all too common for people to downplay the true trauma experienced by those bearing the crisis in real time, telling ourselves and others that "it can't really be that bad" in an attempt to assuage our own emotional pains. By the same token, it is equally as common to be swept up in a moral panic and exaggerate reality to such a degree that it catastrophizes an entire population or demonizes a whole group. Two sides of the same coin, denial and exaggeration are both anathema for the humanitarian diplomat seeking to improve any given situation, as such misrepresentations of reality inevitably erode one's diplomatic capital, both in the immediate run up and the long term, thereby setting policymaking off on the wrong foot. Knowing and presenting the situation without distortion not only allows for an accurate diplomatic response that is relevant to the degree of suffering faced by affected populations but also renders the messenger more trustworthy and respected in the eyes of the international community.

Such a diplomatic commitment to realism may sound ill-judged in humanitarianism, given its innately idealistic, dramatic, urgent, and extreme character within the greater domain of international relations. Surely, one might believe that no headway can be made without at least a modicum of panic or exaggeration, especially since it is well known among those involved in public communications that one needs to shout excessively to attain only half of what he wants. Here, however, we must be attentive not to confuse exaggeration with emotionalization, for these are two distinct concepts. Good humanitarian diplomats must emotionalize suffering so that people on the other side of the world can effectively empathize with the pains experienced by their fellow man. Yet, it is paramount that they avoid exaggerating suffering, as doing so could result in a loss of credibility and undermine their cause. Humanitarian diplomats need to appeal to people's emotions and faculty of reason to help the wider public relate to the suffering of others on a deep human level (Smith, 2010).

Human suffering is only one facet of the political reality that humanitarian diplomats must understand and inculcate into their core. The other facet is a proper appreciation of the politics and politicians exercising control over that suffering. A humanitarian diplomat needs clear political insight into the ideology, interests, objectives, motivations, and needs of the political forces behind the emergence of a human tragedy, as these same forces have the power to relieve said tragedy. This insight is essential for humanitarian diplomats if they are to determine what courses of political action are feasible, which actors are fixed in their policies and why, where these actors might modify their behavior and why, and who within their own party and amongst their allies may be able to leverage real humanitarian influence. Only when humanitarian diplomats have a good feel for the attitudes, incentives, and objectives of decision-makers in the political arena for a given situation will they find the right counterparts, entry points, common interests, pressure points, and diplomatic asks with which they can make practical progress.

This sense of reality about those who suffer and those who shape their suffering is, therefore, the first soft skill that every good humanitarian diplomat needs to possess. Political analysis—a hard skill—cultivates, at least to a certain extent, this political realism in diplomats, especially while mapping, interpreting, and assessing the objectives and interests of involved parties. More than this, however, the best humanitarian diplomats *feel* what people believe, how deep their interests run, and how much they might move ahead with or distance themselves from their current strategy. While analysis sets out the political environment, emotional insight intuits more precisely where change is more likely. This sense of reality appreciates what is politically possible and how and where diplomacy can work most effectively in a given situation. In his famous essay on political judgment, Isaiah Berlin described how this sense of reality and its insight resemble the creative touch of a potter who feels the clay coursing between their fingers, shaping it intuitively as he labors on (Berlin, 2019, pp. 50–67). Like a potter, a humanitarian diplomat must also deploy this sense of reality artistically as he feels his way through the politics and personalities of a crisis. Much of this political sense emerges in individual encounters with political players and their representatives, which is why interpersonal communication is the next important soft skill that makes a good humanitarian diplomat.

Interpersonal Communication

Diplomatic communication encompasses not only addressing and speaking, organizing topics, making strong statements, and ensuring the main ideas are understood in both secret and open meetings, but also undoubtedly includes listening, empathizing, envisioning, networking, building relationships, and developing sincere connections.

Humanitarian diplomacy, like all forms of diplomacy, is frequently characterized as advocating for particular groups and their needs. This, however, gives the dangerous impression that diplomacy is restricted to talking and that its main focus is to draw up speaking points, to issue powerful statements, and to deliver important messages in private and public meetings. This is, of course, a serious misrepresentation of good humanitarian diplomacy and of all good diplomacy. Listening, empathizing, imagining, networking, and relationship-building are essential to effective interpersonal communication, much more than talking and speaking out. If humanitarian diplomats have not listened well before they speak, their key messages are likely to fall flat and their statements either to disappear into thin air or to be championed only by those who already agree with them. If diplomats have not taken the time to forge genuine relationships, they will have no one to work with.

The first rule in inter-personal communications for humanitarian diplomats, therefore, is to listen, and listen well, in order to develop their sense of reality and to discern what is and is not possible. This means listening attentively both to suffering individuals and to those in power. Listening well requires one to be an active listener and not simply waiting one's turn to talk, as Deborah Tannen so famously described male listening (Tannen, 1992). Active listening involves paying very careful attention to what is said, what goes unsaid, the way issues are framed and narrated, who speaks before others, how people are listened to and respected, and the body language that accompanies spoken words. Following speakers' body language is important because it often indicates the opposite of the words uttered. A defensive posture by a humanitarian minister verbally promising humanitarian access, for instance, may reveal a deeper intention of rejecting such access. Similarly, the eyes of a defense minister refusing to alter her government's military strategy may hint at future positional changes.

The best way to listen is not to take notes but to use one's entire being to soak up the full experience, retaining as much of the encounter as possible and then relaying it to others later in a written or oral briefing. Taking notes severs vital eye and body contact. It confines a full sensory experience to a more limited one of reason and words. Note taking also preoccupies an important part of one's mind, forcing the listener to devote valuable mental resources to ordering his notes and thereby distracting him from fully immersing himself in the encounter. Finally, note taking reduces the status of a diplomat to that of a student scribbling away in his notebook, dutifully jotting down words of wisdom imparted on him by his intellectual superiors.

Active listening requires one to use her imagination to place herself in the speaker's shoes and see the world through his point of view. Doing so allows the listener to grasp where the speaker is coming from, what he believes, what his interests are at this moment, what drives him to do what he is doing, and why he is beholden to certain policies. While from a diplomatic perspective, this kind of listening is essential in conversations with allies and adversaries alike, it is especially challenging with adversaries whose point of view one may find obscure, unbelievable, unreasonable, or inhumane. Working cross-culturally or through the mediation of interpreters presents another, more technical challenge, and it may be morally and politically painful to listen to an interlocutor's view that is anathema to one's own. Nevertheless, it is essential to listen and understand. While one need not agree with everything said, the skilled diplomat must start her diplomacy from a place of understanding that can be attained only by listening well and not avoiding, exaggerating, downplaying, or denying the views of others on whom the success of one's diplomacy depends. Indeed, since where one starts her diplomacy is largely determined by the party that wields greater power, listening to others is absolutely paramount.

Beyond listening attentively to all parties involved in a particular conversation, humanitarians need to pay close attention to the wider conversation surrounding the issue on which they are working. Political discourse and the various opinions brought up typically form a complicated conversational landscape around a given topic. Every political landscape soon reveals ideological and political differences that divide diplomatic ground into areas, each of which varies in terms of how difficult it is to navigate. Nations may have radically different views from one another, which may prevent them from working together or even set them in opposition to one another. Groups of cooperating nations, like the Economic Community of West African States (ECOWAS) or the Association of Southeast Asian Nations (ASEAN), may agree on some things but not on others. A properly nuanced understanding of the political landscape enables humanitarian diplomats to determine the best route to take while simultaneously demarcating areas of common ground, bridging gaps, and avoiding chasms of disagreement and insurmountable hurdles within the time available.

Networking is the single best way to develop a sense of reality across a political landscape. Talking only to a single nation or a single group of allied nations will not aid one in developing a successful diplomatic strategy unless he has sufficient hard power to deliver his humanitarian objectives on his own. Since, however, this is a rare occurrence, networking is essential to knit together a good political understanding, a good group of diplomatic partners, and a good reputation as a trusted diplomat ready to listen and contribute creative solutions. Building such a network requires an exceptionally powerful memory for people, names, characters, and faces. It also requires one to keep in touch with others and to know who is important at a particular moment. Good networkers resist the temptation to limit their connections to those with whom they feel most comfortable, seeking instead to build a diverse network and to work with those who will ensure the best outcome, even if they may not be the easiest or nicest people to work with.

One must be careful, however, not to harness networks for exploitative or self-serving purposes. Diplomats who exploit networks to extracting information or who leverage members in it to secure their own interests soon find themselves facing closed doors. Operating an effective network inevitably entails sharing time and information. Humanitarian diplomats, therefore, need to be able to place something on the table. It is not enough to be humanitarian in spirit and to speak truth to power on behalf of suffering individuals. Indeed, people involved in politics are busy, short of time, reluctant to being lectured, and actively pursue their own interests and objectives. Humanitarian diplomats need to make themselves useful while building a network and ensure that are a respected member of said network.

The golden rule in building and maintaining a good network is to make genuine human relationships with the other members in the network and to bring added value to the network. Like most networks, diplomatic networks are built on reciprocity, meaning that humanitarian diplomats need to give as well as take. A network works best if its members truly want to see one another because each one adds value to the group. This value may be informational, analytical, political, material, or reputational. A government official, a representative of an armed group, a religious leader, a humanitarian, or a civil society activist will benefit from a meeting only if she can bring the other members information or new ideas to add to an analysis, or if she has political contacts and influence that can integrate the group into an even larger, more powerful network. One's value may be rooted in his ability to leverage material, moral, or emotional support; in his ability to boost the group's reputation in front of a third party; or in his ability to stir up public ire in the event that one refuses to meet him.

A great deal of diplomacy happens in formal meetings in which chairs, cushions, or sofas are arranged in such a manner so as to inculcate a sense of a diplomatic hierarchy among attendees, with the high-level main players facing one another in the main seats, flanked by a line of their accompanying acolytes on opposite sides of the room who act as observers, note takers, and the occasional purveyor of some technical tidbit. In many meetings, it is diplomatic tradition that these acolytes remain seen but not heard. Their role is primarily to get to know their equally silent counterparts in between meetings so that they may set up effective working-level channels to keep the conversation flowing and to follow up on actions agreed upon by their respective bosses. This highly ritualized form of diplomatic meetings constitutes the norm in diplomacy today and makes good meeting management a key skill for humanitarian diplomats.

Conducting effective meetings is indeed an art, requiring one not only to manage preparations and relations prior to the meeting's convention but also to facilitate its pace, content, asks, and actions as it is ongoing and after it has concluded. Good preparation is essential for an effective meeting. It is imperative to know with whom one is meeting, to have a good sense of their power, roles, personality, political views, and history of engagement with the topic at hand, with one's own institution, and with other relevant organizations. One needs to enter every meeting with a clear purpose, objective, and list of desired outcomes in mind. While the purpose of a meeting may be exploratory and informational in nature, it could also be to forge a new relationship, to collaborate in solving a specific problem, or to ask for a small or even large favor. As a rule, every meeting, even the shortest ones, should be regarded as a potential opportunity for all parties and harbor a well-defined, measurable objective.

Every meeting presents a valuable opportunity to build or deepen a personal rapport with another person. This requires a positive temperament, a healthy degree of curiosity, and sincere empathy while interacting with the other person and inquiring into the objects around him, his capacity in the meeting, and his family. If building a positive rapport is not possible, a meeting should be used to clarify one's differences and affirm diplomatic hostility where necessary or inevitable. Not every meeting is conducted on amicable terms, and there is always a great deal to learn and gain from difficult and unfriendly meetings.

Managing the tempo of a meeting is critical and depends on how much time is available to achieve one's objectives. Some meetings run very long and can therefore be conducted at a leisurely pace with more ice breakers and deeper, more elaborate discussion. Others may last only half an hour, fifteen minutes, or even a staged two-minute "bump-in" between busy people at a conference or summit. Some may take place in elevators while moving around an office, hotel, or conference center. The pace at which the meeting is conducted depends on how much time attendees have and the speed at which interlocutors are moving. In every meeting, however, the underlying objective needs to be coordinated with the time available in order to achieve what one has set out to achieve. This means working at different speeds in different meetings and being both a good sprinter and long-distance runner.

Content, asks, and actions constitute the other three key components of meeting management. During the course of the meeting, humanitarian diplomats must, regardless of the atmosphere of the meeting and the tactics adopted by their interlocutors, prevent discussions from straying away from the specific content and demands they have in mind and then negotiate key action points slated for implementation following the meeting. This requires one to have developed a deft conversational style that allows him to listen carefully and respectfully, to take the lead on content when the opportunity arises, and to deliver his asks without ambiguity. This, in turn, requires firmness, highly adapted active-listening skills, clarity of speech, and the ability to interrupt, deflect, defuse, and redirect the conversation without causing offense. The aspiring diplomat needs to learn new things by listening to his counterparts, explain to them what he wants them to know, and ask them for what he needs. Finally, the diplomat needs to conclude with a plan in mind on how to proceed with the course of action agreed upon during the meeting. The skills involved in handling a bilateral meeting and chairing a multilateral meeting are different. Not all diplomats are equally good at both. Some people are highly adept at navigating bilateral meetings while falling short at leading multilateral meetings, similar to the difference between the solo violinist and the conductor. Nevertheless, chairing and co-chairing difficult meetings are essential skills for a senior humanitarian diplomat leading such a process.

The best diplomats tend to build genuine personal relationships with their counterparts, taking the time necessary to come to know them and allow themselves to be known. Formal diplomacy is covered in a thick veneer of protocol and officialdom. This is by deliberate design to prevent diplomacy from becoming personal to such a degree that politicians are tempted to, for want of a better expression, shoot the messenger. Instead, flags, rituals, rhetoric, and etiquette all reinforce the notion that diplomats are representing their nations and not themselves. Still, many gifted diplomats deliberately show a personal face alongside their official face or organizational persona. This is essential if they are to have genuine human encounters "in the margins" where difficult issues can be thrashed out creatively beyond the public view and without divulging the options available to nations or being seen to make otherwise impalpable compromises. A deliberate commitment to familiarity means that many diplomats become friends as well as counterparts, even when their respective governments have strained political relations. They come to know and like one another as individuals, as well as respecting one another as state representatives. They eat together, play together and even sing and dance together, thereby revealing themselves as individuals outside the ritual space of formal diplomatic meetings and working together as professional colleagues.

These informal meetings in the margins are extremely important in humanitarian diplomacy. They are often symbolized in the media by politicians taking private walks around a garden or relaxing together over dinner. In humanitarian diplomacy, informality also occurs at meals where two or more individuals break bread together, thereby moving from being political counterparts to more intimate companions.[1] In humanitarian settings, similar informality often occurs while cruising around in a Toyota together to travel from one place to another. This commitment to informal, even intimate human contact is very important. It helps diplomats to communicate quickly with their counterparts, seek help more easily, and solve problems together more efficiently. Above all, it helps colleagues trust one another, which is another vital soft skill in humanitarian diplomacy.

Trust

Trusting people is partly emotional and partly calculative (Wheeler, 2018, pp. 25–75). We intuitively feel whether a person is trustworthy or not. We also calculate whether we can trust others to do something based on their previous performance, as past experience demonstrates probable future reliability. We also calculate the likelihood of people following through on they say depending on how much incentive they have to do it.

> **Trusting people and institutions is something we are required to do all the time in our everyday lives, and humanitarian diplomacy is no exception. Humanitarian diplomats are forced to trust people without being absolutely sure of their motives or having any guarantee for successful outcomes. They regularly have to trust the words of politicians, military leaders, and other diplomats simply because they said so and without a solid legal or contractual foundation. Similarly, both the public itself and these groups are required to trust humanitarian diplomats.**

Trusting people and institutions is something we are required to do all the time in our everyday lives, and humanitarian diplomacy is no exception. Humanitarian diplomats are forced to trust people without being absolutely sure of their motives or having any guarantee for successful outcomes. They regularly have to trust the words of politicians, military leaders, and other diplomats simply because they said so and without a solid legal or contractual foundation. Similarly, both the public itself and these groups are required to trust humanitarian diplomats.

The Prophet Muhammad was, throughout his life, lauded as *al-amīn* (i.e., the trustworthy). Indeed, it was his trustworthiness that facilitated him to realize the great feats he achieved during his life. This is certainly true for humanitarian diplomats who are often required to move between different parties to a conflict and to rely on particular information to represent large groups of suffering people. Should one's behavior appear suspicious or unreliable or should the information presented be false or exaggerated, his trustworthiness and reputation will evaporate in the blink of an eye. Considering that gaining and maintaining trust is a vital soft skill in humanitarian diplomacy, we must inquire into the best way to go about doing so.

Personality and performance are key. To be trusted, a humanitarian diplomat needs to be accepted by others as honest, impartial, discreet, effective, and reliable. Honesty is essential; otherwise diplomats run the real risk of not being believed or accused of exaggerating the truth. Impartiality is equally vital, without which other parties may very well doubt the sincerity of a diplomat's motives, possibly leveling accusations of playing favorites or not being driven by purely humanitarian concerns. Discretion is equally important, as one's counterparts need to be sure that he will not divulge private discussions to others or engage in gossip. Should a diplomat be required to work confidentially, discretion becomes an even more important commitment. Confidentiality requires deliberate steadfastness and awareness—well beyond a simple compartmentalization—as one remembers who it is appropriate to quote to whom, and what she is required to know in front of one group of people and to forget in your with others.

Finally, a good humanitarian diplomat needs to be effective and reliable. She must be able to do what she says she will—and then do it. She needs to do this every time she commits to something, not just sometimes. If a humanitarian diplomat is able to be all these things all the time, this consistency in personality and performance will help her ensure that she is perceived as trustworthy. Stakeholders will invest their time and political capital in engagements with diplomats whose personality and performance they can trust, even taking certain risks along the way.

Yet trust in diplomacy is not a one-way street. Humanitarian diplomats must continuously gauge the trustworthiness of their counterparts and maintain a healthy degree of suspicion toward them until they have proven themselves worthy of trust. To do this, one will need to feel out the other party's trustworthiness, meaning that intuition is inevitable, especially in the first and last steps of a deal. Can one trust the other party to make the first move and to see things through to the end? These are the two most difficult parts of a joint endeavor and where one may face the most pressure by those resisting a more humanitarian policy. It is relatively easy for politicians to agree to a specific course of action early on when plans for change are still speculative and private as to later when they are imminent and public.

Beyond intuition, humanitarian diplomats must also estimate other parties' honesty, reliability, and effectiveness using as much evidence of their past performance as you can find. Information into their history of trustworthiness and little tests played out in early confidence-building measures (CBMs) are of immense importance before undertaking a more comprehensive diplomatic endeavor. One must be mindful, however, as these same probes are certainly done by all parties involved. CBMs common in humanitarian diplomacy may include a counterpart's commitment to provide access to a contested area or a test to see whether one will relay confidential messages reliably. Whatever happens, the challenge of preserving mutual trust will endure throughout the entirety of humanitarian diplomacy and remain something needing to be gauged, risked, and proven constantly.

Conceptual Skills and a Knack for Strategy

The strategic aspect of the diplomat's art involves sensitivity and expertise in defining success, setting objectives, and building a wise narrative frame around a problem.

Some soft skills in humanitarian diplomacy are more conceptual than they are inter-personal. If a large part of diplomatic work focuses on working well with people, another aspect of the diplomat's craft involves thinking through angles and options to develop an effective diplomatic strategy. The strategic aspect of the diplomat's art involves sensitivity and expertise in defining success, setting objectives, and building a wise narrative frame around a problem. It also entails a certain dexterity in judging when and how to use evidence, experience, and expertise, thereby striking the right balance between deploying reason and emotion when communicating privately and publicly. The conceptual area of the diplomatic craft requires a talent for strategy: creatively designing the best path to achieve one's objectives all whist ensuring that it is grounded in a realistic sense of the politics and personalities around oneself and the options at one's disposal.

A clear definition of success and ability to set the specific objectives to achieve it are essential in humanitarian diplomacy. Humanitarian diplomats need to have a clear sense of what they want to change in order to alleviate human suffering during a crisis. Success may mean different things depending on the specific situation. It could be about recognition, or the need to bring attention and funding to a hidden crisis. It could focus on access and the need for a siege to be lifted or a roadway to be opened. Less immediately and operationally, success and its diplomatic objectives may focus on global policy change, like convening nations together to devise a new policy or law concerning AI-based weapons, or the complicated challenge of linking climate finance and humanitarian action in places like Afghanistan and the Sahel where conflict and climate change are deeply integrated in their disastrous effect on people's lives. Once success and its specific change objectives are clear, the best way to achieve these must be elaborated in a diplomatic strategy, which usually involves four types of activity and impact: *connective*, *ambient*, *normative*, and *operational*.

Connective impact

Connective impact refers to identifying and connecting with the people and organizations with the power to bring about or influence the change desired. This is the network a humanitarian diplomat needs to build when faced with a particular diplomatic challenge. This specific skill relates to the ability to discern political gold from ordinary metal among a wide array of people who make themselves appear busy dealing with a crisis in an attempt to look important. What is infinitely more important, however, is to determine which people and institutions have the real power, energy, influence, and even desire to play a role in improving the situation. It is these parties with whom one needs to connect and work, as they are capable of exacting meaningful change. They will not always be the most obvious and vociferous of protagonists and may remain relatively hidden from view, opting instead to work in the shadows around a crisis, or be several steps removed from the frontline as financiers, allies, ideologues, and puppet masters. Similarly, one's golden counterparts may not always be formal and high-level politicians. They will often be part of social movements operating more *en masse* among the people than at the elite political level. Good humanitarian diplomacy relies on a multi-track network and engagement that spans tracks one, two, and three. This is especially important because the human suffering that follows a crisis, as well as solutions to this suffering, typically revolves just as much around local communities and leaders as it does around national leaders.

Diplomatic time and energy is limited and good judgment about which people one should invest in is vital. It is all too easy to spend most of one's time talking with the wrong people, especially those referred to in the field as sponges and shields. These officials are deliberately ineffectual middlemen and women deployed specifically as decoys to soak up diplomats' time and energy all while pretending to be useful and engaged. Spokespeople and international liaison officers are often deployed to keep diplomats away from powerful people and to waste their time. Having identified her golden targets, the diplomat needs to design ways to meet and connect face-to-face with them. Gaining access to the right people can be rather tricky and require a substantial amount of time and energy. Good diplomats make and take any opportunity that comes their way in order to gain an audience with or simply appear beside these key individuals.

Ambient impact

Ambient impact constitutes the next challenge to humanitarian diplomats. This type of impact involves the diplomat's artistic feel for framing and narrating a political crisis in such a manner so as to produce the humanitarian response appropriate to the crisis at hand. The International Committee of the Red Cross (ICRC) has a fitting, frequently used phrase for this: "Translating humanitarian concerns into compelling political terms." Still, humanitarian diplomats must make their change objectives politically important, if not politically desirable. Often this means changing the political climate around a crisis recounting it in such a way that resonates with politicians and offers them good reasons to involve themselves in finding a solution. The trick here is to show how the crisis at hand is not simply another inevitable humanitarian tragedy beyond the international community's control, but something of importance to everyone. This is the art of framing, narrative building, and motivating key actors.

Humanitarian diplomacy has a large repertoire of political frames ready at its disposal. Morality is one: As a good person, you must want to solve this problem. Shame can also be played from morality: This behavior is inhumane and disgraceful and makes you a pariah within the international community. Reciprocity is another: If you allow aid in to help their civilians, they will reciprocate for your civilians. Political self-interest is yet another: Working on this humanitarian agreement is either a way-win situation or will afford you a better position at the table of high-level politics. Or, if you and your opponent destroy the whole city and its port, nothing will be left for you to take after winning this war. Law is another: These people have a legal right to protection and your government or armed group is legally bound to cooperate. In fact, you may end up in court if you continue to ignore your legal obligations. Finally, there is self-image and prestige: Would you prefer to be seen as a monster or a heroic leader who acted courageously. The best way to frame something is always the way that encourages politicians to engage in problem resolution instead of avoiding it out of a feeling of disgrace or humiliation. A good frame deals directly with the conflict itself and sets out immediate advantages and disadvantages of cooperating with humanitarian efforts rather than one that appeals to long-term interests or that threatens censure by Geneva or New York. Persuading a belligerent party to allow its enemies to receive COVID-19 vaccinations may best be done by arguing from a frame of self-interest. This can be done by suggesting that civilian vaccinations will prevent one's own armed forces from being severely weakened by the spread of disease and will prevent new variants that current vaccines are ineffective against.

Good framing and narrative building need to be carefully supported by the three Es: Evidence, experience, and expertise. Diplomacy requires much more than mere smooth talking; true persuasion requires hard facts in the form of statistics, trend analyses, and the exact location of suffering. A clear analysis of the crisis' underlying causes as well as well-substantiated claims demonstrating how the solutions proposed will help rectify the problem. It is, therefore, an important part of the diplomat's craft to muster and master the facts of a case. When talking about hunger, displacement, and other atrocities, diplomats must present credible evidence to corroborate their claims and speak from experience while describing what they have personally witnessed in the field. Diplomats must also bring in or at least be able to cite subject experts where appropriate to help build their case and convince people that a response is necessary. The art of the three Es is how best to tailor one's delivery to diverse audiences.

When addressing politicians, given their penchant to look at the wider picture, one needs to slip in a couple of "killer facts" to draw their attention to specific details. With others of a more rational and empirical mindset, on the other hand, one will need to present a highly precise and detailed briefing.

Whereas evidence, experience, and expertise all tend to leverage reason in a discussion, emotion certainly has its place, too. At key moments, whether in private with key figures or in public with the media, it can help to exhibit emotion and to articulate in words how one feels about the crisis. Conveying some of the emotions felt by afflicting individuals is key in showing one's own humanity and to emotionalize the crisis so that one's audience, including those in power, can empathize with the pain and suffering experienced by real people in crisis zones. In short, a humanitarian diplomat must be able both to express things with a warm heart and with cold reason as the situation requires.

Normative impact

Normative impact is the third area that a humanitarian diplomat needs to master. Given the bureaucratic nature of diplomacy and politics, discussion points usually need to be written down. By harnessing the way agreements, resolutions, military orders, and government mandates are worded, humanitarian diplomats have a golden opportunity to develop and reinforce humanitarian norms that then can be used to address crises. This demonstrates how important the choice of words is in order to create a text that sets the tone for real humanitarian change, links words with extant laws and principles, records everything in writing, and ensures that the final document will be approved, disseminated, and easily understood by its target audience. The dexterous art of selecting the correct word for the job is called wordsmithing and is yet another important soft skill in humanitarian diplomacy. Since this skill often requires a very particular type of mind—one that is not always common among the more politically inclined diplomats whose focus rests more in interpersonal relations—this is a prime example of why working in a diverse team is vital in humanitarian diplomacy.

Operational impact

Norms are nothing more than abstract principles until they are acted out in real life. Although the approval process of a normative document is a central part of humanitarian diplomacy, it means absolutely nothing if positive action does not follow from it. As such, being able to have operational impact is the pinnacle of achievement for humanitarian diplomats. They must have the skills needed to ensure that their counterparts follow through on their obligations so that the suffering of affected populations may be alleviated. Humanitarian diplomacy is deemed successful only when it leads to a positive change in people's lives, meaning that simply reaching an agreement on people that does not translate into practical steps that reduce human suffering is meaningless. Once again, it takes a particular kind of diplomat—one who has the determination, patience, and dogged working style—to follow up on agreements until they have borne real fruits. While the envoy gifted in communicative and ambient skills is capable of building the right network, framing the problem well, and sealing the deal, it is highly unlikely that he will have the skills set needed to spend the next few months monitoring, chasing, nudging, and reporting on real life changes in humanitarian conditions. Yet, since this final process is imperative to ensure that people's suffering is actually relieved, humanitarian diplomats' work remains incomplete without it.

Personal virtues

Alongside the aforementioned skills, all of which are needed at particular moments of the diplomatic process, are several positive character traits, or virtues, that humanitarian diplomats must possess if they are to persuade others to work with them and to stick it out over the long road in the face of difficulties, policy reversals, and failures that inevitably accompany crisis diplomacy.

The first of these virtues is authenticity. Humanitarian diplomats typically represent an organization and so manifest some kind of institutional status in their dealings with others. A humanitarian diplomat may represent the UN, a sovereign nation, the Red Cross or Red Crescent, an NGO, a religion, or a private foundation. Diplomats are bound therefore to speak in the name their organization and emphasize its values and goals. At the same time, however, diplomats must be themselves. Bad humanitarian diplomats are very wooden, repeating the language and jargon of their institution at every turn and sticking rigorously to pre-drafted talking points. They resemble the knight in Italo Calvino's famous story who knows all the rules and regulations of his organization but who is non-existent inside his shining armor (Calvino, 1992). Similarly, such a diplomatic is nothing more than an empty suit.

Instead, a diplomat should be himself, show himself as a person, and bring his own personality to the negotiating table. It is important to be authentic and to connect with people as such. The good diplomat seamlessly operates in the name of her organization without sacrificing what makes her unique as a person. This allows others to know the actual person with whom they are dealing and not just the institution she represents. Personal integrity is key to maintaining this authenticity. The diplomat's counterparts need to know that a good person has been sent to them. Since diplomats' personal behavior is subject to careful scrutiny both while on the job and not, their character needs to be beyond reproach. Sending a decadent, shifty, or bad-mannered individual is immediately regarded as an insult in many cultures. Knowing that a diplomat is honest and respectful is essential to achieving trust. This does not mean that all effective humanitarian diplomats are, or need to be easygoing, nice people. Herbert Hoover, the great American humanitarian of WWI, was a notoriously awkward person who often stared at his shoes and had no interest in charm. Yet he was a genius for detail, was extremely persistent, and always had a practical plan at hand. In her campaigning diplomacy against the British concentration camps of the Boer War, Emily Hobhouse could be both charming and fierce. She was well connected, extremely persistent, and had a sense of her own destiny that infuriated others. Bob Geldof, the driving force of Band Aid during the Ethiopian famine in the mid-1980s, dressed in jeans and a t-shirt. He swore profusely, could be rude, and was often hot tempered. Yet he was clever, politically astute, cared deeply for his fellow man, and was very powerful during his day. All of these individuals worked around the clock.

Creativity is a fundamental virtue in humanitarian diplomacy defined by deft framing and hard problem solving. Very few humanitarian diplomats are able to leverage hard power to solve emergent problems. They are, therefore, working mostly with soft and smart power. This requires great creativity as they contemplate new angles, explore new contacts, and make the most of positive and negative developments. Such an approach requires profound patience and endurance given the lack of a quick and easy solution. Humanitarian diplomats must be ready to face more failures than successes and to endure long periods of no progress. They must also be prepared to receive more criticism than praise, most of which is then aired out before the public following the advent of social media. This level of personal attack requires all humanitarian diplomats to have developed very thick skin.

Considering the highly social nature of humanitarian diplomacy, humanitarian diplomats need to excel at being team players. They must not only be valuable members of their own team but also able to navigate the often highly conflicted network they have built with others to solve the problem. A diplomat's network is also his team and inevitably overlaps with local, national, regional, and global networks. The ability to run and mobilize a complex and asynchronous team that stretches across the country concerned, the greater region in which the country is situated, and a conglomerate of capital cities outside of the region can be described as nothing less than an art. It requires successive personal phone calls, crisp email briefings, and constant availability. Members of such widely networked teams can easily feel slighted if they believe themselves to have been left out. While the decision to keep the inner circle tight is often the right move, it is neither always easy to do nor the best option at every step of the process. Above all, humanitarian diplomats should have a reputation of being easy to work with so that others will want to collaborate with them and include them in a diplomatic team.

All of the above requires humanitarian diplomat to have meticulous organization skills. They must be personally organized with a clear agenda and list of priorities. They must also be able to select a good team and to lead and delegate well so that their office runs smoothly and their operations as efficiently as possible. This means having people who are excellent at keeping diaries, traveling, maintaining protocol, preparing and notes, as well as people who are persistently scouting ahead to improve the network and bring in new information and new contacts.

The Interpersonal Challenge of Virtual Diplomacy

Like everything else in life, humanitarian diplomacy is increasingly being practiced on the virtual front. This has significant implications for interpersonal relationships. Digital diplomacy requires humanitarian diplomats to operate increasingly in digital space (Bjola and Holmes, 2015, p. 252). Here, on social media platforms like X (formerly known as Twitter), Facebook, LinkedIn, and Instagram, diplomats need to find their voice, project an authentic personality, build relationships with a mass audience, and create diplomatic effect. This digital space, in addition to offering humanitarian diplomats immediate contact with both their diplomatic counterparts and opponents active on these networks without ever meeting them, allows them to speak directly with the millions of people they represent. As such, social media is an immensely important instrument in their public diplomacy. What is key here is that diplomat be able to portray himself as an authentic person on social media—who cares for the plight of his fellow man and is realistic, constructive, and engaged. Some people perform better than others in this new medium that affords them the advantage of being able to "cut through" to large swaths of people and influence a wide constituency not under their direct jurisdiction. Such diplomats can then leverage this as hard power when necessary. However, many diplomats do not perform well in today's new virtual environment. They delegate their handles to their communications team, which has the adverse effect of making them sound wooden and impersonal and lacking an authentic digital persona. Regardless of whether one is proficient at digital diplomacy or not, engaging in it does carry several risks. A single major fumble or misjudgment can set in motion a toxic chain of responses that damages a diplomat's reputation around the world in mere seconds. Being good at digital diplomacy demands authenticity and care. Holding fast to such common sense rules as "don't drink and tweet," "pause and reflect before sending," "err on the side of caution," and "never say something to someone that you would not say publicly to their face" are essential.

The COVID-19 restrictions pandemic have moved humanitarian diplomacy beyond social media into the era of what has been dubbed Zoom diplomacy. Most bilateral and multilateral meetings are now held in virtual or so-called hybrid spaces, where a small contingent of people sits in a room while others join online. This means real diplomatic business and negotiations are being conducted in digital space and not just the communications surrounding negotiations. Zoom diplomacy comes with many advantages as humanitarian diplomats can meet with numerous counterparts based on different continents in a single day, something that was impossible during the heyday of physical diplomacy and air travel. Nevertheless, gains in geographical closeness and expediency are accompanied by losses in intimacy. Diplomats readily admit that they find it much more difficult to read the room on a Zoom call than in a conference hall or meeting room where they can easily see who is talking to whom in the margins, who is paying attention, and how one's body language reacts to a particular statement. Diplomats also miss the corridors of physical diplomacy where they can meet people for a chat, bump into others, and deepen relationships over coffee and snacks. The interpersonal challenges of Zoom diplomacy are new but they are also here to stay. Humanitarian diplomats will need to discern carefully what can be done well through virtual diplomacy and what still need be done in person. Designing a diplomatic strategy that strikes the right balance between physical and virtual encounters is now essential for humanitarian diplomats and their teams.

Conclusion: Improving Humanitarian Diplomacy

The whole field of humanitarian aid has undergone a profound expansion and professionalization over the last thirty years. Humanitarian diplomacy is the latest element of the field to be singled out for greater attention. Although academic analysis of contemporary humanitarian diplomacy remains under-developed, a new commitment to training and education in this area has made itself apparent. The Clingendael Institute in The Hague offers new short courses on humanitarian diplomacy for diplomats and humanitarian organizations. In Oslo, the Chr. Michelsen Institute (CMI) engages in research and resource gathering on humanitarian diplomacy to further improve the field. The Global Executive Leadership Initiative (GELI) designs and delivers training courses in humanitarian diplomacy to senior-level humanitarians. It is clear that a new focus on improving humanitarian diplomacy now complements the focus on the very humanitarian negotiations spearheaded by several organizations since the early 2000s.

As the field of humanitarian diplomacy continues to develop, it is essential that theory and training not remain confined to Western institutions in Europe and North America. Expertise and education in humanitarian diplomacy need to be developed across Asia, the Pacific, Africa, and Latin America as well. This is especially important as we enter the climate crisis, as this will cause the focus of humanitarian diplomacy to turn to climate emergencies either as much as or more than conflict emergencies. In the decades ahead, humanitarian diplomacy will play a significant role in protecting the interests of those displaced and forced into poverty by climate change.

Humanitarian diplomacy needs to be part of every twenty-first-century diplomatic academy. In this chapter, I have attempted to demarcate several of the main soft skills needed in humanitarian diplomacy and I have no doubt that these will be significantly elaborated in the years ahead as climate crisis and non-traditional security threats become a more central focus for diplomats around the world.

Note

1 Companion derives from the Latin words *cum panis*, meaning "with bread" and so captures that human friendship found in sharing food together.

References

Benham, J. E. M. (2017). *Peacemaking in the Middle Ages: Principles and practice*. Manchester University Press.

Berlin, I. (2019). *The Sense of Reality: Studies in Ideas and their History* (pp. 50–67), H. Hardy (Ed.). Princeton University Press.

Bjola, C. & Holmes, M. (2015). *Digital diplomacy: Theory and practice*. Routledge.

Calvino, I. (1992). *The non-existent knight in our ancestors*. Vintage Classics.

Hall, A. J. (2008). *That bloody woman: A biography of Emily Hobhouse*. Cornwall.

Smith, A. (2010). *The theory of moral sentiment*. Penguin Classics.

Tannen, D. (1992). *You just don't understand: Women and men in conversation*. Virago.

Wheeler, N. J. (2018). *Trusting enemies interpersonal relationship in international conflict*. Oxford University Press.

Whyte, K. (2017). *Hoover: An extraordinary life in extraordinary times*. Knopf Publishing Group.

9 Harnessing the Power of Culture in Humanitarian Diplomacy

Cihat Battaloğlu and Fadi Farasin

While the essence of diplomacy has undergone minimal change, ever-evolving interstate relations and the high conflict environment that has come to characterize the twenty-first century have necessitated the appending of new qualifiers to the term diplomacy. This has resulted in the development of more highly sophisticated techniques to address specific crises or contexts. The scope of diplomatic action has widened, stretching into entirely new arenas, and become more layered. Privileged diplomatic positions have been conferred upon a variety of new actors, such as international organizations, non-governmental organizations (NGOs), humanitarian organizations, and even prominent individuals. Over time, the traditional state-to-state diplomacy in which state institutions had enjoyed a monopoly over diplomatic affairs would eventually become more inclusive. A survey of the recent literature on diplomacy shows many qualifiers appended to diplomacy, such as conference diplomacy, cultural diplomacy, defense diplomacy, humanitarian diplomacy, and, among myriad other iterations, environmental diplomacy.

Here, we must underline that each diplomatic initiative is unique in its own right, boasting its own internal complexities, dynamics, and processes. It is therefore no easy task to define humanitarian diplomacy (HD). This task is further complicated when we remember that individuals are driven to don the humanitarian mantle by different values and motives that resonate with them on a deeper, more personal level. Still, the International Federation of the Red Cross and Red Crescent Societies (IFRC) has put forward a workable definition: "Humanitarian diplomacy as a process which persuades decision makers and opinion leaders to act, at all times, in the interests of vulnerable people, and with full respect for fundamental humanitarian principles."[1] The International Committee of the Red Cross (ICRC) has similarly advanced its own, slightly more sophisticated definition:

> "Humanitarian diplomacy is a strategy for influencing the parties to armed conflicts and others—States, non-State actors and members of civil society. Its purpose is purely humanitarian and it is carried out through a network of sustained relationships—bilateral and multilateral, official and informal".

(Harroff-Tavel, 2005, p. 1)

DOI: 10.4324/9781003503187-9

Whatever the definition, reality dictates that humanitarian diplomats (HDiplomat) work diligently to prove that they are indeed legitimate interlocutors in the eyes of all parties to the conflict in which they are involved. Egeland, Harmer, and Stoddard summarize this as actively building and cultivating good relations and consent as part of a security management strategy with parties to the conflict and relevant stakeholders (2011, p. 18). This means that HDiplomats must have effective skill sets, be attuned to the cultural environment in which they find themselves, and be adept at integrating dialogue, information gathering, and negotiations into their initiatives.

In this chapter, we aim to discuss various HD tools and their rapport vis-à-vis culture. In the first section, we shall explore the importance of culture in HD and discuss how culture should be approached. In the second section, we will then delve into how incorporating culturally sensitive practices can enhance and amplify the effectiveness of the tools HDiplomats have at their disposal. Before concluding, we will discuss why culturally defined HD tools and strategies are necessary not only to understand humanitarian crises but also to assist and resolve them.

How to Approach Culture

Given the difficulty surrounding in any attempt to pinpoint the true nature of culture, the academic literature is rife with contested definitions of what does and does not constitute culture. Nevertheless, we observe a consensus that considers, in broad terms, culture to encompass the characteristics and knowledge of a group a people, such as language, religion, social habits, history, and arts. In addition, there is an agreement that culture works as a set of lenses influencing how and what we do and do not see, in that culture shapes how we perceive and interpret the world. Moreover, culture operates below the surface; it is dynamic, reflexive, and fluid. Culture is open to transformations and transitions that, at least in the majority of cases, occur naturally over time.

Turning to the realm of HD, we need not a definition of culture but an approach to culture applicable in the diplomatic process that incorporates mediation and negotiation in an effective manner.

Turning to the realm of HD, we need not a definition of culture but an approach to culture applicable in the diplomatic process that incorporates mediation and negotiation in an effective manner. Three dichotomies are useful for our purposes: (*i*) individualistic versus collectivist cultures, (*ii*) traditional versus modern societies, and (*iii*) high- versus low-context cultures. While each one of these dichotomies uses a wide brush to describe cultural clusters, we must remind our readers that each of the generalizations has its own limitations and pitfalls (LeBaron, 1998).

The individualist–collectivist dichotomy is one way to approach culture (Kağıtçıbaşı, 1994). Individualist-centered cultures tend to afford greater importance to freedom, frankness, social recognition, hedonism, equity, and self-reliance. In contrast, collectivist cultures tend to value harmony, face-saving, filial piety, modesty, moderation, frugality, equality of rewards, and fulfillment of others' needs. Those from collectivist cultures are inclined to vertical hierarchies and function well within them. They may be more comfortable with wider and more pronounced power discrepancies and reverence to those higher in status. In contrast, those from individualistic cultures give primacy to horizontal relationships; that is, they expect equality and acknowledgment (LeBaron, 1998).

A caveat, however, is required here. Individualist and collectivist values need not be understood as polar opposites. For instance, face-saving is not exclusive to collectivist cultures; it exists in individualistic societies as well, though conceived differently. Whereas legitimate expressions vary from one society to another, certain values transcend cultural boundaries. Honesty, harmony, kindness, and bravery surpass cultural boundaries and are universally valued norms (LeBaron,1998).

The individualist–collectivist dichotomy has many merits in helping to build a robust understanding of culture and, by extension, intercultural mediation. The general insight that these approaches afford one can help facilitate a more culturally sensitive mediation process. Such insight can likewise enhance mediation preparations by fostering an understanding of how to approach the conflicting parties. Mediation where both parties hail from individualist societies, for instance, calls for a particular, more clear-cut mediation strategy. Similarly, in mediation sessions where one party is from a collectivist society and the other from an individualistic society, certain measures and arrangements can help increase the likelihood of successful outcomes. This approach to culture thus offers an umbrella of values that may apply to individualist and collectivist societies, communities, and groups. However, assigning a value to one cultural cluster at the expense of the other can, if not properly guided, aggravate diplomatic efforts as well. This approach to culture should always be taken with a grain of salt, as the values extant in one group may likewise exist in the other, seemingly opposing group with varying meanings and codes attached to it (LeBaron, 1998).

Another approach to culture and diplomacy is to distinguish between traditional and modern societies. This approach, some might argue, conceals an inherent bias because of the connotations attached to so-called traditional and modern cultures. Traditional cultures are commonly regarded with disdain, characterized as backward, tribal, underdeveloped, and rooted in the past. Modern cultures, on the other hand, are celebrated as progressive, civilized, industrial, and superior. Many have criticized the very notion of "pitting modernity against tradition, and assuming that the former will replace the latter" (Kağıtçıbaşı, 1994, pp. 59).

Modern societies are commonly characterized as autonomous, individualistic, impersonal, professional, rational, formal, technical, and specialized. Traditional cultures, on the other hand, tend to feature familial and group dependence, personal and relational priorities, affective and assumed interactions, informal and holistic approaches, and ascriptive and personal networks (Lederach, 1991). Nevertheless, while the innate inequality in the characterization of these two societal conceptions has rendered this approach less desirable in conflict resolution literature because it can exacerbate and deepen conflict, it does offer useful insights.

The difference between traditional and modern approaches to culture becomes apparent during armed conflict and humanitarian crises. Modern approaches tend to regard diplomacy from a systematic task-oriented vantage point whereas traditional approaches emphasize building personal relationships, expressing emotions, and putting greater value on culture and accepted norms. When mediation is taking place between a modern and a traditional actor, misunderstandings compromising parties' likelihood to reach a viable resolution may arise. For instance, modern cultures are most interested in "getting the job done," and may be perceived by a more traditionally minded interlocutor as impersonal and overly concerned with achievement and accomplishment. On the other hand, traditionalists may seem too concerned with relational decorum and too informal to an individual from a more "modern" cultural context (LeBaron, 1998). This is where the mediator's cultural awareness and intermediary skills become particularly salient. The mediator needs to have the right set of skills and expertise to pull the mediation out of cultural deadlocks and present a middle-way that is acceptable and advantageous to both parties.

The third cultural dichotomy distinguishes between high- and low-context cultures. Just as with the previous two dichotomies, this approach offers mediators important insight while analyzing conflicts and designing effective diplomatic action plans. Low-context cultures are characterized by individualism, overt communication, and heterogeneity. Communication in low-context cultural settings tend to elevate the written and spoken word to a position of primacy and, as their name indicates, understand messages directly without the need for much context. High-context cultures, on the other hand, have collective identity focus, communicate covertly, and are homogenous. As a result, communication tends to be associative. This means that more attention is paid to the context of communication, including behavior and environment, the relationship between the two interlocutors, the messenger's family history and status, age, sex, and power (Cohen, 1991).

The use of this specific categorization of cultures has several implications for HDiplomats, given that parties might have different communication expectations. These differing expectations may lead to potential misunderstandings and communication breakdowns that have the potential to derail mediatory efforts completely. As with the individualist–collectivist dichotomy, most societies have elements of both low- and high-context cultures. For instance, most cultures have some unspoken high-context patterns that, while being wholly indiscernible to outsiders, are assumed among insiders. Competencies informed by this approach include the ability to discern the nonverbal behavioral cues specific to different cultures, creativity in questioning and rapport building, the appropriate use of cultural informants, and refined communication analysis skills (LeBaron, 1998).

HDiplomats must acquire a deep insight into cultural differences and recognize the complex and interrelated nature between a diverse set of themes and variables if they are to put these three approaches to effective use during their diplomatic work. This includes understanding how these three dichotomies differ from one another on the macro level and, perhaps just as important, how the internal dynamics and nuances within each individual dichotomy vary. Moreover, HDiplomats must always remember that intra-group differences can be at least as profound as inter-group differences (LeBaron, 1998).

> **Successful diplomacy requires that culture be treated with the utmost sensitivity. In the end, effective diplomacy depends on HDiplomats' flexibility, creativity, and innovative streak in addition to their having a deep awareness of their own and others' culture.**

Successful diplomacy requires that culture be treated with the utmost sensitivity. The three aforementioned cultural approaches provide a foundation that HDiplomats may use to approximate the cultures of parties and then create a space that accommodates all parties involved so that they may reach an acceptable agreement. The objective is not to define the minutia of every culture; it is to comprehend cultural differences, histories, and contexts. In the end, effective diplomacy depends on HDiplomats' flexibility, creativity, and innovative streak in addition to their having a deep awareness of their own and others' culture.

The Importance of Cultural Acumen for Humanitarian Diplomats

Culture is an ecosphere that allows communities to feel a sense of congeniality to those who share the same cultural attributes. This mutual affinity begets a sense of security and stability in a world where power and uncertainty reign supreme. Culture, therefore, has a pervasive effect on all human beings—one that influences one's day-to-day behaviors and responses to new stimuli. Since this naturally holds true for belligerent parties, those involved in conflict resolution and mediation must take into account how culture will affect dealings (Foulkes, 2004). Indeed, just as small hiccups can stall out proceedings, the way mediators handle conflicts arising from cultural differences can sometimes mean the success or failure of the entire diplomatic process.

Conventional mediation or negotiations tend to be characterized by overt communication, structured confrontation, and interventions by neutral third parties with no decision-making power. Such approaches have waned in significance as the nature of conflicts has gradually shifted away from war between sovereign nations toward internal conflict. This has prompted diplomats to afford greater consideration to culture in their work relating to conflict zones. This has in turn increased interest in the cultural element of conflict prevention and resolution within academia.

HDiplomats must take into account the cultural backdrop of conflicts during their conflict resolution efforts, as the informed diplomat will have an edge during otherwise very trying mediation and peacebuilding initiatives (Leeds, 1997). The key difficulty lies in discerning how culture affects how people perceive reality. Cultures construct reality through various codes, boundaries, and beliefs. This means, in short, that there are as many interpretations of reality as there are cultures in the world (Duffey, 2000). Since these interpretations overlap to varying degrees, parties will naturally have certain blind spots that the skilled HDiplomat must be aware of and able to navigate in order to resolve the conflict at hand.

Culture affects actors' perceptions, behaviors, and worldview. Cultures more tolerant of threatening or violent behavior may, for instance, unwittingly escalate conflicts with an action that while in their own cultural context would be considered rather run of the mill, their interlocutor perceives to be an egregious affront. In other words, culture is always an inherent part of conflict resolution as conflicts themselves arise out of human interaction. Indeed, culture affects the way we name, frame, blame, and attempt to tame conflicts (LeBaron, 2003).

HDiplomats must consider several variables during mediation and negotiation proceedings. The way a diplomat comport himself during the initial phase of negotiations or mediation will invariably influence parties' behaviors over the course of the proceedings. HDiplomats aware of parties' cultural dynamics will be in a better position to interpret parties' behavior, interests, and perspectives, which will in turn allow for smoother negotiations more likely to end amicably.

While culture is inextricably linked to the environment in which it is molded and sculpted, humanitarian diplomats will be the most successful at managing conflicts in a neutral environment free from external pressure, especially that of voters and the media (Bercovitch & Houston, 1996, p. 29). HDiplomats need to acknowledge the weight that cultural norms, codes, heritage, and history carry while weighing which strategy they should employ during upcoming mediation or negotiations, as those strategies that appreciate cultural differences are much more likely to result in successful outcomes.

Culture invariably influences how parties assess mediation outcomes. To achieve sustainable resolutions, HDiplomats must therefore remain conscious of the cultural backdrop tinting parties' perceptions. Since some actors may perceive what others consider a fair resolution in a very different light, HDiplomats need to consider whether and where parties can find a common ground to resolve the issues in a universally satisfactory manner. In order to carry out such a feat, HDiplomats must equip themselves with intimate knowledge of the parties involved, their cultural codes, and how their culture might influence their assessment of outcomes (Foulkes, 2004).

To disentangle and manage multilayered cultural conflicts, HDiplomats need to understand three contemporary frames of reference—cultural intelligence, cultural competence, and cultural fluency—as these serve as effective tools in discerning and navigating this complex and diverse landscape.

Here, we must highlight that certain cultures will have an easier time reaching a durable solution (Lucke & Rigaut, 2002). Different mixtures of interests and cultural backgrounds coalesce to allow HDiplomats to induce truly transformative resolutions. For this to be possible, however, HDiplomats must assess parties' underlying objectives, which, once again, requires cultural finesse. To disentangle and manage multilayered cultural conflicts, HDiplomats need to understand three contemporary frames of reference—cultural intelligence, cultural competence, and cultural fluency—as these serve as effective tools in discerning and navigating this complex and diverse landscape (Whatling, 2016).

Cultural intelligence is the ability to engage in a set of behaviors that combines language and interpersonal skills with personal characteristics (e.g., tolerance for ambiguity, flexibility) appropriately tuned to the specific culture-based values and attitudes of people with whom one interacts (Peterson, 2004, p. 89).

Cultural competence comprises four components: (*i*) awareness of one's own cultural worldview, (*ii*) attitude toward cultural differences, (*iii*) knowledge of different cultural practices and worldviews, and (*iv*) cross-cultural skills. Developing cultural competence enables one to understand, communicate, and interact with people across cultures. The upshot is that the more one interacts with new cultures, the more his competence expands to encompass a wider range of cultural blocs (Martin & Vaughn, 2007, p. 31).

Cultural fluency is, in essence, a heightened awareness of the set of lenses through which a culture interprets and articulates the world. As one's cultural acumen increases, or, in other words, as he becomes more cultured, he likewise becomes more open learning from the surprises that life sends his way. This way, we begin to anticipate, internalize, express, and navigate unfamiliar milieus (LeBaron & Pillay, 2006, p. 187).

Capitalizing on Culture: A Catalyst for Expanded Diplomatic Reach and Presence

Individuals and institutions have, even if not by name, engaged in HD for decades. Under whatever name it might have been practiced, the skills necessary to conduct effective HD cannot be reduced to a uniform set of criteria. Still, however, several key skills are requisite for HDiplomats to hone and practice their craft effectively; these include an understanding of international humanitarian law, a familiarity with past efforts, refined interpersonal and communication skills, and a keen sense of timing (Minear & Smith, 2007). More importantly, perhaps, HDiplomats must have developed a mature sense of impartiality, a willingness to consider the opinions of insiders and involve them in ways that will further ones diplomatic goals, and rhetorical prowess.

Personnel Competencies

Humanitarian crises and armed conflicts comprise complex factors that dictate which actors will find themselves playing a part in how crises unfold, evolve, and are resolved. Negotiations and mediation naturally require the participation of diverse parties. Yet, further complicating an already tense situation is the reality that members of individual groups may hold diametrically opposing views. Humanitarians are, by themselves, limited in their ability to grasp the all the complexities of a situation and offer viable, comprehensive solutions to ongoing crises. This being the reality, carefully planned collaboration based in trust and a clear demarcation of duties is imperative for the success of any such initiative intended to be executed in the field. The individual strengths and weaknesses of HDiplomats must be carefully weighed prior to selecting members of any such team. In addition to skills, experience, track record, knowledge, and personal discretion, HDiplomats' cultural background and fluency should be taken into account while deciding the ideal composition of a diplomatic team.

Diplomats' individual characteristics and skills impress heavily on the success of a diplomatic endeavor. The lack of certain interpersonal skills will paralyze any efforts from moving forward. These attributes include empathy, analytical understanding, excellent political judgment, ability to handle criticism, working under stress, high communication skills, and the ability to facilitate during time[s] of tension" (Nathan, 2012).

HDiplomats must display a strong penchant for empathy toward their fellow man and be willing to construct bridges between conflicting, sometimes outright belligerent parties. Empathy requires that HDiplomats be able to leave their own worldviews, biases, and perception at the door and instead seek to understand the situation through the eyes of those in negotiations. Just as salient as empathy is the ability to analyze the cultural context and nuances at play, as this allows the HDiplomat to construct a holistic image of the conflict. Analytical skills allow HDiplomats to collect and interpret information to make better-informed decisions before proceeding with negotiations.

Working in humanitarian crises requires one to have developed hard enough skin to handle criticism leveled against one's person and to work under intense stress and tension. Therefore, humanitarians must be able to field criticism constructively and innovate techniques to defuse stressful and high-tense situations. Finally, HDiplomats must have highly refined communication, rhetorical, and discretionary skills lest they lose the trust of or find themselves accused of partiality by one or more parties involved in negotiations.

Other important, though perhaps somewhat secondary skills include patience, persistence, creativity, and a willingness to take initiative. HDiplomats must listen attentively to all parties to see beyond surface motivations and penetrate more deeply to discern what really drives them underneath the initial façade they have put up. Indeed, it is imperative that HDiplomats be able to grasp the entirety of the conflict and all of its complexities—something that is possible only through careful listening and truly investing oneself into understanding the conflict. This has the added advantage of creating a more trustworthy, impartial, and dedicated persona of the HDiplomat in the minds of negotiating parties. More importantly, humanitarians must retain their independence, impartiality, and dedication to reaching a mutually satisfactory resolution. HDiplomats must then refrain from making judgments, proffering solutions, and offering unsolicited advice. Instead, their role is to guide discussions in such a way that facilitates conflicting parties to identify the key issues of dispute, as these are often blurred and rarely clearly articulated.

Experience is yet another important factor in effective HD. A proven track record instills ever-important confidence in conflicting parties, as it helps ensure them that they have entrusted themselves in the hands of a capable third party able to navigate the situation. This is a result of the amount of trust and credibility parties have in HDiplomats' abilities to fulfill their role as legitimate interlocutors as well as in the rapport they have built between the mediator and negotiating parties over the course of diplomatic efforts, as this rapport acts as the grease that facilitates HDiplomats' ability to manage the process equitably (Bercovitch & Houston, 2000).

Linguistic Prowess, Emotional Intelligence, and Communication

The linguistic prowess—or lack thereof—of HDiplomats working in crisis situations contributes greatly to the success or failure of the diplomatic process. Since language shapes how we interpret and articulate both our internal and external worlds, it has the real potential to function as a barrier to conflict resolution when parties misunderstand or misinterpret one another. As many linguists have aptly pointed out, language includes both direct and latent meanings, many of which are an extension of the culture in which the language is molded. Accordingly, HDiplomats must make a concerted effort to familiarize themselves with the vernacular, customs, and cultures indigenous to the populations with whom they work, even if they are fluent with the language at a more academic level. Indeed, not only are certain things simply lost in translation altogether, many realities may only be expressed through local, often dialectal vernacular. In other words, it is bad practice to negotiate, or engage in any form of interpersonal relation for that matter, through translation, as doing so will inevitably hamstring one's ability to communicate intimately and effectively (Nathan, 2012).

Emotions, and HDiplomats' ability both to control and to employ them dexterously, play an essential role in conflict resolution initiatives. Emotions, as with language, are often sidelined during the diplomatic process; they are either not understood or not properly controlled and managed by HDiplomats. Effective HD must take into consideration all aspects of crises and conflicts, including parties' emotional realities. Accordingly, HDiplomats must refine their emotional intelligence until it has matured to such a degree that it can then be harnessed for the good of all parties. HDiplomats must be aware of, control, and channel their emotions properly so as not to unwittingly sabotage negotiations, meaning that HDiplomats must approach interpersonal relationships with empathy and equity. The HDiplomat who has mastered this will undoubtedly be much better equipped to ensure a more fruitful, less abrasive negotiation process for all involved.

Effective communication requires an acute awareness of language—both verbal and nonverbal—and emotions. Poor communication invariably results in misunderstandings and, over time, may lead to the complete breakdown of negotiations. Consequently, HDiplomats must consider not only what is being said but also how it is being said. Different cultural contexts may impose different ways of communicating that are not always necessarily interchangeable. Communication methods considered "normal" in one context may very well be abnormal or outright offensive in other cultural settings.

The current technological age and the realities to which it has given birth have impelled people in positions of power to pay closer attention to the communication strategies they prioritize both at the negotiation table and during public relations events in general. Since social media platforms have evolved into important arenas for discussion and debate, HDiplomats must consider how they will be perceived by the public when they post or, in some cases, delete a post previously published. Information about the humanitarian operations being circulated on social media can have a negative or a positive impact on the overall process. When devising diplomatic plans, HDiplomats must make extra effort to utilize social media effectively and constructively in their communication strategies in order to increase the possibility of precipitating a successful resolution.

HDiplomats must pay careful attention to how they communicate both with negotiating parties and with one another. Since having a firm grasp of cross-cultural communication patterns, including turn-taking, tone, body language, and facial expressions, is absolutely essential, HDiplomats must consider the cultural ecosystem in which discussions are to take place while devising the strategies they intend to employ. Communication is largely governed by cultural norms and the boundaries set by these norms. Accordingly, fruitful negotiations require a thorough understanding of and well-refined ability to synergize cultural codes, the intricacies of language, and emotional intelligence.

Maintaining Cultural Impartiality

Naturally, antagonistic parties will not place their trust in just anyone; they must have built a minimum rapport with any aspiring mediator. HDiplomats must therefore approach and forge robust bonds of trust with all parties involved. However, building trust takes time, sometimes even taking decades in personal, let alone official relations. In conflict situations, HDiplomats cannot assume that trust will develop overnight, nor can they assume that their relationship will remain set in stone once they have gained their interlocutor's trust. On the contrary, they must constantly strive to ensure the bonds of trust they have built remain kindled.

Since even the slightest trace of duplicity, whether real or perceived, in a diplomat will impair, if not completely derail, the likelihood that a dispute will be resolved amicably, any individual whose ability to remain objective or whose trustworthiness may be called into question during the course of negotiations should not be assigned to that specific case. HDiplomats' credibility likewise rests upon a multitude of factors, including the reputation of the organization for which they work as well as the degree of support they receive both at home and from the wider international community. In some circumstances, negotiating parties' desire or, as is sometimes the case, lack of desire to reach an equitable outcome may clash with that of the HDiplomat assigned to the case. In such situations, HDiplomats will face accusations of harboring ulterior motives, even if they adhere to every core humanitarian principle to a T. Conversely, however, dialogue and negotiations are often just the continuation of an ongoing conflict, only now verbally, meaning that a viable solution can sometimes remain just out of reach.

Still, it falls squarely upon the HDiplomats to earn the trust of negotiating parties. To demonstrate their impartiality and to gain the trust of all parties involved, HDiplomats must see past cultural stereotypes and respect the identities, values, rights, and dignity of all sides. HDiplomats should refrain from making sweeping generalizations, from thinking they know everything about the parties involved before negotiations even begin, and from pigeonholing or caricaturizing culture in a stereotypical or pejorative light. HDiplomats' cultural impartiality seeks to instill in opposing parties the belief that they are dealing with one another as equal partners, thereby leaving no room for any misgivings that one culture might be regarded as superior to another.

HDiplomats must maintain and exude a neutral, impartial demeanor, neither favoring one party over another nor accepting any form of material compensation from anyone with a vested interest in the outcome of negotiations. Moreover, HDiplomats must not make value judgments, criticize parties, or indicate surprise, as doing so would call into question their neutrality and impartiality—the maintenance of which, along with a deep commitment to resolving the conflict equitably, are absolutely integral in building and preserving credibility.

HDiplomats need to be trained to recognize and counteract their own unconscious biases. This means that they should not only be cognizant of how their own cultural background shapes and influences both their personal views and practices but also preempt any potential conflicts arising as a result of differing cultural codes. It is essential that HDiplomats acknowledge and uphold parties' right to espouse values, attitudes, and opinions diametrically opposed to their own. The keyword here is respect—HDiplomats must respect and take into consideration others' opinions regardless of how much they disagree with them.

HDiplomats should adopt an approach that allows them to perceive events from locals' vantage points without imposing their own values or giving the appearance that their personal beliefs are in fact unalienable truths. The role of HDiplomats is not to make binding decisions or to determine which party is in the right, but to inculcate in parties confidence in negotiations and to pursue solutions equitable to all those involved.

In addition to building good relations with all their interlocutors, HDiplomats should understand their perspectives, including their vulnerabilities and their most important points of interest. At the very least, opposing parties must be able to trust that HDiplomats will, from the very get-go, operate in good faith and refrain from disclosing any sensitive information they are unwilling to share with other parties until they are ready.

The Power of Insiders in Humanitarian Diplomacy

Conflicts are often rooted in deeper historical, regional, linguistic, or territorial disputes than what initially meets the eye. This requires one to be aware of the historical and cultural particularities of opposing parties. Working with locals and insiders on the ground offers analysts insight into what they can bring to the diplomatic process. By recruiting locals and cooperating with those on the inside, outsiders are able to penetrate into the more shrouded corners of disputes that would have gone completely unnoticed to their otherwise uninitiated eye.

Working with locals and insiders is essential for any diplomatic endeavor as such individuals enjoy privileged knowledge and insight into the inner workings and machinations of the communities involved. HDiplomats native to the region or who work closely with locals are better equipped to understand disputes' root causes, thus enabling them to play a more active role in negotiations. It is important, however, to highlight that working with insiders comes with its own caveats and potential pitfalls, as their ability to remain neutral and objective can easily be undermined should they have a stake in achieving a specific outcome during mediation. Yet at the same time, insider mediators are often driven by dint of their position in society, intimate knowledge of the cultures involved, access to power brokers, and perceived legitimacy to exert greater energy to instigate change. Insider mediators become powerful vehicles for lasting change when the assets they bring to the table are properly deployed in mediation processes.

Moreover, insiders enjoy not only a greater awareness of internal group politics but also a more acute sensitivity to changes in mood and on-the-ground realities—two things that allow them to navigate negotiations much more effectively that outsiders. In addition to having influence horizontally and vertically with state, non-state, and international actors, insiders are more apt to work toward developing shared connections and mutual points of positive memory. Insiders' multitier access enables them not to mobilize their own supporters to pressure decision-makers to find a resolution. Similarly, because networks are themselves a form of social capital in most cultural settings, insiders' expanded personal and professional networks can be used to garner greater leverage and therefore advance the negotiation process (Mubashir et al., 2016).

The support insiders need differs markedly from that which outsiders need. The first step is to listen, focusing specifically on the challenges and needs at hand. Thereafter, HDiplomats may point out any entrenched limitations they perceive, investigate gaps in support, seek out opportunities, and offer organizational, logistical, and advisory support. While partaking in all these efforts, care should be taken to follow local developments and, when needed reassess needs and the best way to respond as the situation evolves.

Both insiders and outsiders are active in nearly all humanitarian crises. Support networks between the two are vital for there to be any hope of a positive, humane outcome. While both groups can reinforce one another in myriad ways, the best form of support is the dialogic mutual support provided by insiders (i.e., support based on conversation and interaction between the insiders and outsiders), as it nurtures joint learning, knowledge building, and problem solving. Partial, vested insiders can provide important methodological insight to impartial, neutral outsiders—insight that can then be wielded in an unbiased manner. Likewise, insiders value the peer-to-peer support that outside actors with experience in other conflict zones can bring to the table. That said, however, the ideal scenario would be when an outsider carrying a briefcase full of mediation support materials is just as open to peer-to-peer support from insiders as vice versa. If that is not in the mandate, outsiders can simply act as a sounding board for insiders to discuss ideas and mediation strategies to see if they are feasible and make sense (UNDP, 2014).

Insiders can use "gentle initial support and accompaniment [provided] by outsiders" to precipitate push forward constructive change in contexts where "credible national capacities may be absent or eroded because of high levels of polarization" (UNDP, 2014, pp. 12). Insiders are invaluable in situations lacking safe spaces and protracted conflicts. Nevertheless, all support must be expertly tailored through close consultation with insiders to ensure that both local and national assets remain autonomous and, just as important, are prevented from finding themselves trapped in a dependency loop (UN, 2012, p. 114).

Insiders must likewise realize the personal beliefs, views, and biases they bring with them to the table of humanitarian diplomacy. Insiders pervious experiences may, for instance, may aggravate their ability to remain neutral during negotiations and mediation sessions. This should not, however, be the sole reason to avoid engagement with the very insiders who may be significantly more auspicious for ongoing HD efforts than detrimental. A caveat, however, is necessary; HDiplomats must collaborate with insiders to design intricate engagement strategies that will neither unduly complicate nor derail the process entirely when the state apparatus and civil society are at bitter odds with one another, when the state perceives insiders as an existential threat to its authority, and when insiders offer irreplicable value to their society. Moreover, HDiplomats must not hesitate to draw clear redlines against certain actions, such as the propagation and incitement of hate speech or violence.

Inclusivity in Humanitarian Diplomacy

Since every humanitarian crisis is host to its own set of complex factors, an inclusive approach, by dint of the greater diversity of team members involved, is better equipped to identify and address crises' root causes. Inclusivity also increases the legitimacy of HDiplomats' actions, as it promotes a sense of ownership among participants, while simultaneously preventing excluded actors from seeking to undermine proceedings. That said, however, an inclusive process does not mean that all stakeholders participate directly in formal negotiations. On the contrary, an inclusive environment streamlines interaction between all parties involved and creates a forum, so to speak, in which a wider gamut of perspectives may be heard.

While inclusivity is an important element in HD, one must be very attentive where to demarcate limits to who may and may not participate. All stakeholders should be clearly identified and their loyalties, if any, rightfully acknowledged. For example, HD efforts that include armed groups must be careful not to insinuate through their association with such groups that violence is to be rewarded, as this could encourage others to take up arms to gain a place at the negotiating table. Utmost caution should be exercised so as not to unwittingly sabotage the entire process solely for the sake of being inclusive (UN, 2012).

Civil society actors, on the other hand, are important assets that help increase the effectiveness of HD initiatives. Let the name not be deceiving; civil society is not always genuinely civic. This is particularly true for societies embroiled in conflict, as the space for such groups to exist alongside and independently of armed factions is severely undercut. In certain cases, civil society actors may act as an extension of armed groups and their interests. Furthermore, civil society actors differ on which issues they consider important. Accordingly, it can be an uphill battle to include civil society actors in a meaningful, beneficial capacity in such contexts despite the otherwise central role civil society plays in HD efforts (World Bank, 2006).

The presence of a wide range of actors should not jeopardize the healthy functioning of HDiplomats' efforts. On the other hand, however, limiting the spectrum of actors to only those with highly specialized technical skills risks creating an elitist and exclusionary appearance that snubs other actors vested in humanitarian crises. In any case, however, the inclusion of actors can do greater harm than good to the diplomatic process if not applied carefully and as part of an overarching strategy (Shamir & Kutner, 2003).

Several challenges complicate diplomats' abilities to design inclusive negotiations. First of all, parties may outright refuse to negotiate or, even if they do agree to sit at the negotiation table, may lack the knowhow or decorum to engage in negotiations properly. HDiplomats must safeguard their ability to maneuver and to engage with a wide range of actors all while refraining from wittingly or unwittingly crossing legal lines. They must accurately gauge parties' comfort levels and convince them of the value of broadening participation. HDiplomats also need to strike the proper balance between transparency and confidentiality, as inclusivity should enhance the mediation process, not jeopardize parties' ability to trust each other or the mediators involved (Shamir & Kutner, 2003).

While planning for any set of negotiations, diplomats must strike a balance between inclusivity and efficiency. Naturally, HDiplomats will find their work more complicated as the consultation base expands, as different tiers of actors weigh in at different stages of the process. HDiplomats may also find it difficult to engage nebulous interest groups lacking a clear hierarchy, such as social movements and youth groups. Such issues highlight the premium placed on stakeholder mapping, planning, and management of the process (UN, 2012).

Inclusive measures should by no means be regarded as a metaphorical silver bullet or panacea implemented simply for the sake of appearing inclusive. Rather, the particularities of each individual situation will dictate the degree that the pool of participants should be expanded; certain phases of the process may call for greater or lesser inclusivity. For instance, the inclusion of stakeholders beyond the principal political actors in humanitarian negotiations is often considered less crucial than in discussions on the form that a future governmental regime will take. Questions of inclusivity, however, become ever more pertinent as the diplomatic process evolves and begins to transition into new stages. While inclusion might not be appropriate at the beginning of a diplomatic process, other actors may be offered a seat at the negotiation table as the process matures and parties themselves agree to greater inclusivity.

The decision-making process is another element where issues of inclusivity must be properly managed. While preliminary negotiations might include a wide host of actors debating a range of issues, those who actually make the decisions might not so diverse. As such, the course of action decided upon may lack universal backing, thus only to be implemented partially or superficially. In some cases, the entire decision-making process is conducted behind closed doors but subsequently followed up by a broad and inclusive approval process. As all this demonstrates, different inclusion modalities are indeed possible, ranging from having certain more-inclusive phases to being inclusive throughout the entire peace process (Paffenholz & Ross, 2015).

When properly managed, HD can preclude many challenges and hurdles that might otherwise dilute negotiations' effectiveness and efficiency when such a wide range of actors are invited to discuss such diverse issues. While inclusivity can be advantageous when carefully managed, it can just as easily undermine the success of humanitarian negotiations when not incorporated either at all or ineptly. As the above discussion demonstrates, HD is ultimately a complex, multi-dimensional endeavor that requires a well-planned, sometimes very cautious inclusion strategy so as not to unwittingly stonewall the entire process.

Strategies for Humanitarians to Address Culture-related Problems in Diplomacy

Culture-related obstacles can potentially hinder all diplomatic initiatives, causing proceedings to stall or, even worse, break down altogether. As such, a culturally sensitive HDiplomat who possesses the skills necessary to lead and manage the entire diplomatic process will be better positioned to achieve successful outcomes.

Since culture affects negotiating goals, attitudes toward the negotiation process, personal styles of negotiators, communication styles, time sensitivity, emotionalism, agreement form, agreement building process, negotiating team structure, and propensity toward risk taking (Salacuse, 1998), HDiplomats should familiarize themselves with the cultural context surrounding conflicts, as culturally attuned HD strategies not only help cultivate an understanding of the depth and intricacies of disputes but also offer a higher probability of resolving them. Accordingly, the HDiplomats should:

- Identify local norms, traditions, hierarchies, and positions during the preparation phase, as these affect parties' willingness to compromise and, by extension, the overall effectiveness of negotiations.
- Map out what parties consider important. Go beyond the obvious and employ indirect methods, such as asking about dates, symbols, rituals, and monuments, to determine what parties are truly seeking to achieve. Identify potential, often loosely camouflaged issues that may emerge during negotiations.
- Support analyses that incorporate cultural inquiry and that reject a rigid, one-size-fits-all formula to conflict resolution. Individual countries may also be home to diverse cultural contexts, meaning that what works in one community may not in another.
- Identify partners able to help gather information on the cultural dimensions of negotiations. Include individuals able to design a diplomatic process that takes into account cultural sensitivities. Explore the best actions to take and determine the ideal people to take these actions, as this will result in greater commitment levels and satisfaction with procedures among all involved.
- Understand and respect the cultural values that make each party unique. Identify cultural differences influencing how parties perceive certain words and acts as well as how parties might interact with one another, as this will help prevent conflicts from escalating needlessly. Involve cultural informants to help interpret the cultural codes informing parties' words and behaviors.
- Be aware of their own goals and values in undertaking diplomatic talks. Ask themselves whether their own identity and cultural background will harm or enhance their effectiveness. Being aware of one's own beliefs, values, biases, and prejudices helps the HDiplomat regard different cultures and ideas more sympathetically.
- Identify what parties know about the issues at stake, including their root causes, evolution, and potential solutions.

HDiplomats must employ appropriate language, emotional intelligence, and rhetorical techniques to initiate and ensure the smooth flow of negotiations should they have any hope of achieving positive outcomes. These include:

1 The Use of Culturally Sensitive Language and the Identification of Potential Language Barriers

Languages are molded in their own specific cultural contexts that invariably contain elements foreign to other cultures. HDiplomats must therefore identify and preempt any language barriers that may arise during mediation, as they have the potential to undermine or even completely undo any progress made. HDiplomats adequately versed in the local languages will be better equipped to overcome any linguistic challenges threatening to undercut the success of humanitarian initiatives.

2 A Culturally Sensitive Approach to Emotional Intelligence

HDiplomats need to develop skills to discern and interpret the intricate web of culturally embedded emotions, reactions, and norms. They must act with a proverbial third eye that allows them to spot where talks are breaking down at the emotional level and then reinvigorate them appropriately. HDiplomats need to have the proper emotional acumen to read the latent feelings of parties during negotiations and channel them into a rational and constructive policy agendum.

3 The Use of Culturally Sensitive Communication Strategies

HDiplomats must be sensitive to cultural communication codes and norms, as parties may have different understandings of what constitutes approval of and commitment to a proposal being floated during negotiations. One party may outwardly appear to approve, perhaps with a nod of the head or even a verbal *yes*, without intending to agree to whatever is being proposed. HDiplomats must therefore be well acquainted with parties' cultural sensitivities and adept at developing strategies accordingly.

Conclusion

Culture is largely, if not completely, overlooked in diplomacy, and very often at the expense of more tangible elements. Nevertheless, the importance of culture both in diplomatic efforts in general and in humanitarian diplomacy in particular has become ever more evident in recent times. In this chapter, we have summarized several approaches and skills that HDiplomats can employ in cross-cultural settings and have advanced a mechanism to interpret and, more importantly empathize with diverse cultures so as to transform it into an asset, as opposed to a barrier, in one's HD work.

Language, emotional intelligence, and communication skills are of paramount importance should any humanitarian endeavor hope to bear fruit. It is equally important to remember that all three are, by their very nature, contextual and therefore situated squarely within their own unique cultural milieus. Since humanitarian efforts that ignore the cultural aspect are very often doomed to failure, it is imperative that HDiplomats develop their linguistic, emotional, and rhetorical prowess alongside their ability to interpret and interact with diverse cultures on their own terms. Indeed, it is only at the crossroads of cultural appreciation and diplomatic finesse that one's interlocutors—even the most belligerent of which—may be made to feel understood, welcomed, and at ease.

Note

1 Humanity, Impartiality, Neutrality, Independence, Voluntary Service, Unity and Universality are those fundamental principles of the IFRC. See for details: https://www.ifrc.org/fundamental-principles.

References

Bercovitch, J. & Houston, A. (2000). Why do they do it like this? An analysis of the factors influencing mediation behavior in international conflicts. *The Journal of Conflict Resolution, 44*(2), 170–202.

Cohen, R. (1991). *Negotiating across cultures: Communication obstacles on international diplomacy.* US Institute of Peace Press.

Duffey, T. (2000). Cultural issues in contemporary peacekeeping. *International Peacekeeping, 7*(1), 142–168.

Egeland, J., Harmer, A., & Stoddard, A. (2011). *To stay and deliver. Good practice for humanitarians in complex security environments.* OCHA: Policy and Studies Series.

Foulkes, J. M. (2004). *The impact of culture and cultural difference on the mediation process.* http://dx.doi.org/10.26021/4594

Kağıtçıbaşı, Ç. (1994). A critical appraisal of individualism and collectivism: Toward a new formulation. In Kim, U., Triandis, H. C., Kağıtçıbaşı, Ç., Choi, S-C. & Yoon, G. (Eds.). *Individualism and collectivism: Theory, method and applications* (pp. 52–65). Sage Publications.

LeBaron, M. & Pillay, V. (2006). *Conflict across cultures. A unique experience of bridging differences.* Intercultural Press.

LeBaron, M. (1998). Mediation and multicultural reality. *Peace and Conflict Studies, 5*(1), 3–15. Doi: 10.46743/1082-7307/1998.1187

LeBaron, M. (2003). Culture-based negotiation styles. In Burgess, G. & Burgess, H. (Eds.). *Beyond Intractability. Conflict Research Consortium.* Colorado: University of Colorado   https://www.gevim.co.il/wp-content/uploads/2014/01/Culture-Based-Negotiation-Styles.pdf

Lederach, J. P. (1991). Of nets, nails and problems: The folk language of conflict resolution in a central American setting. In Avruch, K., Black, P. W. & Scimecca J. A. (Eds.). *Conflict resolution: Cross-cultural perspectives* (pp. 165–186). Greenwood Press.

Leeds, C. A. (1997). Managing conflicts across cultures: Challenges to practitioners. *International Journal of Peace Studies, 2*(2), 77–90.

Lucke, K. & Rigaut, A. (2002). *Cultural issues in international mediation.* https://www.nottingham.ac.uk/research/groups/ctccs/projects/translating-cultures/documents/journals/cultural-issues-mediation.pdf

Martin, M. & Vaughn, B. (2007). Cultural competence: The nuts and bolts of diversity and inclusion. *Diversitf Officer Magazine* https://diversityofficermagazine.com/cultural-competence/cultural-competence-the-nuts-bolts-of-diversity-inclusion-2/

Minear, L. & Smith, H. (Eds.). (2007). *Humanitarian diplomacy: Practitioners and their craft.* United Nations University Press.

Mubashir, M., Morina, E. & Vimalarajah, L. (2016). *OSCE support to insider mediation.* Bergh of Foundation, OSCE & German Federal Foreign Office.

Nathan, L. (2012). Towards a new era in international mediation. *Policy Directions.* https://www.lse.ac.uk/international-development/Assets/Documents/PDFs/csrc-policy-briefs/Towards-a-new-era-in-international-mediation.pdf

Paffenholz, T. & Ross, N. (2015). *Inclusive peace processes–an introduction* (pp. 28–37). Development Dialogue.

Peterson, B. (2004). *Cultural intelligence: A guide to working with people from other cultures.* MA: Intercultural Press.

Salacuse, J. W. (1998). Ten ways that culture affects negotiating style: Some survey results. *Negotiation Journal, 14*(3), 221–240.

Shamir, Y. & Kutner, R. (2003). *Alternative dispute resolution approaches and their application.* UNESCO.

Tavel, M. H. (2005). The humanitarian diplomacy of the International Committee of the Red Cross. *Relations Internationales, 121*(1), 1–16.

UNDP. (2014). *Supporting insider mediation: Strengthening resilience to conflict and turbulence.* https://www.undp.org/publications/supporting-insider-mediation-strengthening-resilience-conflict-and-turbulence

United Nations (UN). (2012). *United Nations guidance for effective mediation.* United Nations.

Whatling, T. (2016). Difference matters: Developing culturally sensitive mediation practice. *Journal of Mediation and Applied Conflict Analysis, 3*(1), 397–406.

World Bank. (2006). *Civil society and peacebuilding potential, limitations and critical factors.* Social Development Department Sustainable Development Network.

Bercovitch, J. & Houston, A. (1996). "The study of international mediation: Theoretical issues and empirical evidence". In Bercovitch, J. (ed.) *Resolving International Conflicts: The Theory and Practice of Mediation.* Lynne Rienner, 11–38.

10 Humanitarian Diplomacy and the Business Sector

Aygün Karakaş

Whether in Türkiye or the wider world, the private sector invests and supports advances in various sectors, including the food industry, textiles, construction, and industrial manufacturing. This integrates the private sector into the political, social, and economic fabric of the geography in which it is actively engaged. As such, the business world, as a collective whole, bears firsthand witness to the numerous crises that happen around the globe—sometimes as a partner working to ameliorate the otherwise dire conditions of afflicted parties and other times as an aggrieved party in the crisis. In either case, private companies shoulder important responsibilities in the geographical areas in which they operate. These include shaping public opinion, providing emergency aid, and supporting projects that will help stabilize and amend acute situations— all things in which they excel given their long-term presence among and history with the local population.

Ways to Include the Business Sector in Humanitarian Diplomacy

The business world is active in humanitarian diplomacy in two distinct manners. On the one hand, the private sector provides logistical support to ensure that aid materials reach crisis victims, thereby allowing them to live a more dignified life. The private sector serves a more diplomatic function, providing insight, gained through first-hand experience on the ground, into the most effective ways to resolve crises, shaping public opinion, and engaging in negotiations seeking to advance humanitarian principles with decision makers.

One of the reasons explaining why private companies take on an increasingly more active role in humanitarian diplomacy is that they are able to deliver necessary relief materials and assistance faster and without needing to jump through as many bureaucratic hoops. Whether a large multinational corporation or a smaller domestic company, private businesses feel an increasingly deep sense of responsibility toward humanity in our globalizing world. This responsibility, in turn, may arise out of a sincere commitment to humanitarian principles or, on the other hand, a desire to create a positive public image of themselves.

All organizations and individuals involved in humanitarian diplomacy, whether civilian or official in nature, achieve more profound results when they

DOI: 10.4324/9781003503187-10

act in collaboration. In addition to the more traditional actors of classic diplomacy, diverse elements of society play important roles in twenty-first century diplomacy. One of the most important differences between former forms of diplomacy and that of today, however, is that all diplomatic actors have espoused a human-first approach in the resolution of humanitarian crises. Defined as "persuading decision makers and opinion leaders to act, at all times, in the interests of vulnerable people, and with full respect for fundamental humanitarian principles" (IFRC, 2009), humanitarian diplomacy has served as the impetus not only for the aforementioned human-first approach but also for the widely recognized fundamental humanitarian principles, all of which constitute the bedrock for humanitarian initiatives undertaken by the business world. This awareness permits the private sector to act more deliberately and thus more effectively in projects pertaining to humanitarian diplomacy. As this awareness continues to grow, humanitarian diplomacy actors are expected to develop more effective methods to help private sector executives and employees assimilate humanitarian principles into their very being, embody these principles in their actions, and, more importantly, employ the various resources available to them—even those of which they may be unaware—to this end. Even so, it is imperative that these corporations, given their *raison d'être* is to generate profit, exhibit strict adherence to specific moral values and prioritize helping and alleviating the suffering of people in conflict zones while working with organizations involved in humanitarian relief and diplomacy. It follows, then, that humanitarian aid and diplomacy actors, such as the International Committee of the Red Cross (ICRC), are expected to initiate strategic partnerships with the private sector. It should be emphasized here that the majority of the ICRC's founders are prominent members of their respective countries' private sector.

How the Business Sector Can Support Humanitarian Diplomacy

The larger part of the business world's contributions to humanitarian relief efforts and the creation of humane conditions are naturally financial in nature. The assistance, contributions, and support provided by the private sector include monetary and material donations, sponsorships, technical support, professional and operational support, and bargaining. Just as private corporations can deliver materials and support directly to beneficiaries, they can also do so through relief organizations NGOs, public institutions located in the recipient country, or public organizations based in their home countries. In addition to providing monetary aid to afflicted countries, supplying and delivering needed items and materials, sponsoring humanitarian aid projects abroad, and offering technical support in critical humanitarian areas, such as healthcare, private corporations are an integral component of the humanitarian diplomacy policies of their home country. Whereas some nations lose their ability to act effectively in conflict zones, the private sector is often able to maintain its presence on the ground and influence among the local population.

This, in turn, allows private businesses to effectuate viable, humane solutions to ongoing humanitarian problems. In the event that relations with other nations are officially severed, the private sector's continued presence and influence within the country international relations functions as an important lifeline for humanitarian efforts.

The private sector finds itself shouldering increasingly greater responsibilities in international political relations in today's globalized world. By partnering with their own national governments as well as domestic and international organizations involved in humanitarian diplomacy and relief efforts, private businesses can provide logistical support for the transfer and delivery of aid materials either to the target country or region within a specific country. Businesses are able to act as mediators for organizations seeking to devise equitable solutions to issues plaguing individual countries. Similarly, private businesses operating abroad can, when adjudicating between two countries, facilitate humanitarian initiatives by organizations based in their country of origin.

Why Should the Business Sector be Involved in Humanitarian Diplomacy?

Certain moral/humanitarian obligations undergird for-profit corporations' contributions to and support for humanitarian diplomacy and relief. The Kantian concept of *categorical imperative* necessitates that businesses make decisions and act in conformance to humanitarian principles. Given that moral action is inherently rational and therefore constitutes an absolute and unconditional obligation, acting morally regardless of the outcomes and any extenuating factors is an intrinsic obligation. In short, since categorical imperative is unwavering and unequivocal, companies have adopted it into their decision-making and executive mechanisms. The private sector is intimately aware of this fact; companies know very well that their profits will most likely suffer, if not be wholly lost, in the event of conflict or political instability. It is also widely known that conflict, war, and chaos generate massive profits for certain sectors, such as the arms industry. That said, given the inherently chaotic nature of crisis zones, private businesses not involved in the arms trade may find it difficult to turn a profit or even to maintain operations altogether under such precarious conditions. On the other hand, however, the private sector is well aware that those countries and companies that have offered their support during the conflict will naturally be given priority treatment in reconstruction projects once violence has subsided. Consequently, the private sector may, and very well does support humanitarian diplomacy and relief efforts out of *hypothetical imperative*—the contraposition of categorical imperative. Although hypothetical imperative is indisputably conditional and self-serving, it can impel the private sector to contribute to humanitarian work. In other words, humanitarian engagement can help companies safeguard continued profitability and even gain access new markets once conditions have improved. While not being the result of any real moral imperative, these acts can have a powerful humanitarian impact and lead to a number of positive outcomes. This allows human life and dignity to be protected, bodily integrity safeguarded, and the healthcare, nutritional, and accommodation needs of affected individuals provided without impugning human dignity.

Principles that the Business Sector Needs to Observe while Engaging in Humanitarian Work

So as not to mar their credibility, members of the business world must demonstrate that they are unbiased and regard all parties equally while engaging in humanitarian actions. It goes without saying that in order to serve people harmed by those acting in opposition to humanitarian values and to the detriment of weaker, more vulnerable segments of society (e.g., women, children, the elderly, the disabled), all negotiations must conform to fundamental humanitarian principles and harbor no ulterior motives. The same holds true for all forms of communication and collaborative works; they must in no way contradict the principles of impartiality or equality. In any case, it cannot be overemphasized that the very *raison d'être* of such collaborative efforts, both in terms of underlying rationale and aims sought to be achieved, is to serve all of humanity altruistically.

The ICRC, IFRC, National Societies humanitarian diplomacy, and other institutions and individuals engaged in humanitarian diplomacy abstain, out of principle, from cooperating with organizations that act with ambivalence during disputes, that disregard humanitarian values, and that prioritize organizational interests over humanitarian principles. Since, moreover, the Red Cross and Red Crescent do not work with businesses that do not uphold humanitarian principles in their own operations, the public image and reputation of commercial enterprises are of critical importance. The IFRC lists several criteria that guide their decisions to collaborate with the private sector:

- Companies involved in the direct manufacture or sale of arms, or that have a majority stake in such companies, are not sought out for partnerships, nor is their support accepted.
- Companies involved in violations of international humanitarian law are not sought out for partnerships, nor is their support accepted.
- Companies that do not respect internationally recognized human rights and fundamental labor standards, including the International Labour Organization's Declaration on Fundamental Principles and Rights at Work are not sought out for partnerships, nor is their support accepted.
- Companies whose products are widely recognized as deleterious to health or that do not observe to widely recognized rules and regulations, such as those elaborated under the World Health Organization (WHO), are not sought out for partnerships, nor is their support accepted.
- The ICRC takes into account whether a company has come under ethical scrutiny for possible involvement in major public controversies (ICRC, 2018).

In addition to these criteria, companies engaged in sustainable development, are careful in their use of natural resources, and exhibit a sense of responsibility toward the environment are prioritized by the ICRC.

Beyond institutional responsibilities and criteria for collaboration, we should touch upon humanitarian diplomacy and aid organizations. Companies wishing to offer assistance during international disputes, both on the field and otherwise, need to be brought up to speed about humanitarian diplomacy and, more importantly, fundamental humanitarian principles by relief organizations. Moreover, these organizations should take the initiative to encourage companies operating in conflict-affected environments to be more sensitive to the needs of people around them. Humanitarian diplomacy and relief organizations should similarly seek to raise awareness of humanitarian values and principles among private sector employees working in active conflict zones.

The Business Sector's Reservations Regarding Humanitarian Activities

The United Nations Office for the Coordination of Humanitarian Affairs (OCHA) maintains that an air of skepticism surrounds the relations between commercial enterprises and the humanitarian relief community (The New Humanitarian, 2014). This is, in effect, the result of decades of mutual distrust. The various entities making up the humanitarian relief ecosystem regard, somewhat prejudicially, the private sector and commercial enterprises as— given their profit-oriented and mercantile nature—notoriously *heartless*. The private sector, on the other hand, considers humanitarian relief organizations, and especially their personnel, to be complacent and ineffective. Although the ICRC maintains that it is advantageous to work with the private sector, likely a result of the valuable contributions by private enterprises during the formative years of the Red Cross, it has generally been difficult for both sides to form constructive partnerships with the other.

The Humanitarian Policy Group at ODI, known formerly as the Overseas Development Institute, published a series of studies revealing that most of the parties involved lack the necessary know-how concerning how to establish effective communication channels between each other (The New Humanitarian, 2014). This is further compounded by the fact that the two groups share very few venues where they can engage in interact and dialogue with one another.

Citing an ODI project carried out to help people affected by the Syrian crisis in Jordan, a project in which he was personally involved, Steven Zyck argues that the private sector is indeed a major participant in emergency humanitarian interventions:

> *Businesses are often among the first responders to any crisis, opening their stores, opening their warehouses, volunteering their trucks and equipment and machinery to clear roads and get supplies into affected areas [...]*

This isn't a fad. In the future, the opportunities for engaging with businesses in humanitarian action are only going to increase. Many of the challenges that we are increasingly facing—as a result of climate change, as a result of pandemics or technological failures—are things where businesses have a real competitive advantage.

(The New Humanitarian, 2014)

The Turkish Private Sector

Türkiye's private sector has, following the adoption of several national policies seeking to strengthen the position of humanitarian diplomacy, taken an increasingly active role in humanitarian relief initiatives. Working independently and in coordination with various partners that share the same humanitarian values, Turkish businesses support the procurement and/or distribution of relief supplies, materials, equipment, and facilities to disputed territories and conflict zones as well as to people in need around the world. Although the Turkish private sector's humanitarian efforts continue to increase with each passing day, the total amount of contributions and support, when compared with current global demand, need to be greatly expanded.

One project exemplifying the collaborative efforts of Turkish economic organizations is the reconstruction and development campaign organized and carried out by the Independent Industrialists and Businessmen Association (MUSIAD) and twenty-two NGOs, tailored specifically to improving the conditions of displaced Palestinians living in refugee camps in Lebanon (MÜSİAD, 2020).

Representatives from twenty-two different NGOs convened in MUSIAD's Headquarters Building in Istanbul, where, in addition to voicing their condemnation of the Israeli invasion of Palestine in a joint correspondence, they launched an emergency relief campaign for the displaced Palestinians who have been living in refugee camps in Lebanon for seventy-two years.

This meeting was used as a venue to disseminate a report detailing the conditions of the more than 475,075 Palestinian refugees that the United Nations Relief and Works Agency for Palestine Refugees in the Near East (UNRWA) counted to be living in Lebanon.

The report found that seventy-five percent of the people in the region lived in extremely overcrowded conditions, that unemployment and corruption had reached at critically high levels, and that the living conditions of twelve camps had deteriorated to such an extent that their inhabitants were fighting to survive every day of their lives there.

Assorted projects planned to be undertaken in camps

In addition to opening healthcare facilities and polyclinics, this campaign seeks to support education and distance learning opportunities, income-generating programs, landscaping projects, waste collection, household electrification, home repair projects, water distribution, the overhaul of water treatment and supply networks, food distribution, the distribution of COVID-19 hygiene kits and health equipment, drug awareness and prevention programs, scholarships for Palestinian students and opportunities for them to study abroad, Quranic education and memorization programs, and the work of religious clerics.

Twenty-two NGOs support the campaign

Supporting NGOs include MUSIAD, the Confederation of Public Servants Trade Unions (Memur-Sen), HAK-IS Trade Union Confederation (Hak-İş), IHH Humanitarian Relief Foundation, Türkiye Diyanet Foundation, Aziz Mahmûd Hüdâyi Foundation, Sadakataşı Association, Technical Employees Association (TEKDER), Cihannüma Association, Deniz Feneri, Hayrat Humanitarian Aid Association, Fetih Der, Umut Ol Association, Alliance of International Doctors (AID), Orphans Foundation, International Refugee Rights Association (IRRA), Health and Civilization Association, Darüleytam Association, Verenel Association, Hayat Yolu Association, International Water Well Aid Association, and the Federation of International Student Associations (UDEF).

Since it seeks to spread awareness about the ongoing plight of and to advocate for the thousands of displaced Palestinians living in refugee camps in Lebanon, this campaign should be regarded as an important humanitarian diplomacy initiative—one that takes practical steps toward improving the daily lives and dignity of refugees through reconstruction, waste collection, education support, student exchange, healthcare, and income-generating programs.

A Civilian Take on the Relationship between the Business Sector and Humanitarian Diplomacy

Humanitarian diplomacy is, from the purview of the business world, the sum of all the initiatives and collaborative efforts undertaken by diverse countries seeking to ensure continued human flourishing. These include offering a helping hand to all disenfranchised people, promoting human dignity among afflicted and downtrodden individuals, engendering an attitude of philanthropic love for humanity, and ensuring that every single human being, no matter his or her personal background, be able to live a dignified life free of human rights violations. The international business world can serve as a valuable partner during negotiations seeking to persuade decision makers to adopt specific policies—the single most important component of humanitarian diplomacy. They can do this either by engaging in efforts to mold public opinion, advocacy, and arbitration campaigns or through more coercive means, such as financial incentives, pressure, or sanction. The following are a few example initiatives and agreements between Türkiye and The Gambia that serve to demonstrate such cooperation:

- Türkiye and The Gambia signed an agreement in 2018 that has resulted in more than one hundred scholarships being awarded to Gambian students to pursue higher education in Turkish universities.
- An agreement between the Turkish Maarif Foundation and Boğaziçi University Members Association (BURA) has allowed Turkish students and educators to attend and offer instruction in Gambian universities.
- An agreement with Karadeniz Technical University intends to help The Gambia improve her efficiency in fish and seafood production, one of the country's most important sources of livelihood.
- The Turkish Cooperation and Coordination Agency has teamed up with universities in both countries and local Gambian woman farmers to promote more effective moringa tree cultivation techniques. These initiatives have helped create new business opportunities for local communities and allowed moringa tea, another of the country's important sources of livelihood, to be marketed internationally.
- Hospital patients arriving in Türkiye from The Gambia receive free medical treatment. This helps, if only a little, support the country's underperforming healthcare system.

Conclusion

This chapter has demonstrated that the business world has the potential to serve as an effective partner in humanitarian diplomacy and global relief efforts, able, as evinced by the projects undertaken in Africa cited here, to wield its influence and clout to help solve problems blighting humanity. However, Turkish businesses need to take part in certain initiatives to increase their awareness of the need to support international humanitarian causes. As such, Türkiye's official and civilian humanitarian diplomacy actors, such as the Turkish Red Crescent, can disseminate comprehensive memoranda to designated representatives of the business world on a periodic basis, guide them toward the best and most effective course of action, and even conduct collaborative initiatives together. Given the number of crisis zones that continue to dot the world map, there remains much work to be done—highly important work that requires the concerted and systematic effort of diverse partners working hand in hand toward a similar goal.

References

MÜSİAD. (2020). *MÜSİAD ve 22 sivil toplum kuruluşu, Lübnan'da yaşayan Filistinli mülteci kampları için harekete geçti.* https://www.musiad.org.tr/icerik/haber-detay-39/p-978

The International Committee of the Red Cross (ICRC). (2018). *Ethical principles guiding the ICRC's partnerships with the private sector.* https://www.icrc.org/en/document/ethical-principles-guiding-icrc-partnerships-private-sector

The International Federation of Red Cross and Red Crescent (IFRC). (2009). *Humanitarian diplomacy policy*. https://www.ifrc.org/sites/default/files/Humanitarian-Diplomacy-Policy_EN.pdf

The New Humanitarian. (2014). *Business and humanitarian action: Overcoming the language barrier*. https://www.thenewhumanitarian.org/analysis/2014/07/21/business-and-humanitarian-action-overcoming-language-barrier

11 Digital Diplomacy for Humanitarians

Clare Dalton

In 2015, a small group of us at the ICRC's Geneva headquarters began a series of digital breakfasts. We would meet in the Director General's office once a week with coffee and croissants for training in Twitter by the organization's communications team. Each week they would announce the "tweet of the week" and explain why one of our tweets was particularly effective, often because it used an image, engaged policymakers in conversation, amplified a message, or shaped a new humanitarian narrative. We slowly found ourselves becoming digital humanitarian diplomats (HDiplomats).

In the same year, Corneliu Bjola and Marcus Holmes published *Digital Diplomacy*, one of the first books to explore how the new digital infrastructure of the hyper-connected world had already precipitated profound changes in diplomacy (Bjola and Holmes, 2015, p. 238). The authors observed that digital diplomacy has not only transformed the very nature of diplomacy but has also streamlined and broadened the scope of diplomatic processes through modern digital communications. They concluded that digital diplomacy is "nothing less than a revolution in the practice of diplomacy" (Bjola and Holmes, 2015, p. 6).

This chapter affirms the validity of this assessment for humanitarian diplomacy (HD), too. Normal ways of working—like representation, networking and communicating—have been broadened, thickened, and accelerated by digital HD. There is no doubt that the Red Cross and Red Crescent Movement is much more intimately connected with policymakers and publics than we were. But more than just making HD better, digital reach and relationships have transformed the diplomatic arena itself, the diversity of diplomatic actors, and even the personal experience of being a diplomat which feels more "naked" and exposed according to former British diplomat Tom Fletcher (2017, p. 336).

In this chapter, I will draw on the ICRC's ventures into digital diplomacy as I explore how diplomacy has been both improved and transformed with the emergence of this novel form of diplomacy. After this, I will move on to identifying the potential risks digital diplomacy poses to humanitarians.

DOI: 10.4324/9781003503187-11

Improving diplomacy

Digital diplomacy has significantly enhanced the modus operandi of humanitarian advocacy and humanitarian operations undertaken on behalf of suffering populations.

Digital diplomacy has greatly improved the ICRC's *representation* and *recognition*. The organization's purpose, its people, and their work in today's active conflicts have become better known to government officials because of their presence on social media. It is now very easy to learn who represents the ICRC in a particular country and to follow senior ICRC personalities via their social media handles. The former mystique of the ICRC official has given way to a more open and identifiable person who embodies the organization's values and concerns in virtual space. Official ICRC and IFRC handles constantly communicate the Movement's purpose, programs, and policy. The same is true of many National Red Cross and Red Crescent Societies.

The advent of *digital networking* has likewise expanded the ICRC's range of contacts, both within official government networks and across the wider public sphere. The effectiveness of these expanded diplomatic networks is further amplified by their continuous, real-time nature. Anyone with an internet connection—not just those involved in the diplomatic apparatus—can follow diplomats' positions, opinions, and activities on social media as they unfold, and can even reach out to particular diplomats by engaging with their messages publicly or by sending them direct messages (DMs). This effectively allows HDiplomats to do extensive global networking even while waiting to catch the bus.

Digital channels have significantly increased the ICRC's range of diplomatic counterparts and tools. Official government websites, online portals, and secure communication channels enable humanitarians and diplomats to exchange information and share policies. Virtual summits, video conferences, and online fora have become common tools for negotiations and discourse around funding initiatives and humanitarian responses. This is likewise the case in the humanitarian sector, where online platforms like *ReliefWeb* and *Humanitarian Response.info* have made significant strides in standardizing data sharing, facilitating interorganizational coordination, and streamlining information management during emergencies, all of which are integral to the smooth flow of HD. The ICRC has seen its own network expand amongst policy-makers and the public, both by building new contacts through social media engagement, and by the ability to continue a conversation or exchange in the virtual world. This requires an important focus on the engagement opportunities that social platforms offer, not only the information-sharing potential.

Just as diplomatic networking has expanded and intensified in real-time, digital diplomacy has expedited the process of cultivating and maintaining more intimate relationships. Not only are interpersonal interactions on social media more informal than ritualized diplomatic meetings, informal relationships are often more quickly forged on X (Twitter) and LinkedIn than they are in stuffy, protocol-bound meeting rooms. This digital intimacy gives us the impression that we all know each other well, essentially allowing DM discussions to hit the ground running. There is also the moment when a digital relationship "breaks through the cloud" and we meet someone in person for the first time after having known him or her digitally for months or even years. Indeed, the interpersonal intimacy extant in being Twitter friends serves to quickly create a powerful bond during in-person encounters and acts as an impetus to go out of one's way to meet someone properly.

Digital connections often serve as a springboard for more important face-to-face meetings. Several times during my time at the ICRC, an online post sharing a report or speech on a key topic was followed up by a DM from a senior diplomat inviting the ICRC, IFRC, or National Red Cross Red Crescent Society to come and brief a ministry team in-person. As such, informal digital relationships have the potential to morph into formal invitations and closed-door diplomatic engagement.

Digital diplomacy offers exponential opportunities for *agenda setting* around humanitarian information, narratives, and policy asks. While a physical in-person campaign might take weeks or months to organize and orchestrate, a virtual social media campaign can be kicked off fast and wide with a single communication via a social media platform. Indeed, if a critical mass of people "pile on" and "crowd in" around the topic, thereby *amplifying* HD in real-time with voices from all around the world. New agendas and narratives boasted by a global voice can then quickly swarm diplomats and politicians. To give one example, this type of amplification has been effective in highlighting the impact of attacks against health workers or in initiating policy discussions around the ethics of autonomous weapons. In both scenarios, people from around the globe have used their collective voice to amplify and advance these humanitarian concerns.

In a similar vein, digital diplomacy offers new avenues for *alliance-* and *coalition-building* with people and organizations previously inaccessible through conventional in-person encounters. This works especially well within hybrid strategies, whereby physical events—a report, a conference, or an aid convoy—can be amplified virtually by HDiplomats to inaugurate a process of coalition building. Indeed, the ICRC has employed this practice on numerous occasions with respect to our concerns about the use of explosive weapons in urban areas.

The wonders of *messaging tools like WhatsApp, Signal, etc.* have revolutionized communications in multilateral conferences and events, not only within individual diplomatic teams but also between multiple teams. The 2016 World Humanitarian Summit in Istanbul marked the first time that team members of an ICRC delegation at a multilateral conference used WhatsApp to communicate with each other in real-time. Today, it is impossible to imagine multilateralism without this invaluable tool. With a diplomatic team dispersed across various concurrent sessions taking place at events attended by thousands of people like the UNGA or COP, WhatsApp facilitates the instantaneous exchange of information, thereby allowing us to learn what states are saying in different rooms in real-time, observe which coalitions are forming around which events, and coordinate important bump-ins as people maneuver through crowded spaces. "WhatsApp diplomacy" has transformed our capacity to engage in real-time planning, communication, documentation, and coordination during ever-larger multilateral meetings, thus making it an indispensable conduit for private communications among diplomats.

Digital technology has also empowered the ICRC to escalate its *public diplomacy* efforts. This is "the process by which international actors advance their ends abroad through the engagement of publics" (Snow, 2020, p. 4), which essentially entails the use of soft power by government personalities to reach behind and beyond their official government counterparts and garner public support to their cause. The last ten years have seen a veritable metamorphosis in the way that digital platforms allow humanitarians to mold public perceptions and build relationships with people across the world. Digital content continues to become increasingly accessible as opportunities to connect with audiences expand. Some 66 percent of the world's population uses the internet, and ICRC social media accounts have amassed an excess of 14 million followers as of April 2024. Nonetheless, the challenge for many humanitarian organizations who take advantage of this technology is to maintain a neutral, impartial stance while remaining steadfast in their pursuit of a more comprehensive understanding of human need and humanitarian action.

The greater broadcasting of humanitarian concerns to the public sphere has produced a reciprocal increase in narrowcasting from the public to government officials. Individuals in emergency situations can now send highly targeted messages up the digital chain to political decision-makers. Messages concerning the laws of war and harrowing images of suffering disseminated by humanitarians as a facet of public diplomacy are often picked up by citizens who propel these messages up the hierarchy to individual government ministers. As these images become viral, government officials are often "called out," sometimes very harshly, by the average Joe on digital platforms in an interesting bounce-back loop.

Digital HD has also improved operational efficiency. A core HD objective for the ICRC is to secure respect for international humanitarian law (henceforth IHL), which is the law to regulate armed conflict. The ICRC's digital public diplomacy involves using public channels both to promote respect for and to disseminate visual explainers of IHL on platforms like X (formerly known as Twitter), Instagram, and Facebook. These are combined with moving accounts of wartime suffering that drive people to engage digital content and link up with one another in support of humanitarian norms both in their own society and globally. These same digital formats can also be used to target members of armed forces and armed groups directly, many of whom the ICRC is engaging in more specific bilateral dialogue.

The ICRC also uses digital HD to facilitate the necessary access and operating conditions for ICRC field operations. Digital diplomacy can augment more specific messages given personally to authorities in private bilateral meetings by communicating the general conditions needed for safe and unimpeded humanitarian access to a broad audience as well. Publicly communicated messages never reveal a confidential dialogue but can be strategically aligned with operational and legal priorities to show the humanitarian importance of access. Digital platforms are used to highlight, demonstrate, and explain humanitarian needs, often encouraging decision-makers to take the steps necessary to improve conditions on the ground. Curated content helps explain the value and relevance of the work performed by humanitarian organizations, enabling digital diplomacy to be used to garner support for individuals affected by armed conflict and to galvanize popular support for the Red Cross/Red Crescent Movement's mission and mandate.

Digital technologies have also transformed how humanitarians gather and analyze information to use as the meat and bones of their HD. Open-source intelligence, data analytics, and digital tools not only enable humanitarian monitoring of crises in real-time but also aggregate important data on needs, violations, and humanitarian impact. Watching social media trends also helps HDiplomats track political developments, human needs, and public opinion in real-time. Platforms like the Humanitarian Data Exchange (HDX) and OpenStreetMap provide valuable data and mapping resources for humanitarian actors. Data can form the content of HD as they seek to influence powerful policymakers to make informed decisions about war and disaster response. If data alone does not work, government officials can be exposed to virtual reality (VR) or augmented reality (AR) to experience people's suffering and conditions for themselves in their office or meeting room (Buch et al., 2022).

Beyond data, digital technology has deepened people's emotional and empathic investment in modern crises, having dramatically expanded the "affected population" of a crisis by creating a global community of pained observers to raw human suffering. Instagram, Tik-Tok, X, and Telegram in particular have nurtured highly emotional cultures in which people express their feelings out in the open *en masse*. Visceral images of terrible individual suffering that the mainstream media would never dare show are constantly on exhibit on these younger, less-regulated platforms, shared deliberately by both the average person and more popular influencers to elicit the empathy, shock, and outrage of their followers. These individual images, often narrated by citizen journalists who become virtual friends to their followers, avoid the problem of psychic numbing from excessive data and focus instead on the pain or death of a specific person not unlike ourselves. Depending on the conflict, this surge of empathy can prime a global public to support a digital call issued by HDiplomats. It is not always easy to assess the impact of this trend, be it positive or negative, and certainly these tools can increase polarization or be used by one waring side or another to further their own aims. Nonetheless, online support for the daily suffering of civilians affected by today's wars fills the streams of these platforms on a daily basis.

A key part of this digital monitoring is the increased potential for humanitarian listening to affected populations. The digital empowerment of so many billions of people today means that aggrieved individuals can dialogue directly with humanitarian organizations. This can facilitate mutual understanding and give affected people greater agency and dignity in designing responses tailored to their needs. Much of this happens through SMS campaigns, crowdsourcing, and the use of GPS and satellite imagery. These all coalesce to produce a clearer picture of an emergency that HDiplomats can then bring to the attention of political decision-makers.

Changing nature of diplomacy

Just as there are numerous examples of how digital technology has improved conventional HD, there are also clear signs of how it has transformed the very nature of diplomacy.

Diplomacy itself is changing. While once a practice largely reserved for states, today it is a much more inclusive process that involves NGOs, businesses, celebrities, and citizens groups of all kinds. Multistakeholder diplomacy was already on the rise in the big-tent in-person summits of the 1990s and early 2000s when the advent of digital technology started to lower the barriers preventing people from entering diplomatic spaces. A wide range of actors that including humanitarians now have a digital voice with which they are able to influence discourse surrounding foreign policy decisions.

Digital diplomacy has served as the impetus for profound change in the practice and culture of negotiations—a core tenant of diplomatic practice. Several notable cases can be cited in which digital diplomacy has played a crucial role in solving diplomatic disputes, in facilitating negotiations, and in fostering international cooperation. In the Iran Nuclear Deal (Joint Comprehensive Plan of Action), diplomats from the United States, United Kingdom, France, Russia, China, Germany, and Iran used secure communication channels and virtual meetings to discuss and finalize the agreement. Digital negotiations also enable heads of state to "drop in" on processes more easily at key moments, thereby dramatically compressing the timeframe and chains of command involved in diplomatic negotiations. Experts of all kinds are all readily available online, able to weigh in with their opinions in situations impossible only twenty years ago. Digital diplomacy allows a wider range of stakeholders to participate in negotiations as talks unfold in real-time. There are also economic advantages, as digital diplomacy reduces the need for physical travel, translators, administrative support, and logistical staff. A large part of the future of diplomatic negotiations may indeed be digital (Molnar and Robertson, 2024).

Digital technologies have enabled diplomats to bridge geographical distances, exchange information quickly, include more perspectives, and coordinate their positions effectively in real time in ways not previously possible. The Red Cross/Red Crescent Movement's first benefitted from this new diplomatic arena while negotiating the Global Compact for Safe, Orderly, and Regular Migration throughout 2018. Digital diplomacy played a crucial role in the movement's ability to influence the negotiation process because it allowed people from different National Societies around the world to join in throughout the year by communicating internally with the IFRC and ICRC, share proposals with states, and work continuously with governments to reach consensuses on complex issues surrounding migration. Online platforms and virtual conferences facilitated dialogue between countries during the process, which in turn enabled them to overcome differences and commit to collective action.

These two examples illustrate what Bjola and Luijang have identified as the "three new dimensions" that digital diplomacy has afforded to classical diplomacy: Agenda setting; presence expansion, and conversation-generation (Bjola and Jiang, 2015, pp. 71–88).

HDiplomats' potential for *agenda setting* has similarly increased. Individualized digital media frees diplomats from the gate-keeping of the journalist or PR consultant, giving digital diplomats an advantage in their own personal ability to grab the headlines, create news, and drive the narrative as they see fit.

Digital diplomacy also gives a HDiplomats and their organization exponential *presence expansion* by enabling them to be "out there" in the relevant public and political spheres in a way that was, quite literally, virtually impossible for the diplomatic official of the last century. Indeed, they must be out there now lest they cede this space to other influencers.

Finally, digital diplomacy is *conversation-generating*. The ability of followers and others to engage with digital HDiplomats makes it very difficult to restrict diplomacy to statements, speaking points, and monologues. Instead, it drives diplomacy forward as a conversation in private and in the public eye. This shift is transforming the very culture of diplomacy, as digital diplomats have become increasingly recognizable to people outside their home region.

Risks

The aforementioned notwithstanding, digital diplomacy also presents challenges and risks that need to be addressed. Cybersecurity threats, misinformation campaigns, and digital propaganda are some of the enduring problems that diplomats, humanitarians, and governments must navigate in our emergent digital age. Ensuring the security and integrity of digital communications, protecting sensitive information, and countering online disinformation are critical aspects of digital diplomacy that require constant vigilance and investment in cybersecurity measures.

While, on the one hand, the impact of algorithms, bots, and hackers remains woefully understudied, we are currently witnessing a surge in misinformation, disinformation, and hate speech within the public diplomatic sphere, on the other. Being part of the larger diplomatic apparatus, digital diplomacy has naturally seen its fair share of manipulation. Indeed, the digital information ecosystem becomes increasingly embroiled in inflammatory discourse. In addition to being susceptible to manipulation, digital content both mirrors and perpetuates wider polarization trends, with humanitarian organizations and leaders increasingly finding themselves the target of deliberate campaigns.

Although social media platforms are constantly improving their content moderation capacity, developments in AI have facilitated the generation and spread of fake content, which in turn amplifies disinformation and other forms of harmful information. An important counter-balance to these risks is for diplomats to focus on the quality of their online relationships online just as they would do offline. Digital technologies have the potential to empower everybody, regardless of one's underlying intentions. Ultimately, however, the quality of relationships and a certain standard of diplomatic decorum must be maintained in digital spaces.

Nevertheless, digital diplomacy offers a platform for misinformation and hate speech to polarize conflicts and foment distrust between people and media content. Given digital diplomacy's dual nature and use, humanitarian organizations must have in place carefully designed policies and approaches to ensure that these tools actually serve their humanitarian aims. They must also find ways to monitor and curate content accordingly, something that can be done by employing data scientists, cyber experts, and IT technicians with the digital expertise and experience to help HDiplomats maneuver through this new digital landscape.

In conclusion, digital diplomacy has transformed the practice of diplomacy in the twenty-first century, offering new opportunities for engagement, communication, and cooperation among nations and publics. By harnessing the power of digital technologies, governments can enhance transparency, build trust, and promote peace and stability in an increasingly interconnected world. Human suffering, whether be brought on by armed conflict or natural disaster, can be interjected into the diplomatic arena more vividly, more personally, and more effectively today. However, as with all technologies, digital space carries risks and unintended consequences. Digital platforms can be used to spread misinformation and disinformation that undermine HD and can equally present a polarized or one-sided view of a particular situation.

Diplomats, humanitarians, and policymakers seeking to wield digital diplomacy in such a way that will further their aims must adapt to the ever-emergent challenges and opportunities that accompany the digital age. Although we might adapt our tools and enlarge our networks, our humanitarian objectives will remain unchanged. Indeed, we will need to evolve how we engage in HD as even newer technologies emerge. As long as digital diplomacy facilitates our ability to bring a more images and examples of humanity into people's feeds and, as a result, their own personal zeitgeist, it will continue to be an effective tool for humanitarian action.

References

Bjola, C. & Holmes, M. (2015). *Digital diplomacy: Theory and practice*. Routledge.

Bjola, C. & Jiang, L. (2015). *Social media and public diplomacy: A comparative analysis of the digital diplomatic strategies of the EU, US and Japan in China*. Doi:10.4324/9781315730844-13

Buch, A. M. et al. (2022). Engineering Diplomacy: How AI and Human Augmentation Could Remake the Art of Foreign Relations. *Science & Diplomacy*. February 25, 2022. https://doi.org/10.1126/scidip.ade6798

Fletcher, T. (2017). *The naked diplomat: Understanding power and politics in the digital age*. William Collins.

Molnar, L. & Robertson, J. (2024). *Intersection of technology and diplomacy: Foresights and implications?* Anwar Gargash Diplomatic Academy. https://www.agda.ac.ae/docs/default-source/2024/foresights-and-implications.pdf?sfvrsn=47da653b_1

Snow, N. (2020). Rethinking Public Diplomacy in the 2020s. In Snow, N. & Cull, J. N. (Eds.), *Routledge handbook of public diplomacy* (pp. 3–11). Routledge.

12 Utilizing HD to Protect Humanitarian Personnel and Humanitarian Aid

Kaan Namlı

From Diplomacy toward Humanitarian Diplomacy

A historical reading of diplomacy reveals important transformations and innovations to the perceptive eye. Traditional diplomacy was considered the sole prerogative of the state, who held an absolute monopoly over diplomatic efforts. Since states continue to retain their diplomatic clout, many definitions focus on interstate relations, communication, and engagement. Ernest Satow discusses the practice of diplomacy as "the application of intelligence and tact to the conduct of relations between governments of independent states" (Satow, 1979). Hedley Bull, a prominent scholar affiliated with the English School of international relations, describes diplomacy as a form of intercommunication—one that occurs between states and that facilitates the development of international society (1995). Similarly, Adam Watson (2013), in his book that presents an overview of diplomacy from ancient times to the present, simply defines diplomacy as "dialogue between states." Bespeckling the literature, moreover, are definitions regarding how external relations form the core of diplomacy. This understanding of diplomacy, albeit accurate, is incomplete. The issue here is not the great attention afforded to states; it is the insistence that they constitute the sole diplomatic actors.

One key factor that has precipitated the diversification of diplomatic actors is the emergence of new challenges that exceeded individual nations' abilities to resolve on their own. The hegemony over diplomacy that states had traditionally enjoyed began to crack under the growing complexity of global challenges. Whereas foreign policy and national interests had customarily held the reins of diplomacy, emergent issues evolved to include climate change, women's empowerment, minority rights, children's wellbeing, migration, and anti-war campaigns. As increasingly more diverse issues entered into the purview of diplomacy, states' former monopoly over the

DOI: 10.4324/9781003503187-12

diplomatic realm, thereby paving the way for the entrance of new, non-state actors (Turunen, 2020).

Though it certainly cannot be denied that nation-states retain their power among diplomatic actors, it would be equally foolish to attempt to refute the reality of the current multi-actor diplomatic ecosystem. Humanitarian organizations have, for instance, used diplomacy to ensure that civilians, aid workers, and aid items are protected during politically rooted humanitarian emergencies. This would eventually crescendo into the rise of humanitarian diplomacy (HD) in the early 2000s, which once again expanded the scope of diplomacy to encompass, among numerous other issues, the protection of humanitarian workers and aid.

Over time, new diplomacy actors joined the mix, including supranational organizations, international NGOs, the UN, the ICRC, the IFRC, Red Cross and Red Crescent National Societies, transnational actors, prominent scholars and celebrities, social media influencers, and the private sector. The aforementioned organizations began coordinating among themselves and with other actors on pressing issues, thereby molding how diplomacy would thenceforth be conducted. As organizations began to form their own blocs, they found themselves better positioned to contest and influence policy decisions in favor of their interests and objectives (Cooper and Cornut, 2019). Authors have suggested the term *transprofessional diplomacy* to describe this new diplomatic ecosystem, as it emphasizes how diplomacy—no longer restricted to the machinations of state-appointed officials—incorporates a wide host of professions interacting with one another, both out in the open and behind closed doors (Constantinou et al., 2016).

Transprofessional diplomacy, rather than restricting diplomatic efficacy to state diplomats, asserts that diplomatic literacy and skills exist to varying degrees in different professions.

Evolving Diplomacy: New Actors in the Advocacy of Humanitarian Ideals

These veritable revolutions in both the theory and practice of diplomacy have caused the global diplomatic modus vivendi to pivot away from a rigid state-centric endeavor toward an intersection of actors, issues, and ideals. The current politically tempestuous era demands the pooling of resources and joint efforts conducted by multiple actors, both state and non-state, through multifarious networks and relationships to lead effective diplomatic responses (Hocking, 2006). These growing networks and inter-engagements between actors led to an evolution in diplomacy where it was crosscutting into multiple sectors and issues simultaneously.

It was only inevitable that entirely new humanitarian ideals, goals, and mandates would emerge as the diplomatic arena continued to expand. This induction of new ideals and values has, in turn, spurred the further diversification of stakeholders, parties, and professionals involved in HD.

The expansion of diplomacy has led to the coinage of new terms to designate incipient diplomatic practices, such as digital diplomacy, public diplomacy, celebrity diplomacy, military diplomacy, small state diplomacy, and business diplomacy (Turunen, 2020). What makes HD its own unique diplomatic niche is its core focus on humanitarianism and the humanitarian cause. This includes adherence to the humanitarian principles of neutrality, impartiality, and independence while aiming to alleviate human suffering and uphold human dignity. Of course, such objectives can only be achieved with the involvement and, more importantly, cooperation of national governments and policy-makers. The point of diplomatic intersection is, therefore, this very need for humanitarians and the political apparatus to interact and engage with one another (De Lauri, 2020). Nevertheless, HD in its present form should be understood from an emic perspective, in which institutional, state, and non-state actors all employ HD because of it multifunctional character and convenience of use by a wide range of both official and non-official actors (Regnier, 2011).

A brief historical overview demonstrates that as the diplomatic sphere expanded as a result of new challenges, the stronghold of state diplomacy splintered to let in new actors who began to inject humanitarian ideals, principles, and goals into the diplomatic ecosystem. This culminated in the emergence of HD, which is now also used by actors outside of the humanitarian sector. Though not fully defined, HD can, at minimum, comfortably be characterized by its goal to achieve positive outcomes for all of humanity. As we have thus far explored the context surrounding the emergence of HD, I shall move on to a discussion of its more practical elements in order to facilitate an understanding of how it works in action.

HD Practices and Actors

HD can be practiced at the highest governmental echelons while simultaneously depending on support by ancillary actors to achieve its outcomes. The inclusion of local community leaders, volunteers, Red Cross and Red Crescent societies, as well as other grassroots initiatives might be necessary to ensure success. HD is often practiced in stricken conditions where the delivery of aid is severely exacerbated, such as natural disasters, armed conflicts, pandemics, and social upheaval. However, quantitative text analyses imply that HD is most commonly applied during armed conflicts (Clark, 2018).

The harrowing crises that rattled Bosnia, Afghanistan, Iraq, Yemen, Syria, and African nations have shown that the safe havens and corridors that humanitarian action was originally meant to secure may also be targeted during times of political strife. With increasing conflicts around the world, the risks and dangers humanitarians now face are most often those associated with protracted conflicts and prolonged crises where civilians are targeted, where access to remote areas is difficult, and where aid workers are perceived as a threat. It is also important to highlight that HD is employed in other, non-military related contexts. Nevertheless, since these contexts often share similar constraints and realities with armed conflicts, HD can be used to address them as well (Egeland, 2013).

In the ongoing Russo-Ukrainian War, both state and non-state actors have engaged in massive amounts of HD to call for a ceasefire, access to affected populations, the creation of humanitarian corridors, and the strict adherence to international humanitarian law. In a similar vein, Afghanistan fell into dire straits with millions requiring assistance following the 2021 US troop withdrawal from the country. Various actors partook in HD in with the ruling Taliban to secure greater rights for women, access to remote areas, and safe passage while conducting humanitarian operations.

Non-state actors are both more attentive to and, unsurprisingly, more able to practice a greater degree of non-political HD compared to sovereign nations, given the latter's inevitable political baggage. That said, however, the humanitarian diplomatic actions and approaches carried out by non-state actors do not adhere to a well-structured framework are often eclectic and multiharmonic. The UN, for instance, lacks a coherent, systematized approach despite being a prominent non-state actor with powerful diplomatic clout within the humanitarian ecosystem. Although several UN organizations have incorporated HD into their charters and action plans, the UN as a whole lacks a consistent approach to HD, let alone strategies or goals. Though this may be attributed to the fact that UN organizations are often involved in very different, sometimes highly specific spheres, the absence of a unified front in this vein is indeed a glaring stain on the reputation of UN system. The ICRC, on the other hand, is more institutionally involved in HD, engaging in humanitarian causes multilaterally, bilaterally, officially, and informally. As a result, ICRC's diplomatic efforts are more limited in scope compared to individual nations and, to a certain extent, the UN. The IFRC's scope is wider than the ICRC's, as it focuses on influencing decision-makers to work toward the interests of vulnerable individuals and to strengthen Red Cross and Red Crescent national societies' abilities to do the same.

Both domestic and international NGOs have, in recent years, sought to increase both the depth and breadth of their involvement in HD. NGOs fulfill an important role by bringing up issues related to community, development, human rights, social equality, and health emergencies with their respective governments and the wider international community. The Turkish Red Crescent, together with international and domestic partners, coordinated with both the EU and Turkish government to ensure that Syrians under temporary protection received the rights and support guaranteed to them. Another issue, climate change, has gained increasing traction among domestic NGOs, who now actively engage their governments to institute more comprehensive environmental policies. Similarly, many NGOs focus on women's and children's rights, anti-drug legislation, and sexual trafficking. In short, HD seeks to bring about change that would have a positive impact on a specific group of disenfranchised people, a pressing issue, or a pervasive societal ill.

Albeit oft-overlooked, local communities and grassroots activists are highly effective actors in the HD ecosystem. Local communities, constituents, and public opinion are important in shaping and influencing decision-makers. Knowing this, it would be imprudent to discuss HD without mentioning grassroots initiatives' power in influencing humanitarian outcomes. Certain issues impacting communities become the focus of decision-makers either because of their popularity or because of heavy constituent pressure articulated in a unified voice. Although success has been mixed, the demand for aboriginal rights among communities in Canada has had considerable influence on decision-makers. More importantly, when grassroots movements combine their efforts with NGOs, international organizations, or Red Cross Red Crescent national societies, they are more likely to leverage decision-makers to supporting humanitarian outcomes.

The above discussion highlights several key points. It is evident that diplomacy has always played a powerful role in humanitarian affairs. Various actors define HD based on their functions and areas of work, which in turn shapes their HD practices. These practices most commonly involve crises, emergencies, and conflicts. Involvement in HD aims to attain access to affected communities, open humanitarian corridors, and provide assistance to vulnerable groups. As the world becomes increasingly embroiled in climate-related, economic, social, and political challenges, diverse actors have, either deliberately or otherwise, sought recourse through HD to devise viable solutions. Despite numerous conventions' expressed affirmation of humanitarian workers' internationally mandated protected status, humanitarians of all stripes find themselves and the materials under their stewardship subject to different forms of aggression, including physical attacks, economic reprisals, and legal sanctions. Yet, HD has not played a central role in ensuring the safety of humanitarian personnel or items.

Table 12.1 Major Attacks on Aid Workers (1997–2022) (Humanitarian Outcomes, Aid Worker Security Database, https://www.aidworkersecurity.org/incidents/report)

	2022	2021	2020	2019	2018	2017	2016	2015	2014	2013	2012	2011	2010	2009	2008	2007	2006	2005	2004	2003	2002	2001	2000	1999	1998	1997
Number of Incidents	235	268	283	276	229	160	164	150	194	265	170	152	131	156	165	124	107	74	64	63	46	29	42	32	26	35
Total aid worker victim	444	461	484	481	409	315	296	290	340	474	277	309	251	300	278	221	240	172	127	143	85	90	91	68	68	75
Total killed	116	141	117	125	131	140	109	111	130	159	71	86	73	113	127	91	88	53	56	87	38	27	57	33	35	39
Total injured	143	203	242	234	147	103	99	110	89	179	115	127	85	94	91	87	87	96	46	49	23	20	23	15	15	6
Total kidnapped*	185	117	125	122	131	72	88	69	121	136	91	96	93	93	60	43	65	23	25	7	24	43	11	20	18	30
International victims	23	23	25	27	29	28	43	30	33	60	49	29	41	74	51	35	26	14	26	26	17	28	21	25	22	30
National victims	421	438	459	454	380	287	253	260	307	414	228	280	210	226	227	186	214	158	101	117	68	62	70	43	46	45
UN staff	76	55	58	37	70	48	71	44	71	115	48	92	44	108	65	39	61	27	11	31	18	28	31	17	21	23
International NGO staff	162	198	228	260	186	109	161	173	152	142	97	135	151	128	158	133	111	108	71	69	49	48	46	31	11	32
ICRC staff	0	5	8	2	5	14	10	3	16	14	3	5	10	8	5	4	10	3	1	8	7	11	9	7	26	9
NRCS and IFRC staff	9	6	20	14	20	60	11	28	27	44	24	10	1	25	2	8	17	5	11	20	5	3	0	7	7	10
NNGO staff	184	187	168	154	128	84	41	39	71	145	92	67	45	31	43	27	37	27	32	15	5	0	4	6	3	0

HD for Protecting Personnel and Aid

While attacks directly or indirectly targeting aid workers and items are more likely to occur in hostile environments, they may happen at any time and in any part of the world. Though perhaps the first to come to mind, humanitarian workers are subjected not only to violent attacks that threaten both life and limb but also to negative political propaganda, imprisonment, social and economic ostracism, character bashing, and forced unemployment. These sorts of attacks on humanitarian workers threaten the delivery of aid to people in need, which, in the worst-case scenario, can lead to the suspension of humanitarian activities.

Figure 12.1 Mehmet Arif Kıdıman: A vehicle clearly marked with the TRC emblem was fired upon by several masked men wearing camouflage from two untagged vehicles on the road between the two northern Syrian cities of Al-Rai and Al-Bab in September of 2020. This attack resulted in the death of one TRC employee, forty-year-old Mehmet Arif Kıdıman, and the injury of two other TRC personnel. Photo by Türk Kızılay.

REVISED
Aid Worker Security Report
Figures at a glance

2023

444 aid workers were victims of major attacks in 2022   **116** killed   **143** wounded   **185** kidnapped

Overall, attacks against aid workers were marginally lower in 2022, but there was a significant surge in kidnappings.[1] A total of 444 aid workers fell victim to violence in 235 separate attacks, with 116 killed, 143 injured, and 185 kidnapped. South Sudan remained the most dangerous operational context for humanitarian workers, with Haiti and Ukraine newly joining the group of countries with the highest number of incidents.

Attacks affecting aid workers, total victims, and fatalities 2013–2022

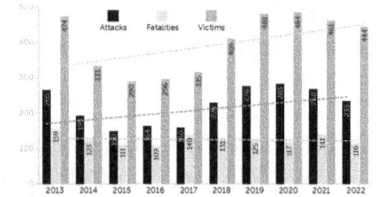

Types of organisations attacked, 2013-2022

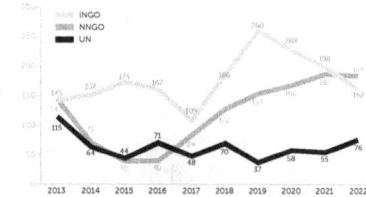

South Sudan remained by far the highest incident context, significantly influencing the global casualty numbers in recent years. Attacks in Mali, particularly kidnappings, remained high in 2022, equaling Myanmar for the second highest total.

In Ukraine, attacks by Russian forces claimed the lives of at least 11 aid workers, mostly in collateral damage from airstrikes and shelling. Moreover, they have illegally detained at least 39 aid workers, many of whom were reportedly abused.

The increase in casualties among national NGOs is especially concerning considering the disparity in security risk management resources between national and international NGOs, including the provision of security training. The upcoming Aid Worker Security Report (August 2023) will focus on security training in the humanitarian sector: what it consists of, who gets it, and how do we know if it works. The report will also analyze the 2022 data, particularly the country-specific trends contributing to the rise in kidnappings, and will provide preliminary statistics for the first half of 2023, a period marked by a surge in violence in Sudan and other regions.

Numbers and types of attacks in 10 most violent contexts, 2022

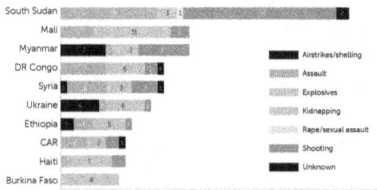

Number of aid workers kidnapped, 2013-2022

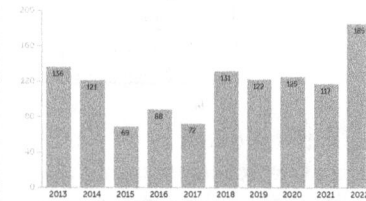

Verified incidents of aid workers being kidnapped, defined as forcible abduction or detention exceeding 24 hours, saw a 58% increase over the previous year, marking the highest total ever recorded.

Another notable trend in 2022 was the continued rise in casualties borne by national and local aid organisations. Despite having far larger staffs, international NGOs have seen a decrease in attacks, while those of their local partners are on the rise.

[1] Includes all forcible abductions and detentions by non-state actors or foreign militaries, where the victim was held for over 24 hours, whether or not a ransom demand was made.

Humanitarian Outcomes

This overview of the latest verified aid worker casualty statistics is based on data from the Aid Worker Security Database (AWSD). The AWSD is a project of Humanitarian Outcomes, made possible by funding support from USAID and available online at **www.aidworkersecurity.org**

Figure 12.2 "Aid Worker Security Report 2023 - Figures at a glance"

Aid Worker Security Database (AWSD)

The AWSD records major incidents of violence deliberately perpetrated against humanitarian workers globally. Incident data is sourced from two main publicly available records that have been systematically filtered by data mining tools and information provided directly to the project by humanitarian organizations and operational security units. The AWSD maintains agreements with a number of regional- and ground-level security consortia to verify and share data on incidents. Incident reports are cross-referenced annually as part of these organizations' verification procedures. While provisional and subject to periodic revision as facts are gradually verified, an up-to-date list of events and relevant empirical data are available on the project's online database.

In addition to cataloguing attacks ending in severe casualties, kidnappings, and other major incidents, the AWSD records data on humanitarian workers involved in these events. The database collects the following data for each incident: Date of incident, country and geographical coordinates of incident, number and genders of humanitarian workers affected, workers' organizational affiliations (e.g., UN, Red Crescent, NGO), type of worker (i.e., national, international), outcome (e.g., death, injury, kidnapping), weapons used (e.g., firearms, IEDs, shelling), incident type (e.g., ambush, armed attack), and any other public details. Data may be sorted by different variables for ease of use. AWSD publishes an annual report after verifying data.

Humanitarian workers deployed in crisis zones and other high-stress environments can seek recourse through HD to advocate for their own safety and that of the materials under their care, just as they do for the interests of vulnerable populations. HD can help facilitate discussions on the protection of humanitarian workers and materials, not only because of how it seeks to engage decision-makers and prominent opinion leaders to support humanitarian causes but also because of how the protection of humanitarian materials goes hand in hand with humanitarian diplomacy itself. Only after having obtained all the necessary permissions from relevant authorities—something that HD, with its heavy focus on persuasion, is specifically tailored to—can aid materials be safely delivered to conflict, crisis, embargoed, and restricted zones.

Humanitarian workers are often deployed in areas over which state control has been largely if not entirely eroded away, where various illegal armed groups might vie with one another for dominance, and where crises continue to pester local populations. HD can, in such contexts, be employed to persuade actors, whether civilian or official, not to attack humanitarian personnel and even to extend protection to them. Since humanitarian workers, medical technicians, rescue crews, social workers, official diplomats, and other government officials cannot perform their duties while under constant threat of attack, the people they serve go without needed aid materials and assistance. Accordingly, actors in the HD ecosystem should, depending on the requirements of their specific positions, should work toward persuading those with power to sign into law agreements granting humanitarian workers diplomatic immunity, providing them with armed protection, ensuring their freedom of movement, developing insurance-like systems that guard against kidnapping and ransom demands, and other similar privileges and protections.

World Humanitarian Day (August 19)

An armed attack in Baghdad on 19 August 2003 claimed the lives of twenty-two humanitarian workers. The UN General Assembly dedicated World Humanitarian Day in response to this heinous incident. This day seeks to recognize people affected by crises around the world and to increase awareness of the need to protect humanitarian workers.

HD can also support humanitarian workers in their professional develop, career advancement, and job security.

HD actors aware of the field's needs and the qualifications required by one to succeed in it are better positioned to convince decision-makers of the need to equip humanitarian workers with the knowledge and skills that will allow them to use the resources and personnel under their supervision to benefit the vulnerable populations they are to serve. Similarly, HD offers more inquisitive minds the opportunity to examine the philosophy on which humanitarian aid is based, thereby enabling them to reach a deeper, more mature understanding of its theoretical and practical application.

By engaging in advocacy, which take place not only out in the open through official channels but also behind closed doors via unofficial channels, HD allows practitioners to gain valuable insight into the realities of international humanitarian law, how it translates into practice in the real world, and, perhaps more importantly, its rapport with humanitarianism, humanitarian principles, and humanitarian aid ecosystem. Through advocacy, actors set the groundwork for the timely delivery of appropriate humanitarian goods and services to those who need them without sacrificing the humanitarian principles they espouse.

A complex web of practical mechanisms acts in synchrony to ensure that humanitarian personnel and aid are protected. These include detailed standard operational procedures bolstered by technical and technological expertise that work to minimize risks for humanitarian workers. Yet, despite the best analyses conducted on regional and emergency conditions and the advances made in transportation, logistics, security, and jurisprudence to prevent them, attacks continue to endanger humanitarian personnel. One way to ensure that humanitarian workers and goods are protected is to collaborate with local, national, and international authorities to the extent that the specific circumstances on the ground require. In this respect, HD is an important, though oft-overlooked, instrument that may be used to strengthen the effectiveness of protective measures. As my literature review demonstrates, although the number of studies on HD in general has indeed increased in recent years, no study concentrates specifically on how to use HD to protect humanitarian workers, and those rare studies that do mention it only do so in passing.

The Gaza Freedom Flotilla, led by the passenger ship Mavi Marmara, was raided by Israeli forces while in international waters on 31 May 2010, resulting in the death of ten volunteer humanitarian workers and the confiscation of the humanitarian goods on board.

HD for protecting aid workers and items is intrinsically linked to the specific emergency, crises, and contexts. Therefore, engagement with partners to forward a valid humanitarian cause can at times be challenging, especially when dealing with non-state actors, aggressive regimes, and more than one group active in the same territory. HD in such contexts must be carefully planned to ensure that it includes humanitarian personnel and aid. Most often this includes engagements with governments, armed groups, and local leaders. Without the proper arrangements and agreements guaranteeing security and access, not only will the lives of humanitarian workers be put at risk, affected populations waiting for assistance will be negatively impacted. As such, humanitarian diplomatic initiatives and arrangements seeking to protect aid workers and items must be finely tuned so that they do not have the reserve effect of increasing the risks posed to humanitarians or affected populations.

Looking specifically at humanitarian personnel and professionals, I must underline that various national and international laws, norms, agreements, and conventions provide special conditions for aid professionals. For instance, international humanitarian law affords special protection to humanitarian workers and considers their security and safety an indispensable condition for the delivery of humanitarian relief items (UNSC, 2000). Another example outlined in the Geneva Conventions is the widely accepted norm stipulating that those tending to injured people or distributing aid shall not be targeted. Though official policy may openly affirm the sacrosanctity of medical personnel and aid workers, for instance, 2022 recorded a total of 444 attacks in which 143 aid workers were seriously wounded, 185 were kidnapped, and 116 were killed (Humanitarian Outcomes, 2023). These figures alone demonstrate the need to increase the number and quality of works seeking to put an end to such violence. HD initiatives seeking to resolve this issue must focus on garnering support and trust within local communities, engage in targeted public and shadow advocacy, and reach agreements guaranteeing access and safe maneuverability with involved parties.

As seen above, the delivery of humanitarian aid items to those in need of them is intrinsically bound to the safety and security of humanitarian aid professionals. Protecting humanitarian aid serves an auxiliary function in addition to ensuring the protection of humanitarian workers, namely, to ensure that aid is used for its intended purpose by the targeted population. HD is, when wielded properly, an effective tool that may be used to achieve both of these goals. As such, it is important to engage whatever group, whether state or non-state, controls an area home to people in need of aid in order to ensure not only that humanitarian aid workers can reach and deliver aid to them but also that the aid will be delivered and utilized for its intended purpose.

In this chapter, I have shown that the majority of discourse, both theoretical and practical, surrounding HD focuses primarily on issues of humanitarian needs, humanitarian law, and vulnerable populations. This constitutes the very core of humanitarianism and humanitarian action. Although this has hitherto bore unequivocally positive results, the need for further academic discussion on the protection of humanitarian workers and materials within the wider field of HD can no longer be overlooked or ignored.

References

Bull, H. (1995). The theory of international politics, 1919–1969 (1972). In Der Derian, J. (Ed.), *International theory*. London: Palgrave Macmillan. https://doi.org/10.1007/978-1-349-23773-9_8

Clark, M. D. (2018). *Humanitarian multi-track diplomacy: Conceptualizing the definitive, particular and critical role of diplomatic function in humanitarian action* [PhD thesis, University of Groningen].

Constantinou, C., Pauline, K. & Paul, S. (2016). Introduction: Understanding diplomatic practice. In C. Constantinou, P. Kerr and P. Sharp (Eds.), *The SAGE handbook of diplomacy* (pp. 1–10). SAGE.

Cooper, A. F. & Cornut, J. (2019). The changing practices of frontline diplomacy: New directions for inquiry. *Review of International Studies, 45*(2), 300–319. doi:10.1017/S0260210518000505

De Lauri, A. (2020). *Humanitarianism: Keywords*. Brill Academic Publisher.

Egeland, J. (2013). Humanitarian diplomacy. In A. F. Cooper, J. Heine & R. Thakur (Eds.). *The Oxford handbook of modern diplomacy* (pp. 286–297). The Oxford University Press. https://doi.org/10.1093/oxfordhb/9780199588862.013.0020

Humanitarian Outcomes. (2023). *Aid worker security report figures at a glance 2023*. Aid Worker Security Database. https://www.humanitarianoutcomes.org/figures_at_a_glance_2023

Hocking, B. A. (2006). Using reflection to resolve conflict. *AORN Journal, 84*(2), 249–259. https://doi.org/10.1016/S0001-2092(06)60492-4

Régnier, P. (2011). The emerging concept of humanitarian diplomacy: Identification of a community of practice and prospects for international recognition. *International Review of the Red Cross, 93*(884), 1211–1237. https://doi.org/10.1017/S1816383112000574

Satow, E. (1979). *Satow's guide to diplomatic practice*. Lord Gore-Booth. Longman.

Turunen, S. (2020). Humanitarian diplomatic practices. *The Hague Journal of Diplomacy, 15*(4), 459–487.

UNSC. (2000). *UN Security Council Resolution, 1296*. http://unscr.com/en/resolutions/1296

Watson, A. (2013). *Diplomacy: The dialogue between states*. Routledge.

13 Towards the Formation of the Conceptual Framework of Humanitarian Diplomacy

Insights from the Veteran Diplomat Christopher Lamb

Hafize Zehra Kavak

Christopher Lamb is one of the architects of the IFRC's oft-cited definition for humanitarian diplomacy. Before he and his team codified their definition, Lamb traveled to nearly forty countries between 2008 and 2009 to conduct interviews with a host of highly respected individuals involved in politics, civil society, academia, and the media.

The IFRC's definition foresees humanitarian diplomats seeking to persuade decision-makers and opinion leaders to work toward safeguarding vulnerable people's interests in adherence to fundamental humanitarian principles.

Hafize Zehra Kavak and Eren Paykal led a two-session online interview with Lamb. The first session of which took place on the ninth and the second on the sixteenth of June 2021. What follows is a transcript of the interview edited by Kavak.

Dear Mr. Lamb, it would be helpful to start with the definition of humanitarian diplomacy. As one of the architects behind the IFRC's definition for humanitarian diplomacy, can you go into how, as a concept, humanitarian diplomacy came into being?

First of all, as you know, I came from being a government diplomatic. I was an ambassador in various places, I had worked in UN settings, and I was also the legal advisor of our foreign ministry. In the [Diplo] course of all those things, one of the things I used to have to do as legal advisor was frequently provide advice to the Australian Aid Bureau—AusAid—about what was expected of the people working on aid projects when they worked in different parts of the world. I'd try to convince the aid people—not always successfully—that they had to give their people some training before sending them off somewhere. If you had a person who was a water engineer working in the back of Tajikistan and something happened there, they needed to know something about how they should act and what they needed to do.

DOI: 10.4324/9781003503187-13

Figure 13.1 Christopher Lamb: In addition to serving as incumbent president of the Australia Myanmar Institute, Lamb directs and teaches humanitarian diplomacy courses offered jointly by the IFRC and DiploFoundation.

So my first thinking about humanitarian diplomacy was before we adopted the name. How do we equip these people to function in a diplomatic setting? Sometimes they worked for the Australian government—and they were there working on a project for the government. Sometimes they were working for a company that was contracted by the Australian government. So how do we define the way they should work and the relationship they should each have with each other? One group, of course, would normally have diplomatic privileges and immunities and the other would not. How do you explain to the host government that these people, even though they might be working on the same project next to each other, are employed differently in Australia, but we want them treated the same way? And so I began to think about how we could have an all-encompassing designation for these people so that they could do their humanitarian work.

The purpose of aid is not to build trade; it is to expedite humanitarian action on behalf of vulnerable people living in the country.

I always thought of aid as a humanitarian program. I always objected when I was with the government to the people who said that one of the purposes of aid is to build trade. I said that it was not to build trade; it's to build humanitarian action on behalf of the vulnerable people in that country—and I worked on that all the time that I was with the government, including when I was an ambassador in the countries where I was. I wanted the aid program, to the greatest extent possible, to be aimed at doing something for vulnerable people in that country or help build the country as a capacity-building exercise for the country as a whole. This doesn't mean, of course, that you are only working with NGOs and civil society. You might need to build the capacity of the ministry of—pick a subject—water supply so that they could actually deliver a particular objective set for the people. One of the things that I always was insistent on was that the aid program always needed to have objectives. You didn't just go and deliver aid in order to get a score sheet with money in the columns showing how much you have done. You would have to produce some sort of humanitarian outcome from the aid program that you had. If they did not come to me with an outcome, I would send them away. I would say, "I'm not going to allow your money to be spent without an outcome being designed." This was a long time ago. This was before the invention of terms like KPIs and all that stuff. I wasn't looking for a check sheet that you could monitor or evaluate from, but those things are now more common and that's no bad thing. I came at all this before the invention of the term "looking for what we could do."

Then I came to join the Red Cross. I arrived at Geneva in the beginning of 2000 after I had retired from foreign affairs in Canberra. I retired when I did because I had been at the 1999 international conference of the Red Cross and Red Crescent in Geneva. What happened there—and I had played some part of that when I was the foreign affairs legal advisor in Australia—was the building of some momentum towards doing something that could bring the Israeli national society—in other words Magen David Adom—into the movement and the Palestine Red Crescent. Although technically, under the rules at the time, neither of them could come in—Palestine because, at the time, there was no State of Palestine that was accepted, which was needed to have a national society, and the Israelis because of their emblem. People said, "Why are you leaving a nice, good job in foreign affairs? You could be ambassador in lots more countries." I said, "No, I want this to be done." And I was quite determined about that. They said, "You're mad." I said, "It's okay. It's only been running in reverse gear for seventy years. I'm sure we can get it to go somewhere." And we did.

In 2005, the international community adopted the third protocol to the Geneva Conventions—with Turkish support I might add, which is a good thing. That was the reason for one of my visits to Türkiye. I went to Ankara and I saw the ministry. We talked what needed to be done through. We also talked about how we needed to find the arguments that would help stop certain people from preventing anything like this from happening because they didn't want the Israelis there. Those people, mind you, didn't care what happened to the Palestinians. Their single objective was to keep the Israelis out.

So, that was an interesting proposition. That took me through to 2005—to the adoption of the protocol. In 2006 we were able to have the international conference of the Red Cross and Red Crescent, amend the statutes of the Movement, and then both those societies came in.

Well, that part of the process—working on the Israeli case—gave me a better understanding of what the word *stakeholders* meant than I'd ever had when I was in Australia or working for the Australian government. As you would've seen, Zehra, during the course, I'm a fascist when it comes to stakeholders.

If you don't do a stakeholder analysis, you can't do your job. I relate that back to my own experience on this Israeli–Palestine issue. Who were the stakeholders? Who wants to keep the Israelis out? Who wants to bring them in? What are their various reasons? How do you take that back into a discussion where you can find areas of common interest? How can you locate an issue which they will both decide—both opposing sides—will both decide that it's a good thing to do?

The point that I decided they would all agree on is that Palestine should become a member of the Movement. If I go and say to the Arab countries that we want Palestine to be in the Movement and the price is the Israelis' coming in, too. However, we will tie that package up this way: If I said to the Israelis, "We want you in the Movement, but we want the Movement to be universal and the whole world to be part of it. Therefore, the Palestinians have to be there."

They both ultimately agreed in separate discussions that the Palestinians were the price—and it was a good price. I had seen the Palestinians many times. I often went to Ramallah and al-Bireh. I even once went to Gaza where I met Yasser Arafat. We worked at all these different levels. I met with doctors, nurses, ambulance drivers, Arafat, and the Israelis at those kinds of supergovernmental levels. Everybody ultimately joined the party. It was an interesting exercise. We talked a lot about things like non-state armed groups and similar actors. I met all those people in the course of this—the non-state and the state people. I saw people in religions. I saw rabbis, imams, bishops, and all these people. They all ultimately came together on that. It was by doing this analysis of who the stakeholders are and what their greatest interest is that enabled us to get to the answers on that. When that was done and both societies were in the Movement, I needed to deliver some things I thought needed to be done because they gave evidence that those stakeholders had their positions met.

The International Conference of the Red Cross–Red Crescent was the first conference of its type. It was an intergovernmental conference as well as one of the Red Cross Societies' to use the word *Palestine* on a nameplate on a desk in a meeting room. People wondered how the hell we were going to do that. So I said to them all,

What you've used since the 1920s when the Movement started is the names of the national societies—using their name. So it would be in order. Australia was 'Australian Red Cross' under A for Australia. The United Kingdom sat under U for the country and B for British Red Cross for the name of the society.

I said, "That's all going to stop now. We're going to do all the signage and next time you go to one of these conferences, have a look at these tables because it's what we designed in 2006." Australia, the country, would have its nameplate with black on white. Australia, the national society, would be red on white. This was the design and that's what went forward. That was the first time the word *Palestine* appeared this way because the Palestinian Authority was there. I said that they would also be called *Palestine*. So, for the first time, the Palestinian Authority came to an international meeting and was called Palestine. I was very proud of that achievement. The Israelis hated it, and I said to them, "It's part of the price you have to pay. In our Movement, everybody is equal. Everybody is out there giving mutual respect to each other. That's how you'll refer to Palestine."

Then others came to me and said, "We want the same treatment." To give you an inkling of what that meant, do you know much about the constitutional situation in Belgium?

Not that much.

In Belgium, there are the Belgian Francophones—the Walloons—and there are the Dutch-speaking ones—the Flanders. They wanted to have their names done that way. I said, "No, you're one country. They're two countries." I found myself having to use all these sorts of wits that you pick up as a diplomat around the world and put them together into something which was sailable as an answer to people. But each time in the case of Palestine, I said that we need to have Palestine and Israel both there together because that serves the humanitarian objectives that the Red Cross has.

Coming back to your question about the ICRC, it said to me, "How can you do that?" I said, "Because we have to think out of the box. We've got to do something that will work and will settle things." They agreed and we did it. We have done it ever since 2006. That's the way the nametags have been and there's no argument about it.

All of these were indeed edifying and I'm sure would come together to form a strong foundation when you would begin your work to define humanitarian diplomacy. What happened next and how did you come up with the definition?

We worked with both the ICRC and the IFRC. The Federation [i.e., the IFRC] is basically a non-conflict organization. If there's conflict, the ICRC deals with that—the law of armed conflict, the four Geneva conventions, nuclear weapons, etcetera. They locate their whole humanitarian response around the laws of war. The Federation needed something that could work for everything else that's done.

The Council of Delegates and the Federation General Assembly were to be held in Nairobi in 2009. Working towards that in 2008, we began a program of interviewing famous people around the world about the concept of humanitarian diplomacy. They included some people who were quite luminous in their own way. One of them was the High Commissioner of refugees, Sadako Ogata, and Jakob Kellenberg, President of the ICRC, and then heads of organizations like the director general of the WHO—the sorts of organizations that the Federation would often deal with—and people in governments, academics, and some newspaper people. We interviewed people from CNN, the BBC, and those sorts of things so that we could assemble as much information as we could. In the end, we probably interviewed forty or fifty people of that level.

Did you conduct these interviews as an IFRC team?

Yes, it was an IFRC team, but we had national societies as a part of the exercise because if you look at the concept of humanitarian diplomacy, the Federation is the sum of its national societies. It's nothing by itself. It's the national societies that make it what it is. I am also very determined about that. We had to have the national societies as the team that was putting it together. We had to have national societies of basically all the cultures we could assemble. So we had Africans, Arabs, Latin Americans, Anglos, Russians—I went to probably thirty or forty countries in 2008 and 2009 to see people. There were probably two or three of us at the core who were doing that work. Then we brought the other people in. They were scattered around, living in their own capitals and countries. We brought them all in. This was before the age of Zoom, so it wasn't easy.

> It's the reference to decision-makers and opinion leaders. If you want the public to appreciate what you're doing and support it, you've got to have the people who will lead those opinions.

So by visiting these countries, you sought to highlight humanitarian diplomacy and cement its surrounding policy. Am I correct?

Yes—well to highlight to highlight what we thought the concept was, to see if they liked it, and to understand that we would develop it into something that wasn't a long document, but one that should be able to be understood by people. So it couldn't be a complicated document. It wasn't going to refer to Section 51 of the initial protocol of the Geneva Conventions or anything. It was going to be something that would make sense. When we talked to newspapers and those people in private, we wanted to make sure that it would come out with results that the media could use and we can take out. It was because of them and those discussions that we introduced something into the concept—into the definition of the policy that had never been in one of these documents before. You would've seen it, Zehra; it's the reference to decision-makers and opinion leaders. If you want the public to appreciate what you are doing and support it, you have got to have the people who will lead those opinions. And so it worked very neatly.[1]

The IFRC's Four Signposts

1 The responsibility to persuade.
2 Persuading with the appropriate diplomatic tools and actions.
3 Focusing on areas of knowledge and expertise.
4 Engaging at appropriate times with partners outside the Movement.

When we finished it, the ICRC said, "Well, we watched this happening and you interviewed our people as well and we've used some of them in the documents as the people who supplied reference material for the policy." But they said, "It's not about what we understand. We understand that it's all about war." So I said,

It's quite alright for you to talk about war because that's your business, but disease has to be talked about. If you go back to the First World War, two or three times as many people died of the flu as died on the battlefield. So let's get real about these humanitarian disasters.

We then built up this idea that it should be humanitarian diplomacy, and it all went very smoothly in the way we drafted it. We produced the policy document and the explanatory memorandum. It's in this memorandum that you see those things like the signposts. You need to read them both to understand what it's all about. However, you really only have to read the definition to know what it you are meant to be doing. We set several discussions about words—if you go back to that definition, you'll see that practically every word has a meaning. It's not a long sentence; it's a set of meanings. So you've got to do your work at all times.[2]

If you take a decision, the fundamental principles must be part of that decision. To do that—to understand where you're taking it, you need to use two more words that are not in there—which I've mentioned before in my fascist belief in them—the story of the stakeholder analysis.[3]

Given their crucial role in humanitarian diplomacy, could you elaborate a bit more on the issue of stakeholders and stakeholder analyses?

So who are the stakeholders? I correct people all the time even in other work that I do outside the course. I say, "Okay, we're working on the situation of Myanmar, which I have spent a lot of my life on these days. The people of Myanmar are the principal stakeholders in what we're doing. What do they want? Who's leading their thinking? The other side of the argument is the military—what are they doing? The answer is that the military is shooting people and the civil society is trying to get a message across, but the people are not skilled in accepting the message. So how do you get out with those who can help design the message you need to take and then work with it? For me, one of the channels back to the people about what they need to be considering is the people in the diaspora. There are a lot of Myanmar people living in Australia, Canada, the United States, Thailand, and some in China. We worked and come together with those people as well. Stakeholder analyses give you what you need and then you know what to do.

As understood from your statements and the discussions we had in your Diplo Course, fulfilling humanitarian principles for vulnerable people shouldn't be a spontaneous endeavor. HD should be a well-planned process that includes a stakeholder analysis and an assessment of needs and objectives. You've discussed stakeholder analyses. Can you go into the assessment of needs and objectives?[4]

A lot of people don't start from the position of need. If you are going to help people in a camp, how do you know what to do unless you've done an assessment? How do you do an assessment? You have got to get out there into the camp and see them. So you have got to persuade the government, the country, or the authority to let you go to the camp and make this assessment. You, the HDiplomat,[5] will also use your diplomatic skills to persuade the government to accept that what you see is a representation of need.

Quite often in this [Diplo] course when we talk about objectives, people say, "What about human rights?" I have worked on human rights nearly all my diplomatic life. But this is not about human rights; this is about humanitarian need. The word human rights—very sadly—is really now much more about political objectives then the real objectives of humanitarian need. If we are talking about the needs of children, we are informed about how to assess those needs by the convention on the rights of the child. Human rights treaties and other instruments conform out of your base for determining need, but they are not necessarily what you are after. That all worked out quite well. The Geneva Conventions are part of that need business as well. That's where the ICRC fell into this. We had started the [Diplo] course; the ICRC looked at it a bit snuffly for a while. Now the ICRC thinks the course is useful and we have people from the ICRC in every course now, which is good.

Mr. Lamb, what do you think about the introduction of diplomacy into the humanitarian field and the marriage of the two concepts?

I should say that people then said to me as we were developing it, "How can you call it diplomacy?" The ICRC was bit struck by the issue of diplomacy. They use the term HD, but they don't actually have diplomatic action in the demonstration of what they do. To which I said—and I often say in talks I used to give when I was in Geneva and in some other places—looking around the people in the room, look at someone and say, "Eren, did you go somewhere on holiday this year?"

Yes, of course.

Are you a married man?

Yes.

So, you and your family went. Who decided where you'd go? You don't have to answer that, but this demonstrates that you had to have a negotiation about where to go. Then you decided where to go, how you'd get there, where you'd stay. You came to an understanding and agreement. To do that, you have to exercise skill. Diplomacy doesn't only mean intergovernmental relations; it means tact—working together harmoniously before governments were drawn into this. The term diplomacy has been used as something related with government for the last 300 years, but diplomacy has been around a very long time. In that sense, HD is diplomacy directed to a humanitarian objective. I would say to the ICRC,

I'm happy to accept that preventing a war is a good, strong humanitarian objective, but it's not the only one. So what I'd be very happy about, ICRC, is that we understand each other very well. Don't try to lock the word diplomacy solely to what you do.

It extends to everywhere you like, including some things you've mentioned in your questions, Zehra.

> **The term diplomacy has been used as something related with government for the last 300 years, but diplomacy has been around a very long time. In that sense, HD is diplomacy directed to a humanitarian objective.**

You played a leading role in bringing various stakeholders like national societies and grassroots initiatives into the process during your field missions. Can you go into more detail about this?

The national societies should know what we are doing in the UN or somewhere and intervene if they want to say something. So I created, as best as I could, a mechanism that would enable the national societies to be consulted by the Federation's regional offices or by us directly. I remember, as an example of that, there was a meeting of the International Standing Committee in New York in 2007 or something like that to talk about cyclones in Bangladesh. We as the organization—the IFRC—went to this meeting. I got to have a speaker at that meeting—the Secretary General of Bangladesh Red Crescent. Some asked, "What's this guy doing here?" I said, "We're a membership organization. He represents one of the members and he is our designated spokesperson." And that was it. I primed him; I said to him,

> This is going to be complicated for you because they've never had anyone come and speak to them at one of these interagency meetings. He's from a national society, but he's sitting at the IFRC seat with an IFRC badge on his coat and you're speaking for us, but you're bringing your experience.

He said, "That's fine." We did that and it was beautiful. But that also was part of what humanitarian diplomacy is—to make the stakeholders feel that they're bringing something forward.

As you've seen, Zehra, in the course, we emphasized to the extent that we can that we want to see the involvement of the members of the grassroots. Grassroots are very hard to bring forward, especially at a meeting of that level. Yet even that we did sometimes. What I would do if I were back there now, I would employ things like Zoom to bring people up from the back of nowhere— to deliver a three-minute intervention on what the floods mean, what the disease means, what discrimination is, the difficulty of getting food, what's happening to us at the moment in Nigeria.

Our next question is about the areas in which humanitarian diplomacy is involved. Are there certain areas on which HD is more focused?

I don't think it's possible to give a one-size-fits-all answer. Different things matter in different parts of the world. In Europe at the moment and for some years now, they've been very fixed on the issue of migration, and so has Türkiye. Think of how many people are still in Türkiye living in tents following the Syrian conflict, and what happens to them. Think about what the impact of these people—these refugees—has been on the ability of your government to make decisions about the directions of Türkiye's growth and development—it's tragic—and then the people themselves. If you are in Southeast Asia—if you are in Myanmar at the moment, the only thing you could be concerned about is the military takeover.

Different things matter in different parts of world. Since the Pacific Islands are going to go under water, the focus there is climate change. In Europe and Türkiye, however, the issue of migration is at the fore.

If you take WHO, in Latin America they have got PAHA—the Pan American Health Organization, which is a regional treaty-based organization that works on what is important for them in Latin America. Very often, disease is something that becomes a regional issue of significance because of an earthquake or a cyclone. Something will start the rapid spread of cholera or some other disease like that. They then get fixed around those sorts of issues. But they also have migration—a tremendous problem.

So the definition will vary depending on where you are. If you are in the Pacific Islands, those places are going to go underwater because of climate change. For them, that's the center of their concern. If you are in parts of Africa, most of them will talk about what we will do about al-Shabab. How do we have a discussion with a non-state armed group? How do we deal with them when they're causing so much damage and destruction to our societies and communities?

I'll tell them about things I have seen once upon a time in Geneva. I went to a meeting. I met some women from Africa. They wanted to meet people and talk about the problem in their country, Uganda. I don't know how they got there or where the money came from to bring them to Geneva. They saw themselves as the best remaining stand-out against the Lord's Resistance Army. I then did the speech for the Federation. I said,

We've got to pay much more attention to what these women are saying when we assess what the needs of people are. Most of the problems they're suffering are caused by men. What do the women say about the future of their families, their countries, their people, and their needs?

People were shocked by this.

So I use that now in Myanmar. I said, "We're talking about war, the army and all that. All the things we're talking about that are bad are nearly all caused by men. I want women brought forward to be part of the discussion about the future."

When Myanmar settles down to a new future, how are they going to fashion the future of the country and who's going to do that fashioning? I think the answer to that is going to be found by civil society—which is practically nonexistent in a real form now but will have to be formed—and *women*.

We have discussed the definition of needs and objectives, stakeholder analyses, and persuasion strategies. Does reaching an agreement mean that the problem is now solved?

Many people would say that if you go into an HD negotiation, you negotiate, you get an agreement, and that's it. That is not it; that's the easy part. The hard part is the implementation and the resources. Think of the Middle East. The Israelis and Arafat signed an agreement in Oslo in the 1990s to solve the Middle East crises. Oslo is about as far as you can go from the Middle East to get a signature done. Look at the impact of that on the people on the ground. You've got to have a way of getting through these things that works. You have got to have a commitment to implementation. Securing that implementation and the resources for it is a job for the HDiplomat, and we use that term fairly loosely. But there will need to be an involvement of HD right through implementation and it needs to stay connected to the time when an agreement is being sought.

I'd like to discuss the risks and challenges faced by those involved in HD. What are the primary difficulties in the field?

If you're talking about physical risks—if you're working in an area where there's conflict or a very disturbed population. Think about the Turkish Red Crescent—think about Kızılay working along the Syrian border. Sometimes maybe crossing the border, although I noticed as I followed that situation recently carefully, the Kızılay, the Turkish government, and everybody else is always very vague when it comes to describing where they actually are— whether they crossed the border or not. But that's dangerous; there's a physical risk in working in that kind of environment. There's also a risk if you're working in an area full of disease, such as this pandemic [COVID-19], that you could be threatened by that. There is the risk of being threatened with corruption—lots of things. If you're standing for something as firm as the bedrock fundamental principles, you are going to make enemies some of the time.

You have experience in both classical and humanitarian diplomacy. Where do these two fields of diplomacy converge and where do they diverge?

If you are a state diplomat, you get your instructions from the government. You operate with the authority of the flag of the state. The HDiplomat is not governed in the same way. The humanitarian diplomat works in accordance with humanitarian principles and to satisfy the needs of the most vulnerable whereas a state diplomat considers that he or she is backed by the power of the state.

If you're a state diplomat, you get your instructions from the government. You operate with the authority of the flag of the state. The HDiplomat is not governed in the same way. The humanitarian diplomat works in accordance with humanitarian principles and to satisfy the needs of the most vulnerable.

State diplomats have certain material advantages. They have diplomatic privileges and immunities. They have got nice cars. They live in big houses. There used to be an understanding that these state diplomats came from best families in Europe, played golf, and were therefore high-level, high-ranking people. The HDiplomat who's working on real programs and support for people is actually in a position to get more strength from that work, but they don't have the privileges, immunities, and benefits of the treaties. Except the ICRC, using its reputation, has been able to get host-country agreements—status agreements—with a lot of places where they have postings—where they have delegations.

On the other hand, HDiplomats can work with state diplomats to help them achieve their [humanitarian] objectives. In some situations, the IFRC is also given privileges. I don't know how it works in Türkiye with the Federation.[6] The ICRC has diplomatic privileges and immunities for its delegation in Ankara. In some countries, like China, the Federation has diplomatic privileges and immunities because it agreed to style its office in Beijing as a regional office.

Is there a widely accepted definition for an HDiplomat? Is it understood the same way that we understand it?

Not really. It's understood why we use it after discussions. But if people just read it, they don't understand it very easily unless they are intimately connected to this kind of work. People in the Red Cross tend to understand it. That varies a little bit; it depends on the national society and how attentive it is to what it's meant to be doing.

HDiplomats are people whose objectives are determined by fundamental humanitarian principles. The principle of humanity stands above them all. That's where your base is. You can then talk about neutrality and impartiality as the next set of principles that feed the principle of humanity.

If you go back to very deep basics, an HDiplomat is somebody whose objective is set by the fundamental principles and, in particular, by the fundamental principle of *humanity*. That's why we have got in the [Diplo] course. We discuss the auxiliary role that national societies frequently play to their respective governments. National societies were granted this auxiliary status in the 2007 international conference, where what they could and couldn't do was clearly defined. As such, governments cannot require national societies to act in contravention to humanitarian principles. HDiplomats are people whose objectives are determined by fundamental humanitarian principles. The principle of humanity stands above them all. That's where your base is. You can then talk about *neutrality* and *impartiality* as the next set of principles that feed the principle of humanity.

To reiterate, HDiplomats are those people who work according to the fundamental humanitarian principles at all times.

At all times, yes. Often, you need an HDiplomat who understands these things—who guides the other people into what they have to do to secure the humanitarian objective. They need to know how to act and have common sense. That is why I put a lot of emphasis on the *Protocol Handbook*.[7]

When discussing HD, we often think more about humanitarian needs, disasters, earthquakes, and wars. Is it possible to enlarge the scope of HD so that, in addition to wars and disasters, it encompasses humanitarian needs?

Yes, of course. Do you remember the question in the course about how we define vulnerabilities? There were a lot of different answers to that. But one thing we came back to some people on was to say that it's not all about the war, it's not all about disease, it's not all about earthquakes—it's about all of these things and much more. As for the vulnerability, it lasts forever because you can never really extinguish it.

What governments recognize HDiplomats and work to improve the qualifications of theirs that you've mentioned?

The ICRC, over the last hundred or so years, has worked to make sure its people who are posted to a country, including, for example, to the delegation in Türkiye, are able to be recognized as people coming and working for an international organization. So they get a diplomatic visa. They carry, although it's technically not legal in an international sense, Swiss diplomatic passports—these ICRC people. Even though the ICRC is by Swiss law not more than a private company, which is accepted by the government, they still can carry these passports and they get a diplomatic visa.

You've been involved in countless humanitarian initiatives around the world. Could you discuss the objectives, stakeholders, and outcomes you achieved in one of such initiatives in which you were involved?

I played a part in the Federation in the issue of road safety, as an issue which needed to be dealt with using HD to get it the recognition and support it needed at the international level. Road traffic issues responsible for killing all people, and guns, needed to be given proper and full attention by governments. It was an international issue. Most countries are not like Australia; we do not have and road borders with anywhere, whereas most countries do. You're a good example of a country that does. You've got all sorts of different traffic conditions in the countries bordering you. If you even go around from Greece to Bulgaria to Romania to Russia to all those Caucasus. You think of the quality of driving, the way cars are controlled, the way emission control works, and climate change. There are a whole of things on the roads that governments need to cooperate on. They shouldn't treat road safety as something like someone had run over a pedestrian crossing in downtown Izmir. It's not like that; it's a worldwide phenomenon. What we did was to engage with an NGO set up in parallel with the Federation, but not as part of it. I worked to bring to the Federation. It's called the Global Road Safety Partnership. You'll find that on the web—the GRSP (GRSP, n.d.).[8] It's been incredibly successful. What we did with them as the Federation was, using our ability to work with the international organizations from the observer status we have, was to get the GRSP into bodies like WHO to agree that there should be a major concentration on road safety, to get the World Disasters Report to have a whole edition devoted to road safety, to get these governments mobilized around the issues of road safety, and then to run it as a particular issue in some regional Red Cross conferences.

I went to an African Regional Red Cross and Red Crescent conference held in Johannesburg in 2008 or whereabouts. African road safety was the big thing. Governments came—international organizations, the UN, aid donors, UNDP—these governments, they all came to this road safety set up to look at what they can do. We got money from people. Toyota was one of our good sponsors, for example. Shell, the petrol company, was another good sponsor of these things. That involved a lot of stakeholder negotiation with people. I remember talking to the Canadian government, who said, "What are you doing this thing on road safety for? That's not important." I said, "Canada, here are your statistics." They said, "Where'd you get these, these are wrong." I replied, "From your bureau of statistics. It produces these things on road accidents in Canada." Then he said, "Why are you involved in the Red Cross? What have they got to do with road accidents?" I said, "Do you know who carries the burden apart from the families—the great burden of road accidents? It's the Red Cross." Out there on that street corner in Izmir, talking with the families, helping people cope with what's happened to them, dealing with the trauma and stress of these deaths bring and, just as bad, the injuries. If you've got somebody who's lost his legs or is disabled because of the accident, the Red Cross carries that. In Canada—I know this because I've talked to the Canadian Red Cross on this—they do this and they get recognition from the Canadian government for what they do.

What cases or positions—both classical and humanitarian diplomacy positions—satisfied you the most in the eighty-five countries in which you worked?

It's difficult to answer something like that, I'm afraid. As you will appreciate when you are a lot older, different things have an impact on you at different stages of life's experience. I remember being very satisfied with a thing I did together with some friends with the UN General Assembly in about 1977—so that's a long time ago. We were working in a committee on human rights and humanitarian questions. We decided we needed to try to do something that would stop the Russians from standing in the way of what we wanted to do on human rights. To do that, we would need to do something the Americans would oppose. We did a resolution together, called Alternative Approaches and Ways and Means to Human Rights, which the Americans hated but couldn't oppose, because to oppose it would be dreadful in their own eyes. They now had President Carter as a new president and they couldn't go against the human rights resolution coming out in this way.

I decided we should borrow some things. One of the things I thought we should borrow, and we've got it in this resolution somewhere, is something conceptually borrowed from the four Geneva Conventions. You know how the four conventions start with the Common Articles—1, 2, 3, and 4. These common articles have got the greatest prominence of all because they're ratified and enforced by everybody four times with the four conventions. We developed some thinking around Common Article 1, which is pretty scanty thinking. What I did in lots of speeches was to refer to Common Article 1 as if it were, therefore, the Bible on human rights. Everybody had to live with that in the end. I was very satisfied in getting it done. When in 2007—I was in Geneva by then with the Federation—we used a lot of those principles in the declaration that we did to set out the objective that all states and societies should ratify in that conference. They include such things as the fact that migrants should all be treated irrespective of their legal status. Governments didn't like that very much; national societies did like it. The stuff on Israel-Palestine was very satisfying and the stuff on Cyprus was also very satisfying. It was also satisfying for me to get the president of the Red Cross in Cyprus to come north with me to Kythrea there to meet the president of the North Cyprus Turkish Red Crescent. It wasn't an official meeting, but I got them to go and do it—the one from the south to go the north and meet him there.

Thank you for this enlightening interview Mr. Lamb. Is there anything you'd like to add or share before closing?

After the Second World War, things like the Marshal Plan and the way that the United States basically rebuilt the world—it was quite extraordinary. You'd never see that happen again. Nor would you see the humanitarian spirit that there was the UN Organization itself was created, with a reasonably rational approach to what went wrong with the League of Nations before it, and how to correct as much as they could in the UN Charter. Australia, in 1948, was one of the countries that proposed the establishment of an International Criminal Court. At the time when the Geneva Conventions were redone, the UN High Commissioner for Refugees was created. The world made enormous strides on a humanitarian front. We have a lot of holding the line to do to make sure that what we have achieved in humanitarian senses remains achieved. That's one of the reasons I feel very motivated by humanitarian diplomacy—because you can actually build people who can do that.

Notes

1 Decision-makers and opinion leaders include individuals and groups that humanitarian diplomats attempt to persuade to implement policies that will benefit vulnerable people. [ed].

2 "Humanitarian Diplomacy Policy" and "Explanatory Memorandum" are set under the leadership of Christopher Lamb in 2009. The two documents of IFRC highlighting the definition, objectives and signposts of HD are among the main references of Humanitarian Diplomacy literature. [ed].

3 IFRC's Humanitarian Diplomacy policy draws a well organized roadmap for Humanitarian diplomats. The stakeholder analysis is one of the pillars of this road map enquiring the interests, position, and needs of stakeholders in the field. According to IFRC, an influential HD policy would only be implemented after the assessment of needs and objectives and stakeholder analysis completed. [ed].

4 Christopher Lamb is the course director and lecturer of Humanitarian Diplomacy training offered jointly by IFRC and DiploFoundation. [ed].

5 HDiplomat is the abbreviation for humanitarian diplomat. Humanitarian diplomats manage humanitarian diplomacy affairs and conduct negotiations with decision-makers and opinion leaders to advance the rights and interests of vulnerable groups. [ed].
6 Red Cross and Red Crescent workers are protected by the Geneva Conventions of 1949, which recognizes them as humanitarian aid workers. Although the workers of national societies may be afforded diplomatic immunity and certain diplomatic privileges in specific cases, there no universal protocol guaranteeing such treatment. [ed].
7 IFRC, *Humanitarian Diplomacy Protocol Hand Book, A manual to facilitate the IFRC's work in diplomacy and the international field*, 2010.
8 Formed in 1999, the Global Road Safety Partnership (GRSP) is an NGO hosted by the IFRC that aims to permanently reduce road crash fatalities and injuries in both low- and middle-income countries. See: https://www.grsproadsafety.org/.

References

GRSP. (n.d.). *Global road safety partnership.* https://www.grsproadsafety.org/
The International Federation of Red Cross and Red Crescent Societies (IFRC). (2010). *Humanitarian diplomacy protocol hand book, a manual to facilitate the IFRC's work in diplomacy and the international field.*

14 Successful Humanitarian Diplomacy Practices and Case Studies

İzzet Şahin

The 2016 World Humanitarian Summit (WHS) organized in Istanbul argued that *humanitarian aid* and *development* cannot be considered independent of the other and that activities in these two areas must be conducted in coordination in order to be successful. After *peace* was subsequently added to this dual ensemble, these three concepts began to be referred to collectively as the *triple nexus* of the humanitarian aid system.

Just as it is impossible for any aid system that does not support development projects to remain viable in the long term, it would be improper to focus entirely on development while simultaneously regarding humanitarian aid initiatives as unnecessary. Similarly, it is difficult—if not outright impossible—to conduct development and humanitarian aid projects in areas bereft of peace.

It is estimated that eighty percent of world poverty and underdevelopment are a result of war, political crisis, administrative problems, and human-induced disasters. This imposing figure thus reveals just how important establishing and maintaining peace truly is.

The same *disaster risk reduction* (DRR) efforts undertaken to mitigate potential damage caused by earthquakes, floods, tsunamis, and other types of unpreventable natural disasters are not common in human-induced disaster prevention, despite the aftereffects of such disasters having significantly more dire consequences. Unlike their natural counterparts, however, it is possible to prevent such human-induced disasters altogether or, at the very least, reduce the gravity of their effects.

Wars and humanitarian crises are responsible for the death, imprisonment, and forced migration of thousands of people each year. Even if crises are restricted to a small geographical area, their effects are of truly global proportions. The refugee crisis that brought such a seemingly unshakable transnational community as the EU to the brink of unraveling is a clear example of how crises can have such a far-reaching impact.

While nearly all crises in the modern world involve either Muslim countries or areas in which Muslims constitute a minority, solutions are sought from powerful third-party nations whose influence extends far beyond their own borders. Crises become significantly more complicated when those affected by

DOI: 10.4324/9781003503187-14

them are excluded from the resolution process, often deteriorating into bloody proxy wars.

Majors hurdles to the swift resolution of crises include systemic problems, such as the UN Security Council's veto power; ineffective stances of the Organization of Islamic Cooperation (OIC), the Arab League, and the African Union (AU); and policies that either prioritize national interests or that see no problem with sacrificing people's livelihoods in order to maintain political power. Instead of a realist approach in which the major actors are nation-states, today's international climate has allowed NGOs, multinational corporations, social media networks, and other non-state actors to play important roles in crisis management and resolution.

IHH Humanitarian Relief Foundation and Humanitarian Diplomacy

Beginning its involvement in humanitarian aid and human rights initiatives during the Bosnian War (1992), one of the greatest human-induced disasters of recent history, the IHH Humanitarian Relief Foundation was but one of the non-state actors mentioned above. IHH's areas of operation exhibit significant overlap with the aforementioned triple nexus. While IHH's various emergency aid and development assistance projects correspond to the humanitarian aid and development wings of the triple nexus, the foundation's (human rights) advocacy and humanitarian diplomacy activities coincide with how this nexus approaches peace.

Projects conducted by IHH's Humanitarian Diplomacy Unit are personally overseen by the foundation's most senior officials. Having completed numerous successful humanitarian diplomacy missions in the field since its inception, IHH continues to play key roles in solving ongoing critical situations. Beyond a truly impressive amount of fieldwork in which it is involved, IHH works to build awareness of and promote humanitarian diplomacy efforts through educational workshops and the distribution of literature on the subject.

Before delving into IHH's involvement in humanitarian diplomacy, it would be beneficial first to define humanitarian diplomacy, identify the fields in which it is active, and discuss the different techniques that practitioners employ. The International Federation of Red Cross and Red Crescent Societies (IFRC) defines humanitarian diplomacy as "persuading decision makers and opinion leaders to act, at all times, in the interests of vulnerable people, and with full respect for fundamental humanitarian principles." (IFRC, 2017)[1] In line with this definition, IHH emphasizes four basic components:

- Decision makers and opinion leaders
- Vulnerable people
- Humanitarian principles
- Persuasion

As stressed in the aforementioned definition, the underlying goal of humanitarian diplomacy is to persuade decision makers to support policies that, in their adherence to international humanitarian principles, will protect the lives and rights of vulnerable individuals, secure their continued freedom, and allow them to lead a dignified life. Several of the central activities of those involved in humanitarian diplomacy are:

• Peacebuilding efforts (e.g., mediation, observation)
• The creation of humanitarian corridors and access to humanitarian relief
• Prisoner and hostage release
• Family reunification
• Evacuation of civilians from areas under blockade to secured zones
• Protection (e.g., women, children, refugees, and other vulnerable groups of people)

Persuasion is a key component in all humanitarian diplomacy initiatives. These efforts include attempts to persuade not only those parties directly involved in crises but also influential statesmen, religious foremen, opinion leaders, and public opinion itself. Naturally, each type of individual requires an entirely different set of knowledge, experience, and skills to be successfully persuaded.

Techniques commonly employed in humanitarian diplomacy in tandem or with persuasion include mediation, advocacy, and collaboration with other organizations working in the same field. Since each situation comes with its own unique circumstances, the efficacy of each technique can vary greatly. One particularly striking example is how IHH employed different techniques in Bangsamoro than it did in Lebanon, Iraq, Palestine, and Syria.

Just as individual nations collaborate with one another to resolve humanitarian crises, NGOs do the same. IHH, for instance, cooperates with a large number of organizations in the various initiatives in which it takes part. These include various UN organs, the International Committee of the Red Cross (ICRC), Geneva Call, the European Institute for Peace, the Centre for Humanitarian Dialogue (HD), Frontline Negotiations, and the Cordoba Peace Institute.

In order to enhance their knowledge and working capacity, IHH employees involved in humanitarian diplomacy are apt to attend educational workshops and seminars offered by, among other institutions, DiploFoundation and Frontline Negotiations as well as Geneva Peace Week organized by the Geneva Peacebuilding Platform. IHH employees then share the knowledge and experience they have gained from these programs and the field both to their fellow coworkers and to NGO representatives of other countries.

To illustrate the difficulties faced by the different actors involved in humanitarian diplomacy, it would be helpful to explore a small portion of the hardships that IHH has had to endure while performing the aforementioned and other related duties. These include:

- Unlike in classic diplomacy, very few rules, if any at all, govern humanitarian diplomacy. As a result, NGOs find themselves on ambiguous legal ground when attempting to intervene in humanitarian causes.
- Since efforts are executed in live crisis zones, engagement in humanitarian diplomacy poses serious risks to all those involved—both for the civilian actors conducting humanitarian work and for the people to whom these efforts are directed.
- Competition between classic and civilian actors not only reduces the total number of areas in which the latter are able to operate freely but also prevents civilian actors from performing certain activities in the areas still open to them.
- Although civilian actors can be mistakenly associated with belligerent, particularly non-state armed groups, humanitarian diplomacy does not seek to imbue any armed group with the slightest sense of legitimacy. That said, however, for any solution to be feasible, non-state organizations involved in the various armed conflicts plaguing today's world also need to be persuaded to cooperate. As such, legal arrangements protecting civilian organizations interacting with non-state armed groups need to be developed if engagement in humanitarian diplomacy is to be viable.
- The number of workers knowledgeable and experienced enough to engage effectively in humanitarian diplomacy is, relative to the number of ongoing crises, severely limited.

Whereas Western organizations are able to compensate for this deficit with retired diplomats well-versed in classic diplomacy, Türkiye feels this shortage in qualified individuals much more poignantly. In the following section, I shall discuss, in thorough detail, specific cases of successful humanitarian diplomacy that IHH has headed.

Case Narratives

Syria Prisoner Exchange

The destruction, massacres, and forced migration so common during war leave deep wounds in all those affected. The Syrian Civil War, one of the most severe humanitarian crises to rear its head in recent times, has left an estimated half-million people dead and excess of two hundred thousand imprisoned. While the majority of prisoners taken by opposition forces have been combatant soldiers and members of pro-government militias, Syrian security forces sought to imprison the civilian family members of the opposition, including thousands of women and children. IHH's Humanitarian Diplomacy Unit successfully negotiated a prisoner exchange that saw forty-eight Iranians taken prisoner by opposition forces in 2012 swapped for hundreds of civilians imprisoned by the Syrian government.

Prisoner Exchange Process

As soon as IHH's Humanitarian Diplomacy Unit was informed that forty-eight Iranian citizens had been captured by opposition forces in East Ghouta on 5 August 2012, IHH offered to act as a mediator between both parties. Work began as soon as the opposition and Iran accepted this proposal. The following are among the various reasons that both parties accepted IHH's offer:

- IHH had maintained an active field presence since the crisis first erupted.
- IHH is an independent organization whose sole objectives are humanitarian in nature.
- IHH is well renowned for its work in diverse crisis zones.
- IHH had proven that it is more than willing to take risks and act courageously in the face of danger when human lives and freedom are on the line.
- IHH had successfully executed similar exchanges that led to the liberation of other countries' citizens prior to this event.

The first step of the prisoner exchange was to ascertain the identities of those who were being held prisoner. This was important because while Iran asserted that all of the prisoners had been taken hostage while visiting Sayyidah Zainab Mosque, the opposition forces claimed that they were soldiers who had come from Iran to fight alongside Syrian government forces. Stressing that they would not accept any "apologies or empty promises" from Iranian officials, the opposition demanded that a significant number of prisoners held by the Syrian regime be released in exchange for the forty-eight Iranian prisoners. Iran, however, hesitated to make any promises concerning those being held captive by the Syrian government.

During the ensuing negotiations, IHH's Humanitarian Diplomacy Unit mediated between the Syrian opposition, the Syrian government, Iran, and Qatar—the last of which was included in negotiations because four of her citizens were being held as prisoners in Iran and the Qataris sought to use this as an opportunity to secure their freedom. Though a portion of negotiations were held in parts of Syria where fighting was still ongoing, this served only to prolong the process and increase the risk to participants. After IHH had hosted dozens of meetings in Istanbul, Tehran, Damascus, Douma, and Doha, however, negotiations finally began—albeit still slowly—to produce results.

As the mediating body, IHH met with each party individually and, in some cases, in pairs (e.g., Iran and Syria, Iran and Qatar, Qatar, and the Syrian opposition). One of the greatest difficulties was that parties were sometimes reluctant to meet face to face. The Syrian government, for instance, refused to sit at the same table as the Syrian opposition and Qatar whereas Iran refused to share a table with the Syrian opposition. In such cases, IHH represented the absent party. Another issue was that although everyone present was authorized to make decisions, more often than not they requested a recess so they could deliberate privately amongst themselves.

IHH would use these negotiations as an opportunity both to secure the freedom of other civilian prisoners who were not included in the original prisoner exchange protocol and to bring up other humanitarian issues pertaining to the Syrian Civil War. For instance, IHH discussed the welfare and possible release of Turkish citizens, Palestinians, and Syrians who had been taken prisoner, ways to end the ongoing bloodshed, access to humanitarian aid, and what roles Türkiye and other regional nations are to play in resolving the Syrian crisis.

For humanitarian diplomacy, efforts to have any impact whatsoever, it is of utmost importance that organizations acting as mediators establish their trustworthiness among the various parties involved. Unsure as to how much they could trust IHH during prisoner exchange negotiations, the Syrian opposition stipulated that seven people—two couples, an imam, and two girls—held in the Syrian-controlled city of Douma be released before agreeing to sit at the bargaining table. This allowed the opposition to gauge IHH's ability to lead negotiations. Should these seven individuals be released, the opposition agreed to share a picture proving that the forty-eight Iranian hostages were alive and well. IHH officials shared photographs and video recordings of the seven aforementioned individuals and facilitated face-to-face meetings with them in government-controlled prisons, thus proving IHH's negotiating credentials to the opposition.

The meeting between IHH's negotiating team and the seven Doumani prisoners showcased to all watching just how dirty the war in Syria was. Two married women were forced to appear in clothes they would never dream of wearing outside instead of the abayas normally donned by Syrian women when leaving the home. The prisoners were brought to the agreed-upon meeting location blindfolded and with visible marks of torture and bondage on their bodies. Similar signs of trauma and stress could be read on the other two girls and the middle-aged imam. None of these individuals had taken part in any armed or political activity; they were taken prisoner because family members or theirs had joined the armed resistance and the Syrian government wanted to use them as leverage to pressure their relatives to surrender.

After weeks of negotiations led by IHH, it was agreed that these seven prisoners were to be transported by minibus to their families living in an area controlled by the opposition outside of Damascus. Iranian and Syrian officials would escort the prisoners and IHH officials until the final inspection point in the Syrian town of Jisrin. All attacks were to be halted for twenty-four hours along the designated transit route and in East Ghouta. Despite these promises, however, no escort was provided and attacks were not halted. Upon arrival at the first of five inspection points, the Iranian and Syrian officials appointed to escort *refused to go any further, stating that their lives would be in grave danger if they did.* After abandoning the minibus, IHH President Bülent Yıldırım took control of the steering wheel and continued forward. Because their escort had abandoned them, however, they mistakenly deviated from the planned route. Although the families in the minibus successfully directed Yıldırım to a neighborhood under oppositional control, a group of armed motorcyclists from the

Figure 14.1 Seven prisoners freed following intense negotiations and IHH President
Bülent Yıldırım.

opposition noticed emblems belonging to Syrian intelligence agencies and
promptly surrounded the vehicle. After identifying themselves and correcting
several misunderstandings, the group needed to convince the motorcyclists to
allow them to return to government-controlled territory so that they could
continue to Douma as planned. Upon receiving promises from the civilians in
the minibus that they were not in any danger, opposition forces agreed to escort
them to an area near Jisrin. Upon arrival at the government-controlled inspection point, the minibus was once again surrounded by several heavily armed
men. Although IHH officials attempted to explain the situation, the guards
objected, stating that they had not received any information about a prisoner
agreement, and threatened to place the families under arrest. At this point,
Yıldırım demanded to speak with their commanding officer. Eventually, an
elderly looking commander arrived, made a few telephone calls, and, upon
receiving confirmation from his superiors, allowed the group to pass through
the inspection point. Finally, after four long hours on a road that would normally take a maximum of twenty minutes to complete, Yıldırım delivered the
seven now-free prisoners to their families in opposition-controlled territory.
Having kept their word, IHH officials met with leaders of the opposition, who
agreed to begin negotiating conditions for the release of the aforementioned
forty-eight Iranian hostages.

Thus began the second phase of the prisoner exchange. Despite the difficult field conditions, IHH met with leaders of the Syrian opposition in an isolated building without electricity—this building, they would eventually learn, served as the opposition's headquarters. The goal of this initial meeting was to convince the opposition that IHH's negotiating team was able to effectuate the proposed prisoner exchange. Just as the negotiating team was coming to terms with the direness of their situation, they found themselves face-to-face with yet another hardship. Negotiations took place in an active combat zone in which conflicts were in no short supply. Refusing to cut meetings short even when the sounds of skirmishes encroached ever closer upon them, IHH and leaders of the opposition were forced to constantly relocate from one building to another. The negotiating team realized that they had come into firing range by the sounds of explosions emitted from the shells that hit their own or adjacent buildings. The team had initially planned to complete two short meetings in Douma on 25 Oct 2012 before immediately returning to Damascus. Since, however, the conditions on the ground were in a state of constant flux, the negotiating team found themselves needing to remain in Douma overnight but had no way to inform either their team members in Damascus or headquarters in Istanbul of their situation. Despite promises to the contrary, government forces continued to subject the region to bombardment throughout the entire

Figure 14.2 Syria destruction: The blatant destruction wrought by the bombing throughout the dark of night became perfectly clear as the light of dawn overtook
the horizon. Hardly any building was spared—most had been completely
obliterated and reduced to mere rubble. Those that were fortunate enough
to survive the shelling, however, were left with no windows to speak of.

night. After a long and stressful night, the negotiating team met one final time to discuss with opposition leaders what they intended to relay back to the Syrian government and then set out for Damascus in the morning.

Following their meeting with the opposition leaders, the negotiating team faced yet another tumultuous journey on the road to Damascus. The opposition sought the release of several important figures and hundreds of male and female prisoners in return for the forty-eight Iranian hostages, adding that they would consider the negotiations to have failed should their demands go unanswered for two days. These demands and the conditions served as omens foreshadowing just how precarious negotiations would be. Over the next two and a half months until the day that the prisoner exchange was realized on 9 January 2013, IHH was required to run a sophisticated form of shuttle diplomacy.

Negotiations began to accelerate come December of 2012. Meetings in Damascus were followed by dozens of sessions in Tehran, Istanbul, and Doha. After much back and forth, the opposition accepted the following terms offered by the Syrian government in return for the release of the forty-eight Iranian hostages:

• All women shall be released from government-controlled prisons.
• A total of 2,054 *unnamed* men arrested after the revolution shall be released.[2]
• Four Qatari citizens held in Iran shall be simultaneously returned to Qatar.

The meetings in Istanbul were attended by several Qatari ministers and other government officials, making them the continuation of the Doha negotiations. The Istanbul negotiations, however, focused more on the organization and execution of the exchange than on the actual terms.

As per the Istanbul negotiations, a nine-person team from IHH would travel to Damascus via Lebanon on 5 January 2013 for one week to finalize the arrangements for the prisoner exchange. As agreed upon by all parties, the exchange was to be realized simultaneously. While the forty-eight Iranian hostages were being transferred from Douma to Damascus, 2,130 Syrian nationals—seventy-six of whom were women—were to be released from prisons located in twelve different cities in Syria, the majority from Damascus, and a private airplane was to pick up the aforementioned Qataris from Tehran.[3]

As the Iranians would be retrieved from East Ghouta, it was of vital importance that attacks conducted by the Syrian government on the area be halted over the course of the exchange. Indeed, it was no easy matter to enforce a complete ceasefire in an area that had become accustomed to an explosion every five minutes. The Syrian government proposed that the negotiating team travel to the oppositions' encampment one day prior to the exchange, stating that they would abstain from shelling the area for one or two hours while the team was en route. There, the team was supposed to find a secure area for the night and the government would once again refrain from shelling the area for a few hours as the team returned with the Iranians. Naturally, IHH rejected this outlandish proposal. Even though the parties had reached an agreement that a ceasefire would endure throughout the entirety of the exchange that was to take place on 9 January, the Syrian government went back once again on its word. The shelling continued without interruption throughout the entire ordeal, even while the negotiating team was in the designated area.

While, on the morning of 9 January, four members of the negotiating team were en route to Douma to pick up the forty-eight Iranian citizens, the remaining five members began working to accept the Syrian nationals held in the Damascus police headquarters who were scheduled to be released. Beyond the difficult field conditions, the abrasive attitudes of the detachments appointed by both the Syrian regime and the opposition to carry out the prisoner exchange further exacerbated the already tense situation.

The four-person IHH team, upon reaching Douma, first visited the hostages held by the opposition. There the team members introduced themselves and explained to them how the exchange would transpire. However, the team did not inform them that they had come to Douma to pick them up and escort them to Damascus because, given how the Syrian government consistently broke its promises not to attack during prisoner exchange operations, they believed it to be impossible to move out safely. Since contacting Damascus directly entailed severe risk, the team informed IHH's Istanbul headquarters of their predicament. Aware of the situation on the ground, IHH senior officials in Istanbul promptly began pressuring Damascus to cease all hostilities in the area. Once there was a noticeable break in attacks, the Douma team returned to where the Iranian hostages were being held to begin preparations to transport them to Damascus.

IHH President Bülent Yıldırım personally remained in Damascus to personally ensure that the more than one thousand individuals scheduled for release from the police headquarters were indeed granted their freedom. The families of those promised to be released waited for their loved ones outside the police station. The poor health and visible marks of torture on the prisoners testify to the importance of humanitarian diplomacy. One of the women prisoners told Yıldırım that her twelve-year-old child was still inside and that she would not leave without him. Though it was impossible to console everyone after all that they had been through, a total of 2,130 people, including seventy-six female prisoners, were freed that day—a monumental step in alleviating the unspeakable amount of human suffering in Syria.

The Douma team carried out the prisoner exchange operations in the opposition-controlled territory with the utmost care and attention to detail. After the Iranians boarded the bus to that would take them to Damascus, the team performed a head count to ensure that no one was missing; for, the absence of just a single person would bear detrimental consequences for the entire process. When, to their complete surprise, they found that one more person than expected was among them, they informed their superiors of the situation. After some investigation, the team learned that this individual was an Afghan guide who had been driving the bus carrying the forty-eight Iranians when they were taken prisoner. Although he was also a Shiite and shared the

Figure 14.3 Freed prisoners: Overcome with both joy and appreciation, the hostages began embracing each other and their captors upon realizing that they were about to regain their freedom. Though their actions may seem rather strange at first thought, this was a very natural reaction given that the opposition had treated them very well and that an emotional bond had formed between the two groups. In Damascus, on the other hand, the prisoners received the same despicable treatment that they had been subjected to in government prisons up until the exchange actually took place. They were constantly bombarded with insults and slogans of "May our lives and blood be sacrificed for you O Assad!"

same fate as the others, Iranian officials had not made a single mention of him nor did they seek his release.

Only after having confirmed with Istanbul one final time that all the Syrian nationals scheduled for release from government prisons had attained their freedom and that the Qataris held in Iran had boarded the plane sent for them and were safely on their way home did the team feel comfortable moving the hostages to Damascus. Though the sound of weapons firing resonated around them, the bus made it back to government-controlled territory without incident.

A large crowd of Iranians and pro-government Syrians welcomed the arriving IHH team and hostages at the government-controlled town of Harasta. Immediately upon arrival, the hostages were unloaded from the bus and evacuated from the area by several smaller vehicles. They were greeted with an even larger program when they reached the hotel where they were to stay. Iran's ambassador to Syria, official delegations, senior military officers, and an army of journalists presented the now-freed hostages with bouquets of flowers before hosting a press conference with them during which the IHH team was thanked for their role in ensuring that the prisoner exchange was completed successfully.

The Release of Adem Özköse and Hamit Coşkun

Turkish journalist Adem Özköse and cameraman Hamit Coşkun traveled to Syria on 5 March 2012 to film a documentary on how local children were affected by and dealing with the ongoing conflict. When, however, their families received no word from them after crossing the border, they sought assistance from IHH on 13 March. Whereas all indicators pointed to the grim reality that the two journalists had been kidnapped by Syrian security forces, the Syrian government adamantly denied that they were in their custody.

IHH President Bülent Yıldırım was engaged in negotiations for the safe release of eleven Iranian citizens who had been kidnapped when he learned that the two aforementioned journalists had gone missing in Syria. As such, Yıldırım made the release of Özköse and Coşkun a condition of these negotiations.

After a series of exchanges, the Syrian regime admitted that the two journalists were indeed being detained and informed IHH that they would release the

Figure 14.4 Freed journalists Adem Özköse and Hamit Coşkun, and İzzet Şahin: "Once we accepted their offer to visit the journalists, we found out that they were not far away and were being held in an underground prison located beneath the center in which we were conducting negotiations."

two into the organization's custody in Damascus. With that, Yıldırım met with Iranian officials and Syrian senior government authorities on 5 May 2012 in Damascus. Several topics were discussed during the ensuing meeting before coming to the journalists' situation. Despite previous promises to the contrary, the Syrian government representatives informed IHH that they would hand over Özköse and Coşkun at the following meeting. This unexpected development brought negotiations to a boiling point. Seeking to alleviate rising tensions, the Syrian authorities decided to allow the IHH team to visit the two journalists.

Since neither Özköse nor Coşkun had been allowed to speak with anyone from the outside until that day, both their families and government were in the dark about their predicament. The two saw, at a time when they had lost all hope of regaining their freedom, IHH officials in front of them. Thoroughly shaken by what they had experienced, the two journalists spoke with the IHH representatives, who further leveraged the Syrian authorities to allow them to speak with their family members via telephone. The IHH took photographs and videos with Özköse and Coşkun to prevent the Syrian government from being able to deny the two were being held in the country. The publication of these images by the Turkish media afforded some relief—if only a little—to the two journalists' families and the wider public. One week after this meeting, on 13 May 2012, Özköse and Coşkun were transferred from Damascus to Tehran, where they were delivered to IHH officials and flown to Istanbul in an airplane sent by the Turkish government to retrieve them.

Case Files for Bashar Kadumi and Cüneyt Ünal

IHH's Damascus-based humanitarian diplomacy team was actively working on several other case files while dealing with the Iranian hostage situation. Two of these case files belonged to Turkish journalist Cüneyt Ünal and Palestinian journalist Bashar Kadumi, married to a Turkish national. On 20 August 2012, these two journalists, along with Japanese journalist Mika Yamamoto, were targeted in an attack in Syria. Whereas Yamamoto was declared dead at the scene of the incident, the two other journalists were taken into custody by the Syrian military forces and not heard from again.

The plight of Kadumi and Ünal came to constitute an integral part of IHH's negotiations with Iranian and Syrian officials. Several influential political and opinion leaders, such as Palestinian President Mahmoud Abbas, offered their support to help liberate Kadumi and Ünal.

Syrian soldiers taken prisoner by opposition forces at the site where Ünal and Kadumi had been last seen were presented as evidence for their kidnapping. After extensive efforts, the Syrian regime eventually provided IHH with a recently taken photograph proving that Ünal was being held in a Syrian prison but denied any knowledge of what happened to Kadumi. Similar to Özköse and Coşkun, IHH shared this incriminating photograph to Ünal's family and employer. Ünal was delivered to Türkiye on 18 November 2012. Kadumi's whereabouts, however, continue to remain a mystery to this day.

Other Issues Brought Up During the Prisoner Exchange

The Syrian Crisis and the Path to Peace

As an NGO, IHH consistently issues calls for calm and restraint both when and after weapons have begun to be used to enforce one's will. Accordingly, IHH made the following recommendations to all parties involved in the prisoner exchange negotiations:

- That a country-wide ceasefire be implemented.
- That artillery and other heavy weapons be removed from city centers.
- That non-violent demonstrations be permitted.
- That a comprehensive amnesty be declared.
- That those alleged of having committed acts of torture be tried in court and, in the event that they are convicted, face due punishment.
- That Law No. 49 mandating that members and sympathizers of the Muslim Brotherhood shall be tried and executed be repealed.
- That channels allowing the civilian population to redress their administrators be opened. That all requests, recommendations, and complaints by the local population be forwarded to the relevant administrator. That individuals acting as liaisons between the country's citizens and administrators be elected. That a service similar to Türkiye's White Table (i.e., Beyaz Masa) program be implemented.
- That the Syrian government articulate its unequivocal support for peace and that the possibility of future foreign intervention be taken off the table.
- That all possible non-violent means be taken as soon to ameliorate the situation as possible to before events reach a point of no return.
- That the Syrian government sit down and open dialogue with the opposition.
- That, if necessary, Türkiye, Iran, and Syria act in coordination to put an end to the ongoing crisis.

Humanitarian Diplomacy and Relief Initiatives in Syria

IHH's Humanitarian Diplomacy Unit conducted several negotiations with the Syrian government and Iran to expand aid delivery services to the entire country instead of solely to territories controlled by opposition forces. During said negotiations, IHH stressed that aid would not only save lives but also serve as a valuable tool paving the way for lasting peace in the country. The following are a few of the recommendations made by the IHH in this regard:

- Humanitarian relief efforts should encompass the entire country.
- Groups conducting relief efforts should be afforded NGO status and their works should be supported.
- Humanitarian relief efforts should be centered in Damascus and be managed locally by branches and representatives in every city.

- IHH officials should be permitted to work everywhere that aid materials are distributed.
- Syrian IDPs and Palestinian refugees residing in Syria should be allowed to work with the IHH in the organization's aid distribution operations.
- Palestinian refugees should have an active hand in relief efforts. Syria's support of the Palestinian resistance has always been the subject of praise from the wider Muslim world. Palestinian refugees should not only continue to receive aid but should also be recruited so that their experiences in humanitarian relief efforts can be benefitted from throughout Syria.
- Victims of violence should receive medical care regardless of who they are or to which group they belong. When necessary, they should be permitted to receive care abroad.
- Potential logistics centers supporting humanitarian relief efforts should be identified and, where needed, established.
- The importation of vehicles (e.g., cars, trucks, ambulances) necessary to carry out relief efforts from Türkiye should be eased.
- Taxation, customs, and other bureaucratic processes should be simplified.
- Logistical support should be provided for humanitarian relief efforts at ports of entry.
- Money transfers should be made streamlined. The goal here is to bolster the local economy by sourcing humanitarian relief materials locally.

Captive Women in Syria and the Conscience Movement

As a mediator, IHH affords the utmost importance to maintaining independence and neutrality during mediation hearings. This manifests itself most concretely when dealing with female and child detainees as well as captives of war. For while IHH strives to secure the unconditional release of imprisoned women and children regardless of which side of the conflict they find themselves, the foundation also engages in what might be called *preemptive protection* by working to prevent women from being used as collateral or some other form of leverage during negotiations.

During prisoner exchange negotiations, IHH requested that all women being held in prisons under the regime's control be released in exchange for forty-eight Iranian citizens held by opposition forces. While Syrian authorities appeared to be acquiesce, the operative word here being appeared, they listed only seventy-six women prisoners, despite IHH's Humanitarian Diplomacy Unit having evidence of there being several thousand women prisoners. When it came time for the prisoners to be exchanged, the regime only released seventy-six women. The most egregious aspect of this was that the majority of these women were, similar to their male counterparts, being held without access to any of their legal rights in underground prisons known only to a select number of high-level officials. These women were unlawfully imprisoned without trial. They were not allowed to contact their families, receive legal assistance from a lawyer, or even defend themselves. Not only was no evidence presented for their alleged crimes, their confessions were extracted after being subject to various forms of torture and coercion. Without a trial or even appearing before a judge, they were locked away to be forgotten to the world. This continued for several years, resulting in the imprisonment of literally thousands of women.

Figure 14.5 Conscience Convoy: Women from different countries of the world made their voices heard with the Convoy of Conscience for Syrian imprisoned women.

Figure 14.5 (Continued)

IHH engaged in a variety of diplomatic endeavors to draw attention to the ongoing suffering of women in Syria. Under the leadership of the foundation, the Conscience Movement organized the *Convoy of Conscience*, which, as the name implies, consisted of a massive convoy of humanitarians from around the world that marched on the Syrian border on International Women's Day of 2018. Then on International Women's Day of the following year, the Conscience Movement arranged a press conference attended by numerous high-level international officials. Also in 2019, the movement organized another event, Female Prisoners in Syria, at the UN Office at Geneva.

The Conscience Movement spearheaded several other initiatives in addition to the awareness and advocacy campaigns discussed above. The movement sent letters to numerous heads of state and opinion leaders and met with ministers, speakers of parliament, and MPs from Iran, Kuwait, Qatar, Ukraine, Türkiye, the EU, and various other countries. On 21 June 2021, IHH President Bülent Yıldırım met with Hezbollah representatives and the Syrian ambassador in Lebanon to discuss the issue of detained women. All of these efforts did eventually pay off, however, as the number of detained women fell from the staggering fourteen thousand when the Conscience Movement first began to voice its concerns on this issue to approximately two thousand by December 2021. The movement continues to work to secure the release of the remaining female detainees.

Reconciliation between Misrata and Zintan

Background

After starting in Tunisia in December of 2010, the Arab Spring spread to Libya by February of 2011, a civil war broke out between Muammar Gaddafi, who had been ruling the country for forty-two years, and dissident forces. Gaddafi's forces surrounded the eastern city of Benghazi where dissidents had congregated. The two western Libyan cities of Misrata and Zintan sided with the Benghazi-based opposition and began to revolt against regime forces, who were preparing an assault on the city of Benghazi.

The fall of the Gaddafi regime in October of 2011 only a short time after the initial sparks of the Arab Spring were ignited opened a new page in Libya's history. On the one hand, a new political authority was established in Tripoli whereas the various ethnic and tribal groups that had supported one another against Gaddafi began to fall into discord while attempting to share power. Several factors contributed to the opposition's fragmentation, including deep-rooted historical issues, the personal ambitions of certain key individuals, and the ripple effects of the 2013 military coup d'état that shook neighboring Egypt. The two cities of Zintan and Misrata, despite having fought on the same side against Gaddafi's forces, now found themselves in conflict with each other.

Figure 14.6 Map of Libya: Map showing the three main regions of Libya - Tripoli, Fezzan, Barqah.

Libya has, throughout her long history, been divided into three regions: Cyrenaica (Barqah) in the east, Tripolitania in the west, and Fezzan in the south. Not only do these three regions boast visibly different social structures and conditions from one another, cities inside the same region are home to different tribal groups and relations. The first two year following the collapse of the Gaddafi regime saw a number of ineffective practices implemented by the authorities that rose to power in these regions. Though these may very well have been caused by a variety of complex factors, the end result was that the public found themselves in ever-deteriorating conditions. Seeking to harness this situation for his own gain, former general Khalifa Haftar returned to Libya from self-imposed exile in the USA, upon which he, with the support of several foreign powers, plunged the country into a new conflict against the Tripoli-based government in May of 2014.

Khalifa Haftar announced the launch Operation Karama (i.e., Dignity), essentially an attempt at a military coup, in Benghazi. In response to this, the Tripoli-based government began negotiations to that no similar conflicts would engulf in the capital. During this same period, the administration and security of the airport in Tripoli under the control the UN-recognized government was in the hands of Zintan groups. During negotiations, the Tripoli government requested Zintan forces agree to share said airport's security responsibilities with them and that they not support Haftar when he staged his coup d'état. Despite this, however, Zintan groups were discovered to have secretly colluded with Haftar's forces and been smuggling fighters and ammunition into the city. After a long and bloody fight in the airport, Zintan forces were driven back to their home city, leaving the airport in an unusable state.

The militia *Fajr Libya*, the largest part of whose military forces was composed of Misratis played a significant role in liberating the airport. After their success in Tripoli, Fajr Libya began to lay siege on Zintan, intending to take control of the city. Although Zintan's geographic position thwarted their efforts in this regard, the Misratis succeeded in cutting off supply lines into the city, thus preventing even the most basic of needs from entering the city. The conflict between the cities of Misrata and Zintan persisted for several months thereafter.

One of the processes in which IHH is involved through humanitarian diplomacy is the ongoing peace process in Moro. IHH is one of the five members of the Third Party Monitoring Team (TPMT) established in 2014. TPMT monitors the implementation of the agreements signed between the Government of the Philippines and the Moro Islamic Liberation Front. TPMT members, who meet in the Philippines every two months, observe the peace process, hold consultations with the parties and share their reports with the public. For a detailed narrative on IHH's role in Moro Peace Process see Oruç, 2023.

Conflicting Parties Sitting Down at the Same Table: Humanitarian Negotiations

After running humanitarian projects throughout Libya from the first days of the country's revolution, IHH ramped up its efforts in the cities of Benghazi, Bayda, and Misrata beginning in March 2015. The humanitarian works that IHH's Benghazi office kept up even during the most violent phases of the revolution allowed the local population to become acquainted with and trust the foundation. Similarly, IHH's humanitarian relief initiatives in Misrata during both the revolution and Operation Karama caused the Misratis to become familiar with the foundation. When, however, the conflicts that overtook Libya in 2014 led to financial loss for the Turkish companies working there, many of them met in Ankara in 2015 to discuss the ongoing situation and the losses they had incurred. During this meeting, they discussed how to institute peace between Misrata and Zintan forces, which, in turn, led them to reach out and seek the counsel of the now late IHH Executive Board Member Ahmet Sarıkurt.

Shortly thereafter, IHH organized an online conference with the Zintanis, who, over the course of negotiations, requested that basic food supplies be allowed into the city and that the siege be lifted. In return, Zintan would refrain from cutting Misrata's electricity, as Gaddafi had constructed an infrastructural grid in which each city was connected to the other.

The following bullet points delineate the steps included in the roadmap drafted during the meetings held in April of 2015 in IHH's Humanitarian Diplomacy Unit intending to resolve the ongoing humanitarian crisis in the region:

- Since the city of Zintan had yet to be consulted, IHH was chosen to establish communication channels with the Zintanis, to gain their trust, and to serve as mediator during peace talks.
- The military arms of both groups were to sit down with one another at the same table. (Since these two groups were responsible for perpetuating the conflict, it would be easier for them to convince the other groups to cease hostilities after they had been persuaded to reconcile with one another.)
- A safe zone between the two sides was scheduled to be created.
- Affronts against either side's dignity were to be avoided. (Both sides will be convinced that they have walked away from the negotiating table having gained something they wanted, as the peace process would be irreparably harmed if one side were to perceive itself the winner and the other the loser.)
- The agreement between parties was to prioritize the improvement of human conditions, not the protection of myriad political interests.

In order to ensure that this plan achieve the goals that it set for itself, one of the more prominent figures of Zintan, the now late Ahmad Tayyeb, was invited to Türkiye by IHH to represent the Zintanis in preliminary discussions. While in Türkiye, Tayyeb helped draw up the final form of this roadmap and articulated what problems could potentially arise during its execution.

While discussions with the Zintanis were still underway, it was necessary to persuade the Misratis—the most powerful armed faction within Fajr Libya—to accept this plan. During the period in question, Misrata was ruled by two groups: the Municipal Council of Misrata and the city's military wing, *the Council of Notables and Elders*. Furthermore, although this council had only recently been elected, processions were sent to numerous cities, including Benghazi, to engage in peace talks. While the country's military wing was civilian in nature, it did act as the driving force behind Fajr Libya. Prime Minister Khalifa al-Ghawil's government was, during this period, close to this group. Similarly, President of the General National Congress, Nouri Abusahmain, maintained close ties with one of Fajr Libya's commanders, Salah Badi. As such, it was necessary to convince all of these different factions sit down together and come to a mutual agreement. To ensure a fruitful process, IHH began sending processions to Libya in April of 2015 to initiate negotiations. IHH's negotiation team met with an MP from *Majlis al-Aʿyān waʾl-Hukamāʾ* known for his earnest efforts to secure peace, several of the more moderate commanders of Fajr Libya, the Libyan Muftiate, and various politicians on several occasions. During the discussions that ensued, not only were the need to improve conditions among the civilian population and, therefore, the importance of instilling an air of peace highlighted. Despite consistent attempts to persuade them to accelerate this process, however, the parties involved continued to drag their feet in this regard. Whereas all of the Misrati representatives stressed their desire for peace, all parties voiced that they no longer trusted the Zintanis to follow through on their word. Deep-rooted tribal rivalries, when combined with Zintan's support for Haftar, greatly frustrated all attempts to build the atmosphere of trust requisite for lasting peace.

After listening to the Misratis' concerns, the IHH procession returned home where they wasted no time in inviting Zintan representatives to Türkiye for peace talks. The sincerity that the Zintani delegation demonstrated over the course of their visit coupled with their receptiveness during initial talks precipitated a sense of trust between the Zintanis and IHH.

While IHH was engaged in talks with Zintan and Misrata, the Swiss-based NGO Centre for Humanitarian Dialogue was making in preparations to meet with several influential Libyan politicians and leaders in Istanbul. Using these meetings as an opportunity to talk with various political and military figures in attendance from Libya, IHH made great strides in strengthening the ongoing peace efforts.

The Istanbul talks were instrumental in demonstrating to all parties just how important mediation is for peacebuilding initiatives. After returning to Libya, in fact, the various attendees found it significantly easier to come together and take the steps necessary to resolve the problems that had been plaguing Libya for the past several years.

Upon their return to Libya, *Majlis al-Aʿyān waʾl-Hukamāʾ* invited an IHH delegation to Misrata. Expressing their willingness to engage in peace talks, *Majlis al-Aʿyān waʾl-Hukamāʾ* selected an envoy to represent them and agreed to meet with the Zintanis in Istanbul during the first week of June 2015. After setting the date for these peace talks, IHH Executive Board Member Ahmet Sarıkurt, IHH Board of Trustees Deputy Chairman Hüseyin Oruç, and IHH Board of Trustees Member Ömer Faruk Korkmaz began preparations to meet with Libyan officials in IHH's Istanbul headquarters. Oruç personally went over what protocols were to be followed while welcoming the arriving delegations, whether the different parties should stay in the same or different hotels, and issues that could potentially arise during negotiations. Korkmaz was elected to chair the meeting because of his previous experience talking with the Zintani delegation. Whereas the Zintanis had informed IHH who from their side would attend the meeting very early on, the Misratis continued to hold back this information even as the date fast approached. Naturally, the Misratis wanted to know the names of those whom they would encounter in Istanbul; however, they were kept in the dark until the very last minute.

When, on 3 June 2015, the parties were scheduled to convene in Istanbul, IHH's humanitarian diplomacy team was, on the one hand, reevaluating its decision to host two mutually antagonistic groups in the same hotel and, on the other, working overtime to identify who from the Misrati delegation would attend the talks. Following several deliberations with the Misratis during the day and intense telephone diplomacy, it was finally decided that talks be placed on hold before they even began. The next morning, however, when the Misrati delegation informed IHH that they would not be participating in negotiations, IHH's humanitarian diplomacy team immediately began searching for other opinion leaders in Libya who would intercede on their behalf. After a series of talks that lasted until midnight, IHH was informed that four local MPs from the Municipal Council of Misrata would come to Türkiye, thereby allowing them to accelerate their technical preparations for the peace talks. The Zintani delegation, waiting patiently in their hotel suites throughout this entire affair, was kept abreast of all developments as they transpired. Eventually, however, all of IHH's efforts—largely supported by the late Mayor of Misrata Mohamed Eshtewi—paid off.

Once all of the parties were present in Istanbul, they took part in a two-day program to spend time and become better acquainted with one another before the peace talks began. This two-day program held in IHH's Istanbul head-quarters was the first time that Zintan and Misrata interacted with one another, even if through foreign delegations, on amicable terms. In any case, the first session of peace talks were held on 6 June 2015 in IHH's Istanbul headquarters. IHH Humanitarian Diplomacy Coordinator Hüseyin Oruç opened the meeting with a speech in which he emphasized that only the Libyans could effectuate lasting peace and that IHH would remain by their side during the entire process. Moderated by IHH Board of Trustees Member Ömer Faruk Korkmaz, this meeting lasted from morning until late in the evening and bore witness to conversations that frequently ended in heated arguments and that required short breaks to bring the discussion back on track. After two long and tense days of back and forth negotiations, the talks ended successfully on 7 June.

The following issues were agreed upon:

- Misrata forces shall lift the siege on Zintan and allow all food items and basic necessities to enter the city.
- Zintan forces shall not partake in any armed operations against Tripoli.
- Both sides shall refrain from speaking negatively of the other in the media.
- Commercial vehicles shall be allowed to pass without hindrance.
- Misrata and Zintan shall accept and facilitate the unfettered entry of visitors.
- Talks shall be led by both sides upon return to Libya.
- This agreement shall, for security reasons, remain confidential for the time being and not be made public in Libya.

The signing of this agreement was instrumental in resolving a serious humanitarian crisis that had plagued Libya for a significant period of time. With the siege lifted and the two cities having begun a process of rapprochement, humanitarian groups began operating in the respective areas with greater ease.

Following this fortunate course of events, the two cities not only refrained from fighting one another until the time of this article's composition in late 2021 but have also coordinated with one another to solve several other problems. Another positive outcome of this rapprochement that was not a part of the original agreement signed on 7 June 2015 in Istanbul was that both sides decided to release the prisoners that they had been holding. Perhaps the most important effect, however, was that this agreement has served as a precedent for other belligerent groups in similar circumstances, especially given the amount of difficulties and hardships that were overcome to reach it.

Notes

1 IFRC, Humanitarian Diplomacy Policy, https://www.ifrc.org/sites/default/files/Humanitarian-Diplomacy-Policy_EN.pdf (Accessed: 25 Dec 2021).
2 The term *unnamed* indicates that the freedom of an agreed-upon number of people was sought as opposed to that of specific individuals.
3 Although the Syrian regime had agreed to release all women held in government-controlled prisons, government officials stated that there were only seventy-six women in prisons on the day that the exchange was to take place. As a result, seventy-six women were liberated from Syrian prisons during this exchange.

References

The International Federation of Red Cross and Red Crescent Societies (IFRC). (2017). *Humanitarian diplomacy policy*. https://www.ifrc.org/sites/default/files/Humanitarian-Diplomacy-Policy_EN.pdf
Oruç, H. (2023). Moro Barış Süreci'nde İHH İnsani Yardım Vakfının İnsani Diplomasi Aktörlüğü. In Kavak, H. Z. (ed.). *Kuramdan Uygulamaya İnsani Diplomasi*, 415–428. Kızılay Kültür Sanat Yayınları.

15 To Be a Humanitarian is to Be a Diplomat

Michael David Clark

Introduction

As the sun rises over a seemingly endless desert road, a convoy of vehicles comes to a halt at a checkpoint manned by an armed group. The lead driver rolls down his window, takes a deep breath, and prepares himself for the unpredictable negotiation. Three days earlier, a few thousand kilometers away in Geneva, the opening of a humanitarian corridor had been negotiated. With no end in sight to this protracted conflict, several states, the UN, the International Committee of the Red Cross (henceforth ICRC), and non-governmental organizations (NGOs) had held direct and indirect talks with the parties to conflict to realize this humanitarian operation. Yet it is here, in the proverbial last mile of the humanitarian operation, that it is up to the driver to persuade this splinter group to respect the agreement brokered in Switzerland.

Halfway around the world, the sun has already set as a first response team steps off of the plane and into chaos. A few hours earlier, an earthquake caused massive destruction; there are mounting fears of mass casualties. The team has been asked to conduct a rapid assessment, and most importantly, to formalize an agreement with a local organization they will partner with during the emergency response. The local NGO is determined not to be relegated to an implementing role, but to lead the assessment, to own the response design, and to limit the presence of expatriate staff. The effectiveness of this partnership will depend on the ability of both parties to practice diplomatic function.

In a time zone somewhere between the conflict and earthquake, a local volunteer is meeting with a group of mothers by the village water well. Her goal is to persuade them to have their children vaccinated to prevent a dangerous disease. Advocacy campaigns by the humanitarian community secured the funding to begin the vaccination drive. A working group of state actors, NGOs, and the UN successfully negotiated the terms of the immunization campaign with the host government's Ministry of Health. Now the operation's ultimate success or failure is up to the volunteer.

The 450,000 aid professionals in the $25 billion humanitarian sector have something in common: to be a humanitarian is to be a diplomat. Regardless of their role—and the context of their work—they practice diplomacy in order to

DOI: 10.4324/9781003503187-15

deliver effective aid. In recent years, as official diplomats are questioning the relevance of their craft in a globalized and digital age, humanitarian diplomacy has emerged as a critical component in achieving aid effectiveness on the local level of humanitarian action, as humanitarian actors incorporate diplomatic function with an emphasis on localization in their work.

This article will briefly present the results of a multi-year, multi-national PhD research project that this author conducted at the University of Groningen on the topic of humanitarian diplomacy (Clark, 2018). The research project involved the (to this date) largest systematic review of literature on humanitarian diplomacy. The empirical evidence from the systematic review, suggested that a *specific type* of diplomacy was the moderator in the relationship of humanitarian diplomacy and humanitarian effectiveness. This observation led to the following research question:

> To what extent can humanitarian effectiveness be improved when the practice of diplomacy in humanitarian action is conceptualized and operationalized as humanitarian multi-track diplomacy?

Three hypotheses guided how the research question was answered:

1 Humanitarian actors incorporate diplomatic function into their job responsibilities during a humanitarian response in order to achieve humanitarian effectiveness.
2 Humanitarian actors adjust their diplomatic strategy depending on the proximity of parameters between them and their counterparts.
3 Humanitarian actors' preference to apply a consensus-based diplomatic strategy has a positive effect on humanitarian effectiveness.

A case study examined the role of diplomacy in the disaster responses of an international non-governmental organization (INGO), namely, Convoy of Hope, and a local NGO, Mission of Hope, in the aftermath of the 2010 Haiti Earthquake. In-depth interviews with representatives from both organizations were conducted to understand how these two counterparts practiced diplomacy during partner negotiations. The case study involved seventeen participants from Convoy of Hope and six participants from Mission of Hope.

During the case study, the researcher had unrestricted access to the presidents of both organizations, as well as other decision-makers, managers, and practitioners on the headquarter and field levels. The case study gathered information through self-reporting exercises (i.e., interviews) and unobtrusive measures (i.e., internal memos and policies, public statements via news interviews, social media posts, email campaigns). The primary focus was to study the perceptions, decisions, and behaviors of those who were directly involved in and who had relevant knowledge of the humanitarian response.

As a result, this research explained the critical link between aid effectiveness and diplomatic function in humanitarian action. Most relevant to this book, the research found that humanitarians incorporate diplomatic function into their job responsibilities because diplomacy is critical to aid effectiveness. The research concluded that humanitarian diplomacy is best conceptualized and operationalized as humanitarian multi-track diplomacy and best is defined as a *multidimensional approach to achieving humanitarian objectives through dialogue, advocacy, negotiation, and persuasion.*

The research makes it evident that humanitarian diplomacy is part of the humanitarian identity and definitively present in humanitarian action because humanitarians consistently and broadly practice it. In the case study, 100 percent of interviewees agreed that diplomacy was critical to achieving humanitarian effectiveness during the relief operation. Since this research, the practice of humanitarian diplomacy has often been intentionally referred to as *diplomatic function.* As the researcher, I make no claim to having coined the term, but it succinctly encapsulates the tension that exists as, despite having received no expressed mandate to practice diplomacy, humanitarians view themselves as diplomats.[1] They practice it because they must to achieve their purpose. Accordingly, it is a matter of function defined as "the natural action or intended purpose of a person or thing in a specific role" (Collins English Dictionary Online, n.d.).

Humanitarian diplomacy is practical not ceremonial, efficient not long-winded, and is mostly focused on achieving short-term objectives. Therefore, humanitarian diplomacy cannot be associated with the Hollywood image of official diplomacy practiced by state actors at grand galas or in stately conference rooms of an embassy. Humanitarians gave examples of how diplomatic function in humanitarian emergencies took place on dusty roads, in smoke-filled cafés, in overcrowded government offices, and in blood-covered makeshift operating rooms. Since humanitarian actors incorporate diplomatic function into their job responsibilities during a humanitarian response to achieve humanitarian effectiveness, humanitarian multi-track diplomacy in the literature and this case study offer a clear picture of the practice as definite, particular, and critical.

1   Diplomacy is **definitive** because humanitarians incorporated diplomacy into their day-to-day job function.
2   Diplomacy is **critical** since the humanitarians interviewed regarded their relationships to diplomacy as essential to achieving their organization's mission, namely, an effective humanitarian response.
3   Humanitarians practice a **particular** type of diplomacy—one that is very different from traditional diplomacy.[2]

Simply put, humanitarian multi-track diplomacy is clearly present in humanitarian action because one can put his or, in just as many cases, her finger on it. Elements of the humanitarian multi-track diplomacy theory were simultaneously present in the literature and case study interviews. Diplomatic function was present in all INGOs' hierarchical and geographic spaces, from the president at the headquarters to the volunteers in the field. Collectively, the conclusive evidence warrants unconditional use of the absolute term *definitive* when referring to diplomatic function in the humanitarian system.

The individual case study participants exposed not only a matter-of-fact association with diplomacy but also a desire to reflect on and learn from particular instances during the responses when diplomacy was especially important to the execution of their duties. There is a sense that when humanitarian professionals and volunteers enter the humanitarian theater, they can seamlessly adapt to the role of the diplomat whenever the situation so requires. Certainly, several of those interviewed reflected on what they or their colleagues could have done differently. There were, for example, a few instances when rather undiplomatic actions were taken, but even these could often be seen as calculated decisions to escalate a particular situation or to call someone on a bluff. Although in the real world of humanitarian action, a rematch is rarely permitted, humanitarians generally believed that their practice of diplomacy resulted in reaching the desired outcomes. It is noteworthy that these men and women showed deliberate and restrained professionalism under highly physically and emotionally challenging conditions.

The evidence of this research presents a system in which humanitarians from all backgrounds, experience levels, and, perhaps most notably, job functions manifest a high familiarity with the practice of diplomacy. Whereas previous scholarly work on the topic has suggested that most humanitarians would not see themselves as diplomats, the overwhelming majority of participants in this case study (90%) strongly associated with the role of a diplomat. Humanitarians comfortably embraced the idea that humanitarians were also diplomats. It should be noted that when the case study interview was conducted with a comparison group consisting of aid professionals who responded to the 2015 earthquake in Nepal and the ongoing Middle East refugee crisis, responses were nearly identical (78% strongly agreed, 22% agreed).

In general, organizations do not clearly articulate what humanitarian diplomacy means to them or how it translates across their organizations. Strikingly, this lack of mandate does not seem to affect the individual practitioner, at least on the micro-level, where diplomatic function is operationalized. Although it emerged during the case study that only three of the ten job descriptions expressly mentioned diplomatic function as a requirement, all humanitarians practiced it consistently. They comfortably associated themselves with the concept and practice of diplomacy, connecting the dots between the idea of diplomacy and its practice in their day-to-day routines. From a higher vantage point, they were able to zoom out and remark the role that diplomacy played across their organization. Humanitarians' relationship with diplomacy raises an important question: Why do humanitarians, despite the lack of mandate and irrespective of job level, type, and location, practice diplomacy? The answer is simple: They view it as mission critical.

Evidence conclusively reveals the existence of a link between diplomatic function and humanitarian effectiveness. Case study participants viewed their personal practice of diplomacy as being essential to humanitarian effectiveness. This substantiates claims made by others in the literature asserting that the unique realities and challenges of the humanitarian sector require diplomacy as an indispensable forte. Since diplomacy is indispensable, diplomatic function is not a choice, but a responsibility. Diplomacy emerges as the X factor—the key ingredient—to humanitarian effectiveness. Where there are threats to humanitarian effectiveness, diplomacy is present. Diplomatic function addressed major challenges, such as acceptance and protection, but also minute operational issues in aid delivery and communications with local communities. Regardless of the type of threat, the participants believed that diplomacy played a critical role in ensuring a positive outcome in the face of these challenges.

The utilization of the four primary diplomacy tools—dialogue, negotiation, advocacy, and persuasion—were regularly practiced in order to achieve an objective. The tools were the means to begin deliberations and to gather intelligence. Dialogue opened channels of communication and when there was no consensus during a negotiation, the tool propelled the conversation. Negotiation, as a wide-ranging utility, was used to reach agreements on how programs were to be implemented and evaluated. Advocacy raised awareness through discreet networks when decision-makers needed to be influenced behind the scenes. When there were clear violations of norms or agreements, humanitarians could employ the last-resort tool, persuasion, to put public pressure on the counterpart in question. In all of these applications, diplomatic function assisted in meeting individual objectives, and together made up the sum: humanitarian effectiveness. Yet, it is not just any kind of diplomacy that these and other humanitarians incorporate into their work. The practice of humanitarian diplomacy is, given it is definitive in practice and critical to humanitarian effectiveness, particularly in type.

Conclusion

This article opened with three short illustrations of humanitarian diplomacy. In the first example, a driver had to renegotiate access at a checkpoint. In the second illustration, INGO first responders were discussing a joint disaster response with a local NGO partner. Finally, a volunteer, at the last mile of aid assistance, was engaging with local villagers to ensure children were protected during a disease outbreak.

Every day humanitarians practice diplomatic function because it is critical to aid effectiveness. Since the responsibility for humanitarian diplomacy is shared, every diplomatic activity, as unique and disconnected as it might appear at first glance, takes place in a dynamic, interconnected system. This system is best conceptualized as humanitarian multi-track diplomacy.

Every humanitarian must practice diplomatic function in order to ensure effective aid delivery. At the conclusion of this research, the statement that appeared in bold at the beginning of this article is now undeniable: To be a humanitarian is to be a diplomat.

Notes

1 Only 29% of job descriptions required or described diplomatic practice. Eighty-nine percent strongly agreed or agreed with the statement, "To be a humanitarian is to be a diplomat.".
2 For example, it was multi-lateral; shared across the system and both geographic and hierarchical spaces; and purely humanitarian in purpose.

References

Clark, M. D. (2018). *Humanitarian multi-track diplomacy: Conceptualizing the definitive, particular and critical role of diplomatic function in humanitarian action* [PhD thesis,University of Groningen].
Collins Cobuild. (n.d.). Function. In *Collins English Dictionary Online.* https://www.collinsdictionary.com/dictionary/english/function

16 Humanitarian Diplomacy and the Turkish Red Crescent

An Exposé on Theory and Practice*

Kerem Kınık and Hafize Zehra Kavak

The Turkish Red Crescent (henceforth TRC) is a part of the larger International Red Cross and Red Crescent Movement. One of the many *national societies* comprising the aforementioned movement, TRC is recognized as an *auxiliary to the public authorities* by the Turkish government and thus engages in humanitarian diplomacy at its own behest. The International Committee of the Red Cross (ICRC) was formed when Swiss businessman Henry Dunant, who after witnessing first-hand the suffering and desperation of countless wounded men following the 1859 Battle of Solferino, called for the creation of an international aid organization (Dunant, 1964). Under similar circumstances, the Ottoman Society for Aiding Wounded and Sick Soldiers (i.e., ʿOsmānlı Mecrūḥīn ve Marżā-yı ʿAskeriyyeye İmdād ve Muʿāvenet Cemʿiyyeti)—the precursor to TRC—was founded in 1868 to provide humanitarian aid to wounded and sick soldiers. The organization was renamed the Ottoman Red Crescent Society (i.e., ʿOsmānlı Hilāl-i Aḥmer Cemʿiyyeti) in 1877 and then the Red Crescent Society of Türkiye (i.e., *Türkiye Hilāl-i Aḥmer Cemʿiyyeti*) in 1923 with the establishment of the Republic of Türkiye. Though the organization's name was essentially solidified in English at this date, it underwent another change in Turkish in 1935, becoming *Türkiye Kızılay Cemiyeti*, before attaining its final and current form of *Türkiye Kızılay Derneği*—shortened to *Türk Kızılay*—in 1947 (Kızılay Tarih, n.d.). Regardless of its name, TRC has remained an active member of the humanitarian community throughout its long history, whose activities include family reunification, prisoner exchange, facilitating the return of seriously wounded and sick prisoners of war, searching for missing persons, civilian evacuation, opening humanitarian corridors, delivering humanitarian aid, crisis mitigation, and providing legal assistance to victims of conflict.

TRC conducts the aforementioned activities in accordance with the International Red Cross and Red Crescent Movement's six fundamental principles—*humanity, impartiality, neutrality, independence, voluntary services*, and *unity*. These principles guide humanitarian workers and officials in their efforts

* We would like to thank Bayram Selvi, Director of Migration Services for the Turkish Red Crescent, Mevlüt Kuş, Manager of Document and Archive Management in the Turkish Red Crescent and his team for their help in compiling the information used in this chapter.

DOI: 10.4324/9781003503187-16

to determine in what areas they should be involved, how they should conduct their operations, and what values they should prioritize while engaging in humanitarian work. This is important because the majority of humanitarian relief work is carried out in areas that have suffered war, invasion, natural disasters, and any other catastrophic event that leaves the local inhabitants in a vulnerable state for a prolonged period of time. Such conditions, when left unchecked, encourage the exploitation of women, children, the elderly, and other vulnerable groups. Similar to every other constituent of the humanitarian aid ecosystem, TRC adheres strictly to international law, international humanitarian law, and human rights in addition to the aforementioned humanitarian principles as it goes about its endeavors. Adherence to these principles and legal frameworks allows humanitarian workers to serve all people in need, irrespective of religious, linguistic, or ethnic differences. This furthermore prevents humanitarian aid from being politicized, from being manipulated for ideological purposes, from being the means for perpetuating armed conflicts, or from serving the political or military interests of benefactor nations, while simultaneously increasing the credibility of humanitarian organizations working on the ground in the eyes of beneficiary, stakeholder, and benefactor nations.

TRC has, from its very first days, striven its utmost to tend to the wounds of humanity and lend a helping hand to the downtrodden wherever they may be. TRC has treated the sick and wounded in field hospitals, hospital ships, and first aid stations; facilitated the delivery and distribution of medical supplies; provided rations, clothing, and medicine to military deployments; worked to contain contagious diseases; seen to the needs of refugees; and protected women and children left in destitution by war during the Russo-Turkish War (1877–78), the Greco-Turkish War (1897), the Balkan Wars (1912–1913), World War I (1914–1918), the Turkish War of Independence (1919–1922), the population exchange between Greece and Türkiye (1923–1930), World War II (1939–1945), and the Cyprus Peace Operation (1974). More recently, TRC has stood by the side of disadvantaged people in Afghanistan, Bosnia, Iraq, Syria, Yemen, and other areas of the world wrought by crisis. These include the 1966 Varto earthquake; the 1999 Izmit earthquake; the 2005 Indian Ocean earthquake and tsunami, the 2005 Kashmir earthquake; the 2011 Van earthquakes; the earthquakes that rocked Elazığ, Bingöl, and Izmir in 2020; the 2020 Giresun flood; the fires that ravaged Türkiye's Mediterranean and Aegean coasts in 2021; the 2021 Kastamonu deluge; and the floods that inundated Türkiye's Black Sea coast in 2022.

Examples of TRC's Humanitarian Diplomacy Activities

Family Reunification and Tracing Services

TRC's Restoring Family Links (RFL) Unit works diligently to safeguard the rights guaranteed by the Geneva Conventions, Türkiye's Temporary Protection regulations, and other relevant statutes. One facet of this is the reunification of first-degree family members who have been separated after having been forced to abandon their homes and relocate to new lands in the wake of armed conflict or humanitarian crises. TRC works hand-in-hand with national and international government organizations, NGOs, and the various constituents of the Red Cross and Red Crescent Movement to bolster the success of its RFL efforts.

Family reunification refers to when one or more family members migrates to join another member of the family residing in a different country and seeks, first and foremost, to maintain family integrity. The reunification process is initiated upon the expressed request of an estranged family member. Several conditions, one of which being the degree of kinship between the family members issuing the request, dictate whether relevant authorities will pursue a family reunification case.

Domestic requests to initiate family reunification procedures in Türkiye are handled by the nineteen TRC Community Centers located in eighteen of Türkiye's eighty-one provinces and by local TRC branch offices in those provinces lacking community centers. International requests are forwarded to TRC by the National Red Cross and Red Crescent Society of the country where the request originated.

Cases that meet the necessary criteria laid out by TRC's RFL Unit are pursued on a priority basis, with cases involving higher degrees of vulnerability and sensitivity afforded greater precedence. Family reunification procedures are carried out jointly by the Presidency of Migration Management and its subordinate provincial directorates, the Ministry of Family and Social Services and its subordinate branches, and the governors of Türkiye's border provinces.

Case Study: A Turk in Guantánamo Bay

Aziz [name changed to maintain anonymity], who had been living in a village in Türkiye's province of Trabzon, set out for Afghanistan via unofficial routes over Iran in the summer of 2001. Leaving his mother, father, and five children in Trabzon, Aziz decided to seek employment in Afghanistan to pay off the debts that he had accrued. Aziz was detained by American armed forces during a routine identity check while working under the table in Afghanistan. Upon realization that he was not an Afghan citizen, Aziz was first detained in an Afghan prison before being shipped off to Guantánamo Bay Detention Camp.

Aziz was issued an ICRC number when said organization visited the detention center during his third year of detainment. Shortly thereafter, Aziz decided to send his family a Red Cross Message, Given Aziz's Turkish nationality, this heartfelt message was immediately forwarded to the coordinator of TRC's RFL division, Bayram Selvi, by the ICRC. In turn, Selvi had Aziz's letter delivered to his family in Türkiye accompanied by an official TRC letterhead.

Upon receiving a letter from the father and son they thought they had lost, Aziz's family contacted Bayram Selvi to express their immense gratefulness and glee to know that he was alive. Selvi then informed the family that TRC would forward whatever message they wanted to send to Aziz. From that day forward, Aziz and his family were able to communicate with one another on a regular basis. At the behest of Aziz's family, TRC appealed to Türkiye's Ministry of Foreign Affairs and the ICRC to seek Aziz's release and return to Türkiye. Following several meetings held over a specific period of time, Aziz was returned home and reunited with his family.

Message exchange services allow family members deprived of normal communication means to maintain contact with one another—a right guaranteed by the Geneva Conventions. Means of correspondence include Salamat Messages, Safe & Well Messages, Red Cross Messages, and video conferences.

Families forced to abandon their homes as a result of natural disasters, human-induced catastrophes, political chaos, or socioeconomic crises often lose contact with one or more members while relocating elsewhere. Given the precarious nature of the roads and forms of transportation used during sudden and irregular immigration, all migrants, especially minors, are at risk of falling victim to predators and of losing their way. Domestic and international family tracing services help families locate members separated by conflict or other emergency situations, thus playing an active part in alleviating human suffering and upholding human dignity as per the spirit of the Geneva Conventions.

Between February 2014 and June 2022, a total of 1,954 tracing cases were received by our bureau. Of these, 101 families were able to reestablish contact using their own resources and another sixteen cases were solved by the Red Cross.

National and international government agencies, NGOs, and National Red Cross and Red Crescent Societies work in collaboration with one another on the ground to locate family members who have been separated from one another while en route to their intended destination. Requests made by other countries' National Societies or the ICRC to initiate an investigation into individuals gone missing in Türkiye are handled by TRC's RFL division. Requests for investigations into missing individuals outside of Türkiye are taken by TRC Community Centers and local branch offices and forwarded to the ICRC and the National Society of the country where the investigation is requested to take place. TRC has signed several protocol agreements with various government agencies and organizations to encourage cooperation between them and its RFL division, thereby increasing the quality and success rate of the division's operations.

To increase awareness of available RFL services, TRC:

- Provides educational workshops and seminars to its own personnel, national and international NGOs, and employees working in government-run social service centers,

- Prints Turkish, Arabic, Farsi, and English-language brochures available for pick up from Community Centers and affiliate organizations,
- Plays a looped video depicting RFL services in Community Centers, and
- Has filmed and distributed a short documentary informing humanitarian organizations and potential beneficiaries of available RFL services.

Case Study: In November of 2019, the German Red Cross submitted a formal request to TRC asking the organization to investigate into a missing persons case involving a mother and daughter who had not been heard from since 2017. TRC informed Türkiye's Ministry of Family, Labor, and Social Services of the situation in an official letter containing a list of unattended children—including the girl in question—who had gone missing in Türkiye and whatever personal details were known about them. The ministry responded, however, that they could find no information on any of these children in their databases, possibly because of confusion in how the names were rendered into the Latin alphabet across different languages or because nicknames or pseudonyms may have been given when records were first created.

Despite this initial setback, TRC's previous experiences had shown it that collaborating with other organizations produced positive results. Thinking that the mother and daughter in question may have benefitted from services offered by Community Centers, TRC began scouring the databases of the Community Centers located in the provinces in which they were known to have spent time. Their search, however, returned no positive results. Eventually, however, TRC found a promising lead; the mother was a holder of a Kızılaykart (Red Crescent card). After a telephone conversation and home visit to ascertain that the correct individual had been located, TRC contacted the German Red Cross to inform the organization that they had made contact with the individuals in question.

Facilitating Correspondence between Prisoners of War and their Families

The national societies making up the International Red Cross and Red Crescent Movement were, pursuant to the First Geneva Convention signed on 22 August 1864, made responsible for managing affairs related to prisoners of war (POWs). The actions taken by TRC's precursor, the Ottoman Red Crescent Society, to facilitate the exchange of correspondence between POWs and their family members serve as a powerful reminder of how the spirit of the Geneva Conventions might manifest in the real world. Set up during the Balkan Wars, the Prisoners' Commission (*Üserāᶜ Heyᶜeti*, 1912) was responsible for ensuring that POWs were provided the means to correspond with their families. The same commission resumed this role during World War I and the subsequent Turkish War of Independence. The Ottoman Red Crescent Society worked to facilitate correspondence not only between Ottoman POWs held in Cyprus, Egypt, India, Myanmar, Russia, France, Italy, and the United Kingdom and their families but also between Russian, British, Australian, Romanian, and Indian POWs held in Ottoman lands and theirs.

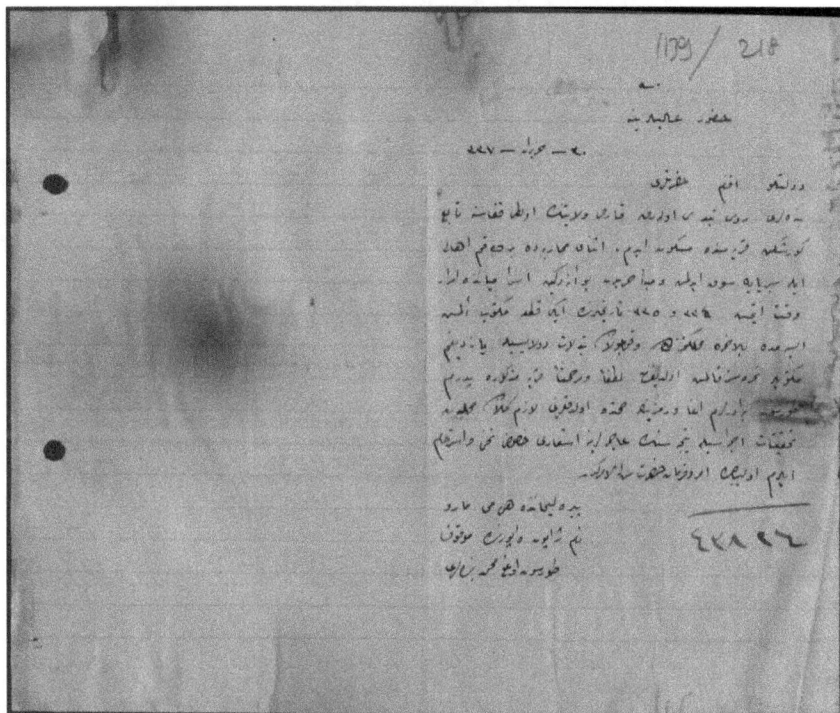

Figure 16.1 Letter by prisoner Mehmet:

In His name.

TN: This letter was translated from Ottoman Turkish. All of the years mentioned are written in accordance to the solar-based Islamic Rumi calendar commonly used in the Ottoman Empire during the period in question. For reference, the year 1337—the year that the letter was written—corresponds to 1921 AD.

His Sublime Presence

30 June [1]337

O Exalted and Illustrious Master

I, your humble servant, had been living in the village of Göreşken in the Oltu District of Kars Province. I, along with several other residents, was sent to Siberia when the fighting first broke out. I have spent my time in prisoner camps since the onset of the war. I received two letters in [1]334 and [1]335, respectively. Because of the upheavals that have shaken our homeland, however, the letters I wrote in response failed to reach their destination. As such, I respectfully request that you investigate into the health of my father Ţursun and my brothers Āgā and Remzī in the aforementioned village and then inform me, your humble servant, of what you learn. Verily the command belongs unto Him to whom all commanding belongs.

Your servant, Meḥmed, son of Ţursun, prisoner on the Japanese ship Heimei Maru moored in the Port of Piraeus.

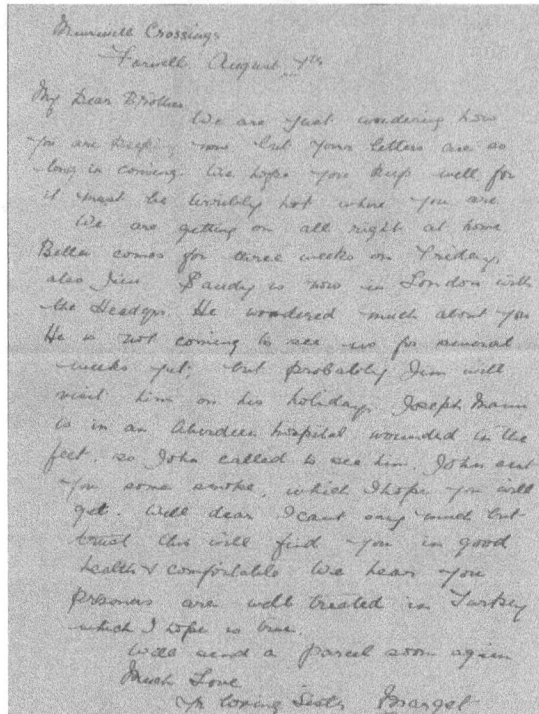

Figure 16.2 Letter by a prisoner's sister, Margel:

Murwill (?) Crossings.

Faruell (Last Name?). August 7th

My Dear Brother,

We are just wondering how you are keeping now. But your letters are so long in coming. We hope you keep well, for it must be terribly hot where you are. We are getting on all right at home. Bella comes for three weeks on Friday, also Jim. Saudy (?) is now in London with the Headgr (?). He wondered much about you. He is not coming to see us for several weeks yet; but probably Jim will visit him on his holiday. Joseph Maun is in an Aberdeen hospital. Wounded in the feet. So John called to see him. John sent you some smoke, which I hope you will get. Well dear I can't say much but trust this will find you in good health and comfortable. We hear you prisoners are well treated in Turkey which I hope is true.

Will send a parcel soon again.

Much Love.

Your loving sister Margel

Prisoner Exchange

Over its history, TRC has spearheaded a host of humanitarian initiatives that ended in the release of untold numbers of POWs. Prisoner exchanges during World War II are but one example of TRC's work in this particular regard. While overseeing prisoner exchange procedures at the two Turkish ports of Izmir and Mersin, TRC provided humanitarian aid to POWs awaiting repatriation. TRC's

Figure 16.3 Prisoner exchange, 1942: Photographs from the 1942 British–Italian prisoner exchanges—Mersin and Izmir, Türkiye.

actions not only earned it recognition among the greater humanitarian community but also were instrumental in raising awareness of the plight faced by POWs among the international community.

While the bloodshed of World War II was at a high point, prisoner exchanges between the United Kingdom and Italy were organized twice at Türkiye's Mersin Port and four times at the Izmir Port from 1942 to 1943. The first exchange took place on 8 April 1942 at Izmir's seaport just one day after British and Italian POWs—many of whom were severely wounded—had arrived there. The exchange of 1,797 British and 5,593 Italian POWs was supervised by Garrison Commander General Hakkı Akoğuz, a procession of military officials, the Red Cross delegation in Ankara, and personnel from TRC's Izmir branch.

Several other exchanges would take place at these same two ports in 1943: (i) 863 German and 863 Italian POWs were exchanged with 863 British POWs at Mersin on 21 March, (ii) 1,205 Italian POWs with 150 British POWs at Izmir on 4–18 April, (iii) 1,200 Italian POWs with 200 British POWs at Izmir on 5–8 May, and (iv) a mixed group made up of 2,269 Italian officers and petty soldiers, including five generals, with 455 British officers and petty soldiers at Izmir on 2 June.

Another example showcasing TRC's diplomatic prowess is the prisoner exchange that took place following the Korean War (1950–1953). TRC was a member of the multinational commission formed to oversee the upcoming prisoner exchange slated to take place in Japan. In addition to TRC, this commission included the American, Soviet, Chinese, Japanese, Danish, Canadian, and Australian Red Cross Societies. During the run-up to the exchange, TRC Director General Fikri Akurgal led a three-person team charged with ensuring that all of the necessary preparations were made.

Two decades later, TRC helped facilitate the prisoner exchange between the Turkish Cypriot POWs held by the Greek Cypriots and the Greek Cypriot POWs that had been brought to Türkiye during the 1974 Cyprus Peace. These prisoners were repatriated to their respective territories in Cyprus under the supervision of the Red Cross, the Red Crescent, and the UN Peacekeeping Force in Cyprus.

Yet another prisoner exchange in which TRC was involved is that which took place following the Iran–Iraq War. A few weeks after the conclusion of said war in 1988, Iranian forces withdrew from Iraqi territory and regrouped behind the borders proposed in the 1975 Algiers Agreement. Article 3 of this agreement and to the Geneva Conventions required that all POWs be repatriated without undue delay. As Türkiye was entrusted with seeing this through, TRC was made responsible for handling the prisoner exchange slated to take place in the cities of Adana and Diyarbakır. Pursuant to the bilateral agreement signed between Iran and Iraq, the final exchange that TRC would oversee took place in 2003.

Legal and Social Assistance

Support services need to be offered to immigrants to prevent rights violations against them as they attempt to acclimate to an entirely new setting. Linguistic barriers, cultural differences, and social introversion frequently cause immigrants to experience social exclusion and, especially with respect to the new bureaucratic system, alienation. Faced with an influx of immigrants fleeing the carnage of the Russo-Turkish War during its formative period, TRC's forerunner, the Ottoman Red Crescent Society, strove to meet the various needs of the incoming immigrant community. This and subsequent wars, further exacerbated by the ethnic cleansing endeavors that would follow, forced the Muslim Turkish population living in the Balkans to immigrate to Istanbul and Anatolia. As a result, the Ottoman Red Crescent Society worked overtime to help the incoming Muslim refugees integrate into their new communities and to ensure that their day-to-day needs were met. By coming up with truly inventive solutions to such novel issues, the Ottoman Red Crescent Society was able to turn the initial hardships into a blessing. The unique experience that TRC has accumulated over its long history has bolstered the organization's ability to provide government agencies effective support in their humanitarian relief efforts during crisis situations. The Community-Based Migration Programs Department, in tandem with nineteen Community Centers, has dispensed various forms of humanitarian aid and support services to Syrian refugees since 2015.

In collaboration with the UN High Commissioner for Refugees (UNHCR), TRC began providing specialist lawyers and translators in 2017 to ensure that immigrants were aware of their rights and had access to the legal assistance they needed in order to seek proper legal recourse in Türkiye's complex legal apparatus.

Since this project's inception in 2017, a total of 5,976 people have received legal assistance and 43,137 have attended legal seminars led by specialist lawyers. Of the total beneficiaries, 90% were Syrian immigrants, 6% were immigrants of other nations, and 4% were citizens of Türkiye. Those issues for which legal assistance was sought were, in descending order, legal status—including citizenship and temporary protection—at 23%, pro bono legal assistance services at 21%, family law—specifically marriage and guardianship—at 16%, and civil registry procedures—such as the application process for identity cards and signature requirements—at 15%.

As a final note, the effects of COVID-19 forced officials to reevaluate immigrants' needs with respect to their ability to access legal assistance given the linguistic hurdles they face, the fact that they often live further away from urban hubs, and their general lack of awareness of the opportunities at their disposal. As a result, forms that could be used to request legal assistance were made available online.

Humanitarian Corridors and the Delivery of Humanitarian Aid

Pursuant to the authority vested in them to provide relief to people in distress, humanitarian aid organizations strive to use their resources to help populations in need of assistance after natural or human-induced disasters. As such, national and international humanitarian relief organizations prioritize being adequately prepared for complicated situations often requiring emergency intervention. TRC's extensive work in the field of humanitarian relief has earned it worldwide acclaim, especially among other humanitarian organizations. In the last ten years alone, TRC has furnished the food and shelter needs of countless people affected by natural and man-made disasters in more than one hundred countries. Beyond providing emergency assistance and basic essentials, TRC has had a hand in constructing houses, schools, community centers, places of worship, and other public facilities through the development programs it runs. TRC has helped create opportunities for affected communities to earn a living and regain some sense of continuity in their lives by supporting health, education, social assistance, agriculture, and irrigation projects. Indeed, all of these initiatives are made possible through negotiations and collaboration.

The delivery of the aid materials that people suffering the effects of natural and human-induced disasters are in dire need of, the transport of wounded individuals, humanitarian actors' ability to reach civilians, and civilians' ability to make itself heard to the outside world are all issues of critical importance. Through the various tools at its disposal—namely, persuasion, negotiation, advocacy, and collaboration—humanitarian diplomacy seeks to facilitate these services and, when the gravity of the situation necessitates it, to open humanitarian corridors. TRC has taken the initiative to open such corridors in diverse crisis zones throughout its history—a prime example being the corridor opened during TRC's humanitarian initiatives in Syria. Together with Türkiye's Ministry of Family and Social Services, the Disaster and Emergency Management Presidency (AFAD), the UN, the IFRC, the UNHRC, and the World Food Programme (WFP), TRC opened and oversaw the administration of a humanitarian aid corridor and lifeline that the lives of 4.5 million Syrian refugees. Since preexisting humanitarian corridors are among the first places that individuals living in vulnerable areas turn to in order to source their needs, TRC utilizes extant humanitarian corridors to distribute relief items to vulnerable populations, such as how it did in 2011 with the Afgooye corridor in Somalia. Established in 2007 along the eighteen-mile road between Mogadishu and Afgooye as fighting began to peak in Somalia, this corridor provides basic humanitarian and alimentary aid to internal and foreign refugees who were forced to abandon their homes in the wake the massive drought that overtook the entire region.

The fighting that exploded a short six miles east of Damascus in Eastern Ghouta on 14 November 2017 left a large number of civilians dead or wounded as a result. When this region, home to roughly four hundred thousand people, was laid siege to by Syrian government forces, TRC delivered 8,650 emergency rations, 10,500 hot meals, and 1,400 baby healthcare kits to the civilian population. As the more intense fighting began to subside, eighty thousand people were carefully evacuated from the parts of Eastern Ghouta still under siege. TRC resettled evacuees in six camps established near Syria's border with Türkiye (i.e., Elbil, Elbil 2, Kafar Lousin, Mahmudiyah, Dayr Ballut, and Bardaklı) and began operations to provide for their basic human needs.

Advocacy and Awareness Building

Two integral components of humanitarian diplomacy, advocacy and awareness building seek to mitigate the effects of crises on vulnerable and disaster-stricken populations and to create the most conducive conditions for the successful delivery of essential items to them. Humanitarians work to raise awareness among international organizations, governments, NGOs, opinion leaders, and other decision-making authorities either directly or indirectly, such as through individuals and institutions able to influence decision-makers' opinions. Initiatives range from advocating for emergency funds and other forms of support for humanitarian projects on one end of the spectrum, to lobbying for policy changes on the other. In one instance that took place in

2017, TRC successfully persuaded the Bangladeshi government to allow the establishment of the Hope Village Community Center for Rohingya refugees residing in Bangladesh. After receiving authorization of the Bangladeshi government, a total of 1,200 temporary shelter units were constructed and turned over to the aforementioned refugees. Another example involves Bosnia and Herzegovina: Toward the end of 2019, Bosnia's Vučjak migrant camp came under intense and sustained criticisms for the deplorable conditions in which refugees attempting to enter Europe lived. After a series of inspections confirming these allegations, TRC successfully lobbied the Bosnian government to relocate refugees to camps that offered their inhabitants better living conditions. As TRC continues to its efforts to raise awareness among the general public and opinion leaders about the traumatic realities faced by those living in Syria, Palestine, Ukraine, Rakhine, and other areas beleaguered by seemingly unending humanitarian catastrophes, its success in persuading decision-makers to take action to ameliorate the situation offers encouragement to humanitarians the world over.

Protection of Civilians

Humanitarian law mandates that civilians and other non-combatants shall be protected in all circumstances and shall not be targeted during military operations. The Geneva Conventions of 1949 and the Additional Protocols of 1977 contain special rules for the protection of civilians. These agreements enshrines the protection of civilians in the event of internal conflict, appealing to international law, the principle of humanity, and the inalienable rights guaranteed to all human beings under human rights law.

As part of its efforts to protect civilians living in conflict zones, TRC has led numerous operations to mitigate the devastating effects of the ongoing crisis in Syria. One such example is when, following a chemical attack on the town of Khan Shaykhun in Syria's Idlib province that killed more than 170 people and injured many more, TRC delivered 33,467 first-aid materials acquired through donation to Syrian hospitals and humanitarian NGOs deployed in Syria. In addition to providing medical supplies, TRC provided civil defense organizations with equipment to protect themselves from chemical attacks in the future and put together workshops to educate these organizations against chemical, biological, radiological, and nuclear (CBRN) threats. The negotiations and collaborative efforts in which TRC has engaged throughout the Syrian crisis have greatly expedited its works in assessing needs, identifying partners, and delivering aid to those in need in an effective and equitable manner.

Civilian Evacuations

Civilians living in areas plagued by war, internal conflict, and terrorism are at constant risk of death or property loss. Protecting such people, which, in certain cases, may require their evacuation from crisis zones, is among the primary responsibilities of national and international humanitarian organizations. In line with the Geneva Conventions and other relevant international agreements, TRC has advocated for civilian rights, amplified the voices of the disenfranchised and downtrodden so that they may be heard by a wider audience, and executed evacuation operations when the situation required it, such as those it carried out throughout the Syrian crisis. TRC's historical role in the massive civilian evacuation of Aleppo (2016–2017) is a prime example of its operations in this regard. As the lives of the civilian population in Al-Waer, a suburb of Homs, were under constant threat because of the brutal conflict that plagued the area, TRC began making plans with the Syrian Arab Red Crescent to evacuate tens of thousands of civilians from Al-Waer to Jarabulus and Idlib so that TRC could continue to provide them desperately needed aid. As part of evacuation operations, TRC had 1,450 tents and 1,899 truckloads of aid materials sent to the region to prepare for the influx of refugees. Evacuations began on 12 December 2016 in coordination with the Syrian Arab Red Crescent and saw a total of forty-five thousand civilians evacuated.

Another civilian evacuation in which TRC was involved occurred in 2011 in Libya. As the ongoing domestic armed conflict and deteriorating security conditions began to threaten the lives of Turkish civilians in the country, Türkiye's Ministry of Foreign Affairs, Chief of General Staff, Disaster and Emergency Management Presidency (AFAD), Turkish Cooperation and Coordination Agency (TİKA), and TRC began making preparations for a large-scale evacuation. Communication was established with the Libyan Red Crescent to coordinate evacuation operations, which saw a total of 18,621 Turkish citizens and an additional 6,000 citizens of third countries evacuated by air and sea. As part of the operation, TRC dispatched one hundred personnel to Marmaris Port and Dalaman Airport to see to the various needs of the arriving civilians, providing them with rations, blankets, beds, hygienic items, and psychological support.

Transport and Treatment of Wounded Individuals

As part of its wider humanitarian efforts, TRC provides medical services to people injured in natural and man-made disasters, which sometimes entails that severely wounded people be transported to facilities where they can receive proper care. An example of this involved the Gaza Freedom Flotilla led by the passenger ship Mavi Marmara. On 31 May 2010, said flotilla was boarded and attacked by Israeli forces in international waters, culminating in the arrest, detention, and injury—some of which were so severe as to have ended in death—of the civilian volunteers aboard. In response, TRC mobilized immediately to help these ill-fated volunteers, particularly those who had suffered injuries. Following negotiations with TRC's Israeli counterpart, Magen David Adom (MDA), the two organizations began working together to ensure the safe evacuation of the detained civilian volunteers. Together with MDA personnel, a team of TRC professionals composed of two doctors, a disaster management specialist, and a delegation of international relations officers was permitted by Israeli officials to examine the wounded individuals. When the twenty-three wounded Turkish citizens were stabilized, medical evacuation procedures were initiated on 3 June 2010 and completed the next day. The IFRC and ICRC lauded both the success of this operation and the cooperation exhibited between national societies.

As part of the organization's humanitarian works in Palestine, TRC was dispatched to Ben Gurion Airport to retrieve 104 Palestinian citizens injured during an Israeli attack on the Gaza Strip and transport them to Istanbul where they were scheduled to receive medical care. Upon their arrival to Istanbul, Türkiye's Ministry of Health remitted the wounded Palestinians to nearby hospitals for treatment.

Following a terrorist attack involving two truck bombs in Somalia's capital of Mogadishu on 14 October 2017, Türkiye's Ministry of Health, AFAD, and TRC began discussing the best way to proceed. After deliberating, they decided to form a team that would serve as a vanguard for the delivery of humanitarian relief materials. Shortly thereafter, a military cargo plane under TRC authority was dispatched to Somalia laden with aid items. While the cargo plane was grounded in Mogadishu, thirty-five people injured during the aforementioned attack were approved for medical treatment in Türkiye. Accompanied by thirty-four next of kin, these individuals were airlifted to Türkiye on 16 November 2017 by the same cargo plane.

References

Dunant, H. (1964). *Bir Solferino hatırası* (N. Arpacıoğlu, Trans.). Türkiye Kızılay Derneği.

Kızılay Tarih (n.d.). *Dünya'nın ilk Kızılay'ı, dünyaya hilali armağan eden Kızılay.* http://kizilaytarih.org/dosya001.html

Afterword

Alpaslan Durmuş

I solemnly pledge, in the name of humanity, to serve all humanity!

Humanitarian diplomacy is the act of seeking humanitarian solutions, undertaken by men and women driven by a deep sense of personal responsibility to help their fellow human beings who are suffering under inhumane conditions because of unfounded differences projected onto them.

Allow me to make a point by negation: Humanitarian diplomacy is not a revamped, more glamorous version of traditional public diplomacy, nor is it a tool designed to empower or promote disadvantaged individuals and organizations. On the contrary, it is a collective call to action by those willing to sacrifice their own comfort and well-being to defend the weak, the helpless, the impoverished, the oppressed, and the marginalized. Yet it is a silent but powerful call, so quietly deafening that it grates the ears of those who dare to ignore it. It beckons those who hear it to virtue and righteousness, with a solid rational foundation and an undeniably humane and noble spirit.

A Universal Human Nature

We are one and the same; there is no difference between us. We all share in life and death, prosperity and adversity, joy and sorrow. We all experience sadness, heartbreak, happiness, longing, and the joy of being reunited with our loved ones. These emotions and experiences, even if they occur only once in a lifetime, have enriched the inner world of humanity since time immemorial. We are the offspring of parents we did not choose, born in a time and place we did not choose, and in bodies whose dimensions we had no say in. We live lives over which we have little control. No child of Adam can claim to be different; even Adam and Eve share this experience with us. Given the reality of our physical existence, can there be any doubt that our environment should be different? Trees, rocks, soil, streams, mountains, and the sky... the four cardinal directions, the seven climes of classical geography, the entire cosmos itself... None of these were created with our input.

DOI: 10.4324/9781003503187-17

Therefore, let us declare our intention to stand as a barrier between humanity and all that can cause suffering: *Neither the land on which I stand nor the sky above me is my property. I did not inherit them from my ancestors, nor will they ever be mine. I am willing to share them without objection.*

Every man and woman is personally responsible

Perhaps we do indeed live in a solipsistic universe, though I am not sure. While many may assert the existence of such a universe with great authority and volume, no one can definitively confirm or deny this claim. At most, we can acknowledge the eloquence of these speakers and the logical coherence of their arguments. However, fire still burns, rocks still fall, and iron still rusts. These are fundamental truths, as clear as the full moon on a cloudless night, truths that a solipsistic universe cannot accommodate.

What we do know, however, is that no individual is the ultimate arbiter of right and wrong. If someone were to claim otherwise, that only they could define right and wrong, every other human being would have the right to challenge them. At the very least, the hearts of all people, regardless of their individual upbringing, would rise up against such bold claims, even if they lack the will, strength, or courage to voice their objections.

Nevertheless, the importance of each human being cannot be underestimated. Without human consciousness, the universe cannot even be imagined, let alone contemplated. As Omar Khayyam wrote in one of his quatrains:

When I am here no more, gone too will be roses and cypresses. / No red lips, no fragrant wines. / There will be no dawns or twilights, no joys or sorrows. / The world exists only as long as I am aware of it; when I am gone, it too will cease to exist…

With this in mind, let us proclaim: *Anyone who dares to raise a hand against another human being will find me standing between them and their intended victim, no matter how inhumane or reprehensible their actions may be.*

Acting Humanely Makes a Man a Man

No matter how precise, clear, or airtight the language we use to codify laws, there will always be something overlooked or undefined. Even if we have reached the end of times or the eleventh hour, we must remember that until the last trumpet sounds, something new and unprecedented can emerge at any moment.

Going forward, let us agree on a fundamental principle in the event that we encounter such an unprecedented reality in uncharted territory: *I will, for as long as there is breath in my lungs, adhere to my commitment to mankind—to all humans no matter how far or wide.*

So let us all make a promise to each other: *We will stand with the oppressed against the arrogant and tyrannical who delight in subjugating the weak. We will advocate for our oppressed brothers and sisters in humanity in negotiations and actively seek opportunities to uplift them whenever, wherever, and however those opportunities present themselves.*

Index

Pages in *italics* refer to figures, pages in **bold** refer to tables, and pages followed by "n" refer to notes.

For Product Safety Concerns and Information please contact our EU
representative GPSR@taylorandfrancis.com
Taylor & Francis Verlag GmbH, Kaufingerstraße 24, 80331 München, Germany

www.ingramcontent.com/pod-product-compliance
Lightning Source LLC
Chambersburg PA
CBHW050336270326
41926CB00016B/3487